Forest of Pressure

VISIBLE EVIDENCE

Edited by Michael Renov, Faye Ginsburg, and Jane Gaines

Volume 18 :: Abé Mark Nornes
Forest of Pressure: Ogawa Shinsuke and Postwar Japanese Documentary

Volume 17 :: Alexandra Juhasz and Jesse Lerner, Editors
F Is for Phony: Fake Documentaries and Truth's Undoing

Volume 16 :: Michael Renov
The Subject of Documentary

Volume 15 :: Abé Mark Nornes
Japanese Documentary Film: The Meiji Era through Hiroshima

Volume 14 :: John Mraz
Nacho López, Mexican Photographer

Volume 13 :: Jean Rouch
Ciné-Ethnography

Volume 12 :: James M. Moran
There's No Place Like Home Video

Volume 11 :: Jeffrey Ruoff
An American Family: A Televised Life

Volume 10 :: Beverly R. Singer
Wiping the War Paint off the Lens: Native American Film and Video

Volume 9 :: Alexandra Juhasz, Editor
Women of Vision: Histories in Feminist Film and Video

Volume 8 :: Douglas Kellner and Dan Streible, Editors
Emile de Antonio: A Reader

Volume 7 :: Patricia R. Zimmermann
States of Emergency: Documentaries, Wars, Democracies

Volume 6 :: Jane M. Gaines and Michael Renov, Editors
Collecting Visible Evidence

Volume 5 :: Diane Waldman and Janet Walker, Editors
Feminism and Documentary

Volume 4 :: Michelle Citron
Home Movies and Other Necessary Fictions

Volume 3 :: Andrea Liss
Trespassing through Shadows:
Memory, Photography, and the Holocaust

Volume 2 :: Toby Miller
Technologies of Truth:
Cultural Citizenship and the Popular Media

Volume 1 :: Chris Holmlund and Cynthia Fuchs, Editors
Between the Sheets, In the Streets: Queer, Lesbian, Gay Documentary

VISIBLE EVIDENCE, VOLUME 18

Forest of Pressure

Ogawa Shinsuke and Postwar Japanese Documentary

Abé Mark Nornes

University of Minnesota Press
Minneapolis
London

The University of Minnesota Press gratefully acknowledges a grant from the University of Michigan that contributed to the publication of this book.

Portions of the book originally appeared in "The Postwar Documentary Trace: Groping in the Dark," in *Open to the Public: Studies in Japan's Recent Past,* ed. Leslie Pincus, a special issue of *Positions* 10.1 (Spring 2002): 39–78; copyright Duke University Press; reprinted with permission. Portions of chapter 5 were originally published as "The Theater of a Thousand Years," *Journal of the International Institute* 4 (2) (1997), a publication of the University of Michigan International Institute, www.hti.umich.edu/j/jii/; reprinted with permission.

"Yajiri no mura, kai no mura" ("Village of Spearheads, Village of Shells") is reprinted by kind permission of Kimura Michio.

"Toge" ("A Mountain Pass") is reprinted by kind permission of Makabe Kuniko.

Published by the University of Minnesota Press
111 Third Avenue South, Suite 290
Minneapolis, MN 55401-2520
http://www.upress.umn.edu

Library of Congress Cataloging-in-Publication Data
Nornes, Markus.
Forest of pressure : Ogawa Shinsuke and postwar Japanese documentary / Abé Mark Nornes.
p. cm.— (Visible evidence ; v. 18)
Includes bibliographical references and index.
ISBN-13: 978-0-8166-4907-5 (hc : alk. paper)
ISBN-10: 0-8166-4907-3 (hc : alk. paper)
ISBN-13: 978-0-8166-4908-2 (pb)
ISBN-10: 0-8166-4908-1 (pb)
1. Ogawa, Shinsuke, 1936–1992—Criticism and interpretation. I. Title. II. Series.
PN1998.3.O33N67 2007
070.1'8—dc22
2006015941

Printed in the United States of America on acid-free paper.
The University of Minnesota is an equal-opportunity educator and employer.

12 11 10 09 08 07 10 9 8 7 6 5 4 3 2 1

for Ogawa-san

Contents

Acknowledgments

This book was many years in the making. My starting point was a series of stays at the Ogawa Productions apartment in Ogikubo, Tokyo. The apartment was a short walk from the postproduction studio (itself a small apartment with an office, editing room, projection booth, and screening room for sound mixing crammed into what was otherwise a typical Tokyo rabbit hutch). On my visits, Ogawa Shinsuke was generous enough to let me stay while I finished my business. It was especially kind of Iizuka Toshio; this was his home whenever he was in Tokyo, which was most of the time. My best memories of those stays are not the charged talks with Ogawa but the quiet chats with Iizuka at the end of each day. We would often go to the nearby public bath (the apartment's bathroom was being used as a storage closet) and later end the day by pulling out beers from the tiny refrigerator in the apartment.

My evenings with Iizuka-san were eye-opening. The little I knew about Ogawa Productions came from English-language books by David Desser, Joan Mellon, and Noël Burch. Their relatively short passages concentrated on the films. What I learned from Iizuka was the unique circumstances of their production. I found his stories fascinating, even spellbinding. There's a book in there, I thought.

However, my inclination was to understand the larger context of Japanese documentary before attempting to describe the role of Ogawa Productions in it all. This little diversion resulted in many years of research and my first book, also published by the University of Minnesota Press in the Visible Evidence series. Along the way, I had countless discussions with members of Ogawa Productions about their life and work. I am particularly indebted to Iizuka Toshio, Shiraishi Yoko, Nosaka Haruo, Fuseya Hiro, and, of course, Ogawa Shinsuke. Over the years, they have gone far out of their way to help my research; more important, their friendship is very precious to me. I also received gracious help from Hatanaka Hiroko, Fukuda Katsuhiko, Tanaka Nobuko, Kawada Yumiko, Honma Shusuke, Kato Takanobu, Otsu Koshiro, and Tamura Masaki. I thank these people for the documents, pamphlets, and other ephemera they have lent and given me. It is not often that the historian's subjects simply hand over key pieces of the archive.

As for the more formal archives, such as they are, Shiraishi Yoko allowed me to rummage through the boxes stored in Furuyashiki Village. Nosaka Haruo showed me the Jieiso boxes (and even let me borrow one). He was also instrumental in helping me achieve access to the Sanrizuka materials. For the latter, Hatano Yukie and the rest of the members of the Rekishi Densho Iinkai were unusually obliging in granting me access to the as-yet uncataloged boxes of papers in the airport. Their guidance included conversations over soba during our pleasant lunch breaks. Hatano took me on powerful tours of the Sanrizuka area, pointing out the spots where the films were, giving me a sense of the lay of the land, and introducing me to the Uriu and Ishii families. I received help with materials from Kageyama Satoshi and Erikawa Ken (both editors of *Eiga Shinbun*) and Patricia Steinhoff and the Takezawa Collection at the University of Hawai'i.

I enjoyed many public events and retrospectives that discussed the collective after Ogawa's death, and over the years many serendipitous bar discussions took on the heady feel of good symposia. The opinions, speculations, and stories I heard are woven into every page of this book. Colleagues who read the manuscript in part or whole include Aaron Gerow, Livia Monnet, Leslie Pincus, and Mitsuhiro Yoshimoto; most of this help has been received through casual conversations. The most influential people on my thinking have been Tsuchimoto Noriaki, Yano Kazuyuki, Sato Makoto, Suzuki Shiroyasu, Hara Kazuo, Yomota Inuhiko, Makino Mamoru, Kogawa Tetsuo, Ishizaka Kenji, Ikui Eiko, Adachi Masao, Nakajima Yo, and Ueno Toshiya. There are so many more I could name—it seems as though I meet people with Ogawa connections whenever I go out, whether to hotspots of the independent-film world like Shinjuku's Jutée and Gingakei or to restaurants just about anywhere in Japan.

My trips to Japan were possible thanks to generous grants from Fulbright, the Japan Foundation, and the University of Michigan's Center for Japanese Studies. Kim Dong-won and PURN supported my trip to Korea, and Nick Deocampo brought me to the Philippines with the help of the U.S. State Department.

Above and beyond this, my work with Yano Kazuyuki and the Yamagata International Documentary Film Festival has always been a constant source of encouragement and material support. On my many trips to

Yamagata, I relied on, and thoroughly enjoyed, the kindness of people such as Kato Itaru, Masuya Shuichi, Miyazawa Hikaru, and so many others associated with the festival. The ever-resourceful Yasui Yoshio of Planet Bibliothèque de Cinéma shared much of his library and saved me in more than one tight spot.

Writing this book has been a humbling experience.

Ogawa and friend, shot in Takashima, Yamagata, June 1975.

Introduction

The creation of beauty thus begins with an act of publicity. . . . The duplicity of the artist, the grandeur as well as the misery of his calling, is a recurrent theme closely linked with the theme of infamy. . . . The poetic impulse in all its perverse duplicity belongs to man alone, marks him as essentially human.
:: Paul de Man

Sometimes I wonder if this Ogawa Shinsuke really existed.
:: Shiraishi Yoko, Ogawa's wife, 1999

This book is about one of the most astonishing filmographies in Japanese cinema, the work of Ogawa Shinsuke. To be more specific, if somewhat obscure, this is a critical biography of his collective, Ogawa Productions (or Ogawa Pro, as it is known in Japan). The book takes its title, *Forest of Pressure,* from a mistranslation of one of the collective's film titles from 1967. The original Japanese title literally means "the forest that crushes one to death" and was initially rendered in English as *The Oppressed Students*. This language exemplifies the breathless, over-the-top rhetoric of the day, but the image of a "forest of pressure" offers a better fit for the conditions within which Ogawa Pro worked. I will look closely at the many pressures that bore down on the collective, the political, economic, aesthetic, institutional, and interpersonal conditions of their practice. And inspired by the method of history writing forged by Ogawa Pro in its last films, I will play with multiple avenues of approach, shifting between conventional narrative, close analysis, first-person narration, poetry, historical contextualization, and tall tales.

Ogawa Shinsuke began his career in high school in the 1950s as the member of a film study group and joined one of the largest PR film companies after graduating from college. As it happened, this company was the

The sweeping view at the entrance to Heta Village, where Ogawa Pro set up shop. By the turn of the century, the families living in the foreground all sold their property, and airport authorities destroyed the homes and removed every scrap of wood. Photograph by Naito Masatoshi.

breeding ground for some of the finest political filmmakers of the 1960s and 1970s. Ogawa left it in the early 1960s and electrified the student movement with a series of documentaries made among the students, behind the barricades. When he formed his own production company, he moved to a village outside Tokyo that the central government had designated as the site for Narita International Airport. The farmers there were just starting what would be one of the most traumatic social struggles in modern Japanese history. In the course of eight films shot over nine years, Ogawa and his production company documented what was, for all practical purposes, a small-scale civil war. Ogawa's Sanrizuka Series remains one of the monuments of Japanese cinema history.

In the midst of the turbulent 1970s, Ogawa Pro made the unlikely decision to leave Sanrizuka and resettle in a small village, Magino, in the northern Japanese mountains. The filmmakers lived collectively in a borrowed farmhouse, making rice and another series of films for sixteen years. As in the Sanrizuka Series, the films of the Magino Village Story[1] were made with a commitment to develop deep relationships with their subjects

Yamagata, where Ogawa Pro shot seven films during its sixteen-year stay. This is Furuyashiki Village in the middle of winter. The collective lived in Magino Village, a ten-minute ride down the mountain at the edge of a broad valley.

and with a patient leisure that few filmmakers besides Flaherty have indulged in. It is difficult to imagine any future filmmakers with the ambition (or insanity) to match the scale of Ogawa Pro's conception of documentary practice, particularly now that video has transformed the economics of independent production.

Toward the end of his life, Ogawa helped establish the Yamagata International Documentary Film Festival. He was shooting footage for a new film, and had ideas for many, many others. He was also reaching out to nonfiction film and video artists across Asia to share experiences and films and to begin collaborations that would jump-start a new era committed to documentary in Asia. However, at the height of his powers as a filmmaker, Ogawa died of cancer at a youthful age of fifty-five on February 7, 1992. With his passing, the collective that bore his name quickly dissolved.

Aside from Eric Barnouw, few historians have considered the documentary outside of Europe and North America. Thus, a recent film on cinema verité could portend to offer an authoritative and comprehensive history without acknowledging the work of Ogawa or other Japanese filmmakers, which in some cases precede verité's Western appearance. By contrast, all histories of Japanese cinema—including those by Western scholars like Donald Richie—never fail to cover the contribution of Ogawa. Although overlooked by too many scholars, film festivals, and colleagues, the people that did come into contact with the man have strong memories. Ogawa exuded extraordinary energy. His gregariousness was matched by his love of food, drink, and most of all *discussion*. He loved to talk, overflowed with ideas, and was fascinated with everything within his magnetic reach. He possessed a kind of mesmerizing charisma that charmed most of the people who came close to him, most especially the people who joined his collective. Even the foreigners who struggled to communicate through his broken English never failed to be touched by his passion. Joris Ivens, who visited the Sanrizuka house back in the late 1960s, told Ogawa, "You are my youngest son."[2]

In undertaking the telling of this biography, I find myself compelled to repeat what so many of the former members insisted whenever we talked: Ogawa Pro was no typical organization. There was something inexplicably unique about it. What exactly was so out of the ordinary is extremely hard for me to nail down and communicate, but anyone who came in contact with it over the years understands my quandary. Perhaps by the end of this book, I can give the reader a sense of what sets Ogawa Pro apart from all the other collectives in film history.

In a first attempt at this, and to find an emotional center for this history, I offer the following anecdotal evidence for Ogawa Pro's peculiar character. Over the years, more than one hundred men and women entered and left Ogawa Pro. Some spent a short period of time without making much of a mark on the group. Others stayed for twenty years. Incredibly, none of them received proper salaries; budgets left in the archives reveal they spent more on film screenings than daily life necessities! They committed themselves to Ogawa Pro for other reasons, usually political ones, and they left for as many other reasons. However, the typical way they quit is revealing. As former member Nosaka Haruo explains:

> Ogawa Pro had some 125 people in it, and when it folded there were only three or four left. Most of these people did not announce they were leaving. One night you would go to sleep next to someone, and in the morning you'd wake up and they were no longer there. They would just disappear without saying, "I quit," let alone "Sayonara." It is like certain love relationships; the only way out is to run away. Some stayed only a few days or weeks before disappearing. Others stayed for decades. It was a crazy, unusual group. Impossible to describe![3]

During the shooting of *Winter in Sanrizuka,* even Ogawa disappeared without telling anyone his whereabouts. It drove the staff insane; however, cinematographer Tamura Masaki, who was never a member of Ogawa Pro, found it all entertaining. After a long while, Yoshida Tsukasa, Honma Shusuke, Fukuda Katsuhiko, and several other core members decided to leave, in the middle of night as usual. They got as far as a coffee shop in Chiba before they settled down and decided to return to Sanrizuka. Ogawa himself returned after more than a month, offering no explanation.

This hints at how Ogawa Pro was no ordinary film production company. The inability of these core members to abandon the group intimates the degree to which Ogawa entered into the core of their existence. Their experience working with Ogawa left all of them with powerfully complicated memories, especially in the context of the movement's failure. Although I was not a member of Ogawa Pro, I came to know him well enough to sympathize with the contradictory feelings of the former members.

I first met Ogawa at the 1988 Hawai'i International Film Festival, where he was showing *The Sundial Carved with a Thousand Years of Notches: The Magino Village Story* (*Sennen kizami no hidokei—Magino-mura monogatari,* 1986). The film had impressed me, and I wrote a short piece I'd rather forget for the festival catalog. Ogawa liked the essay, and we immediately struck up a friendship. When I finished my master's degree, he helped me take some time off from school by introducing me to the Yamagata International Documentary Film Festival, where I have worked as a coordinator ever since. In my many trips to Japan, I often stayed at Ogawa Pro's apartments in Ogikubo, Tokyo, or in Magino Village in Yamagata. My relationship to Ogawa felt—and feels—so intense that I am shocked when I consider that it was only for four short years. This book was a deathbed promise.

I write this introduction—on the eighth anniversary of Ogawa's death—in a town not far from the village of Magino. I am finding it difficult to sort out what I can and cannot write. Although nearly a decade has passed, the intensity of people's feelings has not necessarily weakened. What has changed with the passing of time is their willingness to express them. In many cases, these feelings were inflamed by the revelation after Ogawa's death that most of his public biography was a fabulous construction having little to do with reality. Everyone knew that Ogawa was a bullshitter, but even his best friends were surprised by what they found out. A typical biography starts something like the one in Tayama Rikiya's reference book on Japanese film directors:

> Ogawa Shinsuke was born on June 25, 1935, in Gifu Prefecture. His family owned land and were well-off. However, at the dividing line of the war's end, they were dispossessed of most privileges as landlords. Furthermore, his father moved to Yamanashi Prefecture after the war because of trouble within the family, and Shinsuke accompanied him. After that he returned to Gifu, and after studying at Ena High School, went to the capital. Entering Kokugakuin University, he studied ethnology under Yanagita Kunio. However, he waved the flag of the left wing there, and for this was expelled from the university at the beginning of his third year.[4]

Some of the lies were petty. For example, he told people he was born in 1935 instead of 1936, making him slightly older than all of his best friends. Other fabrications radicalize what was otherwise a fairly conservative looking profile. He claimed he studied ethnology at this major center of folklore studies, when he actually was in the department of economics. And he told people that he never graduated, a badge of honor in the days of the student movement, although he did in fact receive a diploma. Ogawa's later reputation for hands-on farming while filmmaking, for example, was also half-fiction; he spent most of his time home reading while the staff did the farm work.

Ogawa told neighbor Kimura Michio that he studied at Kokugakuin because he wanted to major in ethnology with the famous anthropologist Origuchi Shinobu. Once Kimura happened upon the scholar's profile and noticed that Origuchi had retired by the time that Ogawa got there. Unlike many of Ogawa's other friends, Kimura did not feel as though he had been tricked or lied to when he discovered that he was actually older than the director, or that Ogawa hadn't studied ethnology but the decidedly conservative field of economics. Instead, he saw it as Ogawa's way of engaging someone in discussion, of energizing the give-and-take of human interaction. As an example, Kimura recalls the first time they talked about their childhoods. Ogawa's experience resonated against his own: terrible, rural poverty at the end of the war, eating only potatoes and pumpkins. After Ogawa's death, Kimura learned that the director's father was actually a drugstore owner—in Tokyo's city center—and that the family led a relatively comfortable life until the end of the war. To Kimura, this was a way Ogawa built intensity and sympathetic feelings into his friendships. Likewise, producer Fuseya Hiro (Hiroo) asserts that this tendency to elaborate mundane reality is what made him a great documentary filmmaker. Many of Ogawa's friends, however, found the lies unforgivable.

This forces me, in too many cases, to consider stories tinged with everything from glowing happiness to dark bitterness, from hazy confusion to seething anger. Where does one draw the line between gossip and legiti-

Ogawa celebrates his rice harvest in Magino.

mate history? Perhaps all biographers are confronted with this problem, but in the case of Ogawa Pro, the emotional affect of people's contact with Ogawa was particularly potent.

In the course of their filmmaking, they had to strike a balance between what stories to include in the films, and what was best left in the *ura* (backstory). In Sanrizuka, for example, Tamura shot the cruelty of the farmers against their neighbors who sold out to the government. These sequences never made it into the films. The true complexity of the relationships between those who sold and those who fought is one of the structured absences of the film. It is hinted at, but never explored with the dedicated intensity of other aspects of the struggle.

In the case of their time in Furuyashiki, the backstory included the suicide of one young woman who, excited by her contact with the collective, wanted to move to the big city against her father's wishes. Another family we do not learn about sold their daughter into prostitution during the war. Both Sanrizuka and Magino had back stages filled with such stories and very much engaged with the themes of the films. However, determining what their films needed, and what would break them and the people they described, was a difficult task. I find myself in the same position as a historian approaching Ogawa and Ogawa Pro.

The house they lived in at Magino is now gone. Some members (from here on I shall drop the adjective "former," as emotionally no one ever seemed to leave Ogawa Pro) wanted to preserve the house, which was as much a *"sakuhin"* ("work") as any of the films. They envisioned a memorial housing Ogawa Pro's traces, an archive to stop the experience from receding into the past. Others wanted to tear down the house as soon as possible, sell the prints, pay off long-standing debts, and attempt to mark a material ending. They desperately wanted to put the prints, stills, rushes, posters, graphs, clippings, notes, diaries, receipts, scripts, everything, in someone else's archives and relegate Ogawa Pro to the past once and for all. Ogawa died so young and left so little, leaving some clinging to memories others would just as soon purge.

The collective left a prodigious amount of primary material. In the production of just the Sanrizuka Series, it accumulated over sixteen hundred hours of audio tape, two hundred hours of film, and some thirty boxes of paper materials. Today, thanks to the complicated relationships left in Ogawa's wake, the notebooks, diaries, photographs, and films have been split into four pots. The student movement era materials are in the garage of one member's family in Yamagata City. The Sanrizuka era materials are carefully preserved, ironically enough, in an archive *inside* Narita Airport. The Magino era materials are in an old barn in the mountain village of Furuyashiki. The films themselves—the rights, prints, and negatives—have been sold to a film school in Tokyo. I am deeply indebted to all the people who have worked hard to allow me access to these materials.

While searching through these yet-to-be-cataloged boxes, I came across traces of my own encounter with Ogawa. Aside from carefully logged receipts of every expense incurred by the collective on my account, there was a photo album with snapshots from Ogawa's trip to the Hawai'i International Film Festival in 1988. There I was, an intern at the festival and ten years younger, with this intense little man I found almost magnetic. Last night, at a bar with friends who were volunteers on the first Yamagata International Documentary Film Festival in 1989, I was given a photograph taken at that same bar with the same people on my first trip to Magino nearly ten years ago to the day; Ogawa sat in the front row, arms crossed, looking very pleased. Along with this photograph, they told me what they called a "famous story." Before I arrived in Yamagata, Ogawa told the volunteers who I was and why I was going to participate in the next film festival. When we met in Hawai'i, Ogawa felt a strong sense of connection with me. We quickly developed a friendship, but what really cemented things for Ogawa was that he couldn't believe he met an American who didn't own a single credit card! This was someone he could really work with, he thought. From that point on he considered us good friends.

In retrospect, I knew Ogawa for an incredibly short time, but it feels quite long, involved, even intense. What must it have been like for the people who worked and lived with him? No wonder they all have such complicated and present feelings so many years after his passing from this world. His magnetism is still strong, which is exactly why some members are trying hard to establish new lives independent from that vortex of memories while others are so willing to give in.

While this is ostensibly the biography of Ogawa, it is just as much about the film collective that bears his name. At the same time, it is the

In 1990, Ogawa took me to Yamagata to meet the network of festival volunteers, people who would soon become good friends. My main memories are the humbling hospitality of Ogawa Pro, the enthusiasm of the volunteers, the giddy nonstop talk of Ogawa, and the utter cold.

story of postwar Japanese documentary and is ultimately a slice of the social history of postwar Japan. The stance this project takes requires an accounting of the larger context in which the films were imagined, produced, and watched. Kitakoji Takashi has suggested two broad reasons why people like Ogawa's films.[5] Some spectators are keen on the films' politics of resisting power by standing firmly on the side of protesting students and farmers. Others sidestep or ignore the politics to assert that they are simply good movies; for them the films' significance lies in their rejection of the shackles of objectivity, which brought a new creativity to documentary film. In other words, they try to apprehend the films primarily as "cinema," downplaying whatever politics might have informed their production and consumption.

However, I work under the assumption that even these two basic responses are products of a certain moment in the history of Japanese society and its relationship to politics and art. Both readings are available today, and are certainly supplementary to each other, but this does not mean that they were always or evenly available over the course of the past several decades. The films themselves are not equally political, or aesthetically or emotionally pleasing, and that is part of our concern here. Something momentous happens in the midst of Ogawa's career. It is marked by the collective's move from Sanrizuka to Magino, but has everything to do with one of the most difficult problems facing historians of postwar Japan.

Something happened in the early to mid-1970s.

Something happened in the larger frame of history, something that I can only take rudimentary steps toward unpacking. In the end, I can only expect that my explanation will be circumscribed to the subject of postwar cinema. We start our initial approach to this problem by considering a fascinating discussion at the 1998 Yamagata International Documentary Film Festival. The occasion was a major retrospective of Japanese documentary films from the 1980s and 1990s. This was the last installment in a biennial series that painstakingly covered the one-hundred-year history of nonfiction filmmaking in Japan. Previous retrospectives confidently displayed a national heritage and its sure but steady growth, but the title of the 1995 edition suggested a less than optimistic attitude: "The Groping in the Dark—Japanese Documentary in the 1980s and Beyond" ("Nihon Dokyumentarii no Mosaku—1980 Nendai Iko"). Nowhere was the cautious uncertainty more evident than in the accompanying symposium.

On the stage were four filmmakers representing various generations in Japanese film history. In the middle sat Kanai Katsu (who started filming in the 1960s) and Ise Shin'ichi (from the 1980s). On either end were Iizuka Toshio (1960s) and Kawase Naomi (1990s).[6] Iizuka joined Ogawa Pro in the 1960s and served as his assistant director from the late 1970s until Ogawa's death in 1992. He has since become a director in his own right. Kawase had recently returned from the Cannes International Film Festival, where her first feature (shot, incidentally, by Ogawa's cameraman Tamura Masaki) surprised everyone by taking a special jury prize. The media—of which a sizable contingent sat at Kawase's feet in Yamagata—was calling the Cannes coup an indication that a new generation of filmmakers had attained international recognition and that Japanese cinema had entered a new era. This claim has far more to do with Japan's anxiety about its place in global cultural production than with any sense for film history. However, as I hope to demonstrate, it is right on the mark . . . from a certain perspective.

The seating arrangement at Yamagata was a piece of history writing in and of itself. It did not take long before the generational structure bared itself onstage. Any "groping" that evening would be between those on either end of the platform. Iizuka and Kawase would have it out over the question posed by moderator Yamane Sadao, one of Japan's best critics. Taking a

The "Groping in the Dark" panel at the 1998 Yamagata International Documentary Film Festival. The seating arrangement expressed the historical structure of postwar Japanese documentary. From left to right: Yamane Sadao (critic), Kawase Naomi, Kanai Katsu, Ise Shin'ichi, Iizuka Toshio. Photograph courtesy of Yamagata International Documentary Film Festival.

cue from audience member Fukuda Katsuhiko (an ex–Ogawa Pro member who stayed in Sanrizuka after the collective left), Yamane suggested that in the mid-1970s, something happened that transformed Japanese documentary, leaving it in its present, seemingly precarious, state.

As in any serious discussion of documentary in Japan, the words *shutai* (subject) and *taisho* (object) constantly came up. They are rarely, if ever, defined, yet are repeated like the mantra of postwar documentary; functionally, they generally serve to demarcate historical articulations of difference, usually to the end of constructing a periodization. The artists on stage quickly staked out the territory. Iizuka laid out the generally accepted view that the filmmakers of the 1960s and early 1970s had a political commitment and took their engagement with the world seriously. They assumed a filmmaker subject *(shutai)* that was thoroughly social, one that required visible expression on the film and at the same time acknowledged its delicate relationship to the object *(taisho)* acting before the camera. Younger filmmakers, argued Iizuka (in an obvious critical swipe at Kawase), are too wrapped up in their own little world. They either focus on themselves or their family without reference to society, without engaging any political position or social stance. Kawase responded defensively that her own documentaries about her aunt and the search for her lost father had the kind of social resonance Iizuka claimed for his own work. In the end, the two offered only implicit criticism of each other. For all the groping, which included contributions from the floor by Tsuchimoto Noriaki (director of the famous Minamata Series) and Fukuda, almost everyone felt they had been left in the dark, especially on that question, "What happened to the exciting Japanese documentary world of the 1960s?"

This book provisionally accepts Fukuda's periodization. Following the filmmaking of the 1960s and early 1970s, which was spectacular in both quality and quantity, something *did* happen, and the Japanese documentary went into a steady, sure decline. At the very least, all historians accept that the sheer number of stirring, creative documentaries in that earlier period was unprecedented, that the present situation pales in comparison. And how ironic that of all the art forms to experience decay in the bubble economy of the 1980s—in the age of *johoshihonshugi* (information capitalism)—documentary would lose its confidence and end up groping in the critical darkness for a toehold in Yamagata at the close of the 1990s. Few films today are as compelling or as daring as the prodigious work straddling the year 1970. Today's films and videos in Japan represent a turn to the self, a movement that appears strikingly similar to developments in Euro-American film and video making. However, where the latter is rigorously political and theoretically informed, its Japanese counterpart documents the self from a vaguely apolitical place. The intertwining histories of documentary and its conceptualization largely took their own course in Japan. They developed with relative autonomy vis-à-vis Euro-American nonfiction film. Japanese writers and directors were aware of verité, direct cinema, third cinema, and developments in the Western avant-garde, but remained resistant to slavish imitation. As will soon become clear, this independence was a correlate of the pre-1980s vigor of debates in the field, the innovations of the filmmakers, and the perception that the local social and political stakes were high.

Thus, tracking the twists and turns in Ogawa's career and the transformations in debates over *shutaisei* (subjectivity), this book will grope for the "something" that did happen, the thing that seems to divide the filmmaking collective shooting other groups and the camera-toting individual documenting the self, the public and the private, the *shutai* and its *taisho*—the 1960s and the present day.

[1] *Ogawa as Postwar Documentarist*

Prologue—The Occupation (1945–1952)

With this chapter, I begin by sketching out the history of the Japanese documentary form from the end of World War II to the point at which Ogawa Shinsuke started making films. The student of Euro-American film will find many interesting points of synchronicity, convergence, and divergence within this story. With little or no exposure to foreign documentaries, the film culture the youthful Ogawa grew up in centered upon educational films *(kyoiku eiga)*. This undoubtedly shaped Ogawa's understanding of documentary. It was the filmmaking that he absorbed first as a spectator, then learned formally in an institutional setting, and then critiqued through the aggressively independent form he helped pioneer. One cannot understand where Ogawa came from without considering this broader institutional and theoretical context. There are three broad periods in this prehistory to Ogawa Pro: the Occupation's propaganda documentary, the PR and educational film dominated by the Communist Party, and the challenge thrown up by Ogawa's emergent, New Left generation.

As a form of filmmaking, documentary has been attractive to those at both ends of the political spectrum since the 1920s. This is arguably because of several qualities specific to the medium. First, by the interwar era, the infrastructure for the movies had developed sufficiently to allow for quick replication and distribution of images to masses of people scattered across vast distances. This gave cinema an easy national, even international (if too often colonial), reach. A further reason lies in the indexical quality of cinematic representation. The onscreen image is an index in the Peircian sense, like a fingerprint or a thermometer. It possesses a striking spatial and temporal immediacy in relation to its indexed object, a quality that documentary filmmaking uses to set itself far apart from the fictive film. Exploiting this seemingly privileged link to reality, filmmakers with a sense of social commitment developed an arsenal of rhetorical devices to move those newly formed masses of moviegoers. These special qualities were initially evident to filmmakers involved in primary education and the proletarian culture movement in the late 1920s and early 1930s, and stylistic artifacts of their early efforts survive in the conventions of today's documentaries.

These two tendencies in the documentary—pedagogy and sociopolitical enlightenment—converged as Japan went to war in the 1930s. At the very same time, differences between the Japanese Left and Right became increasingly ambiguous as the government cracked down on all forms of dissent, and filmmakers either jumped on the military bandwagon or slipped into obscurity in other professions. However, with the end of World War II in 1945, independence for filmmakers meant new possibilities for deploying cinema as an oppositional force in society. Leftist activists gravitated toward the documentary form, particularly those aligned with the Japan Communist Party (JCP), which became a powerful force behind the organizations devoted to film. Like their predecessors in the prewar and wartime eras, these leftist filmmakers were strongly attracted to the possibility of a medium based on an indexical representation of the public arena.

Through this newly democratized apparatus, they intended to construct an alternative space of the nation, one capable of *moving* people in every sense. The resulting films from the late 1940s and the 1950s generally look pedestrian today, but that was partly the point. This new attitude about moving people's passions—although it can easily be seen as a continuation of wartime practice—seemed to demand a straightforward realism. Nevertheless, Ogawa's generation of filmmakers would come to assert that this documentation of democratic reality also required the suppression of individual expression in favor of larger categories, such as people, citizen, and class.

The immediate transitional period after the end of the war is marked by controversies over two films, *The Effects of the Atomic Bomb on Hiroshima and Nagasaki* (*Hiroshima, Nagasaki ni okeru genshibakudan no koka,* 1946) and Kamei Fumio's *The Tragedy of Japan* (*Nihon no higeki,* 1946). Both of these extraordinary films slipped through the bureaucratic flux of the new government just as the American Occupation was preparing an elaborate system of regulation and censorship. And both films saw only glimpses of the projector's light before being suppressed to unknown film vaults in America. *The Effects of the Atomic Bombs on Hiroshima and Nagasaki* endured a complicated set of "transfers," "confiscations," "suppressions," and "secessions" before final repatriation by a citizens' movement in the 1970s and 1980s.[1] Kamei's *The Tragedy of Japan* was shelved at the request of none other than Prime Minister Yoshida.[2] Aside from its stringent attack on those responsible for the war and its full-frontal Marxist critique of the wartime system, the film's infamous climax drew particular attention: after panning over the photographs of the Japanese leaders doomed to capital punishment at the war crimes trials, Kamei shows a photograph of Hirohito in full military regalia and slowly dissolves to a postwar photograph of a hunchbacked emperor in a business suit.

The incidents and circumstances surrounding these two postwar productions point to the way one censorship system was simply displaced by another. However, these two films also belong specifically to the short, chaotic transition period at the beginning of the American Occupation. More typical are two aspects of the Occupation that provided foundations for the postwar documentary movements from which Ogawa Productions (Ogawa Pro) emerged: the film program of the Civil Information and Education section of the Occupation (CIE) and the eventual dominance of the nonfiction film world by left-wing filmmakers.

After World War II and during the American Occupation of Japan, most documentaries were produced with one thing in mind: the democratization of Japan or the de-fascistization of the citizenry by enlightening the populace to the beneficence of Western democracy. To this end, the Americans sprinkled 16mm projectors across the country and distributed documentaries through a variety of new and old routes. It was estimated that by 1948, the CIE had given away more than 1,300 Natco (National Company) projectors, all stamped with the white lettering *Property of the U.S. Army*. They also established CIE film libraries across Japan, a continuation of prewar film libraries except for the new ideological agenda driving their selection process. The Americans' aim was to spread democracy to the hinterlands, where the realities of the Occupation and the driving forces behind the transformations in the nation were only weakly felt. This was particularly true in the regions that had yet to be penetrated by the electrical grid, so the CIE served these citizens their first glimpses of MacArthur and the postwar version of Hirohito through traveling outdoor film shows.

Bilingual study-discussion guides accompanying these CIE prints hint at the kind of reception context they aimed to create. These guides always start with a list of "seven steps for a successful meeting":

- Preview the picture. Study your materials before the meeting.
- Have several people in the audience ready to start discussion when the picture ends.
- Have everything ready in advance. Start on time.
- Introduce the picture and give reasons for showing it.

- Encourage the bashful. Don't let one or two people dominate the meeting.
- Stop the discussion while it is still interesting.
- Summarize briefly the main points of discussion.

This comes from the study-discussion guide for *Children's Guardian* (1950), a typical educational documentary of the time.[3] The film tells the story of a corrupt member of the Board of Education who used his position to profit from wartime to the present day. A small movement led by the school janitor—who lost his son in the war—deposes the scoundrel through democratic election. Like most documentaries of the Occupation era, it uses largely fictional narrative embedded in actual settings to argue a point. In this case, the objectives are, in the language of the guide itself, "To focus true understanding of the functions of the Board of Education and the important role it plays in the sound development of democratic education. To emphasize that the members of the Board of Education must be persons of virtue, sincerely dedicated to the public interest. To show that the future of education and culture lies in the hands of the people who elect the members of the Board of Education."[4] This forty-minute morality tale hints at many of the themes through its use of fiction, leaving the more complicated explanations of Occupation policy to the after-film discussion.

Information about Occupation educational reforms is supplied in great detail in the study guide, which explains the letter of the law, the functions and structure of the board, its relationship to the local polity, and even describes several case studies. With this information in hand, anyone could lead a reasonably intelligent discussion of the film and supply the rhetorical arguments for a decentralized educational system as the basis of a "democratic and cultural nation." The film leaves its ideology mostly implicit, but the guide constantly drives home the contrast between the centralized, corrupt system of the war years and the current educational agenda. The guide, and presumably the after-film discussions, particularly emphasize that the success of the people's franchise depends upon a conscientious stewardship that protects itself from abuse and dedicates itself to an education responsive to individual and local needs. In its most baldly ideological moment, the guide concludes, "We the people must live up to the ideal of democracy, sovereignty by the people, when the long-awaited peace treaty has been signed. We the people should exercise our franchise and do our utmost to fulfill our responsibilities and duties to prevent our educational reform from becoming a superficial one."[5]

The discussions were also accompanied by other materials, suggestions for which are provided by the guide. They included other films or filmstrips, books, pamphlets, posters, photographic models, and the like. If a local exhibitor did not have such materials, the CIE would provide them upon request. The guides also provided newspaper stories and radio spot scenarios for PR purposes. All organizers had to do was fill in the time and place. In these texts the articulation between locality and national space is most pronounced; by filling in the blanks with one's hometown, the film screening becomes thoroughly interpolated by the Occupation project.

While hardly the kind of master filmmaking memorialized in film histories, the CIE documentaries came to take a significant place in the movie culture of the Occupation period. According to the CIE's own figures, their films were seen by 13,017,973 Japanese spectators in 1947; 92,847,545 in 1948; 280,910,727 in 1949; 342,211,521 in 1950; and reached 472,341,919 viewers by the end of the Occupation.[6] One of the largest audiences for the films was children. A major study by the Ministry of Education revealed that in 1951, 78.6 percent of schools were showing CIE films in the classroom, and 95.2 percent borrowed them for special activities and recreation.[7] The films have survived to the present day, deposited along with the paper records of prefectures as part of their locality's historical archive (in Tokushima, a rural city in Shikoku, the prefectural archive holds over two hundred prints from the U.S. government). This system continued until recent years under the management of the USIS, but became utterly insignificant compared to its role during the U.S. Occupation of Japan, where it introduced young students like Ogawa to democracy while laying the infrastructure for the distribution of Japanese documentaries with quite different politics.

It is rather ironic that this massive project, instituted by an occupying foreign power, eventually became dominated by the Communist Left. Initially, the Americans restricted their new distribution system to CIE and Department of Education productions, however, this resulted in immediate shortages, and they opened it up to smaller Japanese companies. By the end of the Occupation, the CIE shortage of productions constituted a crucial niche market for Japanese documentary film and filmstrip companies like Nichiei Shinsha, Riken, and Sakura-Koga.[8] As one might imagine, it was not an entirely smooth relationship. One gauge of this is the 1948 strike at Toho studios, which shook the foundations of the Japanese film world. The aftershocks of this event contributed several factors to the development of Japanese documentary. First, a new distribution route opened up with the creation of a nongovernmental, noncommercial network in the form of cine-clubs. And second, an independent film production sector emerged as left-leaning filmmakers were purged from the studio system and began carving out their own independent space in the industry.

The strike was seen as a serious threat to the film culture of Japan, and in response to the union's call for help, support spread among student and labor groups.[9] This support became formalized with the creation of the Association to Protect Japanese Culture (Nihon Bunka o Mamoru Kai) on April 22, 1948. It continued to grow, leading to the formation of the Tokyo Film Circle Council (Tokyo Eiga Sakuru Kyogikai) in August, a group that was nationalized in October 1949 as the National Film Circle Council (Zenkoku Eiga Sakuru Kyogikai, or Zenkokueisa). This was the first leftist film appreciation organization since the Proletarian Film League of Japan (or Prokino, for short) in the early 1930s and was many times larger. In the midst of these developments, the Toho strike reached its notorious climax with the deployment of over seven hundred police in military garb, bulldozers converted into barricade-busting machines, as well as military aircraft, four Sherman tanks, and fifty soldiers borrowed from the Americans—"everything but the battleships," as actress Akagi Ranko so famously put it. The strikers left the studio grounds singing labor songs, and by October, at least twenty of the most talented people at Toho had quit.

This talent formed the core of a new independent sector in the film industry. The model came from Kamei Fumio's *A Woman's Life* (*Onna no issho,* 1949), which funneled profits into the production of the next project, *City of Violence* (*Boryoku no machi,* 1950) and the establishment of the first of the independent production companies, Shinsei Eigasha. This became the prototype for the independent film movement of the 1950s. One cannot minimize the contributions of filmmakers like Imai Tadashi, Kamei Fumio, Shindo Kaneto, and Yamamoto Satsuo. Despite the fact that they were only releasing a couple films a year, the quality of their works and the innovations of their production methods often stood out from the studio practices of the 1950s. Instead of owning their own theaters, they created new organizations and networked old and emerging groups. A synergy developed as a range of new organizations related to film appeared in the 1950s, such as the Kyoto Society for Viewing Documentary Cinema (Kyoto Kiroku Eiga o Miru Kai), Society for Japanese Film Art (Nihon Eiga Geijutsu Kyokai), Japan Film Directors Guild (Nihon Eiga Kantoku Kyokai), Union of Education Film Producers (Kyoiku Eiga Seisakusha Renmei), Tokyo Association of Film Lovers (Tokyo Eiga Aiko Kai Rengo), Kyoto Council of Film Workers (Kyoto Kinrosha Eiga Kyogikai), not to mention the resurgence of student film study groups on campuses across Japan. The National Council of Film Circles experienced explosive growth after mid-1954 when an entertainment tax system went into place giving members a one-third discount at the box office window. By the late 1950s, they changed this name to the Tokyo Association of Film Lovers and had over

100,000 members at the end of the decade. The system broke down around 1959, just when young directors like Nakahira Ko, Masumura Yasuzo, and Oshima Nagisa were shaking up the Japanese feature film world. By this time, film circles, independent production routes, and the idea of independent exhibition (*jishu joei*) were in place; and the option of working within or without the mainstream industry—fiction or documentary—had become a real, if difficult, choice.

Simultaneously, an independent documentary cinema emerged, and, once again, the Red Purge and events at Toho played a decisive role. This new independent documentary scene was being forged by some of the same feature directors, most notably Kamei Fumio. They used many of the same strategies for production, distribution, exhibition, and organizational networks as the independent feature film. One of the typical ways they raised production monies was through labor unions. Examples include *The Whistle Won't Stop Blowing* (*Go fue nariyamazu,* 1949, directed by Asano Tatsuo) by the national railways union, *We Are Electric Industry Workers* (*Warera wa denki sangyo rodosha,* 1948, directed by Takeuchi Shinji) by their own union, and *The Statements of Young Women* (*Shojo no hatsugen,* 1948, directed by Kyogoku Takahide, screenplay by Atsugi Taka) by the union for the textiles industry. One of the best of these films is *Living on the Sea* (*Umi ni ikiru,* 1949, directed by Yanagisawa Hisao and Kabashima Seiichi). It was funded by a union for people working in fishing and records the life of men fishing on the open ocean. It is somewhat reminiscent of Grierson's *Drifters* (1929), but has a far more dramatic treatment of the rough seas these people work in. The same groups often sponsored newsreel-like films about actions, incidents, and events they were involved in.

There was also a strain of science films that largely escaped the politics of the Occupation. These include Ota Nikichi's *Life of Rice* (*Ine no issho,* 1950), and *Butterfly* (*Agehacho,* 1948), and Okayama Dairokuro's *Living Bread* (*Ikiteiru pan,* 1948). They were among the most visually interesting films made before the 1960s, mostly for their creative use of time-lapse photography and photomicroscopy. However, they did not escape the standard conventions of the CIE education films in any significant sense. Their beautiful photography not withstanding, they are mostly interesting as examples of the possibilities and limits of the day's documentary.

In general, the style of the American documentaries distributed by the CIE was closely attuned to Japanese modes of documentary. The logic of the narration was dictated primarily by the temporal order of the events recorded or the "enlightening" voice-over. Because of this, the films are dominated by matter-of-fact description and rarely take advantage of the resources available in the filmmaker's toolkit, from editing to other kinds of logic for construction. One filmmaker referred to the style as "moving *kamishibai*."[10] This practice was propped up by theoretical writings on realism that relied on a rather instrumentalist conception of the apparatus.

Despite the prestige of Imamura's writing, the ultimate frame of reference for documentary style during the Occupation must be traced back to the 1930s. Most of the Occupation filmmakers started their careers during or just before the war. When Ogawa's generation took the stage in the late 1950s, they harshly criticized these Occupation filmmakers by drawing a line of stylistic continuity between the older generation's wartime and Occupation work. This was theoretically informed critique, in which we shall engage at the end of this chapter; however, the key plank of the platform was simple: the generation filming through war to Occupation performed an ideological about-face (*tenko*) in 1945 without undergoing any serious self-criticism. Without a thoughtful self-reflection about their role in World War II, it was a matter of course that they would reproduce the approach to filming reality that they deployed to wage war. The agenda they proselytized simply shifted from the Great East Asian Co-Prosperity Sphere to American-style democracy and capitalism. At a nuts and bolts level, this is certainly understandable, considering Occupation filmmakers were literally filming under the gun—punishment for going against American policy could be as severe as imprisonment or banishment to Okinawa. However, despite the continuity in style, the subject matter of independent documentaries substantially, sometimes radically, changed with the end of American rule.

The New Documentary of Subjective Assertion

Near the very end of the Occupation in 1952, left-wing filmmakers started making documentaries with increasingly oppositional politics. Initially, these films tended to be simple documents of events. They were made with the assumption that one would capture the actions of the day directly, reproducing them later for far-flung audiences. Some of the first efforts were from a group called the Youth Culture Association (Seinen Bunka Kyokai), which made 8mm shorts as part of their activities. Its most important films are *Mitsukoshi Strike* (*Mitsukoshi sutoraiki,* 1951) and the ironically titled *Sightseeing in Tokyo* (*Tokyo kengaku ryoko,* 1951) about conditions surrounding the American military bases.

This short period also saw a few May Day films, shot for the first time since the early 1930s before police crackdowns destroyed the Left. Marked by parades and demonstrations, this labor celebration was first outlawed by the Japanese government during the Fifteen Years' War and then again by the Americans in 1945. The first postwar May Day film was shot in 1951. At Tokyo University a student club called Free Cinema Research Group (Jiyu Eiga Kenkyukai) shot *May Festival Record* (*Gogatsu sai no kiroku,* 1951). This group simultaneously set the stage for the reinvigoration of another tradition that was interrupted by the war: the amateur productions by student film clubs from which Ogawa would emerge at the end of the decade. Another example of May Day documentary comes from the cameramen, directors, and scenarists who lost their jobs at the Kyoto studios during the Red Purge. They formed the Kyoto Filmmakers Group (Kyoto Eigajin Shudan) and shot the local May Day in 1951. They later shot films about a local rail strike, an incident in which hard questions were asked of the emperor on his trip to Kyoto, and Kyoto's 1952 May Day.

A similar group of purged filmmakers shot the violent police riot at the 1952 May Day events in Tokyo, and the film they made sparked a movement that constituted the core of the documentary cinema for the next decade. This was the first large-scale May Day celebration since the early 1930s. It ended up on the grounds of the Imperial Palace, where riot police suddenly attacked protestors with vicious force. The demonstration was being shot with multiple cameras by the professional cinematographers left unemployed by the political events at the studios. The film they created has the rough quality of the Prokino parade films from twenty years before, but it also features the brutal spectacle of police attacking demonstrators that would fill the films of Ogawa Pro twenty years later. The film about the event was a simple record of the incident, but featured shocking police violence that had been kept from Japanese movie screens through the censorship apparatus. It was screened all across Japan in independent theaters and met enormous success. The filmmakers began to think that they had discovered a route to engage the passions of the Japanese masses and started nurturing their discovery. To this end, they created the Documentary and Education Film Production Council (Kiroku Kyoiku Eiga Seisaku Kyogikai) in 1952, which itself was constituted by the membership of the Association of Japanese Filmmakers (from the Nichiei purge) and the New Filmmakers' Association (from Toho Kyoiku Eiga).

The films of the Production Council were usually funded by labor-related organizations and invariably toed the ideological line of the Japan Communist Party (its feature film analogs were being produced by directors like Yamamoto Satsuo). One could split the films into two broad groups: those that centered on political incidents and those that focused on everyday life through a narrative movement from the particularized local to the generalized national. The former films would take an action, incident, or event and record it on film. The Production Council documented strikes, rallies, and demonstrations, faithfully including the latest slogans of the JCP. The solutions to the problems would inevitably involve the forming of solidarity between proletarian groups, especially farmers and workers.

The other group of films has come to constitute the Production Council's historical legacy, a reputation attributable in part to its own writing of documentary history. Ironically, these films are different from the organization's starting point on that Bloody May Day of 1952. The most famous of the films is *Tsuki no Wa Tombs* (*Tsuki no Wa kofun*, 1954), its first production after formation. It is ostensibly the simple documentary record of a citizen's group in Okayama Prefecture that organizes to conduct its own excavation of an ancient tomb. The film is free of flag-waving and heavy-handed rhetoric, but it essentially boils down to a social education film meant to enlighten the moviegoing masses to democratic ideals and the power of people who form into mass efforts.

Iwanami's *Record of a Single Mother* (*Hitori no haha no kiroku*, 1956, directed by Kyogoku Takahide, screenplay by Iwasa Hisaya) was made by a number of Production Council members and is a far more interesting film, particularly for the rousing debate it ignited over the role of reenactment in documentary. For this reason, the film also reveals sharp tensions in the Production Council's politics of representation. Films like *Tsuki no Wa Tombs* and *Record of a Single Mother* make significant choices of subject matter. They focus on a single locality, or in the latter film a single individual, to make an argument about the nation or about capitalism. This movement between the particular and the general is tricky for documentarists, especially those operating under the assumption that their cameras can directly transmit reality. For the producers of *Record of a Single Mother,* the answer was to resort to fiction.

The film deals with the potential destruction of Japan's villages through urban flight. It approaches this theme in a roundabout fashion, using the potent trope of the suffering single mother, presumably alone because her husband lost his life in the war. Set in a village in the mountains of Nagano Prefecture, it describes the daily life of a peasant family cultivating silk worms and rice. The Miyazawas are posed as a typical family from the countryside. Of their five children, the eldest daughter left the village to work in a factory in the city. The remaining children help out on the farm. Silk production is considered women's work, and the mother is constantly worried about her worms. In addition to these duties, she also cleans, cooks, and helps in the fields. The difficulty of her position is shown in a poignant scene where the family sleeps while the mother works into the night. Following the cycle of the seasons and the harvest, the film ends with the sale of her cocoons. At the end, the film drives home its point when one son goes off to work as a day laborer on a road crew while a daughter takes an exam to work at a factory. Life for the mother is already difficult; if her children leave, her life will be unbearable, and ultimately the village itself will die.

As Noda Shinkichi points out, *Record of a Single Mother* implicitly argues that the contradictions of society are shifted onto the points of weakness and least resistance—in this case village Japan—and that they would be most concentrated on the weakest people there, thus, the choice of a single mother. By zeroing in on the suffering of this woman, the filmmakers assumed they could uncover the reality of present-day Japan. However, Noda suggests,

> When moving to an ordinary individual as material one must express that person's inner aspects; otherwise, the sense of a social totality within the individual will not come out. There is no way to do this with a simplistic documentarism. So they season their film with various techniques from the fiction cinema, and end up making a documentary-like fiction film.[11]

Many other critics aired similar complaints, especially regarding the profilmic family's constitution. Basically, the filmmakers entered the village with script in hand, sought out farmers who matched their preconceptions, and built their family from these nonactors. While it was shot entirely on location, it is clear that every scene was carefully staged. It is essentially a fiction film shot in a manner strongly reminiscent of neorealism. Despite (or perhaps because of) the controversy that the film stirred up over reenactment, it met with some success. Kyogoku's handling of the melodrama was obviously effective enough to garner the top award on the *Kinema Junpo* best-ten list for nonfiction films, and it is now considered one of the finest documentaries of the 1950s.

Other prominent films using fictional modes of narration followed, most notably Yokota Keita's *The Children of Kujuku Ri Beach* (*Kujuku ri hama no kodomotachi,* 1956) and *The Children of a Town of Soot and Smoke* (*Baien no machi no kodomotachi,* 1957). This is the kind of filmmaking the Production Council is remembered for, not the more newsreel-like films following the agitprop call to arms of their Bloody May Day documentary. This set the stage for a generational confrontation led by filmmaker Matsumoto Toshio that would tear the group apart and shake up the documentary world. Before this would happen, however, the energy of all nonfiction filmmakers—including the Communist artists—was drawn into a close collaboration with the industries of Japan's high-growth economy, which was enjoying booming growth after the Korean War.

In the latter half of the 1950s, the independent film movement reached the peak of its prestige, in both fiction and documentary. At this very moment, a boom in nonfiction production occurred when large companies threw their weight behind PR films. They thought this would be the best method for representing themselves to the nation and the world. Television had yet to reach into enough homes to compete with celluloid for this purpose. As a result, the PR film reached epic proportions, more ambitious and expensive than similar films in any other national context with which I am familiar. Films like Takamura Takeji's three-part *Sakuma Dam* (*Sakuma Damu,* 1954–1957) were exhibited in major theaters for feature films, where they were discovered by a filmgoing audience open to something new and different. The country was pulling out of the desperate poverty left in the wake of World War II, and spectators were content to fulfill their desires to know the unknown, to see things they had never experienced before. *Sakuma Dam* and Nishio Zensuke's *Kurobe Valley* (*Kurobe keikoku,* 1957) thrilled people with their twist on the "man against nature" theme. Rather than a Japanese Nanook battling a seal, they pitched construction workers and their machines against natural formations being transformed by massive public works projects. The war receded to the past in these films filled with images of prosperity and growth. Ise Chonosuke's *Karakoram* (1956) even removed spectators from Japan by following a Japanese research team to the Himalayas. It was followed by films like *People of the Mekon River* (*Minzoku no kawa Mekon,* 1956), *Beyond the Andes* (*Andesu o koete,* 1957), Hayashida Shigeo's *Antarctica Adventure* (*Nankyoku tanken,* 1957), *Unexplored Himalayas* (*Hikyo Himaraya,* 1957), and Kuwano Shigeru's *Mesopotamia* (1956). In a related vein, the successful release of Disney's *Living Desert* (1953) led to domestic attempts at similar nature films like the controversial *White Mountains* (*Shiroi sanmyaku,* 1957).[12]

Two filmmakers stand out in the documentary world of the 1950s, Kamei Fumio and Hani Susumu. The most important director in the history of Japanese documentary is unquestionably Kamei Fumio.[13] During the war, he was one of the few directors to take daring chances with the films he produced. Kamei was a brilliant editor, and he regularly subverted the overt politics of his documentaries to include subtle critiques of wartime ideology. In the end, he was not subtle enough as he was finally imprisoned on the eve of World War II. As noted earlier in this chapter, Kamei found the American Occupation less than libratory, and after it ended, he directed some of the finest films of the 1950s in both fiction and documentary. Kamei's first documentaries dealt directly with subjects that had been placed off-limits since his immediate postwar brushes with the

Americans, most notably atomic warfare (*Still It's Good to Live* [*Ikite ite yokatta*, 1956] and *The World is Terrified—The Reality of the "Ash of Death"* [*Sekai wa kyofu suru*, 1957]). In 1953, he directed the first of two documentaries on the problems that inevitably follow the American military wherever it sets down roots. Immediately after the Americans handed the country back to Japanese control, movements sprouted up to protest the situation surrounding all the military bases. Poverty, violence, and prostitution were endemic. The bases were restricted subject matter during the Occupation, and in the spirit of the red scare, Eirin established the Four Regulations Concerning the Evaluation of Base Films (Kichi Eiga Shinsa Yon Gensoku) on July 24, 1953, which stipulated in part, "The treatment of the base problem as a special political problem shall be avoided."[14] However, this was the same year that Kamei directed *Children of the Bases* (*Kichi no kotachi*, 1953), which reveals the shocking conditions outside of the base fences in Hokkaido, Yamagata, Ishikawa, Yokosuka, and Tachikawa.

Kamei Fumio's *The People of Sunagawa* (1956) presages the struggle and the films of Sanrizuka. Photograph courtesy of Yamagata International Documentary Film Festival and Japan Document Film.

Kamei's 1955 film is even more important in the landscape of the postwar documentary. *The People of Sunagawa—A Record of the Anti-Base Struggle* (*Sunagawa no hitobito—Kichi hantai toso no kiroku,* 1955) was the first entry of his Sunagawa Series. The American Air Force asked the Japanese government for help in expanding one of its runways because their new jets required more space for take-off and landing. Prime Minister Hatoyama accommodated the Americans' request and then proceeded to take the necessary land by force, ordering the farmers working outside the fences to vacate their land. They resisted, and were quickly lent the support of various anti-American organizations and networks of activists. Soon there were large demonstrations around the base involving thousands on both sides of the fence. Kamei was on the scene to record the violence that ensued when survey teams staked out farmland with the protection of thousands of riot police. He stayed with the local farmers and continued to document the evolving struggle in *The People of Sunagawa: Wheat Will Never Fail* (*Sunagawa no hitobito: Mugi shinazu,* 1955) and *Record of Blood: Sunagawa* (*Ryuketsu no kiroku: Sunagawa,* 1956). The struggle was perceived to have national importance, and Kamei's third film was blown up to 35 mm and distributed to regular theaters across the country. When the farmers began rising against the government's plans for Narita Airport a decade later, delegations moved between Sanrizuka and Sunagawa to share information and learn from the earlier experience. Kamei's series not only set an important precedent for the connection of film projects to tumultuous social movements, but it foreshadows Ogawa Shinsuke's Sanrizuka Series, even if its production method and style was conventional by comparison.

Kamei's other films tackle controversial subjects, such as survivors of the atomic bombing, nuclear proliferation, the plight of minorities, and environmental pollution. He was relatively inactive starting in the 1960s, making a few PR films and then a couple films on environmentalist just before his death in 1987. It is uncertain why Kamei basically quit filmmaking in his later years and retired to run an antique store. There is speculation in the film world that as punishment for making films that did not necessarily tow the party line, he was purged in the late 1950s. Since his major sponsors were all tied to the party, he simply could not raise enough money to mount expensive productions. In the end, he left a legacy that appears one step removed from the mainstream movement of Japanese documentary history.

By way of contrast, the other major figure of 1950s nonfiction film, Hani Susumu, contributed documentaries that set the film world off-balance. These were the kind of seismographic film events that Bazin describes, where the river of cinema begins carving new routes after the equilibrium of their bed is upset. Although Hani is best known for features films like *Bad Boys* (*Furyo shonen*, 1961), *He and She* (*Kare to kanojo*, 1963), and *Nanami: The Inferno of First Love* (*Hatsukoi: Jigokuhen*, 1968), he started his film career with documentaries that decisively revealed the conventional rigidity of the dominant style. He made his first film in 1954, and it was entitled *Children of the Classroom (Kyoshitsu no kodomotachi)*. This was a Monbusho-funded education film designed for people who were interested in becoming teachers. The initial idea was to make a documentary in the usual fictive educational film manner, using a child actor to play a problem student. However, this presented an extremely difficult role for a child so Hani began to consider using a real school and real children. Everyone thought it was impossible, but he went to a school to find out. In the first half hour of observation, his presence agitated the students, but after two or three hours, they forgot about him.[15]

Audiences were stunned by the spontaneity captured in *Children of the Classroom*. Close to direct cinema,[16] which it predates, this was actually much smarter filmmaking. While American filmmakers like Richard Leacock and the Maysles brothers initially clothed their work in the rhetoric of objectivity, Hani used observation to approach the subjectivities of the individuals he filmed. This is the decisive difference between the postwar conception of documentary in Japan and that of the Euro-American traditions. It was this core difference that Tsuchimoto and Ogawa would elaborate in their subsequent work, and which was embodied in Hani's first films.

For example, Hani's sequel, *Children Who Draw* (*E o kaku kodomotachi*, 1955), simply shows children interacting in an art class. As we begin to recognize different personalities, Hani cuts to the paintings they are in the process of creating. This jump from apparently objective, observed phenomenon to vivid representations of the children's inner worlds is accompanied by an astounding shift from black and white to brilliant color. Far from the stodgy realism of his contemporaries, Hani's films won international awards and were distributed across Japan through Toho Studio.[17] Other Iwanami filmmakers followed with impressive projects, particularly Tokieda Toshie's *Town Politics—Mothers Who Study* (*Machi no seiji—Benkyo suru okaa-san*, 1957), Haneda Sumiko's *School for Village Women* (*Mura no fujin gakkyu*, 1957), and others. These were the first rumblings of massive change. Hani's stunning work attracted the attention of a number of young filmmakers, who joined Iwanami and would make it one of the epicenters for change in the era of the New Wave. A typical example is Tsuchimoto Noriaki, who recalls, "I had never entertained a thought about becoming a filmmaker, but when I saw Hani's films I was amazed—so this kind of thing is possible in documentary!—and I went to Iwanami."[18]

Iwanami is a prestigious publishing house, and it formed its film division in 1950 with an eye on the considerable amount of money flowing into PR film companies. Its film unit became one of the most successful documentary film companies in the postwar era.[19] There are a number of factors in its success. First, Iwanami had strong ties to the Japan Communist Party, and when the film unit was created it became a haven for intelligent, left-leaning filmmakers, young and old, who had been recently purged from other sectors of the film industry. Another was that Iwanami's audience grew up on its paperbacks in the lean war years, so they were predisposed to admire, purchase, and rent Iwanami's films.

Probably one of the most crucial factors in Iwanami's success was the leadership of veterans like Yoshino Keiji and Kobayashi Isamu. Tokieda Toshie felt that Kobayashi's creativity had something to do with his wartime experience as a documentary filmmaker:

> Only later did I start to understand why Kobayashi said we shouldn't call our films "culture films" or "science films," but simply "documentary" films instead. Before Japan lost the war, Kobayashi was caught and arrested through the Maintenance of Public Order Act because of his publications, in what was called the Yokohama Incident. From that experience he learned that books and text could be censored or crossed out, but you can still find a way to communicate even if you say less . . . in other words he believed that there were ways to express what needed to be said without getting censored. I think that was accomplished in some of the Iwanami films and Iwanami Photographic Publications books.[20]

The Iwanami management was keen on nurturing new talent across the board and making good films. To that end, they created a work atmosphere that was among the more egalitarian and nonsexist spaces in the Japanese film world, particularly when compared to the rigidly hierarchical and authoritarian structures propping up the mainstream feature film. The film department quickly became a hotbed of creative filmmaking. Building room to maneuver within the structure of what was essentially a PR firm, the managers allowed their filmmakers the (relative) freedom to stretch the limits of the PR film. Ironically enough, however, Iwanami's biggest contribution to postwar cinema came from when its best filmmakers quit to make many of the great independent films of the 1960s, both fiction and documentary. Ogawa was among this group.

A key factor in this scenario was one of the most unusual research groups in the history of documentary, Iwanami's Blue Group (Ao no Kai). It formed spontaneously in 1961 after censorship problems with two of

Tsuchimoto's films, issues of an Iwanami series on the geography of various prefectures of Japan. Tsuchimoto's contributions to the series tended to be more gritty than glossy, and upon completion, the television network that ordered them demanded revisions that the company was prepared to acquiesce to. Tsuchimoto stood by his original versions and arranged in-house screenings to show the other Iwanami filmmakers and discuss the merits of each side. A heady debate ensued, and it was clear that other filmmakers were having similar problems. The discussion naturally enlarged to include other issues and transformed into regular meetings. An identity formed around these meetings, and they started calling themselves Blue Group.

They met about once a month. Its membership reads like a roster of the best directors and cinematographers in Japan: Ogawa Shinsuke, Tsuchimoto Noriaki, Kuroki Kazuo, Higashi Yoichi, Tamura Masaki, Iwasa Hisaya, Suzuki Tatsuo, and a couple dozen more. They met formally and informally at bars—particularly the tiny Shinjuku snack called Narcisse—racking up enormous tabs and holding raucous discussions that lasted four, five hours, even through the night. Kuroki Kazuo recalls,

> At first, Tsuchimoto Noriaki, then an assistant director, was brought there by cameraman Segawa Jun'ichi. Then, one after another, Higashi Yoichi, Suzuki Tatsuo, Otsu Koshiro, Iwasa Hisaya, Ogawa Shinsuke, and I trickled into the bar. It was as if we'd set up camp in the bar every night after finishing work in Tokyo's Jinbocho district. The beautiful, determined proprietress had opened shop amidst the ruins immediately after the end of the war. It was known for as the favorite meeting place of young literati like Noma Hiroshi, Inoue Mitsuharu, and Haniya Yutaka. We filmmakers were newcomers raising a commotion in the crannies of this narrow space, and thinking about it, I'm impressed that such impoverished young filmmakers were able to drink at such a place. It would have been unthinkable without the kind and generous heart of the proprietress, who put aside her business mentality for use . . . Even after its members retired from Iwanami Productions, the Blue Group continued to meet with this bar as our headquarters. On some days, we'd rent out the whole bar and have meetings from morning to night. Even Miyajima Yoshio, Kamei Fumio, Matsukawa Yasuo and Matsumoto Toshio showed up from time to time. It's no exaggeration to say that the ideas for films such as *Silence Has No Wings* (*Tobenai chinmoku*, 1965), *Forest of Oppression—A Record of the Struggle at Takasaki City University of Economics* (*Assatsu no mori—Takasaki Keizai Daigaku toso no kiroku*, 1967), and the Minamata series were born at Narcisse.[21]

Aside from their meeting style, their agenda was also highly unique. Instead of discussing famous films, they would use the time as a laboratory for their own life as filmmakers. Members would present projects that were still on the drawing board, the stage where anything is possible because it is mostly in people's heads. They wrestled with the merits, problems, and possibilities of these ideas. They would look at rushes or rough cuts, analyzing what they saw and debating in highly technical terms. What was the cameraman thinking when he made that shot? Why use that lens? What kinds of meanings are produced by the cameraman's pan at that particular moment? How could a certain scene be re-edited? What would happen if the editor put these two shots together? The discussions were spirited, contentious, and alcohol-driven. In an interview with Kato Takanobu, also known as "the Last Ogawa Pro Member," cameraman Otsu Koshiro described the atmosphere:

> We would draw on topics like Eisenstein's collision montage theory for our discussions. For example, what was the best way to connect a long shot with another long shot, we asked. Back then long shot/medium/bust/close-up was a king of orthodoxy, but why can't you just go from a long shot to a close up? It might be cool to skip the mid range and go straight from a close-up to a long shot too. We were still very green, but we had free discussions about all sorts of things. The effect of ideology on the feel of a film, the relationship between art and politics, abstract issues like that. It got very theoretical when we started debating what made a movie like [Kamei Fumio's] *Kobayashi Issa* (1941) interesting. What in [Alain Resnais'] *Night and Fog* (*Nuit et brouillard*, 1955) is interesting and why? . . . It was a very free atmosphere . . . I suppose we grew up a bit and we kept doing film research under Ogawa's leadership like always, but we could always discuss things ranging from one person's specific production problems to politics and film, film and art. We had our hands full of things to debate seriously.[22]

Today, everyone who participated in these gatherings looks back at Blue Group with fond nostalgia as a formative moment in their careers. They assert that the experience made them better filmmakers, and there is evidence that they might be right. When these filmmakers quit Iwanami, they scattered into various parts of the documentary and feature film industries and had a deep impact on Japanese cinema of the 1960s and beyond—an influence that has yet to be adequately charted and accounted for.

The efforts of these young Iwanami filmmakers brought the PR film to unusually spectacular levels, deploying interesting montage, narration, and even stunning 35mm cinemascope color photography. Nevertheless, their subject matter was restricted to steel factories and construction sites—a limit on their ambitions that would soon intersect with other pressures. Working within an industrial context forced the filmmakers to aestheticize the human-made, industrial spaces created by the high-growth economy. Riding the coattails of Japan's spectacular rise of economic power proved problematic for this group of filmmakers because of their sympathies with those social elements bringing capital and government under critique.

While Iwanami filmmakers made industrial strength commercials for some of the most corrupt, polluting corporations in Japan, social movements of every sort were taking to the streets. Chafing under the weight of these contradictions, the members of the Blue Group abandoned Iwanami for a politicized, independent documentary.

On the Subject of Documentary

The Blue Group members' individual decisions to quit Iwanami and strike out on an independent path cannot be understood outside of the context of the decisive push coming from an audacious young filmmaker named Matsumoto Toshio, whose contributions to the critical sphere were as influential as his filmmaking. In the late 1950s, Matsumoto started publishing numerous missives and manifestos, contributing to a critical turbulence that would shake the foundations of the film world in the next decade. Matsumoto and others critiqued the approaches of old and renovated documentary practice by turning the term *shutai* (subject) against the grain. We must approach the translation of this word with considerable caution. Its meaning varies depending on the context of the utterance or inscription. Every field treats it differently, making any easy correspondence to the English word *subject,* a tricky word itself, an impossibility. The term *shutai* appeared in film theory of the prewar period in various essays by philosophers like Nakai Masakazu and in debates over the scientific or artistic merits of the nonfiction film. However, it was during the Occupation that it entered film discourse in an engaged way, and apparently then towed the Japan Communist Party line. Film critics basically borrowed the terms of the debate over war responsibility raging within the Left and transported them to the film world.[23] Much of this discussion occurred in the Association of Education Filmmakers (Kyoiku Eiga Sakka Kyokai), the primary organization of nonfiction filmmakers that was decidedly leftist. This group had formed in 1955, shortly after the dissolution of the Production Council. From 1958, they began publishing *Kiroku Eiga (Documentary Film)* as their monthly journal, their "movement magazine" where the conceptualization of documentary's future would be worked out. Many of the key writings debating the issue of authorship and subjectivity were published here.

The controversies started shortly before this in the December 1957 issue of *Kaiho*, the newsletter that preceded *Kiroku Eiga*. In this issue, Matsumoto Toshio published "On the Subject of the Filmmaker" ("Sakka no Shutai to Iu Koto"). This was the first essay in a decade-long series of political and aesthetic critiques by Matsumoto. It also stood as a declaration of generational difference. He began this initial dispatch with the following words:

> During the war, (documentary filmmakers) uncritically produced films collaborating with the war, changing course because of absolutely external power and transitively switching directions *(tenko)* without any serious internal criticism. In that period of political promotion they quickly and hysterically, in the manner of a rapidly spreading disease among children, engaged in a biased practice that subordinated art to politics. Lacking principles, they subsequently adapted to the PR film industry in a period of retreat. Here, consistent from start to finish, there are only slavish craftsmen lacking subjectivity. One might say that, from the beginning, there were no artists here.[24]

The furor that followed the publication of "On the Subject of the Filmmaker" contributed to the shake-up of the organization. Matsumoto's criticism was the lightning rod for a backlash led by the organization's leader, Yoshimi Tai. In a series of articles published in the first three issues of *Kiroku Eiga,* he defended the work of filmmakers whose careers straddled 1945:

> On the one hand, we use film production as a weapon of citizens' movements—in other words, we widely spread the idea of making film belonging to the people, and the results from this experience have been epochal. It is also extremely meaningful that we have uncovered this route for making works featuring independent planning and independent expression. Moreover, for artists in particular, the experience gained from this period has been precious. The majority of artists, through the pursuit of both realism and a creative method, were certainly able to accumulate experience.[25]

However, it was precisely this continuing commitment to realism that bothered Matsumoto, partly because of its continuity with wartime approaches to documentary, but also because of the suppression of the artists' subjectivity that it implied. A cinematic style that presents itself as a privileged referential representation of the lived world ultimately rests on a set of conventions. These conventional constructions hide the work demanded by realist styles, and this amounts to a suppression of the subjective procedures at the heart of filmmaking. For Matsumoto, this was both irresponsible and dangerous because it inevitably involved a veiling of politics as well. The realist agendas of nonfiction filmmaking "for the people" hid an authoritarianism Matsumoto associated with a Stalinism at the heart of the JCP. He vigorously attacked these older leftist filmmakers in a series of articles, the most famous being an essay on Alain Resnais' *Guernica* (1950). This was a short documentary on the Picasso painting, and in this—both the film and the painting—Matsumoto found traces of what he believed to be missing in

Japanese films. His writing shares much with the earlier film theory of Nakai Masakazu to the extent that both positioned modernist aesthetics in relationship to shifts in both consciousness and politics, and both were ultimately interested in the *art* of documentary film;[26] at the same time, it could be said that in spite of the real-world effectiveness of Matsumoto's critique, he lacked the rigor of a philosopher like Nakai. Consider the following passage:

> Internal consciousness is the decisive disengagement of the subject and the external world of today, the idolatry of the relationship between the two. It is the consciousness established upon recognition of the collapse of the classical human image. Naturalists should bear in mind that capitalist alienation exists, more than anywhere, in the process of materializing one's internal self and dismantling the subject. When they rely easily on the outer world without an awareness of their own internal world, then they cannot but grasp matter itself through attributes and atmosphere. They end up drying up their imaginative power and developing a pattern of helpless emotion. The documentarists who capture the *taisho* (object) with an unemotional eye cannot gain a total grasp of reality without using an inner document as a medium. Sharply confronted with avant-garde art, to which at first glance they have no connection, they fail to aim for a higher realism as an opportunity to negate the self. This is because of the artists' own lack of subject-consciousness.[27]

Attacking the highly lauded realism of 1950s Golden Age cinema by advancing a somewhat rough theoretical critique grounded in subject relations, this is a kind of statement of principles for the emerging battle between Old and New Left filmmakers. When Matsumoto's writings were collected in the book *Eizo no Hakken (Discovering the Image)*, they quickly became a bible for the new cohort of artists and spectators. Matsumoto supported his written critiques with some fascinating filmmaking. In works like *The Song of Stones* (*Ishi no uta,* 1960) and *Security Treaty* (*ANPO joyaku,* 1960), he blurred any easy distinction between documentary and the avant-garde, bringing the realism of nonfiction film together with moments of shocking surrealism.

Security Treaty was particularly controversial. Funded by Sohyo (The General Council of Trade Unions of Japan), it is a collage film editing together found footage, captured documentary imagery, photographs, and drawings related to the 1960 security treaty between Japan and the United States. Rather than simply presenting the images in a matter-of-fact fashion (as you would see in a television documentary, for example), Matsumoto mutilates still photographs of Japan's leaders and literally spits on the projected, moving image of an American soldier and a prostitute—although the liquid oozing over the image of the couple could also be read as a different bodily fluid. This was aggressively experimental filmmaking that politicized film style itself. It caused an uproar for both its cinematic approach and the political position Matsumoto took in relation to ANPO. The film was originally meant to explain the terms of the new treaty, but it struck a far different relationship to its potential spectators than gentle enlightenment. The last scene was among the most controversial. It shows families playing in a park and people out fishing at the ocean followed by the cry of a siren. Matsumoto clearly was treating these stand-ins for the masses with sheer contempt for their ignorance and commitment only to leisure during a time of crisis. For many of his critics, this placed Matsumoto in the same space as Prime Minister Kishi, who once remarked that "they say the citizens are opposed to the security treaty, but the professional baseball games are sold out."[28]

For Matsumoto, it was a far more radical position that flew in the face of the older generation of activists with strong Communist Party ties. The tide against Stalinism had started some years before with the Soviet Communist Party's Twentieth General Meeting in 1956 and Nikita Khrushchev's harsh attack on his predecessor's policies. This started an anti-Stalinist sea change across the world of the Left. It manifested itself in the resurgence of Trotskyism and struggles within most groups with Communist identities. The new groups—fractured though they were into factions from petit-bourgeois radicalism to anarchism and terrorism—were lumped into the unstable category of "New Left." In his history of Japanese documentary, filmmaker and critic Noda Shinkichi described the new situation as the difference between "the group supporting the JCP line advocating an organization protecting the livings of filmmakers" or "the group of filmmakers supporting a creative movement for postwar film while fighting commercialism and politicization, and protecting the rights of filmmakers."[29] In a roundtable discussion in the pages of *Kiroku Eiga*[30] Sasaki Mamoru posed the situation as a choice between supporting Yamamoto Satsuo or supporting Oshima Nagisa (this is coming off the tails of an essay by Oshima criticizing Yamamoto's *Matsukawa Incident* [*Matsukawa jiken*, 1961] in the March 1961 *Eiga Hyoron* entitled "*Matsukawa Incident* and the Problems Surrounding It"—the discussants agreed that they should "get rid of Yamamoto Satsuo").[31]

As this indicates, the power on the editorial board of *Kiroku Eiga* had shifted to Matsumoto and his supporters by early 1959, most notably to Noda Shinkichi. They began publishing work by strong writers outside of the organization, creating alliances with intellectuals in other fields who positioned themselves in opposition to what they called the Stalinist mainstream of the Left. These contributors included Sato Tadao, Hanada Kiyoteru, Uriu Tadao, and others. This was a turning point for documentary in Japan, particularly because the field was experiencing a growth even more explosive than the late 1930s. In 1959, documentary short production was about to surpass nine hundred films a year, marking nearly 500 percent growth over the course of the decade.[32] Made-for-television educational films constituted another nine hundred films a year, up from none at the beginning of the 1950s.[33] Within this healthy industry Matsumoto's pressure to innovate, both through critical attacks and artistic example, met massive institutional weight and strong resistance from those working within established organizations. The ultimate solution for reformers was independence, whatever that might come to mean in 1960.

The decade of the 1960s represents ten years marked by public passion, the spectacle of governments struggling to contain their people's energies, and the shifts in consciousness that lead toward new approaches to artistic expression. In Japan, historians have the convenient bookends of the American security treaty renewals, but for our purposes, we must place "the sixties" in quotes. The (early) 1970s are also considered "the sixties" because it was then that *something happened*. From a certain perspective, the second ANPO security treaty in 1970 was an escalation, not an ending.

Documentary film fascinates because of the claims it makes to represent our world. Its easy alliance with centers of power and its national, even global, reach make it a crucial ground for contestation in times of pressure. This complex of forces bearing down on the cinema was precisely where Matsumoto and company positioned themselves in the late 1950s. By their reasoning, the realism espoused by the older generation of filmmakers was a sham. It was deeply implicated in the propaganda of the government and the public relations of industry; it was a specious realism aligned with oppressive forms of power. The editorial board members of *Kiroku Eiga* announced a new direction for their efforts in 1960, a reconfiguration premised on an intertwining triplet of platforms:

- the logical interrogation *(ronrika)* of the relation of the setting and the filmmaker's subjectivity,
- the logical interrogation of representation and the filmmaker's subjectivity, and finally
- the logical interrogation of the deep correspondence between subject/setting and subject/representation.

Upon these three pillars they would attempt to revolutionize nonfiction film.

At the seventh general assembly in December 1960, they changed their name from Association of Education Filmmakers (Kyoiku Eiga Sakka Kyokai) to Association of Documentary Filmmakers (Kiroku Eiga Sakka

Kyokai). The change sloughed off the "education" and emphasized their identity as documentarists, indicating a broadening of practice and a shifting of identity. But partly through the quality of the writing in *Kiroku Eiga*, the movement came to emphasize documentary as less a recording medium than an artistic one led by strong personalities. In 1961, the journal cover went color, and the board began thinking about selling *Kiroku Eiga* on newsstands thanks to thoughtful writing by authors like film critic Sato Tadao and philosopher Hanada Kiyoteru, as well as contributions by high-profile filmmakers like Teshigawara Hiroshi, Oshima Nagisa, Atsugi Taka, Kuroki Kazuo, and Yoshida Kiju. By the late 1950s, the organization was attracting people who simply liked documentary. This coincided with the massive upheavals taking place around the upcoming ANPO security treaty renewal in 1960, in the wake of which a tumultuous ideological debate ensued within the JCP. Since most of the people writing for *Kiroku Eiga* were either party members or sympathizers, similar struggles occurred within the journal. Party members met regularly to receive orders from the leadership in Yoyogi and debate the direction of the movement and the editorial orientation of the journal. In the course of these meetings, an antiparty group coalesced, ultimately leading to their departure, the formation of the Image Arts Society (Eizo Geijutsu no Kai) and the *Record of a Marathon Runner* Incident (discussed at length in chapter 2).

The critical buttressing of their filmmaking remained the debate over *shutaisei* (subjectivity). As noted earlier, Marxism in general engaged in a lengthy and complicated debate over its meaning in the context of war responsibility. Matsumoto, Noda, and others attempted to turn the vocabulary in a new direction, apparently ignoring previous debates in their assertion of new definitions. This is one of the most striking aspects of this discourse: its fragmentary nondevelopment. Writers freely changed the character of subjectivity, switching contexts with little regard to previous incarnations, within or without Japan, in film or in other discourses. From another perspective this could be seen as multifocal and exceeding the strict bounds of a hermetically sealed debate; however, this disconnected plurality of discursive loci lent itself to a particular kind of careless appropriation with concrete effects in the film world.

Within film, for example, feature film directors Masumura Yasuzo and Oshima Nagisa were discussing *shutaisei* in articles about feature film. However, this seems strikingly disconnected from what was going on in documentary circles. One of the few linkages between the mainstream fiction filmmaking and nonfiction discourses is Oshima's "What Is a Shot?" in the November 1960 issue of *Kiroku Eiga*. Oshima argues for a recognition of authorial subjectivity built into the temporal limits of the shot.[34] Most other writers placed emphasis on montage when thinking about authorial intervention in filmmaking (*Kiroku Eiga* published a special issue on editing just months before).

Matsumoto worked in similar territory, but his activities signaled the direction the documentary discourse would take in the 1960s. In what is probably the most intriguing of his articles, he drew on psychoanalysis and Freud's essay on the uncanny *(unheimlich)*. "Record of the Hidden World" ("Kakusareta Sekai no Kiroku") was published in the June 1960 issue of *Kiroku Eiga*. Here, Matsumoto attempted to turn the debate surrounding documentary toward the very existence of the *mono* (thing) recorded by the filmmaker:

> The existence of the *taisho* is, finally, nothing other than a *heimlich* (intimate) thing. There, the estranged facts of reality are suppressed by the stereotypes of everyday consciousness, and become *heimlich* (concealed) things. Rather, precisely because of that, the existence of the *taisho*—what could be thought of as everyday consciousness or as the law of causality—is powerfully negated by the non-everyday, hidden reality that our consciousness still cannot grasp. It is overturned by the world reproduced [*utsusu* in *hiragana*, thus, it could mean "to reproduce" or "to remove" or "to film" and/or "to project."—AMN] as something nonexistent in our everyday consciousness. When this happens, our consciousness, touched for the first time by that kind of reality we have never experienced directly, dismantles its balance with the outside world. We take it as strange, or as an *unheimlich* (unearthly) thing.[35]

It is with the untapped energy of the "hidden" world that we must resist the very structures that "hide," that oppress through veiling apparatuses like cinematic realism. In this respect, he was edging toward a film theory with interesting parallels to post-structuralism, where his *unheimlich* may roughly correspond to Althusser's structured absence or perhaps the Lacanian abject. Furthermore, he was calling for a politicized avant-garde cinema with essentially the same contours as that which would be valorized in the West some years later after the events of May 1968. Thus, while feature filmmakers like Oshima and Masumura were concerned with the subjective expression of the artist in fictional forms, as a documentarist Matsumoto naturally wanted to account for the existential force of the very real people he was dealing with. While Matsumoto never developed these ideas further in print, and no one else picked up where he left off, his 1960 essay held the promise of inserting psychoanalysis into the debate. It is both surprising and unfortunate that this was another route largely abandoned.

While its specifics went undeveloped, we can see Matsumoto's essay expressing the transformation that the nonfiction film was undergoing. It signaled a new emphasis upon the *taisho* (object) in the debate on *shutaisei*.

Ogawa Shinsuke during the shooting of *Winter in Sanrizuka* (1970). Photograph courtesy of Shiraishi Yoko and Athénée Français Cultural Center.

This part of the equation was largely missing from previous theorization. Its significance lies in the conceptualization of the documentary image as a *document of a relationship* between the filmmaker and the object—this latter term usually referred to as the "subject of the film" in English-language film criticism. This would have wide-ranging effects on documentary practice in the following decades. At the same time, Matsumoto's impulse to draw on psychoanalysis would also prove important, if only because the move went nowhere. It meant a discourse on subjectivity that did not take into account the most important and richest body of thought exploring the contours of the human mind. The implications of this omission were multiple and varied. The fact that various writers and artists did not share a common language and conceptual framework meant the *shutaiseiron* would inevitably splinter into many directions at once. From the distance afforded by time, we can look back and see a seemingly endless variety of positions with people deploying words like *shutai* and *taisho* to significantly different ends. Without the substantial buttressing from an external body of theory, there was no need or pressure to engage in pointed arguments to advance a common line of thought. This dearth of structure enabled a popular conception of *shutaiseiron* to circulate in the documentary world—a malleable version that ironically may have been more productive than a "high theory" comprehensible primarily to specialists. We might speculate that the fact that psychoanalysis was so swiftly raised and dropped from the equation would contribute to the *something* that happened in the coming 1970s. But this would be getting ahead of ourselves.

Enter Ogawa

Previously, I attempted to describe the context in which Ogawa came to know and love film, and aspire to become a filmmaker. As most accounts would have it, Ogawa started out life in much the same way he would end it, off in an obscure corner of Japan, collecting things. The typical biographies start with his birth on the June 25, 1935, in a rural area of Gifu Prefecture. However, as I noted in the introduction, this was one of many tall tales Ogawa perpetuated until his death. He was actually born a year later and raised in the heart of Tokyo and only came into contact with rural Japan when sent to the countryside to avoid the American strategic bombing of the cities at the end of World War II. Ogawa's father was an intellectual with no deep allegiance to school or political party, an independent bent that Ogawa inherited. His grandfather, Ogawa Suzuichi, was the mayor of this village during World War II (and would be thrown out of public office during the American Occupation). His primary job, however, was lifelong teacher and principal at Ogawa's high school. The grandfather was quite the amateur scientist. He exchanged letters with the famed anthropologist Yanagita Kunio, acting as an informant about their local customs and stories. He was also a great admirer of botanist Makino Tomitaro and helped the scientist collect specimens on a visit to Gifu. Ogawa is said to have been deeply influenced by his grandfather's pension for collecting and helped out on these projects. Decades later, Ogawa would come full circle in his life trajectory through his move to rural Japan for the latter third of his career.

As the war in the Pacific intensified, it affected his family in profound ways. On the one hand, Ogawa was the prototypical national youth. He was taken by the war films of the day, and, like most children, he was anxious to join the war effort as a recruit. Ogawa himself aspired to the navy. On the other hand, the reality of the war turned bitter as the years dragged on. As the American forces began their island hopping across the Pacific Ocean to the Japanese home turf, the Ogawas were struggling to feed an extended family with eight children. Ogawa's lifelong memory of August 15, 1945—the day of the surrender—was of neighborhood friends who happened to be Korean. He remembered being puzzled by their suddenly bright faces. In 1946, his parents took him, his brother, and two sisters to live in Shioyama, Yamanishi Prefecture, where he entered Shioyama Primary School.

In 1955, Ogawa entered Kokugakuin University's Economics Department, although he always told people he was in the more politically acceptable Literature Department. He did what most young, radical students did: read, talked, and skipped classes. Studying at this particular institution offered him the opportunity to experience the lectures of Yanagita Kunio and Sakaguchi Norio—or at least that is what he claimed. He had discovered leftist politics in high school thanks to a reading of Lenin's *Imperialism*, which helped explain many things about the world, and he began dabbling in activism in college. He participated in student government, passed time at a nearby coffee shop called Carnegie Hall, and saw many, many movies. Ogawa also performed a variety of part-time jobs, including gopher work at Shin Toho Studio and Asahi Broadcasting. He took assistantships on various independent productions, including an Imai Tadashi film. It is said he even spent some time as a fire lookout. Ogawa told people that the university expelled him for political activities in 1957—bragging rights any radical filmmaker would be proud of. Unfortunately, he had no right to boast, as he actually graduated as planned and scheduled.

With the help of Umeda Katsumi, who would go on to a successful career in independent film and television documentary, Ogawa established a film club at his university. This sort of school-based *eiken* (film research club) has a long tradition extending back to the 1920s. Kokugakuin had had an *eiken*, but it had been dormant for two decades. Typically, *eiken* took their filmgoing seriously and often concentrated on certain kinds of cinema. Ogawa and Umeda's group, which had around twenty-five members, made a point of watching and discussing documentaries and the latest works by the filmmakers of the 1950s independent film movement.

They also started making films. Ogawa was a movie maniac, and from the beginning, his friends often suggested that he was, in the final instance, more interested in cinema than politics. As a youth, he wanted more than anything to make movies himself, and Eiken gave him that chance. Their first production, entitled *A Small Illusion* (*Chiïsa na gen'ei*, 1957), was an eighteen-minute short that played off the Japanese title for Renoir's *Grand Illusion* (*La Grande illusion*, Japanese title: *Oi naru gen'ei*, 1937). However, the connection beyond this film-fan homage is hard to imagine. Made to emphasize the importance of education, it shows a shy, young boy going to a doll theater. He becomes absorbed in the fairy tale world of the narrative, and the dolls come to life thanks to actors wearing animal costumes. The theme on education had to do with the fact that many of the students at Kokugakuin aspired to teaching careers, and the Ministry of Education was deeply concerned with education in the hinterlands. Above and beyond this, it is safe to assume they also thought an educational film might actually have a chance to be taken seriously and have a life outside of the club. As we have seen, the educational film was an important form of documentary production in the late 1950s and was historically the domain of the independent production companies. Its elaborate distribution system could probably accept the level of production a serious film club was capable of.

Eiken's second film was also about rural education issues, and much more is known about its production. *Children Living in the Mountains* (*Yama ni ikiru kora,* 1958) was a fairly involved production for a student film. It began with a long exchange of letters between Eiken members and a rural teacher who had written a book on education in the hinterlands. Umeda, Ogawa, and a few other members made extended trips to live in his village in Gifu and conduct research for their scenario. Kokugakuin University contributed a hefty 20,000 yen, which was supplemented by part-time work and hits on club members' parents. They borrowed the ethnology club's 16mm camera, an old Bolex. Ogawa took the role of producer and Umeda was director, but Ogawa didn't spend much time around the photography, preferring to drink tea and chat at villagers' homes.[36] Even at this early moment in his career as a filmmaker, Ogawa showed a talent for breaking down interpersonal distance and forming close relationships. Umeda describes a process something along the following lines: "Ogawa would chat with some old village woman over pickled vegetables, and after the information garnered from this conversation was narrativized into the scenario they would go and shoot the scene."[37] Ogawa also had a penchant for dominating discussions that were nominally part of a collaborative production process. It seems many aspects of Ogawa's quirky approach to documentary were in place from the beginning.

Children Living in the Mountains flew in the face of Ministry of Education policy by design. However, when they arrived in the village to conduct research and write their scenario, the villagers did not fit their preconceived image from bookish study in the capital. This difference became the theme of the film, the power relationship of the periphery and the center. The perspective of the film is of an outsider looking in. It grounds the voice-over narration and the positioning of the children as others to an urban viewing subject. What is significant, however, is the underlying structure, which forces a constant interplay between the familiar and the strange. In this way, the film critiques the policies of the Ministry of Education and the homogenizing ideologies of nationalism that they were founded on.

The narration repeatedly exposes the contradictions between curricula and textbooks written from the point of the city-dweller (and, by extension, the national center) and the life experiences of youth in the country's rural periphery. For example, how are children in a land-locked region like Gifu to process a textbook that makes much of Japan as an island nation with deep connections to the sea? How does one talk about stairways to children living in structures without second floors? These contradictions are heightened by recontextualizing conventional scenes of school life in the unusual setting of a village deep in the mountains. These typical elements—lunchtime duties, sports day, classes, etc.—provoke identification, while the hardships imposed by the geographic and cultural setting push things off balance. Thus, the typical walk to and from school is more of a hike; a child reading an essay aloud on the topic reveals they must pick up firewood on the way home. Once back, they must begin their farm work for the day. The school itself looks like so many other schools in other education films of the era, but it is obvious they lack many of the essentials of good pedagogy: space, teachers, and even teaching materials. Grades must be combined, and teachers must make their own materials with whatever is at hand.

The film offers other readily emblematic scenes of Japanese education. This is the prototypical education film style, with its roots in the *bunka eiga* (culture film) of the prewar era. The cinematography is surprisingly accomplished but nothing novel. Like mainstream fictional cinema, it starts scenes politely, offering establishing shots before entering homogeneously constructed cinematic spaces. Like the documentaries of the day, the scenes shift fluidly between staged and spontaneous photography in order to set up the film's underlying argument. This is an approach to documentary Ogawa would help shatter in the coming decade.

At the same time, with their attention to the subject position of rural villagers in a nationalized space, these two student films seem to be in a place Ogawa would ultimately return to at the end of his career. Indeed, our look at these first two films has revealed what will become very familiar in the coming pages: the interplay between staging and spontaneity foreshadows Ogawa's explorations of documentary method in his last films; there is also his fascination for the life of farmers; his dedication to standing on the side of his *taisho* in the face of hardship and discrimination; his joyful indulgence in relationships with his *taisho;* his collaborative method, which he couldn't help dominating; and his troubling willingness to risk debt.

Children Living in the Mountains also set his relationship with the government and traditional distribution institutions off to a bad start. Upon completion, the Eiken members sent their film to the Ministry of Education for its official recognition. Ever since the late 1930s, the Ministry of Education "recognized" films they deemed appropriate for education. The ministry's mark ensured a fairly wide audience, since schools and film libraries were likely to acquire films with the government's stamp of approval. The industrial structure relied on sales of prints more than rental distribution so this enabled the government to wield its recognition system as a censorship apparatus.

This de facto censorship system went back to the war, when films like Kamei Fumio's brilliantly critical *Kobayashi Issa* (1941) were denied recognition. It also became a mark of pride; ads for Kamei's film were sure to mention the denial to assert his film's departure from the officially sanctioned norm. Umeda and Ogawa's documentary joined the ranks of well-meaning films kept out of classrooms when *Children Living in the Mountains* was denied recognition status. Ogawa also claimed the accompanying bragging rights, making an appearance in the film group of Communist critic Yamada Kazuo to show the film and discuss the Ministry of Education's indirect and unfair exertion of power. In an article Ogawa wrote for Yamada's journal *Sekai Eiga Shiryo* in 1958, the director noted that while there was no official reason given, officials expressed off-stage indignation that a local school would ignore or subvert the central policy directives of the Ministry of Education. They singled out one sequence where the film criticizes the lack of textbooks and teachers, and suggests that teachers in rural areas should be allowed to write their own textbooks.[38]

Most small production companies submitted their films to the Ministry of Education secretly. Recognition was highly desirous, but rejection virtually guaranteed slamming doors to the companies owning distribution networks. However, Ogawa made an issue of it, preferring the ethics of exposure to the pursuit of profit.

Ogawa's profile suggests a rabble-rouser with a penchant for organized troublemaking. Once out of university, he worked shortly for his father before setting his sights on the film industry. In June 1959, he joined his friends Wakayama Kazuo and Yasuki Yasutaro at Shinseki Film Studio. After half a year of office work, he quit and returned to his father's company. However, thanks to Wakayama's efforts, he landed an assistant director job for a shoot in Nagasaki's Omura Prison. This film wrapped up in early 1960, about the time Ogawa formed a film research organization with some friends called Kinema Alpha. This group dissolved when right-wing activists assaulted some of the members at the height of the security treaty protests in June. In the fall, Ogawa finally secured a job at Iwanami Productions. As was typical, a budding filmmaker would start in the slave-like position of assistant director and move upward when he could.

One of Ogawa's first jobs was to replace Higashi Yoichi as Kuroki Kazuo's assistant director on *Hokkaido, My Love* (*Waga ai Hokkaido*, 1960). Sponsored by Hokkaido Power Company to celebrate its anniversary, it was to glorify the natural beauty of the northern island (and, naturally, the industries exploiting it). The film was three-fifths completed, but it was a position Ogawa wanted, for reasons that escaped Kuroki to this day. Other members of the staff included Tamura Masaki as assistant cameraman, Kubota Yukio on sound, and Watanabe Shigeharu as chief camera assistant, people who would have close connections to Jieiso Ogawa Pro in the future.

Ogawa's arrival in Hokkaido was a favorite story for Kuroki. The crew had prepared a small party to welcome the new staff member, but the honored guest did not arrive as expected. They waited and waited, and finally Ogawa appeared. The jaws of all present dropped when he made them listen to an audio tape he had just recorded. The train had arrived on time, but Ogawa stopped everyone from the stationmaster to passersby to ask, "What do you think of Hokkaido?" It annoyed Kuroki, but left quite the impression. Ogawa surprised everyone with his boundless enthusiasm and raucous love of talk, both of which he subsequently brought to the discussions of the Blue Group.

Hokkaido, My Love was Kuroki's last film for Iwanami, thanks to trouble with the sponsors (and the company that sided with them). Kuroki threw a love story into this PR film as a structural ploy and an attempt to make it more interesting: a young man surveying and admiring various regions of Hokkaido falls for a local girl. We only see her in fleeting glimpses as he waxes eloquently about the beauty of the land (and its business potential) and the woman (who works in a boot factory). Shooting in dazzling widescreen, Kuroki subtly situates the film in a place between fiction and documentary. The old *bunka eiga* and PR filmmakers did their best to hide the fiction, but here Kuroki gives the artifice of fiction a palpable primacy. One feels an attraction to its possibilities, its magic. The sponsors found a number of things wrong with the film, beginning with the scene where the couple, fully nude, makes love. This exasperated the Iwanami management, who cut the scene. Kuroki was bemused by the spin this put on the PR aspect, as it left the man wandering aimlessly across Hokkaido with no consummation.

Ogawa followed Kuroki's lead in more ways than one. The typical pattern for aspiring filmmakers was to enter a company, choose a track like direction or cinematography, and work like a slave. After accruing a certain amount of experience, the filmmaker would move up the ranks. Like Kuroki, Ogawa tampered with the limits of the PR film and immediately got into trouble. He worked on a variety of projects, most of which are not known. One was *Japan's Postal Service* (*Nihon no yubinkyoku,* 1961), which he worked on with then camera assistant Otsu Koshiro. As veteran Ise Chonosuke edited the rushes, Ogawa and Otsu expressed their dissatisfaction with the results and published their own version of the scenario in the newsletter of Iwanami's research group (the forerunner to the Blue Group).[39]

As his first directorial effort, Ogawa was to head up *Shinjuku Story (Shinjuku monogatori)* for Odakyu, the owner of department stores and a train with a major terminal in the Shinjuku district of Tokyo. Suzuki Tatsuo was assigned to the cinematography, and, in this production, we can already see Suzuki's penchant for experimentation, long before his famous collaboration with Terayama Shuji. They tried a variety of tricks, including a time-lapse camera that left the shutter open long enough to effectively eliminate anything that moved; the result was the unimaginable: one of the busiest train stations in the world completely devoid of people. When they shot the standard pitch of the company president, they used only a close-up of his mouth, gold fillings and all. These experimental qualities went over the line, flexible as that line was at Iwanami, and two-thirds of the film was reshot. Another film he was to direct, *Mayonaise* (also with Suzuki on camera), met a similar fate. He was finally shunted back to assistant director and stayed there for his term at Iwanami.

As these examples suggest, Iwanami appeared to have changed. On the other hand, it could simply be that the filmmakers had. In the middle of Ogawa's tenure at the company, Blue Group coalesced and attracted the filmmakers interested in testing the boundaries of documentary convention. It could also be that the film world itself had changed. Filmmakers were enchanted by the advances of European art cinema, especially the French New Wave. The feature film industry was in the midst of its own revolution, which only intensified as the filmmakers of the Shochiku New Wave went independent. The filmmakers of the Blue Group mirrored this movement toward independence. Ogawa was one of the last to go. Upon the completion of his contract in 1964, he quit Iwanami for an uncertain future.

Ogawa's initial strategy was to research, write, and shop around scenarios for PR films. He is said to have written up to seventeen scenarios a year. Those who have read the scenarios call them impressive, but none were made into films. Ogawa did give details about a couple of the scripts, and a glimpse at the nature of the projects suggests why they were never made. As in Kuroki's PR films, they often featured ulterior motives lurking beneath the overt values of public relations. For example, he wrote a script for Komatsu Bulldozer Company that celebrated its machines' ability to clear the forests up in Hokkaido. However, this area was also inhabited by people who had immigrated to Japan from Manchuria after the war, which was what actually piqued Ogawa's interest. He learned of this situation on his visit to the island for *Hokkaido, My Love*. The bulldozer story was a pretense to return to the north to document the problems faced by these former colonists.

By all accounts these were excellent scripts for films that could never be made. On the side he found other work, such as assistant on Kuroki's 1966 feature film *Silence Without Wings*. One of the results of this situation was that Ogawa watched friends like Kuroki and Tsuchimoto rise in the ranks to director while he sat on the sidelines itching to take up the megaphone. In the meantime, he edged deeper into poverty, and his wife and child decided to return to her home in Hokkaido to save money.

Ogawa's strategy of writing scenarios on spec appeared poised to take off with a film about a brewery, *Beer Factory (Biiru o tsukuru kojo)*. His initial premise was that he would find a Marxist-style alienation at the plant. When given a tour, he found quite the opposite. The workers thought their beer tasted delicious and were receiving a decent wage. As Ogawa described it, he went looking to creatively treat reality, but reality was the problem. There was, however, one area his guide steered him away from. Ogawa happened to see that it was where returned beer was processed. When stores couldn't sell the beer, the bottles ended up in the hands of women who emptied them into reservoirs for processing. Here lay the real film, but it was something that was difficult to touch on in a PR documentary.[40]

People who have read the script praised its originality and promise. A minor producer expressed interest in backing the project, and Ogawa devoted months to preproduction. He secured the talent of soundman Kubota Yukio and cinematographer Suzuki Tatsuo, whose just-completed work on *Silence Without Wings* was causing a stir among those who saw the rushes. Kubota now tells the tale of one cold winter evening when the three went to the producer's office in Shinagawa. Kubota and Suzuki huddled around a heater in the outer office while Ogawa went back to talk to the producer. He came out looking dumbfounded, and said, "Let's just leave."

Back on the dark street, the three walked in a harsh wind while Ogawa explained what happened. The producer had taken Ogawa's script and preproduction materials and handed them to a different director, who promised to make the film for half the cost. The producer had stolen

Ogawa's idea, his months of planning, and his hopes that *Beer Factory* would launch his career in the PR film world. As the three walked down the gloomy street in the bitter cold, Ogawa Shinsuke started sobbing.

"Starting that night," reasons Kubota, "Ogawa Shinsuke set his sights on fighting for documentary cinema and never looked back."[41] In a coincidence that seems strikingly serendipitous today, Ogawa's intense longing to become a free filmmaker happened to coincide with the rise of a mass of students who were experiencing a similarly fervent desire to become free human beings. And in that moment, when massive passions stirred in the population and many of the most conservative structures of the old order began to crumble, these two groups experienced a synergy that led to one amazing film after another. If Ogawa had been born at any other time, it is easy to imagine him working at Iwanami until his retirement—or giving up on filmmaking altogether. Instead, he forged his own route of independent cinema by throwing himself into the turbulence of the student movement.

[2] *Jieiso: Ogawa's First Collectivity*

One cannot separate *Sea of Youth* from the problems at Iwanami—people quitting Iwanami on the one hand, and the formation of the Image Arts Society on the other. Iwanami amounted to a space with rules restricting creativity; Image Arts Society was a space liberated from such rules.
:: Otsu Koshiro

Records of a Turning Point

The twelve-month period from mid-1964 to the summer of 1965 marked a shift in the meaning of independent documentary in Japan. This was the period that JCP forces led by Yoshimi Yasushi successfully wrestled power from the Noda-Matsumoto Group within the Association of Documentary Filmmakers, and disaffected filmmakers fled to form the Image Arts Society. Its core leadership included Kuroki Kazuo, Matsumoto Toshio, Nagano Chiaki, Noda Shinkichi, Matsukawa Yasuo, and Tsuchimoto Noriaki. Another group (Film Independent) devoted to independent and experimental cinema formed; it included people like Adachi Masao, Donald Richie, Iimura Takahiko, Obayashi Nobuhiko, among others. In this same short period, the few Blue Group members still under contract with Iwanami—including Higashi Yoichi and Ogawa Shinsuke—quit the company, and Blue Group naturally dissolved. Ogawa started preproduction on his first film, and Tsuchimoto made his first important independent films, including the first installment of the Minamata Series. These developments resulted in the redefinition of nonfiction cinema.

This yearlong interlude began with the troubles surrounding Kuroki Kazuo's *Record of a Marathon Runner*, which came to a head at the beginning of the summer.[1] This controversy resonated institutionally against the struggle ensuing within the Association of Documentary Filmmakers, since the public, postproduction phase of the incident was provoked by a request from the Blue Group to screen Kuroki's film at an Image Arts Society event. Kuroki had been asked by Tokyo Cinema to make a film on one of the competitors for the upcoming Olympics and his relationship to his coach. Kuroki accepted the job on the condition that he would receive artistic freedom. There were conflicts between Kuroki and the management of Tokyo Cinema (which included Yoshimi), but things came to a head when Blue Group asked to borrow the film for a May 4, 1964, screening. It was clear to the Blue Group that *Record of a Marathon Runner* and two other films by the group—Tsuchimoto's *Document: On the Road* (*Dokyumento: Rojo,* 1964) and Higashi's *Face* (*Kao,* 1965)—were breaking new ground for the documentary, and this would be a chance to make these developments public in a forceful way. Tsuchimoto and others approached Fuji Film (the sponsor) and Nikkatsu (the distributor) for permission to show *Record of a Marathon Runner,* which they received. However, Tokyo Cinema declined the request in a rather rude fashion and went out of its way to ensure that other organizations did not cooperate either. In obstructing the screening, Tokyo Cinema made clear that its motives were directly related to the troubles between the Association of Documentary Filmmakers and the Image Arts Society, or what was provisionally being called the Documentary Arts Society (Kiroku Geijutsu no Kai) at this formative moment. From management's perspective, Tokyo Cinema was not obliged to cooperate with a group that it did not recognize. The show went on, except in place of Kuroki's film, Tokyo Cinema held a symposium featuring speeches by Kuroki, Higashi, Tsuchimoto, Matsumoto, Oshima, and others.[2]

There were a number of major planks in the protest. After the first screening of a rough cut, the sponsor asked for changes. The production company acquiesced, making the changes on the sly without consulting Kuroki. The sponsor claimed the voice-over was obscure; Yoshimi, the original screenwriter, wrote a new narration behind the director's back. They unilaterally changed the title, dropping the word *Youth (Seinen)* because of its close association with the student movement and the recent political turmoil over ANPO. When Kuroki and others got wind of these machinations, they raised vigorous protests. Tempers flared as the producers refused to preview the film, even for those who worked on it. And finally, perhaps as a kind of retribution, Tokyo Cinema cut all the staff credits and substituted a commercial for the sponsor. This was the form in which it was distributed.

A petition handed out at the May 4 screening hints at the larger issues behind the controversy. Listing some of the events of the incident, they write, "In the world of common sense [any of these reasons] would be nothing but an unfathomable madness. However, that madness represents the fear of filmmakers making individual, artistic works, and the fear that those works will be shown publicly to spectators and provoke a deepening interchange between filmmakers and spectators. It is clear these people's plan is based on the intent to threaten we creative filmmakers' livelihoods and rights through the power of management."[3] The word *management* in this case is tipping the hat to the political struggle generating the conflict. The unilateral control being exercised by the leadership in Tokyo Cinema—which also happened to be the leadership of the Association of Documentary Filmmakers—was seen as clear-cut evidence of the Stalinist tendencies of the older generation of filmmakers. At the symposium, Matsumoto said that if one were looking for the most essential problem here, it is simply that "There Is a Communist Party."[4] Theirs was a style that demanded acquiescence to top-down directives and central planning. The association itself became involved in the incident midway and issued a controversial response in its newsletter entitled, "The Rights of Filmmakers and Their Social Responsibilities," which sided with the company.

Among all the other signs of change between the summers of 1964 and 1965, two other film productions stand out as symbolic markers. One is *Tokyo Olympiad* (*Tokyo Orinpikku,* 1965), a truly massive production underwritten by the government and corporate Japan, directed by a hired gun from the feature-film world, and designed as the first cinematic display of national power since the debacle of World War II.[5] In contrast to this apotheosis of the PR film, the far more important film is Tsuchimoto Noriaki's minuscule *Exchange Student Chua Swee Lin* (*Ryugakusei Chua Sui Rin,* 1965).

Tsuchimoto's efforts are emblematic of the incipient transformations. As they quit Iwanami, Blue Group filmmakers began recrafting their careers for a life outside the relatively secure position of salaried filmmaker. Of the cohort, Ogawa and Tsuchimoto forged the most unusual, and in the end, most influential routes. Tsuchimoto took the first step, and on his lead Ogawa took the plunge. The former had worked as an actual Iwanami employee for just over a year, from 1956 to 1957, but many of his films were produced for the company. In May 1965, Tsuchimoto made his first Minamata film, a television documentary for Nihon Television's *Nonfiction Theater* (to which he was a frequent contributor). While the subject of Minamata would be the overwhelming concern of his subsequent career, it is his 1965 production that deserves attention at this key moment in Japanese documentary.

Tsuchimoto made *Exchange Student Chua Swee Lin* in June. Initially planned as another television documentary, it reports the predicament of the title character: a Malaysian student studying abroad who ran into political trouble while in Japan for his participation in an antigovernment political movement concerning the independence of Singapore. He was traveling on a British passport and when the British government requested his repatriation to newly independent Malaysia, the Japanese Ministry of Education acquiesced. They revoked his scholarship and put him on notice. It was clear that deportation meant imprisonment. Tsuchimoto met Chua when his movement was a one-man show. He thought an appeal through television would be effective, and Tsuchimoto was sympathetic to the student's plight. He began preproduction for a television documentary; however, just before photography was to begin, the network pulled out when Malaysian relations soured, leaving Tsuchimoto high and dry. He responded by stepping firmly onto the side of Chua. They canvassed production funds for completion and the documentary became, financially and stylistically, centered precisely within the subjectivity of the individual and his budding movement. This is a movie that started a movement rather than represented it. Chua was eventually able to stay in Japan.

From a Sea of Youth to the Forest of Pressure

At this very moment, Ogawa was taking a similar step. After meeting no success with his scenario writing, he turned to distance learning as yet another possible subject for a television documentary. Actually, this amounted to more of a *return* to the subject since he initially discovered the topic as an assistant director on Iwanami's *Young Life—Hosei University's Students* (*Wakai inochi—Hosei Daigaku no gakuseitachi*, 1963). For his new project, he chose a highly unusual approach to preproduction. Beginning in February 1965, just after the traumatic rejection of *Beer Factory*, Ogawa began gathering young Hosei students around him. He met them at coffee shops, proposing to collaborate on a television show on distance learning. Together they formed a group with the remarkably awkward name of "Daigaku Tsuchin Kyoikusei" no Kiroku Eiga o Tsukuru Kai (The Organization for Creating a Documentary Film on "Distance Learning Students").

By May 1965, their plans began exceeding the framework of television documentary in both time and content restrictions, a development relatively independent of Tsuchimoto's coincident experience with the Chua Swee Lin film.[6] This turn of events was, in retrospect, fateful for the future of Japanese documentary. Ogawa was hardly the organizer and political activist, especially compared to those around him. Tsuchimoto, by way of contrast, had participated in the formation of Zengakuren at Waseda in

1948. Ogawa was, at heart, a film fanatic, so it is quite easy to imagine a very different, very conventional career in PR and television had this first film been produced for television as initially planned. Instead, it became the first of Ogawa's films made by and for political activists. From this first step, Ogawa would go on to make the definitive "movement cinema" for the next decade.

As their plans developed, the Hosei and Keio University students around Ogawa came to organize themselves and expand their ambitions. In the summer, they changed their name to the Jishu Joei Soshiki no Kai (Independent Screening Organization), or Jieiso for short. As the name suggests, this was probably an outgrowth of discussions about where to actually show their film upon its completion. Since Jieiso was the precursor to Ogawa Pro, it is worth taking a close look at this group before turning to the three films it spearheaded.

Jieiso was essentially an *eiken,* similar to the film research group Ogawa himself started in. This was a time when students were looking for a place to direct their energies, to find a goal to commit their passions to. These students gathered around Ogawa, whom they felt was far more interesting than most of their teachers (many of them never graduated in the end). Members included the people featured in *Sea of Youth—Four Correspondence Course Students* (*Seinen no umi—Yonin no tsushin kyoikuseitachi,* 1966), along with students from Waseda and Keio Universities. Ogawa was a curious figure to them. He was unusual for being an adult

The main characters in *Sea of Youth* (1966) became core members of Ogawa's subsequent collectives. From left to right: Tateishi Yasuaki, Yamane Makoto, Kuribayashi Toyohiko, and Kobayashi Hideko. Photograph courtesy of Athénée Français Cultural Center.

whom they could actually talk to. Since their actual age was not so far apart, many felt he was something like an older brother. Some of these students ended up becoming longtime Ogawa Pro members, including Kobayashi Hideko, Nosaka Haruo, and Yoshida Tsukasa.

Jieiso left an unusually extensive paper trail to history. The group published newsletters, like *October* (*Jugatsu,* from February to September 1968) and the mimeographed *Jieiso News* in 1969. It sent mimeographed letters of protest to its enemies in the major media institutions along with letters of support to those it felt had been wronged. Jieiso's archives include ambitiously written notes, outlines, agendas, and proposals from its many meetings. Together, the documents provide a complex snapshot of this most unusual organization.

From the beginning, Jieiso's members divided themselves into various working groups: the screening group, the production group, the investigation group, and even a theory group. Each drew up reports that it would share with the others. As Jieiso produced its films, the group's ambitions grew to network organizations committed to the distribution of independent films. In the first issue of the newsletter *October* they clearly state their aims:

> Only independent production can secure the subjectivity (*shutai*) of the filmmaker and the content of the film, properly delivering it to the spectators. The position of our screening movement is at the site enabling a reciprocal relationship between the filmmakers and spectators. The right of spectators to select images freely, their desire for the image, secures the next production. Our solidarity with regional screening organizations is also found there.[7]

In addition to the production of its own films, Jieiso lent its support and energies to other films that encountered troubles. One of these was Iwasa Hisaya's *A Search for a Youth—Within the Peace Movement* (*Aru seishun no mosaku—Heiwa undo no naka de,* 1965), which was abruptly canceled by Fuji Television's *Documentary Theater*. Iwasa showed Beheiren members in the film, despite instructions to avoid them by the management, and his scenes of demonstrations were too long for the taste of the television studios. Jieiso issued a protest that was eventually published in a pamphlet with an official protest letter from the Image Arts Society. It mounted a similar campaign for Kuroki's *Silence Has No Wings*. Jieiso also protested when TBS nixed one of its own television productions, *Narita at Midnight (Narita 24 ji),* which was to be broadcast on March 2, 1968. And it participated in the Suzuki Seijun Problem when the director was fired from Nikkatsu. These were the causes Jieiso's members devoted themselves to actively, but they also tracked an eight-page list of films suppressed or unilaterally changed by television networks.[8]

Presumably, the decision to forego television broadcast for *Sea of Youth*—by far the most lucrative and influential distribution route—was deeply connected to the desire for a production context unconstrained by the narrow conventions and political spectrum acceptable to the networks. Giving this up was both liberating and daunting. While it freed Jieiso filmmakers to craft the film to their desires and ambitions, it also committed them to the hard work of finding and producing their own audiences.

The film they imagined self-reflexively intermingled its own production with the movement of the students striving to reform the distance-learning system. The Japanese government issued a law in 1947 permitting accredited universities to offer their services to students who live and work off-campus. The programs started in 1950, with only five participating universities, and grew to accommodate sixty thousand students across the country by the time of filming. Their rapid growth accentuated built-in problems and created new ones. The Ministry of Education began proposing reforms to the system, which provoked the frustration and anger of many students. For example, the Ministry wanted to extend the number of campus stays from four to five summers, even though the hardship of leaving home and work already resulted in an 80 to 90 percent dropout rate.

There was an organization to engage these issues and represent the students to the government. However, it was ineffective, so a group of students organized to bring people together. In the process of forming this movement, four students came to form the cohort that *Sea of Youth* centers on. They include Kuribayashi Toyohiko (Hosei University, economics), Kobayashi Hideko (waitress; Keio University, history), Tateishi Yasuaki (cram school teacher; Keio University, economics), and Yamane Makoto (steel worker; Keio University, literature). The film poses their activities as grassroots activism without overtly stating that they were also the filmmakers, a strange, watered-down self-reflexivity.

The film does include the trappings of movement politics: banner waving, demonstrations, pamphleteering, and the like. Interviews with hairdressers, priests, and a bag maker reveal the special hardships faced by correspondence students. They are contrasted with regular students at band practice, football practice, and normal group activities that require extended training together in order to function and lend people their identity as students.

Well into the film, the focus settles intimately on these four students. The camera accompanies them on a series of coffee shop meetings that were the basis of Jieiso's own activities. Their soul-searching discussions address the possibilities of success or failure and the importance of self-conscious reflection about what they were doing. The questions they ask are good ones: What is the nature of academic freedom? Are work and study compatible at the college level? What good is actually coming of their efforts? How does the current structure, which marginalizes the correspondence students and stigmatizes them socially, serve their interests, if at all? What is the relationship between the nation and education? In many ways the film feels like a propaganda piece for the JCP, considering it aestheticizes students who are also workers. However, there were reportedly problems with the Minsei—the JCP's youth organization—attempting to crash Jieiso and the production, efforts Ogawa intervened against. With such vast questions on the table, it is no wonder that the film ends without resolving much of anything; consciousness raising was the point.

It may be that such direct critique of the Ministry of Education and engagement with the sensibilities and life experiences of working-class correspondence students precluded its broadcast on national television. What remains perplexing is the film's style, which—despite the unfettered path they chose—is conventional by any measure. The staff was imminently competent, featuring the talents of Ogawa's Iwanami colleagues like Okumura, Otsu, Tamura, and Kubota on sound. The straightforward style is doubly curious considering Ogawa's ties to the Image Arts Society, which gave Jieiso office space, and the innovative documentary being pioneered by people like Matsumoto Toshio at this very time. Ogawa had yet to completely escape the confines of the PR film.

Virtually the only place Ogawa's subjectivity peeks out is the huge white board used as a prop book-ending the film. The students carry it into the first scene; its blank surface reduplicates the white of the movie screen. By the end, both film and board have been filled in by the filmmaker and the students. In the final shot, Ogawa trucks around the four students standing on their big, white board in the middle of an empty athletic field writing things on it; getting paint all over their feet, hands, and faces; and tearing up paper and putting it over the surface. Ogawa trucks in circles around the group as they play on the surface of the board=screen. In the archive, anonymous, handwritten notes from one of their subsequent meetings ruminate in third person on what they were striving for in this device:

> When attempting to fix the hopes and desires of the filmmaker in one image, they probably had to attempt that performance using the signboard, which was something like a white canvas. In this way, they deepened the degree of transparency in the film while more vividly representing their own deviation from reality.[9]

It must be pointed out, however, that the deviation from reality essentially reduplicated the conventions of the old *bunka eiga*. The film's reflexivity is "pale" because it is not entirely straight about its portrayal of the collective self. The rhetoric of the film, in terms of narration and image manipulation, is never quite pitched in the first person. One could watch the film and be left with the impression that it is "a film *about* a group of four students," not *by them*. The voice of the documentary is basically rendered in the voice of God typical of the *bunka eiga*. It is precisely in this gap between the subjectivity of the collective producing the documentary and its textual voice that an ounce or two of fiction surreptitiously slips into the film. For example, one of the four students, Kobayashi Hideko, harbors great regrets about the way she was portrayed in *Sea of Youth*. The film poses her as a waitress struggling to attain a degree, but in actuality she wasn't working: "I couldn't see myself in the film. The Kobayashi Hideko there was largely the creation of Ogawa Shinsuke." The Jieiso filmmakers had yet to break completely from the *bunka eiga* conventions, an advance they would decisively make in their next film.

Upon the completion of *Sea of Youth*, the hard work of finding and creating an audience began. Ogawa was fond of telling a story about the film's first screening. I must have heard it three or four times in the short time I knew him. Ogawa rented a screening room at Shochiku Studios and issued invitations to the press and prominent critics. Although he had no money, he splurged on a taxi to take the print to the studio. When he opened the doors, he ended up with only three spectators: one reporter (an acquaintance), his brother, and his sister. Ogawa always ended this story with the same joke: "This is how I started my career as a filmmaker, and from that point on, no matter how hard things became, I decided that if I ever found less than three people in the audience it was time to quit."[10]

Sage advice for any independent filmmaker, but it is also a narrative that veiled hard fiscal realities. The little story's first-person narration hides the fact that the task of raising the money and responsibility for returning the debt fell on the collective shoulders of Jieiso. One fruit of this dilemma is the organization's elaboration of a system for independent distribution. It identified sympathizers across Japan and divided the country into blocks that organized the reach of its growing network. Jieiso often created its own screening spaces and the audiences to fill them. As the notes from one of Jieiso's meetings states, "This film does not exist in places we do not."[11]

This was more than simply network-building. Jieiso was also redefining what a film movement could be. Most film movements in the history of cinema are centered on production, the promotion of new styles, or certain politics—Italian Neo-realism or the French New Wave as prototypical examples—but Jieiso made the postproduction process the object of action.

Ask an Ogawa Pro member about its "film movement" and he or she will assume you are talking about the screenings, not the film. The real activism of the collective centered on the reception context. These images evidence the wide variety of audiences and venues, from urban art houses to rural gymnasiums to homemade theaters.

This meant forging networks that collaborated on the task of bringing people to the film. It involved publishing newsletters, pamphlets, tracts, and the like. After-film discussions became a condition of screening. We have seen this practice with the CIE, but here it would be redirected toward raising consciousness for radically different politics. And all these interlocking activities would feed back into the production of new films. This redefinition of the film movement around the distribution process came to deeply inform the subsequent organization of Ogawa Pro. To this day, ask a former member of Jieiso or Ogawa Pro about their "film movement" and he or she will inevitably assume you are talking about the *distribution and screening of films,* not their production.

At this very same time, the filmmaking itself was undergoing an equally profound transformation. We might render this change spatially, a movement from outside to inside, and it is most pronounced in the films of Ogawa and Tsuchimoto. This new approach to documentary reaches its most refined and profound development in the Minamata and Sanrizuka series, but the two directors' films at this early point in their careers reveal the actual shift from one mode to the next. This was increasingly an era when being on the inside meant something—perhaps everything.

With Tsuchimoto, we may chart the shift in three of the major films he made up to this point. In *An Engineer's Assistant* (*Aru kikan joshi,* 1963), Tsuchimoto took the position of the typical documentary filmmaker of the era, who comes to a topic from an external position from which he never substantially departs. The film is remembered primarily for its impressive photography and editing. Tsuchimoto moves closer to his object in *Document: On the Road,* building a strong sense of sympathy—in the strongest sense of the word—with the daily frustrations of his taxi driver. His relationship to the driver is qualitatively different than with the train engineer of the previous film, who appears overly aestheticized (and thus objectified) in comparison. Finally, Tsuchimoto completes the movement inward with *Chua Swee Lin.* With this film, there is no question that its textual voice is centered on Chua's own voice on the soundtrack. The fact that Tsuchimoto severed ties to institutionalized structures of production and distribution was decisive. This enabled him to build the film soundly on the subjectivity of the student. There is little question that the film belongs to its *taisho* in ways that had not been seen in Japanese documentary up to this point.

The same transformation is apparent in the differences between *Sea of Youth* and Ogawa's next film, *Forest of Oppression* (*Assatsu no mori,* 1967). As noted previously, *Sea of Youth* is close to the international norm for pre-verité documentary, with its rhetoric of distance and "sly" employment of fiction for the sake of argumentation. *Forest of Oppression* also centers on a group of students and their discussions about education and movement politics. However, the film has a new raw quality, as if shot under the gun. It does not spin a subtle web of fiction through its structuring, which probably accounts for its rough edges. The rough-hewn quality is partly stylistic. The look is unmistakable today; and while one can trace it back through the Sunagawa Series to Prokino in the 1930s, it really achieves the status and identity of a distinct aesthetic at this point. Make no mistake, the directors longed for synch sound and finer equipment, but the jagged style unquestionably announced their difference from the norm as well as their resolve to make films no matter the obstacles. Many first-time viewers of the films of Ogawa and Tsuchimoto enter the theater expecting smoothness and completeness. Being familiar with the film's prestige, they are often shocked by what they see. Those familiar with the codes of verité easily forgive the handheld, rough-and-tumble cinematography. However, most new viewers are vexed by the soundtrack, which is not synched to the lip movements of speakers. The lack of synch sound equipment did not stop these filmmakers from making long discussions and speeches a central part of their cinema. Rather than hiding what conventional documentary marks as deficiency, Ogawa and Tsuchimoto made these rough-hewn qualities the sign of their independence from the demands of capital. The films' roughness increased according to the degree the filmmakers approached their embattled and powerless *taisho*.

The sense of the films being spatially located within an "inside" also comes from their production, which often involved the crossing of actual lines, climbing through barricades being the most spectacular. *Forest of Oppression* provides the prototype. It documents one of the many student risings in the mid to late 1960s. After finishing its first film, Jieiso turned its energies immediately to this new project. The Jieiso members decided to look at the troubles brewing and threatening to explode on the college campuses. They split up and embarked on research trips to many schools, making contacts and returning with notes to share their findings. The written presentations of the scenario section show what a complex and highly organized undertaking this was. They made research trips to Meiji University, Waseda University, Rikkyo University, International Christian University, and many other schools. They networked through universities and even high schools throughout Japan, and made calls on organizations like Zengakuren and other political groups.

As part of this effort, Jieiso held screenings of films during which members would share their findings. Some of these were remarkably involved. The record of their eleventh screening event in May 1966 at Waseda University featured four films, including *Exchange Student Chua Swee Lin,* and lasted six hours. It also featured an extended report of the situation at Takasaki University. This was the month they began concentrating their re-

A protest snaking through the streets in *Forest of Pressure* (1967). Photograph courtesy of the Athénée Français Cultural Center.

search activities on this particular school. The Jieiso members were very clear about how these screenings were designed to network the various student movements into a synergistic whole, something their current production would do at a scale they could not have predicted at this early point.[12] When they finally decided to shoot at Takasaki, the Jieiso members were highly self-conscious about the spatial position of their filmmaking, as their notes clearly attest: "It goes without saying that the movement to make a film about the struggle at Takasaki is built on a solidarity of the *shutai* of the students at Takasaki Economics University and the *shutai* of Jieiso."[13] The language of the memoranda and notes clearly demonstrates how they were building their efforts at independent cinema on the theoretical foundation laid for them by Matsumoto and others.

Judging from the energies devoted to spelling out their intentions, the move to the inside was no easy matter. They gave the project the provisional title *Student (Gakusei)* and created a *Takasaki Keizai Daigaku* Jishu Seisaku Jikoiinkai (Organizing Committee for the Independent Production of *Takasaki Economic University*). They drafted proposals and planning papers, interesting documents sprinkled with quotes from Brecht and Dostoevsky. The following passage from a billet reveals as much about Jieiso as it does about Jieiso's films:

> To all of you fighting at Takasaki University: This is a movement challenging, through filmmaking, the inhumanity always produced by the domination of power. We [Jieiso] have no status, wealth or power. What we do have is the very, very strong support for, and solidarity with, the students fighting at Takasaki Economic University . . . committing your struggle to film through our own efforts recaptures the cinema—which has been privatized in the class system—for our side. Furthermore, making this a possibility through filmmaking will, to be sure, mark a breakthrough in today's movie world. Moreover, the document we affix on film has a profound duality in that it is not unrelated to all the students fighting across Japan.[14]

That this kind of struggle was analogous to many other schools' accounts for both the possibility of its production and the film's eventual success. Jieiso tapped its network to begin the filming (which had a projected ¥2,914,800 budget in March).[15] This was a serious amount of money in 1967, but when the film came out, it was explosively popular and former Jieiso members estimate it turned a healthy profit in the end. The film successfully tapped the energies running through the campuses, and the requests for screenings poured into Jieiso's Tokyo office. A year-end report on its screening movement noted that in the month of November (1967) alone, Jieiso had roughly sixty screenings in every part of Japan.[16] Newspapers of all sizes published reviews, and even inquisitive adults found the film one way to access what was going on in the day's youth culture. *Asahi Journal* went further than a simple review, expressing a curiosity about the new screening strategy and virtually joining the movement itself:

> Both *Forest of Oppression* and *Document: Power* [the preproduction title of *Report from Haneda*—AMN] are not shown in regular movie theaters, and are proceeding through a screening movement that lends prints to groups that want to hold shows. However, shouldn't this kind of film also show in the regular theaters? These are films that hit the blind spot of tepid television, theatrical art cinema, and the entertainment film. Here we can see a method of filmmaking that keeps pressing for sincere thought.[17]

One of the most interesting traces of the older generation's perspective was left by Yamada Kazuo, the well-known, JCP-aligned film critic who supported Ogawa back when *Children Living in the Mountains* was rejected by the Ministry of Education. With the release and what was for his generation the alarming success of *Forest of Oppression,* Yamada was no longer sympathetic. In a review from the JCP's cultural organ *Bunka Hyoron,* Yamada argued the film evidenced the disturbing fact that the film world had been infiltrated by the "'left' right wing elements of opportunism" vis-à-vis Japan's social movements. He criticized the Takasaki students for failing to organize their collective anger correctly, instead simplistically attacking the university administration, city officials, and riot police. He ridiculed the students' rhetoric, and criticized their isolation from other citizens and unions and their propensity to meet force with force. The film amounted to an "ugly self-portrait of the Trotskyites"—an indication of how far inside Ogawa had moved.[18]

These were the very qualities that appealed to the students themselves. This was their own self-portrait. And until this film, they had not seen this kind of representation of their own culture in the media. Athénée Français' Matsumoto Masamichi fondly recalls watching the film as a student and calls *Forest of Oppression* a *seishun eiga,* the youth film that was so popular at the time. Normally, this genre calls up images of love stories, popular music, and action. *Forest of Oppression* offered a different kind of romance. Like the youth film of the feature film, Ogawa's young people sport the fashion specific to their generation—T-shirts, jeans, and helmets emblazoned with slogans. These youth speak in a language of their own concoction—phrases from Lenin, Marx, and Brecht in a heady mix of street slang and academe. And their fights were not over love but over issues and taken to the real streets. Takasaki may have been a minor, rural school with a minority of activists behind the barricades, but this was precisely why it had so much power. The politicized youth culture was centered on the major schools of Tokyo and Osaka, but Ogawa chose Takasaki. It was way off the map of everyday consciousness, so small and far away. Spectators were amazed by the passion of the Takasaki youth and *Forest of Oppression* became one of the biggest films energizing the student movement in the years immediately preceding the 1970 ANPO.

Police Report

Jieiso began its next project in the midst of the excitement generated by *Forest of Oppression.* Its genesis came while Nosaka Haruo and Kobayashi Hideko were sitting in a coffee shop and heard a news broadcast on television about the death of a student from Kyoto, Yamazaki Hiroaki. The death occurred during violent clashes between riot police and demonstrators attempting to stop Prime Minister Sato's departure to Vietnam from Haneda Airport. Jieiso assembled an organizing committee for a film project out of representatives from Jieiso, Iwanami Film Union, Image Arts Society, and Group "Vision" (the labor union for Nichiei Shinsha, one of the oldest documentary production companies in Japan). Kuroki Kazuo, Tsuchimoto Noriaki, Haruma Ko (Nichiei Shinsha), and Higashi Yoichi led separate film teams around the capital for a month, along with stellar cinematographers like Suzuki Tatsuo, Otsu Koshiro, and Tamura Masaki. Their initial title was simple: *Document: "Power" (Dokyumento: "Kenryoku").* They eventually changed it to *Gennin Hokokusho,* which ironically refers to the daily activity reports kept by police. The English title is usually rendered *Report from Haneda* (1967). In one sense, the title is an inside joke, since by now Jieiso was under police surveillance, and the film documents its activities better than any police report. In another more serious sense, the title is an indictment of the police for slaying a student with excessive force.

Ogawa and his collaborators used the film to investigate *precisely* what went on. This meant more than a reiteration of the "facts" or the careful reconstruction of events. These are the approaches of documentary aligned with power, the television report being their own object of comparison. Rather, the filmmakers mix painstaking detail with evocative imagery of past events, shifting between the mundane, the beautiful, and the dreadful. Ogawa comes into his own as a major, innovative documentarist in the first part of this film, even if the last half compromises the whole.

From the spectacular introduction, the film goes on to flesh out both the ongoing struggles on the street and the circumstances surrounding

Yamazaki's death. The skirmishes with police are spectacular and often frightening. In one impressive scene, the cinematographer positioned the camera near the area where they were booking young people who had been arrested. One by one, the protestors, all of them bloody and nursing wounds, are led past the panning camera by riot police. Intercut with these scenes are interviews with Yamazaki's mother about their last conversation in which she begged him not to go to Tokyo, as well as a failed attempt to talk to the doctor who performed his autopsy.

These scenes are of great interest. However, their assemblage failed to consolidate their power. After an impressive start, the film devolves into a somewhat confused assemblage. Most commentators considered the film a failure, and Ogawa seemed to agree. The film was, however, hastily produced under difficult conditions in little more than a month. By way of contrast, their next film would require a year of *sake*-fueled relationship building with the farmers of Sanrizuka. Nevertheless, the first part of the film hints at Ogawa's talent.

Ogawa Shinsuke (center) leading a discussion during the production of *Report from Haneda* (1967). To his immediate left is cameraman Otsu Koshiro, who sits next to Matsumoto Takeaki. Photograph courtesy of the Athénée Français Cultural Center.

The opening of *Report from Haneda* is a stunning montage of sound and still images. In a shot that lasts two and one-half minutes, the camera circles above a hundred still photographs and contact sheets scattered in a mess. Hovering like a police helicopter, the camera's movement causes the images to dissolve in and out of focus. Upon becoming sharp, they reveal still images of violence, police attacking young people on the streets of Tokyo. The documentary noise of protest supplements the violence of the photographs frozen in time, injecting the images with a sense of motion. Jet planes on takeoff from Haneda punctuate the sound mix, from which agitated human voices emerge:

"Riot police are taking their helmets!"

"We'll arrest everyone!"

"Use the batons!"

"Please stop!" cries a woman's voice.

A police siren drones in, and the camera settles on the still image of a young man. The camera trucks up to an extreme close-up of his eye while a subtitle reveals his identity. It is Yamazaki Hiroaki, who was killed in the riots, and this is an image of his corpse. This disturbing photograph, which Jieiso also used in its publicity, was captured shortly before his autopsy. The uncanny quality of Yamazaki's inert eye is soul-shaking. As the sound fades to silence, the film's title is superimposed over the image. This report is for—or perhaps from—the dead.

After an explanation of the incident by Ogawa, we are thrown into the midst of the riots between students and police. A crowd of riot police race into the frame and spread out as they reach the camera, attacking people indiscriminately. Refusing to keep the safe distance of a typical news cameraman, the cinematographer simply plunges into the melee on the street. People are left laying on the pavement bleeding. And then Ogawa abruptly repeats this very same shot. This time he suddenly freezes the image, pauses, then moves the film a few frames, pauses, moves again, returning to full motion, then freezes again. His experimentation analytically heightens the dynamic movement, turning the street fight into a ballet of violence. Bodies—only half of them in riot gear—flow in every direction, limbs askew, faces frightened, batons swinging, and the scene ends on an extreme close-up of a human skull, brain exposed, sitting on a table.

For some, this may evoke the descriptions of student riots in Barthes, only Ogawa was criticized for depoliticizing the events. Indeed, the ethic in Ogawa's American counterpart, Newsreel, proudly rejected any form of slick aestheticism. While their various reception contexts were different, the subsequent scene in *Report from Haneda* points to the decisive difference. From that shocking segue a doctor explains, in excruciating detail, the physiology of a police baton blow. Head in hand, he describes exactly how young Yamazaki perished. This shifting attention to surface, process, and detail may well embody the qualities Matsumoto called for in evoking the *unheimlich* lurking beneath the sure surfaces of documentary realism, for Ogawa's innovative use of freeze-frame is what calls our attention to what is usually hidden by the 24 frame-per-second blizzard of images thrown on the screen. Furthermore, the analytical attention to procedure and development parodies the superficial analysis of television news, while the experimentation with documentary style asserts the subjectivity of the filmmakers in the tissue of the image and sound. Ogawa was a film fanatic, and his cohort worked with a proud professionalism that never settled into a reactionary defense of documentary convention. They were making politically engaged films that simultaneously strove to be emotionally and aesthetically engaging experiences for their audiences. This was the attitude that Ogawa brought to his Sanrizuka films, although with a difference from his New Left colleagues that only gradually became apparent.

[3] The Sanrizuka Series

When Ogawa Pro was formed in early 1968, it was relatively unusual to name a documentary production company after oneself. Tsuchimoto asked Ogawa why he chose this name, and Ogawa replied that it signified his intent to take ultimate responsibility for the films they made. "Hmm," thought Tsuchimoto, "I guess that's one way of looking at it." Ogawa's cameraman, Otsu Koshiro, thought it was improper to attach the name of an individual to social movement films like this, and he jumped over to Tsuchimoto's group. These anecdotes hint at the complexity of authorship in this collective mode of filmmaking.

Ogawa's example troubles the critical impulse to assign the production of meaning to an individual film artist. This is obvious in nearly any article or book about him. The references to authorship inevitably exhibit an unusual slippage between Ogawa, the director, and Ogawa Pro(ductions), the collective. Ogawa's method was predicated on intense collaboration. In fact, when his crew went out, he often stayed home. To Ogawa, their objectives had been decided in advance through extensive discussion, and he clearly trusted the competence of his staff; he also privileged the process of editing. Staff members often jotted quotes from Ogawa in their notebooks; one reads, "Ogawa: 'The foundation of directing is elimination. In contrast, photography is about discovery. This is the fundamental contradiction. On location, if the director insists on "finding things" the film will never end.'"[1] Even this process of elimination was carried out surrounded by staff, and sometimes with the people in the films. Ogawa may have been the director, but his role was conceptualized as collaborative at a number of levels.

Because of this, Japanese authors usually modify *Ogawa* with plural suffixes such as *ra* or *tachi* or *Puro* (short for *Productions*). This book will be no different, except that it will explore the issues of collective production of documentary art in a rapidly changing society. Indeed, we could say

Poster for *Heta Village*, from a community center in 1973.

that this relationship to collectivity is one of Ogawa's contributions to the world of documentary.

Ogawa Pro was the inspiration of Jieiso members Kobayashi Hideko, Nosaka Haruo, and Yoshida Tsukasa, who came up with the idea while chatting at a coffee shop. They took a proposal for this new production company sporting the Ogawa name to the director himself, and he was understandably honored and thrilled. Nosaka Haruo, who participated in *Sea of Youth* and remained a central member of Ogawa Pro until after the move to Yamagata, suspects that there were several unusual reasons behind his enthusiasm. One was that during the recent production of *Report from Haneda,* Ogawa was surrounded by colleagues and many of them were senior to him. These included Tsuchimoto Noriaki and Kuroki Kazuo as quasi-directors, Tamura Masaki and Suzuki Tatsuo shooting the images, and Iwasa Hisaya in the editing room. Nosaka distinctly remembers Ogawa—a master of the one-way conversation—acting unusually reserved around these professional filmmakers, something one can sense in the scenes in which the director appears. Ogawa hated being anywhere but on top, and the best way to accomplish this was to run his own production company and lend it his own name. Nosaka also suspects that another reason for dissolving Jieiso into Ogawa Pro is probably that he needed the receipts from continued showings of the first three films to mount the expensive production of the first effort of the Sanrizuka Series.

Another factor is Ogawa's relationship to Jieiso. There is no question that that organization came together and continued through Ogawa's efforts. He was the students' big brother, whose animated conversation bound them. At one point, their memoranda lists him as *"kyokucho,"* or "chief of staff," although the films credit him as *"kantoku"* ("director"). At the same time, what is remarkable about the newsletters, pamphlets, fliers, memos, reports, and notes left in the Jieiso archive is Ogawa's virtual absence. They rarely mention his existence, let alone outline his responsibilities as they did with other members. Although many of the internal documents in the archive are signed by Ogawa, he did not generate any of them. He rarely contributed to their publications, which barely mention him at all. Former Jieiso members do remember Ogawa at the center of things—talking away—but considering all their rhetoric about protecting the *shutaisei* of the director, Ogawa is curiously absent from the archive. The documents express a different kind of *shutaisei.*

Sea of Youth, Forest of Oppression, and *Report from Haneda* are popularly attributed to Ogawa Pro, despite the fact that they predate the organization. However, they were produced by the efforts of organizing committees set up for each film, a common practice in Japanese documentary to the present day. These three films ultimately belonged to Jieiso (which is also the reason Jieiso's archive is preserved separately from the Ogawa Pro materials). Indeed, we often speak of Ogawa entering the student movement to make his first films, but the situation looks far more like the Jieiso students hiring Ogawa for their productions. Certainly a film like *Forest of Oppression* could never have been made without the networking, research, and careful approach of the youthful activists staffing Jieiso. At the same time, Ogawa had gone so far inside, it is difficult to separate his contribution from the staff's efforts.

Perhaps the group began feeling Ogawa's centrality around the completion of *Report from Haneda.* In April 1967, Jieiso organized screenings of its three films, packaging them as an "Ogawa Shinsuke Retrospective." The leaflets advertising the retrospective speak of Ogawa in glowing, even heroic, terms:

> Amidst today's tumultuous fluidity and polarization of left and right, there is a single artist who secures a space to throw himself into the struggle with his own method (cinema). That artist is Ogawa Shinsuke. Only through guaranteeing the creative acts of such combative filmmakers can a combative cinema be born and liberate us from this cultural condition of bewildering stagnation.[2]

The Jieiso membership founded Ogawa Pro in this spirit, and immediately investigated the options open for their first film. The construction site of New Tokyo International Airport appeared to be their best prospect. Ogawa visited the villages at the proposed construction site on the invitation of an activist from Zengakuren, who took him to the site in actor Mikuni Rentaro's red sports car (the connection to Mikuni is unclear, but Ogawa indulged in the contradiction in subsequent tellings of the story). There, he met Tomura Issaku. A deeply religious Christian named after the prophet Isaac, Tosaka led the organization running the still-small protests. At the time, no one knew the scale that they would reach, but Ogawa recalls Tomura telling him, "This will be no ordinary fight. I'm going to make this a great struggle for the ages. Ogawa-san, if you don't have the stomach for that, you'd better not shoot it."[3]

For a short period, as Ogawa began concentrating his efforts on entering Sanrizuka, Ogawa Pro and Jieiso ran side by side. The newly established Ogawa Pro had a separate office in Shinjuku and borrowed a house in the town of Sanrizuka Crossroads (close to the proposed runway). This house was recently torn down. Today, the neighborhood is filled with apartment buildings for airport workers and the luxurious homes of farmers who sold their land to the airport authority (Public Corporation for the Construction of the Airport, hereafter Kodan). At this starting point, the staff of Ogawa Pro consisted primarily of Yoshida Tsukasa, Nosaka Haruo, Kobayashi Hideko, followed shortly by the addition of Fuseya Hiro (Hiroo). The Jishu Joei Soshiki no Kai continued its efforts from a separate office in Shinjuku, with Sato Kyoko as its main staff member. However, Ogawa soon managed to fold it—the staff and the films they had made—into

The Ogawa Pro crew on location, with a line of riot police waiting in the wings. Yumoto Mareo walks toward a television crew (no helmets necessary)

Ogawa Pro. Until that point, Jieiso maintained at least a partial independence from Ogawa in terms of its identity. After that, however, everything centered around Ogawa.

Summer Heat

The construction of New Tokyo International Airport, commonly called Narita Airport, constitutes a traumatic episode in modern Japanese history.[4] It began two years earlier in June 1966, when NHK scooped the news that the government had made a surprise decision to construct a major new airport in a place near Narita City called Sanrizuka. This was actually an abrupt change in plans, as the original site was to be nearby Tomisato; however, the farmers there had immediately marshaled strong resistance so the government felt compelled to move the site. They could not have foreseen the level of resistance mounted by the farmers of Sanrizuka, which eventually escalated to a kind of civil warfare, just as Tomura predicted.

Most people who fly into Narita wonder why—as they make the one- to two-hour trip into Tokyo—such a distant site was chosen for an international airport serving one of the world's largest cities. There are a variety of reasons. Sanrizuka lies some sixty kilometers from the city center, but it was topographically attractive. While difficult to appreciate from the train, the airport sits on tableland surrounded by a maze-like collection of short hills cut by steep ravines. The broader drainages are carpeted with rice paddies and edged with homes. Fields on the higher tablelands, at least what is left of them, grow a wide assortment of vegetables. Although farmers regularly turned up pottery from the earliest periods of Japanese history in their fields, this area remained relatively undeveloped until the Meiji Era (1868–1912). One factor was that the volcanic soil was poor for farming. Another was that feudal lords had used it as a range for their horses. With the Meiji Restoration, large parcels of Sanrizuka were set aside as the imperial pasture estate. As the capital grew, so did the need for nearby food production, and farmers were granted land for reclamation. They spent one hundred years of hard labor making the barren soil fertile for their wheat, peanuts, taro, ginger, watermelons, onions, and rice.

Sanrizuka attracted the government for far more than its flat terrain. Because the farmers had worked the land for only one to three generations, it was assumed that they would feel less connection to their land and gladly accept generous offers of inflated prices or trades for 50 percent more land elsewhere. Furthermore, their homes were relatively scattered, thanks to the original land distribution plans, so they didn't live in concentrated, traditional hamlets that would foster close bonds of solidarity and inclinations toward collective resistance. This would presumably make it all the easier to divide the farmers against themselves. Finally, the remaining imperial pastureland and adjoining national forest represented large parcels of the airport site, which were easily transferred to the Kodan authorities.

A complex political dynamic underlying the protests contributed to their scale along with the farmers' ability to attract national attention and the support of a wide array of political interests. First, the locals assumed that the airport project represented far more than the natural outcome of the metropole's growth. Farmers across Japan were questioning agricultural reforms of the Sato government. These policies appeared to be the result of a reorganization of the economy. The new structure favored urbanization and industrialization, resulting in the conversion of agricultural areas to heavy industry networked with ports and factory centers along nearby coasts. Sitting near the neck of a peninsula and a short drive from massive industrial areas, Sanrizuka fit this bill perfectly. The farmers were reacting to what they perceived as the transformation of farmers into factory workers by uprooting people from their land and local culture. As an activist journal from the time put it, "The Sanrizuka Struggle is not only in opposition to the airport itself, but is a battle against the entire Hokuso Development Plan. It is a struggle of the local people against the tendency of monopoly capital to explain, modernize, and rationalize for its own benefit."[5]

The Sanrizuka Struggle was also deeply imbricated in the ANPO security treaty with the United States and the rapidly escalating war in Vietnam. The government's rationale for a new international airport centered on the overcrowding at Tokyo's Haneda Airport, which is located in the city on Tokyo Bay. However, one of the reasons for Haneda's busyness was the intensification of the conflict in Indochina. The security treaty guaranteed landing rights to American military flights, and these demands were rising. An added factor was the treaty's provision that reserved a flight path (called Blue 14) for the exclusive use of U.S. military aircraft. This route entered the region from the Pacific Ocean, skirted the coast along Yokohama, and penetrated the interior between Tokyo and Yokota Air Force Base. This made a public airport to the west of Tokyo impossible, so they turned to the region above the Chiba Peninsula where Sanrizuka sits.

Narita's New Tokyo International Airport would fall under the same free use rules of ANPO, basically turning Japan into a huge aircraft carrier for the Pentagon. Thus, the Sanrizuka Struggle became a magnet for the antiwar and student movements as the 1970 renewal date for the treaty neared. Student movements based at universities generally followed the pattern documented in *Forest of Oppression:* emergence, barricading, clashes with police, and eventual dissipation. This boom-and-bust cycle occurred at all the major schools, and many of the smaller ones. The Sanrizuka problem developed in the midst of this process, along with the horror of the Vietnam War and the student solidarity leading up to the second ANPO. As campus-based protests ran out of energy, student activists and their sects flocked to Chiba to join in the farmers' fight.

The farmers found the activism of the students inspirational. One of their critical clashes with police occurred on October 10, 1967, only days after the events of the Haneda Incident. Up to this point, the Sanrizuka-Shibayama Anti-Airport League (Sanrizuka-Shibayama Rengo Kuko Hantai Domei, or Hantai Domei for short) had chosen a strategy of peaceful, nonviolent resistance under the de facto leadership of the JCP. In an attempt to obstruct surveyors from conducting their jobs, the farmers sat on incoming roads. However, the survey teams arrived with two thousand riot police who cleared the roads with brutal force. The farmers watched the JCP retreat singing songs. In the face of this frightening show of force, the tactics of the students in the Tokyo streets started looking attractive. The Hantai Domei subsequently rejected the JCP's attempts at attaining leadership of their struggle and expelled the organization from Sanrizuka. In their place, the students and sects of the New Left flooded in and were welcomed by the farmers, who simultaneously made it clear that the students were invited guests.

Ogawa's own move from Takasaki and the streets of Tokyo to the fields of Sanrizuka must be seen against this larger phenomenon. They entered the site on February 26, 1968, when the situation was reaching the boiling point, and clashes with riot police were becoming a part of everyday life for area farmers. The radical sects were also making their presence known, having established solidarity huts across the construction site. The farmers who had conceded to the conditions of the Kodan were receiving visits from officials to negotiate the sale of their land. The Hantai Domei interfered by gathering at these homes and attempting to prevent the officials from reaching their meetings. The riot police would be called in, clash with the assembled antiairport farmers, and chaos would ensue. The deals steadily proceeded, one by one, in this manner.

This is the tense situation that the filmmakers stepped into. Ogawa wanted to structure this documentary in a new fashion. This first effort would be, from the very start, nothing but a first chapter. By its distant end, this first film would be the entryway to a sprawling work of many parts. Ogawa likened the plan to a *taiga shosetsu* (epic novel). In November 1968, he is quoted as saying, "Spring, summer, fall, winter, and then continuing with spring, summer again. . . . That's how I want to watch the struggle at Sanrizuka. People will change completely, I suppose. Where will the farmers find their own philosophy?"[6] Ogawa was one of the many outsiders joining the struggle in Sanrizuka, but he would—in the process of writing his epic—work his way into the depths of the farmers' existence. By the time they left Sanrizuka for good, they would finish seven documentaries over nine years, a total of twelve and one-half hours of film that sees the power of the state from the farmers' eyes. The Jieiso of *Forest of Oppression* was about to become the Ogawa Pro of the Sanrizuka Struggle.

From their base in Sanrizuka, Ogawa and his crew quickly scoped out the situation before the commencement of shooting in April 1968. At this initial stage, the farmers watched the soil of their livelihood mapped out as a prelude to being cemented over. Their resistance was met with raw state power—a police force fully armed while the farmers themselves had little more than rocks and sticks. Alongside them were the newly arrived students, who perceived the battleground of rice paddies and fallow fields as a new, pure, political landscape on which to confront the state. Ogawa endowed the film that documented their explosive meeting with a bold title that evoked the conflict in Vietnam: *The Battle Front for the Liberation of Japan—Summer in Sanrizuka* (*Nihon kaiho sensen—Sanrizuka no natsu*, 1968).

Like their previous films, *Summer in Sanrizuka* deploys a raucous aesthetic, both in photography and editing, and focuses on the confrontations between airport employees, their police escorts, and protesters. The first shot shows riot police running at full hilt across a field in the distance. The camera gently pans across the field with them. This is the last time we see such a stable shot of the police. It is cinematic chaos from here on out. Everything about Ogawa's representation of the Sanrizuka struggle is extreme: the handheld shots, the loud jumble of sound, the close-ups of people during discussions. And when the fights break out, cameraman Tamura Masaki throws himself into the melee like a fan moshing at a punk concert. Hani Goro told Ogawa he thought it reminded him of an "action film" along the lines of a John Ford Western, with the epic proportions of a violent confrontation between representatives of national power and local

Dressed for battle in 1970. Tomura told Ogawa, "I want this to be a war remembered by history. Ogawa-san, if you don't have the stomach for that, you'd better not shoot it." From left to right: Tamura Masaki, Shimizu Yoshio, Yumoto Mareo, Ogawa Shinsuke, Fukuda Katsuhiko.

residents fighting for their ancestral lands—but with the documentary difference. Noël Burch called it a "rather indigestible assemblage."[7]

The film *is* rough, but it does have structure. More precisely, it has episodic microstructures that the filmmakers do not necessarily weave into an elegant, overall package. A simple example: in one scene where the farmers talk amongst themselves, Ogawa cuts to a long take in a storage shed filled with sickles. The agenda of the discussion was the degree and speed of the escalation of violence and the efficacy of the nonviolent methods they had used for a year with no obvious results. One man had his ribs broken at the protests, so the topic under debate was over matching police force by taking up weapons. The cutaway to the shed with its assemblage of tools recalls early modern peasant riots where farming implements were converted into instruments of war. The film then marks the escalation in the struggle by showing the farmers striking out for the fields with large sticks and sickles—armed, just like the police. The filmmakers are clearly devoting great care to the local editing without necessarily thinking at the global level or striving for smooth transitions and logical progression. However, this nice touch does not mitigate the chaos of the rest of the film, both in content and form.

A more complex example may be found in the many scenes of people communicating by walkie-talkie. Visually, they show little more than groups of men sitting at a table listening to the electronic chatter, occasionally adding to it by speaking into handheld devices. Far more is going on because Ogawa uses these scenes to map the budding space of the struggle through aural means. Most of the communiqués are descriptions of "troop movements," and they make the simple maps these men examine come alive. In this way, the walkie-talkie scenes generate bleeding between the sections. They invite the spectator to chart out the action occurring off screen, an invitation readily accepted since the referent of the soundtrack is usually police clashing with farmers and students. In the first long instance of this walkie-talkie scene structure, Ogawa starts with an extreme close-up of a map with penned-in marks representing the barricades the farmers were erecting. They then cut from the simplified iconography of the map to documentary images of the site; the men put the final touches on a barrier of logs and barbed wire while women pile up fist-sized rocks to lob at the incoming police. The natural sound of the soundtrack is interrupted by squawks from a walkie-talkie. The previous group of men warns them of massing police forces. When the police arrive to an incredible racket of cat calls and flying rocks, Ogawa curiously cuts to the bare feet of the women before becoming embroiled in another violent contestation.

This microstructure creates an analog for other scenes, for example when farmers bang on drums as an alarm. Visually, there is little information to deal with, but we immediately and palpably sense police movement somewhere, out there, in offscreen space. Our imagination searches for it. And when we see the fight commence, we also know it is connected to a nerve center of men sitting around a small table with a map, directing counteraction toward our position. By the end of the film when farmers gather at night to talk about the day's events, one has the eerie feeling of riot police out there, somewhere, doing exactly the same thing.

Faced with the difficulty of portraying such a fluid and ephemeral subject with a minuscule budget, the tactic of deploying the soundtrack to heighten often unexceptional images and energize offscreen space is brilliant. At the same time, its use does not appear to fit into any overall plan. This unusual formal feature—tactics without strategy, as Bourdieu would suggest—is ultimately the trace of their reaction to authoritarian deployments of film form, which always value smoothness and completeness. The apparent explanatory power of the newsreel, the television news, or the PR film is served well by film form that radically simplifies lived reality. Ogawa, by contrast, is less explaining than *inviting* experience. This fractiousness in the film's very structure also contributes much to the way the film marshals tremendous affect while appearing to be out of control; generally, we expect roughshod films to produce lukewarm effects. However, like *Forest of Oppression* before it, this rough-hewn quality is undoubtedly one source of its uncommon power.

Of course, its subject matter is a factor that cannot be ignored. How can one fail to be moved by the spectacle of farmers fighting the enormous repressive apparatuses of the state? At the same time, the intensity of their struggle is immeasurably amplified through Ogawa's predilection for interrupting the epic confrontation with mundane details and odd asides. *Summer in Sanrizuka* has many transcendental moments. The one burned indelibly into my own mind is the tense standoff on a quiet country road between farmers and police decked out in riot gear. The situation seems to ask only one question—when will the two sides tire of glaring at each other and have at it?—and suddenly the two parties stream to either side of the road to make way for a line of children biking to school. Elsewhere, the filmmakers interrupt the swift pace to pause on a peripheral personality. A uniformed man working for the Kodan, clearly out of control and trying desperately hard to clear a way through the crowds for cars to pass, berates and pushes people out of the way, and then starts irrationally pushing the cars themselves. He is a little mad, actually. Or there is the "shifty little bastard" with the police who snaps photographs of the women protesters. Or the old farmer berating the police, whom he calls the "lap dogs of the corporation," with questions like, "You call yourself Japanese?!?"

This attention to small, seemingly peripheral moments is one of the key differences between previous documentary forms and the experiment of Ogawa Pro in Sanrizuka. The films eschew didactic political commentary to closely examine the immediacy of events as they unfold on the ground. As we shall see, these apparently insignificant actions at the edge of the fighting will edge toward center stage and eventually take over their cinema.

Another key aspect of Ogawa's cinema has to do with their cinematic representations of violence. We can explore this issue by closely looking at the moment—caught on film—when the representatives of the state turn their angry attention to the filmmakers themselves and cameraman Otsu Koshiro and his assistant Otsuka Noboru are arrested. Ogawa Pro was well-known to the police from the Jieiso films, and this incident demonstrated the extent to which the filmmaking activities worried the government. The arrests clearly signaled a new intolerance for freedom of speech provisions and troubled the film world, which immediately mobilized to fight the arrests on constitutional grounds.

A close look at this famous incident reveals how Ogawa rendered the various levels of violence that surrounded him. We can tease out some of the specificities of film and its documentary qualities by comparing and contrasting the scene from *Summer in Sanrizuka* with a qualitatively different kind of document, the affidavit. While in jail, Otsu, Otsuka, Matsumoto, and several witnesses filed affidavits with the court. They describe the incident in the dry verbiage demanded by the justice system, yet still manage to communicate their authors' seething anger. They also render palpable the level of violence the farmers, students, and filmmakers were exposed to on a daily basis. The following montage of affidavits narrates the incident:

> OTSU KOSHIRO (OGAWA'S CINEMATOGRAPHER): On July 11, 1968, approximately 11:20 AM, our staff found out that the Kodan, plainclothes police and riot police had entered a private home . . . for assessment and we arrived on the scene to photograph it. At the location there was some trouble between the Kodan and Hantai Domei, although I do not know the details. There were 70 people that appeared to be Kodan members and plainclothes policemen, about 80 riot police and 70 or 80 Hantai Domei members forming a standoff on the narrow road next to the Farmer's Association. . . .
>
> The distance between us and the house being surveyed was 150 meters. I started moving the camera. Finally, about 20 people that appeared to be plainclothes police suddenly came out of the house being surveyed by the

Kodan and headed toward the Hantai Domei. I continued to push the switch on the camera. After about 40 seconds, I heard Matsumoto's voice to my right asking me to pan to my right side. Upon turning the camera to the right, two men wearing masks ran toward me waving police batons.

OTSUKA NOBORU (OTSU'S ASSISTANT CAMERAMAN): The plainclothes policemen started heading toward us, so I thought this was odd. When the plainclothes policemen got within five meters of us they started waiving their batons at us while we shot them. It is likely that Otsu was also thinking this was strange. He cut the shutter and held the camera to his right breast.

MATSUMOTO TAKEAKI (OGAWA PRO'S ASSISTANT DIRECTOR): The plainclothes policeman pointed at us with his baton and said, "Waddya you doin'?" and blocked the lens. I stepped in front and said, "We're journalists shooting a film," but before I had a chance to finish a plainclothes policeman hit me on the right side of the face with his baton and my glasses went flying.

OTSUKA: At that moment, 14 or 15 riot police had already surrounded the three of us.

OTSU: I stopped the camera switch, hugged the camera to my chest with both hands, and moved a couple steps thinking I'd look right for the next object to film. . . . In the instant I was taking my third step I was suddenly thrown to the ground . . . and repeatedly beaten . . . as if they were after the camera. In this way the lens mount on the front of the camera was partly damaged, and at the same time one lens became detached from the mount and its exterior damaged. While I was being beaten, four or five riot police kicked my thighs repeatedly, and they repeatedly struck my upper body with their fists and shields and so on.

MATSUMOTO: In that instant, I saw Otsu and Otsuka being beaten to my right side with wooden shields, batons, and fists, and finally I fell into the watermelon field.

OTSUKA: My arms were pinned by the riot police around me. And then I was kicked and beaten with feet, fists and shields by seven or eight riot police. While being subjected to this kind of violence, I was taken to the road around the front of Sekiguchi's home.

MATSUMOTO: I was dragged back to the road where we had been photographing when they grabbed my head and both hands. At this time, I protested, "Why are you using this kind of violence? Tell us exactly why, please!" The plainclothes police said, "Aren't you disturbing the execution of public affairs? Eh?" I replied, "We didn't throw rocks. We only photographed what was going on." And three plainclothes police shouted "What? Aren't you always making movies with the Hantai Domei? You have to do things from an objective position. You've gotta shoot from an objective position." [As they spoke they were] shoving my body and hitting my arm with metal batons. Since the reason for this violence was not at all clear I said, "Who can judge objectivity and what standards to use violence?" And as I said this, about 70–80 riot police came from the road and one of them said, "Shut the fuck up! Don't talk dirty, you bastard!" and I was punched in the face, thrown against a fence, and kicked repeatedly around my knees. Then four or five riot police behind this one also took advantage of the situation and continued punching my face and hitting my arms. Throughout this I was protesting, "Why are you using this kind of violence on us? Please tell us why." However, they gave no reason, and then my hands were held by three plainclothes policemen and a mug shot was taken of my face.

OTSU: I fled into a field chased by two or three riot police . . . I ran out of the field and into the rear of farmer Sekiguchi's home. At the time I didn't know the Sekiguchis; however, a housewife saw me from inside and beckoned me in so I fled inside the house.

WATANABE HISASHI (FARMER): Anyway, he entered the house. The glass door was closed. Then the riot police rushed up and quickly shattered the glass with their shields—*baaan!*—and kicked the lower part to shatter it. Then four or five riot police entered the house. They dragged Otsu out of the house, and he protected his camera by holding it as tight as he could.

OTSU: The riot police following me had no idea whether the glass door was shut or not and shattered it with their shields and feet. They pressed me to the ground, started strangling my throat with their hands, and then dragged me to the garden holding both hands and legs. Dragged to the garden, I was dropped on my back. While being dragged, I was finally told that I was being arrested for "the crime of throwing stones/the crime of disturbing the execution of public affairs." The riot police increased by seven or eight, surrounded me and kicked me repeatedly on my back, thighs, and other places.

WATANABE: Shattering a door, entering the house, and doing all that is quite a crime.

OTSUKA: [After watching Otsu being dragged away] I was kicked and beaten even more viciously by seven or eight riot police. At that time, even in the midst of such violence, I clearly remember a riot policeman directly in front of me slamming his small shield horizontally right into my face with all his strength. The first time, I reflexively lowered my face and he hit my helmet (green with large, white characters saying "Film Crew"). It broke the glass of the wind visor. The second time, I dodged my upper body slightly to the left so his blow glanced off the right side of my helmet and hit the face of the riot policeman who was holding my right arm. At that time, the riot policeman who threw the blow called out to the riot policeman that received the blow, "Are you OK?" After that the shoulder bag on my right shoulder (which I had prepared for the day's shooting), the Filmo camera I had in the same right hand, and my helmet were taken by riot policemen.

MATSUMOTO: [After my photograph was taken] a young farmer "enthusiastically" protested, "The riot police shattered my glass door. What are you going to do about it?" Two or three minutes later, seven or eight Hantai Domei members came and started protesting, so the three plainclothes policemen holding me let go and ran away.

OTSUKA: [After being taken to the garden of the Nakazawa home] my arms were pinned by riot policemen, and a man wearing the cream colored helmet of Kodan officials went around my left side to the rear and kicked me in the behind. At that time, even though the riot policemen who were holding my right arm saw this, they did nothing about that man. . . . Three

> or four minutes after being taken to the Nakazawa garden, the film crew's director, Ogawa Shinsuke, arrived on the scene. "Why are you arresting the people on the film crew?" he repeatedly protested to the riot police and plainclothes police. They gave no answer. Until I was taken to the interrogation room of the Chiba Central Police, I had no idea why I had been arrested.[8]

Despite their lack of understanding about the direct causes and justifications for this attack, the authors of these documents faced no problems in constructing straightforward narratives of what they experienced. They simply had to set pen to paper. When they crossed out a mistake, grammatical or substantive, they simply affixed their personal seal to guarantee the documents' authoritative representation of their individual experience. The same people faced a panoply of challenges in representing the very same slice of history on celluloid. We will explore a number of these differences in a moment. For now, we should begin with the scene they finally assembled for *Summer of Sanrizuka.*

As the previous documents testify, Otsu captured the first part of the attack and a second cameraman shot the resolution of the incident. These chunks of time constitute the raw materials for the scene, but they did not amount to much. The cameramen were concerned primarily with surviving the beating, not filming it. Thus, in stark comparison to the affidavits—not to mention their footage of farmers and students being attacked—they could not depict the violence in a straightforward manner. Anyone familiar with the film will be surprised at the viciousness depicted in the court documents, as this is only gestured to in the final sequence.

Ogawa and his crew struggled with this problem. In a fiction film or a written narrative, filmmakers can freely construct such a scene. Documentary filmmakers are limited to the images they manage to capture as a starting point. The materials Ogawa and his crew had prepared for editing were unusually elaborate. They made blow-ups of every frame they had to work with. They drew maps plotting out the spatial relationships between all the figures. They sketched out the timing and sequences of events. They even went so far as to return to the site and recreate the attack with still cameras; apparently, they considered working around their lack of footage with reenactments of the history they failed to capture as the violence unfolded. In the finished film, they eschewed reenactment for gestures like freeze-frames, intertitles, and voice-over narration—"violent" interjections in the context of their mostly straightforward documentary realism.

In the finished film, the scene starts with a skirmish near the camera; farmers flow from right to left. Suddenly, a line of riot police trudge down a

Cameraman Otsu Koshiro captures his own beating on film in *Summer in Sanrizuka* (1968).

row of crops in the far distance. The camera pans back and forth as the two groups keep pouring into the field. On one of the pans right, Otsu stops on the image of two men running straight at the camera wielding clubs. The image seizes in freeze-frame on one of the clubs, which hovers inches away from the lens. An anonymous, voice-of-God narrator comes out of nowhere to explain, "On July 11 our cameraman shooting this scene was arrested for no reason. We kept shooting with another camera." The frozen image is replaced by an intertitle with beautiful calligraphy: "B Camera starts running."

A crowd of riot policemen surrounds cameraman Otsu. As they lead him away, an offscreen witness on the soundtrack describes the beating that had just occurred in the temporal gap marked by the intertitle. The description continues as Otsu is led away, and a second freeze-frame highlights Otsu's face glancing back at the camera. His eyes lock on the camera's gaze with a look of helplessness or mischief, it is difficult to say. Pulling out of the freeze-frame, the aural witness becomes increasingly agitated, and it becomes evident that he is speaking to an official.

"They beat him with batons. What do you mean, you don't know? Who are you? What is your name?" the witness asks in agitation.

"I am a policeman. I don't have to tell you," replies the listener, who up to this point had only been implied.

"You're a civil servant. Give me your name!"

A gloved hand flies into the lens; the filmmakers counterattack by freeze-framing the black hand for a split second. As the shot returns to motion, the scene transforms into a power struggle between the police and the cinema on the grounds of civil society. While the editors make their power felt in postproduction, the B cameraman reveals that the soundtrack had been in synch from the beginning of this sequence shot, as he turns his attention from Otsu to the witness (who turns out to be the sound recordist). Now on camera, the witness appears with microphone in hand. He continues to follow the policeman he was talking to, now badgering him with a barrage of questions and accusations. He wields the microphone like a weapon. The policeman dodges the questions, the microphone, the camera. "Why did you arrest them? Why did you arrest them?" The camera feints this way and that, as hands and clipboards swoop into the lens. And suddenly the riot police run in every direction, leaving the empty field from the first shot. Another beautifully painted intertitle closes the scene noting fifteen people had been imprisoned since April, along with scores of casualties.

The violence at the construction site was vicious, often scandalous. Field hospitals were necessary for the wounded. People on both sides of the lines were killed. However, the cameras could never adequately capture the extent of this violence, spatially (what goes on beyond the visual field of the lens) or temporally (what happens before and after the running of the camera). A comparison of the two documents—court affidavits and documentary film—opens up a number of new perspectives on the Sanrizuka Series and its representation of state violence. First, there is the decisive difference of the camera's presence or absence. Where violence occurs in offscreen space or, in this case, when the cinematographer himself was prevented from filming, the documentarist is at pains to represent through other, necessarily creative, means. In contrast, the crew could write their affidavits unburdened by technology; their ultimate recording machine was mind and memory. For their film, they could only narrate the history between and beyond the shots with intertitles, voice-over narration, and on-the-spot testimony by a witness.

More significantly, the two sets of documents mentioned previously speak to a very different power dynamic, one that emerges thanks to their strikingly similar structure here. Each bit of narrative from the affidavits, strung together in a progressive, temporal development, comes to feel like shots within a scene. Reading through them, one may recognize the basic structure of cinema itself: seemingly objective slices of history stitched together with montage into a seamless temporal flow. The pose of objectivity in the affidavits reveals a representation strategy that renders history on terms called for when one is held in the teeth of power. It is a strategy that toes a line, exuding an anxiety about the rules checking their angry passion as open exposure would surely be unproductive and probably result in retaliation. Significantly, this is roughly the same position that traditional media in so-called free societies—television especially—voluntarily places itself in when it comes to depicting police brutality. However, while journalism celebrates its pose of objective balance, the affidavits barely conceal their brimming anger.

By way of contrast, Ogawa uses a set of heightening strategies specific to the medium of film to lend his documentary visceral impact and suggest what lies beyond the temporal and spatial bounds of the screen. The shots he had to work with were as dispassionate as the affidavits' representation of the incident. However, the freeze frames are accusatory. The voice-over is tinged with acid irony. The matter-of-fact intertitles cannily provide spectators novel footing upon which they may look and think beyond the spatiotemporal limits of the immediate documentary sound-image. None of these strategies are radically disruptive; yet their cumulative effect is powerful and complex. They handily provoke the rage of spectators. This is the ultimate difference between, on the one hand, a document on celluloid in a cinematic language of rebellion perfectly legible to its spectators and meant for projection in the darkened halls of villages and college classrooms, and on the other hand a paper document written in the cool, detached style demanded by authority, circulated in the halls of government and in the grip of its considerable power—or for that matter, a broadcast medium dependant on advertising income and government noninterference.

The scene immediately following Otsu's arrest is even more revealing. After Otsu is dragged away, the second cameraman turns his attention and the camera lens toward a line of riot police. He draws near, but they refuse to budge in the face of his advance. For the first time in Ogawa's films, we are able to confront the police as more than robotic enforcers rendered anonymous by their exoskeletal armor. The cameraman slowly walks from policeman to policeman, shooting each in close-up. Rather than achieving the close-up from a "safe" distance by using a telephoto lens, he quietly points the camera in each face and confronts each person with the unblinking eye of the machine. Their armor cannot protect them from this lack of distance, and one by one they avert their eyes. When they look aside, the cameraman shuttles sideways to catch their gaze once more; nailed once again by the accusatory gaze of the camera, and *us* by extension, they shift

A photograph snapped on July 16, 1968, at the celebration of Otsu Koshiro's release from jail, during the photography for *Summer in Sanrizuka*. Front row from left: Yoshida Tsukasa, Otsu Koshiro, Tamura Masaki, Ogawa Shinsuke, Matsumoto Takeaki; middle, right: Kuribayashi Toyohiko; back row from left: Otsuka Noboru, Nosaka Haruo, Jin Kohei.

their own look away into a safer space as though obeying a new twist in the first rule of home movies: "Don't look at the camera!"

This extraordinary scene reveals the vast power of the camera's gaze. In this the most significant scene of the film, they reveal the piercing power built into the axis of the lens. Much has been made in narrative film theory of the camera's "look" as an analog for (gendered) human looks and their investment with social power and privilege. Documentary sharpens the ethical edge of these debates by virtue of dealing with real actors in the phenomenal world. This astonishing scene from *Summer in Sanrizuka* points to the terms of the power invested in documentary looking and reveals what it ultimately means to "make the camera a weapon."

However, what Ogawa has really put on display is a collection of human beings split into two factions, and this might be the essential structure of the Sanrizuka Series and the way it positions its spectators. The side the riot police have chosen to stand on places them in a grip that binds them to the line separating them from the farmers and forces them to defend that line's integrity at all costs; the other side condemns their choice and holds them up to ridicule and responsibility, challenging the boundary at every chance. As spectators, we are asked to search our own lives and the positions we have chosen to take in relation to this same line, or centers of power analogous to those at Sanrizuka. "Which side are you on?" asks Ogawa in every film.

Summer at Sanrizuka represents a turning point in the Japanese documentary for the way it positions its spectators. As Kitakoji Takashi has suggested, it is something like "'We' haven't 'arrived'—'they' have."[9] Ogawa has somehow managed to objectify the riot police and the airport officials they are protecting. This is accomplished by edging us closer to the subjectivity of the farmers, folding us into a nominal "we" that includes the farmers and students and the spectator(s). At the same time, the staff was highly conscious that they, indeed, were the outsiders arriving on the scene. In a report published in Jieiso's *October* at the height of the photography, an uncredited staff member writes, "In the struggle against the imperialistic robbery of the entire tablelands for the summit of the New Narita Airport we can exist, in the first place, only as outsiders. We must implicate *(naiho)* ourselves into this struggle against imperialistic divide and rule."[10]

The profundity of this movement from "outside" to "inside" can only be understood by watching the entirety of Ogawa's filmography. The filmmakers appear to signal the direction they have embarked on in the penultimate scene of *Summer in Sanrizuka,* where the last word is given to a middle-aged woman we will come to know quite well in the coming years. She stands in front of the camera, in the doorway of her embattled house, barefoot and leaning on a very big stick. Her long monologue ranges over many ideas and issues. She is too young to remember World War II, but admits she can imagine fighting foreigners for her survival. But these are Japanese! These riot police have been raised to think this way. They have mothers! At the end of her long monologue, she adds that she enjoys talking with all the women. The protests are great fun! What is more, she takes pride in her son, who has turned into a man thanks to the fight. She talks of the difficulty of her present life, but promises to be strong and not run away. Her speech, privileged by virtue of its placement at the end of the film, holds a certain, curious irony when considered in the context of Ogawa's previous films. What is going on at Sanrizuka is at its heart political so the farmers suddenly had to figure out how to think and act politically. This provokes recollection of a discussion among the men several minutes earlier, when they talk about fear—theirs—and how it drives their rebellion. For them, the struggle is not served by a theory, Marx's or Lenin's, but they know it *through their bodies.* These telling comments point to the real structure of the film, as well as the journey the filmmakers have embarked on: Ogawa wants you to *feel* both the agony and the fun. And as I will argue below, he wants you to feel it *bodily*.

This is precisely why the final few minutes of the film are so mystifying, even off-putting. After these two powerful scenes featuring farmers struggling to make sense of the situation they've found themselves in, having brought us to something so earthy and fundamental about the confrontation out in the fields, Ogawa pulls back to a distanced view. The camera soars over the fields of Sanrizuka in a light plane, showing the turf being fought over so passionately. Far from the messy politics and squabbles of human beings, we see fields stretching out to the horizon, and as the plane flies lower, we recognize the tower from which farmers beat out their calls to action. For the first time in the film, music fades in from the background. Much to the consternation of most of today's spectators, it is the all-stops-pulled climax of Beethoven's Ninth Symphony. The final chorus overpowers the soundtrack as the camera glides over the landscape. It is completely bizarre and roughly perfect: is this, as the music suggests, the perspective of a god surveying the follies of humankind . . . or could it possibly be nothing more than an airplane with nowhere to land?

Beyond the Barricades

Every country that experienced massive student protests in the Vietnam War era contributed representatives to the canon of "1968 films." Japan's would certainly include *Summer in Sanrizuka* and Ogawa Pro's next film, *Prehistory of the Partisans* (*Paruchizan zenshi,* 1968). As Ogawa Pro began shooting their next film in the Sanrizuka Series, a smaller crew set out with Tsuchimoto Noriaki to Kyoto to produce the latter film, a documentary about the infiltration and occupation of Kyoto University. Although on first glance *Prehistory of the Partisans* would appear to be a seemingly straightforward record of the protests, this is a remarkably dense film. Tsuchimoto packs it with allusions to the complex political landscape that produced the struggle, which had iconic significance for all the school occupations sweeping the country.[11]

As in all of Ogawa and Tsuchimoto's films of this period, this is a privileged view of the bustle behind the barricades. Tsuchimoto reinforces the significance of this positioning through visual analogs for the crew's interior position. For example, after scenes of practice on the athletic field—helmeted students marching in formation carrying pipes like rifles—Tsuchimoto reveals recent renovations to Kyoto University's stately grounds. A gentle pan moves across makeshift barricades made of boards, plywood, and furniture "borrowed" from classrooms and offices. Broad surfaces are decorated with huge words like *revolution*. With a smooth cut, the camera begins to truck through the barricade to the students holed up inside, past a group doing calisthenics, and ends up in a room littered with piles of helmets emblazoned with the characters *Zenkyoto*.

This office once belonged to the chair of the literature department, but had recently been seized by students and converted into the occupation's central command. Ogawa Pro's impressive access to the inside of one of the most important actions of the student Left was spectacular for audiences at the time. Perhaps Tsuchimoto was the only filmmaker who could have accomplished it. Aside from his credentials as a radical filmmaker sympathetic to the student movement—most notably the recent *Exchange Student Chua Swee Lin* and the Ogawa Pro calling card—Tsuchimoto was also known as one of the founders of Zengakuren when he was a Waseda University student in 1948.

This did not mean, however, that his deep sympathies for the students evacuated all critical thinking. Back when Tsuchimoto helped create Zengakuren, the efforts to nurture a movement outside of the JCP's sphere of influence were hampered by factionalism. Tsuchimoto became frustrated when the infighting only got worse. The first umbrella organization, the Bund, repeatedly split into at least eight major sects, such as Chukakuha, Kakumaru, Hansen, to name just a few (all of which established solidarity huts at Sanrizuka). Tsuchimoto was further frustrated by the paradox that everyone felt the need for an organization to push for progress and fight oppressive structures from the past, yet these very groups would too often replicate these structures in their own organization, most notably the top-down exertion of power in an analog to the Communist party in Yoyogi—or the emperor system they abhorred.

In 1968, Tsuchimoto found himself attracted to the 150-odd Kyoto students that called themselves the Partisans because he thought they represented something new, thanks in part to their relationship to Professor Takida Osamu (Takemoto Osamu). This professor did not function as a leader of the Partisans, but rather as an intellectual source of inspiration. They avoided the production of a "leader," or even an "organization" as such. In the film, Takida and his students explain their experiment at creating a *gonin-gumi* (party of five). The idea was that if any five people could come together to throw themselves into a project, anything was possible. It could be the occupation of a national university, but it could also be something more modest like a newspaper or a film. This explains the moniker "partisans." They resolutely avoided thinking of their efforts as sect formation. Instead, they thought of themselves as "buddies."

Tsuchimoto also found himself attracted to the Partisans' commitment to interrogating the role of violence in social struggle. The film shows extended discussions of this issue. How should they meet the increasingly violent, even deadly, force of the police? Can we achieve revolution without violence? Tsuchimoto felt a relevant need to resolve these kinds of questions, which are as pressing in today's so-called War on Terror as they were in the traumatic year of 1968.

The film does not provide easy answers. Instead, it questions the role of violence while accompanying the students on their actions. One day they barge in on entrance examinations—one of the points of contention in many of the campus struggles—and dismantle the desks of the testing rooms with their pipes as befuddled high school students look on. There are startling sequences of the famous water cannon attacks on the tower, when the riot police storm the building with helicopters circling overhead. The most memorable scenes document the nighttime protests. Otsu's photography has an unforgettably eerie quality that is spatially disorienting, not unlike the adrenaline-driven experience of a real riot's unpredictable flow. The light from the scenes comes only from blazing automobiles and the fiery plumes of Molotov cocktails. Tsuchimoto went so far as to show the step-by-step process of making Molotov cocktails, a scene that ends with a full-screen title giving spectators the recipe. I can think of no better example that demonstrates how these were no simple, objective records. These films were, by design, meant to incite action.

At the same time, the film is no direct, unmediated communication of the students' methods and philosophy. It is, ultimately, Tsuchimoto's commentary on the state of the student movement in Japan, encouraging spectators to read the film at this meta-level by framing the Partisans' story with reportage from the famous rally at Tokyo's Hibiya Park that inaugurated the Zenkyoto movement. On September 9, 1969, representatives from all the sects from every part of Japan converged on Hibiya Park in downtown Tokyo, near the Imperial Palace. The new organization was to network all the campus struggles into a united front. Sixty Partisans joined the sea of protestors. The film shows riot police giving students body searches, followed by typical documentary footage of demonstrations: massive crowds, waving banners, helmets, and passionate speeches.

Before long, Tsuchimoto focuses on complications steamrolling out of control. The Bund's speaker shouts over the sound of helicopters using a bullhorn, and he is suddenly interrupted by a commotion in the back. It is the Red Army. This organization had recently formed in the Osaka area (and had connections to the Partisans). It criticized the spirit of Zenkyoto as meekly defensive, and called on the students to—as the slogan went—

"incite uprisings and seek victory in war." The group firmly advocated raising the stakes through the use of arms, and shortly thereafter staged various robberies to collect guns and money. It sent 200 members to Tokyo to disrupt the Zenkyoto rally. The Red Army's noisy protest in the back quickly deteriorates into fisticuffs, and Tsuchimoto leaves the scene on that note.

Of all the ways he might have chosen to represent the formation of this promising new stage in the student protests, Tsuchimoto emphasized the fissures in the movement, not its solidarity. In subsequent scenes he quietly goes further. Throughout the film, Tsuchimoto crosscuts between the clashes with police, intense discussions behind the barricades, and scenes of everyday life for the rest of Kyoto's population. The latter category of images includes scenes such as schoolgirls strolling through old Kyoto, a yucca plant in full bloom with a *sukuramu*[12] passing by in the background, a peaceful street with the university's clock tower jutting above the roofs of the homes. Tsuchimoto subtly suggests a fatal disconnect here. The students, in their attempt to "dismantle the imperialistic university" through violent confrontation and occupation, never leave their own hermetically sealed world. With no serious links to other social movements or the masses of people living around the university, their rhetoric and violence appear out of balance.

"Because of this," says Tsuchimoto, "I thought this might be the end of hope for any real revolution." Some believe this film hastened the dissolution of Zenkyoto. One by one, the student activists quit, devoting their energies to other causes like Sanrizuka or Minamata, or giving up on politics altogether.

As for Takida Osamu, he subsequently became a fugitive in what came to be known as the Takida incident. In January 1972, reporters for *Asahi Journal* and *Playboy* were arrested for their connections to a man accused of stabbing a soldier to death. The murder occurred August 21, 1971, and police claimed to have found two red helmets with the word *Sekieigun (Red Guards)* and a pamphlet entitled *Red Flag—Declaration of World War,* a title highly reminiscent of Adachi Masao and Wakamatsu Koji's film on the Red Army.[13] The pamphlet was signed by the "Red Guard Army," which no one to that point had ever heard of. Thus, everyone assumed this incident was simply a ploy to crack down on radical activists, sympathetic journalists, and intellectuals. The latter became obvious when writers for *Asahi Journal* and *Playboy* were arrested for supposedly harboring the suspect, and Professor Takida was put on the wanted list for being their ringleader. Takida went into hiding for a number of years, much of it spent in the closet of Tsuchimoto's production office. The filmmaker received unannounced visits by the police more than once, although they never caught Takida there. On one occasion Tsuchimoto's address book was taken away as a guide for choosing other people to search. However, neither he nor Ogawa was ever arrested. He suspects such a move would have been seen as further oppression of the people of Minamata and Sanrizuka, but as we will see, the police surveilled the filmmakers well into the 1980s.

Into Winter

While Tsuchimoto and Kansai Ogawa Productions filmed *Prehistory of the Partisans* in Kyoto, Ogawa and the main unit continued their "Taiga Drama" behind the barricades in the fields of Sanrizuka. Up until this point, Ogawa and his crew were living in an apartment in the larger town of Sanrizuka. This building, near Sanrizuka Crossroads, was outside of the construction site itself, and they hoped to move into one of the nearby *buraku* (hamlets) as soon as possible. The staff spread out across the entire area, looking for possible places to live as they researched the development of the struggle. They soon settled on two strong possibilities, Komaino and Heta. Both were adjacent to the airport boundary, but the resemblances ended there. In Heta, virtually everyone refused to sell; in Komaino all but one farmer had joined the so-called *joken-ha* (which might be translated, "the side that sold out on concessions").

They chose to live in Heta Buraku, where the Uriu family offered to lend them a small outbuilding to live in and work out of. Heta sat in a small, narrow, remarkably beautiful valley and was home to thirty-three families. Two of these were empty homes (one left the village, and the other was Kichiyoin Temple). Of the remaining families, twenty-eight were in the Hantai Domei and refused to sell. This was a particularly politicized village. Above and beyond this impressive statistic, the women were known to be tough and spirited. Neighbor Ishii Setsuko, one of the most familiar faces of the Sanrizuka Series, proudly told me, "Ogawa always said he came here because we Heta women were always the first to arrive at the very front lines."

In stark contrast, virtually all of neighboring Komaino was being sold to the Kodan without a fight. The lone exception was Seimiya Chikara, a grizzled old farmer who refused to move. Ogawa Pro was intrigued by this man and wanted to make him the centerpiece of its next film. Much to the dismay of the filmmakers, however, Seimiya himself would have nothing of this and refused to cooperate. Honma Shusuke took up the cracking of Seimiya's resistance as his personal project. At the end of every day, he would bike the twenty minutes over to Seimiya's home and talk and drink for hours. Aside from learning about the village and Seimiya's life, Honma tried to make the filmmakers' position clear to the old man. The problem was that Seimiya could not distinguish between fiction and documentary. He figured the film was entirely about him; that made him an actor, and this was a task he had no interest in. Honma tried in vain to teach him the difference between fiction and documentary, but the man was stubborn. Honma's nightly visits continued for an entire year, testament to how far Ogawa Pro was willing to go for its films. Ogawa Pro members often joke that Honma's own evidence for this became his battered face. After one long night of drinking and discussion, he returned home to Heta knock-down drunk and lost control of his bicycle, smashing his mouth into the handlebars and losing his front teeth. After that, he called this toothless smile his memorial to Sanrizuka.

Ogawa finally became impatient with the lack of progress, ordering Tamura and Honma to shoot Seimiya one way or another. By this point in their relationship, both sides completely understood the other's position. It was time to shoot or forget it. The film had already expanded far beyond a singular portrait of Seimiya, but at least they could include an interview. They muscled their way into an interview in the end, which became a moving conversation. It is worth noting that Seimiya was also featured in one of Ogawa Pro's most powerful posters (part of a triptych with images of a helmeted youth and a wasted construction site). His ruddy face looks to the heavens with a quote from his interview: "When a farmer sells his land, that's the end."

This extraordinary effort for a single interview evidences the commitment of Ogawa Pro to build its filmmaking on honest relationships with their objects. Nothing could be further from the hit-and-run exploitation of television news, or the vast majority of the world's documentarists for that matter. While implicit in every shot, they foreground their stance on the farmer's side in the first minutes of the film when a plainclothes policeman asks them, "Are you reporting? Are you reporting?" The crew snaps back, "Whaddya want?"

"Are you reporting? Are you reporting?"

"What's wrong with shooting with a camera?"

"Are you journalists? Are you journalists?"

"Who decides if we're journalists?" they retort, "*You* decide if we're journalists, don't you?"

After taking a year to make *Summer in Sanrizuka,* the method identified with Ogawa's name had taken hold. In the course of the Sanrizuka Series, the filmmakers would continue to develop and refine it, but the major features

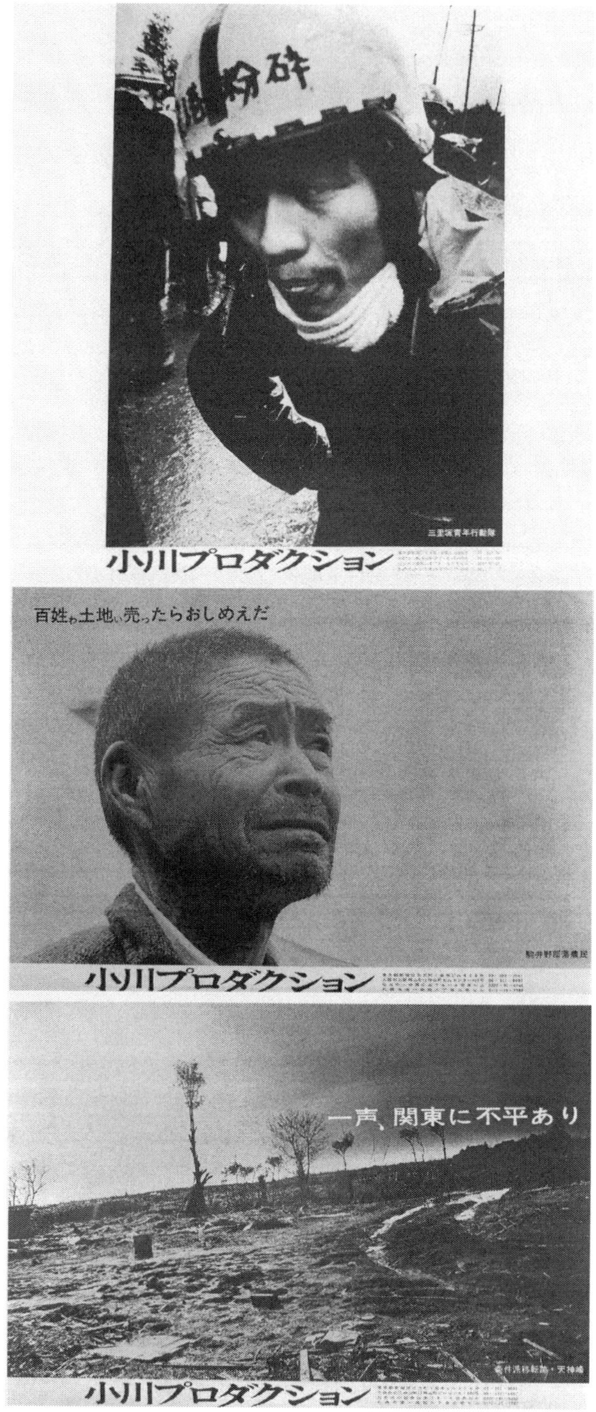

Three posters advertising Ogawa Pro (not a specific film). They list the addresses and telephone numbers of all the regional offices in the lower right corners. The anonymous young farmer leaning into the camera (top) is from the Youth Action Brigade, his helmet emblazoned with "Annihilate the Airport." The middle poster features Seimiya Chikara, the grizzled old man Yumoto Mareo befriended for *Winter in Sanrizuka*: "When a farmer sells his land, that's the end." The third poster shows the absolute devastation of a shrine near Heta after the work crews cleared the ground, along with a famous saying: "In one voice, there is discontent in Kanto." These are the words of politician Tanaka Shozo, who was involved in the protests against environmental pollution caused by the Ashio copper mine in the late 1800s. One of the government's responses to this first popular uprising against modernization was to relocate residents. Photography by Kitai Kazuo.

are in place by their second issue in the series. This method assumed that one could not make a film by invading the space of the *taisho* with the camera. It takes time to build an honest relationship, especially when there are cameras involved. Without that relationship, all one can expect is either rejection or unnatural performance. It also deeply affects the way documentarists shoot the people before them. Former Jieiso members often recall a scene from *Forest of Oppression* where the movement leader was being persuaded not to quit. The situation was delicate so they chose to shoot the discussion from outside the room with a telephoto lens. Cameraman Otsu recalls,

> Later on when the rushes were done the staff were all holding their heads saying, "We shouldn't have done it like this . . ." I think Ogawa and Tsuchimoto both stopped using "hidden camera" techniques after that. That was some pretty bitter medicine, to be honest. There was a debate over whether or not to use the shot, but in the end we did use it. It was a strange cut. Let's say we had a camera here with us as we're talking, with a cameraman to do the shooting. If there's no mutual trust—not necessarily a contract, but an agreement with the person being photographed that there will be a camera present—we probably shouldn't be filming. The problem is whether or not that question was considered, and in this case it wasn't. We weren't serious enough about building a relationship between the camera and the subject.[14]

Ogawa often used the example of shooting an apple. The method he rejected circled around the apple without penetrating the surface; his method required the filmmaker to slowly work his way into the apple, down to the core, and if he comes out the other side, a film is possible. If he doesn't, that's it. Without this kind of effort, Ogawa would have made *Summer in Sanrizuka* and then moved on to other projects—or quit filmmaking altogether. Nosaka called it fixed-point observation *(teitenkansoku)*. Thanks to this, the Sanrizuka Series stands as a truly unique set of films. Considering the commitment and time span the method demanded—and its coincidence with an era when that devotion was possible to imagine—it is unlikely Ogawa Pro's achievement will be replicated anytime soon.

In 1969, their approach was still developing in the process of practice, and the roughness of these first two films suggests Ogawa Pro members still had a lot to learn. *Winter in Sanrizuka* (*Nihon kaiho sensen: Sanrizuka,* 1970) is a far more accomplished film than their first work of the series, even if it has always been considered a failure. One reason for the jump in quality may be attributed to the beneficence of historian Hani Goro (Susumu's father). Impressed by *Summer in Sanrizuka,* Hani told Ogawa he had achieved something with the sense of scale of an American Western. Because of that, the next film should really be in 35mm widescreen Technicolor, and he gave them five thousand dollars to that end. They had to settle for 16mm color, but used a seemingly endless supply of it. As sound editor Asanuma recalls, "I've never seen so much film used. No one makes movies like that. Usually, the cameraman never comes to the dubbing studio, but Tamura did because it was so hard to tell who was talking. I needed his help timing up the sound to image track."

The fruits of this larger budget for color film and more refined post-production work are evident in the dramatic opening of the film. It is November 1969, and the bulldozers have finally arrived to level the furrows and scrape away all plant life. A noisy group of Heta farmers physically blocks one of the massive machines as Tomura Issaku attempts to push past riot police to dissuade the driver from working. He insistently tells the driver that walking away is the responsible thing to do, that a driver can find other work if he loses his vehicle, but when a farmer loses his land there is nowhere to go. The camera turns to the newly exposed red earth, so striking in color film, and settles on two old men sitting on the big blade of the bulldozer. The main characters of the film, the farmers of Heta Village, are rowdily insulting the workers and police. Rich orchestral music swells on the soundtrack, drowning out their noise. A final shot shows the farmers following a bulldozer up a hill scraped clean of vegetation, and it is replaced by the title credit: *Sanrizuka—Front Line for the Liberation of Japan*. Tomura must have liked this opening because it has the feel of an epic confrontation of biblical proportions.

For a film coming out of the tradition of fiercely independent documentary, this was wildly ambitious to say the least. The most striking advance was on the soundtrack. It was still nonsynch, but the sound editing by Asanuma Yukikazu drew on counterpoint and silence in creative and clever ways. Particularly notable is the use of nondiegetic music. From early on, Asanuma wanted to use more music in these independent films. At precisely that time, an acquaintance, Manabe Riichiro, told Asanuma that he wanted to try writing for documentary. Manabe was a well-known scholar and composer of feature film music—most notably for Oshima's films—so the staff balked at the potential cost. Asanuma went ahead and told the composer that, while there may be no music budget, there is Ogawa's Sanrizuka film currently in post-production. Manabe composed the music as they finished the editing and also wrote a score for Tsuchimoto's *Minamata Revolt—A People's Quest for Life* (*Minamata ikki—Issho o to hitobito*, 1973) a couple years later. The music is in nineteenth-century Romantic mode, making it fairly conventional film music. However, to experience this kind of independent social movement film with a well-crafted soundtrack

The famous title calligraphy for the Sanrizuka Series, from *Winter in Sanrizuka.*

was unheard of. Filmmakers were usually at pains simply to make lips match voices.

This was also the first of such independent documentaries to use color. With Otsu now paired with Tsuchimoto, Tamura was on his own here. His cinematography pushed limits. During the interview with Seimiya, the old farmer from Komaino, Tamura starts with a view of his beautiful, rugged face as he begins, "When a villager sells his land, that's the end." Obviously drunk, he rambles on about how even famous leaders like Prime Minister Sato or "Germany's Eisenhower" all go back to their home villages in the end. As he reaches a particularly moving moment in his talk, Tamura zooms in. While this is a typical convention of interview cinematography, Tamura keeps zooming and zooming until only Seimiya's eye fills the frame. In another long interview about the struggle outside, Tamura suddenly pans the camera out a window as if distracted or bored; the sunlit scene registers blindingly white. When he finally cranks down the lens aperture, he reveals tall cranes on the horizon, dipping into the earth as the men talk about strategies to stop it all. And when the women and children surround Kodan officials, pushing nose to nose and screaming "Go home! Go home!! Go home!!!," Tamura's approach to the photography is every bit as confrontational. He shoves the camera into the faces of the officials. This is extreme camerawork throughout.

Like the films that preceded it, *Winter in Sanrizuka*'s stunning action scenes alternate with static discussions. The contrast between the two is distinct and lends the films a striking rhythm contrasting movement with stasis, or audio-visual dissonance with pauses for quiet contemplation. These discussion scenes are not the typical interviews we are accustomed to in the documentary. Generally, the image track takes on the appearance of serial still lives. One person talks—almost to him- or herself—as the others silently sit in thoughtful repose. The shots are extremely long and static. They are almost visual analogues for the spectators in the theater: quiet voyeurs on the scene. The editing of these scenes is also odd. They lack the conventionally tight structuration that propels the viewer through the interview and into the subsequent sequence. One reason is their sheer length, but it is more complex than that. The film progresses in a roughly temporal manner, with subtitles and intertitles marking the passage of time (the last image of the film is an intertitle duly noting that the construction was behind schedule). However, the editing does not necessarily make this chronological progression felt, probably because the film is so people-centric. They pass information concerning the state of the airport construction and the concrete efforts to obstruct it, but one could watch the entirety of the Sanrizuka Series without actually learning much about the struggle and its political backdrop. In journalistic accounts and conventional documentary films, "what happened and why" is precisely the center of attention; here that kind of information is merely background to the farmer's reflection on these historical events on the timeliness. After all, the contemporary spectators learned their *news* from the major outlets, alternative presses, and teach-ins. And Ogawa Pro's newsletters and pamphlets often supplied comprehensive information about a given film's setting. In the films themselves, Ogawa probably did not feel the burden of explaining the details.

One may achieve a sense for this by reading the thick catalog Ogawa Pro published for *Winter in Sanrizuka*. It features two running columns. The bottom is a spare scenario for the film, and the top column strings together a collection of historical narratives about the struggle, letters to and from the Kodan, the texts of relevant laws, manifestos, and other items that flesh out the specifics of what appears in general and vague terms in the film itself. Indeed, to a spectator with no background in the Sanrizuka Struggle, the film probably feels like history out of time. There does not seem to be a "story" here in any conventional sense. Ogawa is not presenting a legible chain of events, let alone constructing a logical argument of any complexity.

What *do* they do? Now into the second film of the Sanrizuka Series, it becomes evident that they are presenting a pastiche of strong emotions and half-formed ideas, all scrambled by editing. In the broadest sense, there is a curious bifurcation between paradigmatic and systematic levels in the structure of the film. One achieves a strong sense for several categories of narration—the group discussion, the interview, and the violent protest—but the logic governing their combination is somewhat obscure. The subtitles chart a progression through time, but that progression is marked by those stark differences in paradigmatic scenes. In the broadest sense, the film's syntagmatic structure is marked by riots and discussions, surges and suspension. However, the bald simplicity of this rhythm plays into other, more subtle structures. In *Winter in Sanrizuka,* Ogawa assembles an array of threads into a weave so intricate the pattern is barely visible. To begin to see it, one must reach back to the previous film. This is a viewing protocol whose complexities and pleasures grow exponentially with every film in the series. It is an intertext that erases meaningful distinctions between films and makes this group of films into something less than a series—and something close to one seventeen-hour epic with intermissions of indeterminate length that we conventionally call "ends" or "beginnings." For contemporary spectators, those intermissions lasted until the next film appeared; in our case, it is usually when one finds access to the other films. As Noël Burch writes, the Sanrizuka Series is "one long 'work in progress.'"[15]

If *Winter in Sanrizuka* fails, as most people felt at the time, it is because *Summer in Sanrizuka* was hardly enough of a base upon which to perch this textual edifice. The intertext was still too weak. But it is also because the filmmakers were not sufficiently self-conscious about how their own intertext was beginning to function in the films. Indeed, in this film, Ogawa was trying to say it all. This one film would sum up the Sanrizuka Struggle. It would be a total representation. Ogawa was so confidently enamored of this idea that at the last minute he proposed changing the title to simply *Sanrizuka.* One word. He was abandoning the idea of a multichaptered *taiga* drama. This was no longer "Winter" because *Summer in Sanrizuka* effectively disappears, absorbed by the one film that says it all.

The staff argued forcefully against the name change. Their fundraising had always used *Winter in Sanrizuka.* They had already advertised the film under this title and even printed tickets, pamphlets, and fliers. More substantially, they had doubts about their ability to render a "total representation."

One would have to agree that Ogawa's idea was misguided and fundamentally wrong. In retrospect, we may see how this production hints at the direction they were going, a vector as opposed to end point. It was the first time that they had turned from the struggle at hand to more peripheral matters of daily life in the farming community. Tamura often recalls how Ogawa started sending him out to photograph thirty-second shots of flowers and butterflies, this in the midst of massive social upheaval. They also interviewed people who were only marginally involved in the Struggle. This is the strategy they would cultivate, a methodology culminating several years later in *Sanrizuka—Heta Village* (*Sanrizuka—Heta Buraku,* 1973)—a singular masterpiece entirely dependent upon and inextricable from the sum of the Sanrizuka Series. It is an approach they would take in novel directions when they left Sanrizuka for Yamagata. *Winter in Sanrizuka* presents these developments in nascent form.

Laying on his deathbed, Ogawa told his friends that one of his regrets in life was changing the name of this film. They told him to forget about it, but it suggests that Ogawa fully realized the impossibility of seeing these films as discrete, that in 1969 he still had many films to make before he understood either Sanrizuka or village life, and even that he had yet to realize what he was accomplishing in these films. This is why I have reinstalled the original title, *Winter in Sanrizuka,* which many members continue to use to this day as well.

Ogawa Pro's next two films dropped the seasonal markers and plunged into the escalating warfare at the construction site. *Sanrizuka—The Three Day War (Sanrizuka—Daisanji kyosei sokuryo soshi toso)* was released in October 1970, only three months after *Winter in Sanrizuka.* The unusual speediness of this production had something to do with Ogawa Pro members' contact with foreign visitors during the production of the second film.

In 1969, Joris Ivens and Marceline Loridan toured Sanrizuka. Ivens had been invited to a major symposium on political cinema in Tokyo, where he was shown a number of contemporary Japanese films. After seeing *Summer in Sanrizuka,* he rearranged his schedule to visit the group that made what he thought was an extraordinary film. This was a relationship that continued to the end of Iven's life, when he accepted Ogawa's invitation to attend the first Yamagata International Documentary Film Festival in 1989. Unfortunately, he passed away just before the event, and Loridan attended alone to show their film *A Tale of the Wind* (*Une histoire de vent,* 1988).

Another foreign visit came from two members of the Black Panthers, Elbert Howard and Roberta Alexander. Howard, otherwise known as "Big Man," was one of the eight founders of the Black Panthers and came to

Ogawa Shinsuke taking Joris Ivens and Marceline Loridan on a tour of Komaino, June 1, 1971. To Iven's left is Hataya Naoko, Shimizu Yoshio, and Yumoto Mareo.

Japan with little money at the invitation of Zengakuren. Alexander came along as someone who could speak to women's issues. Upon arrival, they found themselves being fought over by various factions in the New Left. They were supposed to speak at a Zengakuren symposium; however, their hosts, Shigenobu Fusaku and Shiomi Takaya of the Japan Red Army, had just cut off ties from other organizations and been disinvited themselves. They arranged for other speaking events, but Big Man and Alexander became frustrated and suspicious when someone told them their interpreters were mistranslating to serve Red Army ends. After being pulled this way and that, the Panthers left and became the guests of Ogawa Pro. They toured Sanrizuka and the Tokyo political scene with Nosaka Haruo serving as guide. They also visited the farms of Sanrizuka and watched Ogawa Pro in action. They went to schools and attended protests at Haneda Airport, Sanya, and an outlying military base area. Nosaka recalls, "Ogawa Pro had carefully staked out a position that was on the side of the students and the farmers while studiously avoiding participation in or advocacy of violence; however, here they were playing hosts and tour guides to the Black Panthers!

I don't remember much about what we did, but it was very fun." The intersect rivalry over the two Panthers dominates Howard's memory of the visit. He also recalls the older fellow that everyone treated with such respect, presumably Ogawa. He remembers Nosaka struggling to interpret with his nearly nonexistent English, and being constantly nervous about the carloads of plainclothes policemen that were always and obviously on their tail.

Howard and Alexander found themselves with Ogawa Pro through the introduction of Steve Chain, a Berkeley-based journalist. Chain traveled regularly to Asia and was familiar with the landscape of the Japanese New Left. He was probably the most influential of the visitors because on one trip he engineered a print swap between Ogawa Pro and the American Newsreel. The films they received were *Off the Pig (Black Panther)* (1968), *Columbia Revolt* (1968), and two French shorts credited to the Societé des Trente (*Les Cheminots* and one other film on the events of May).

We can get a sense for what the films meant to Ogawa Pro from the minutes for a October 5, 1969, meeting held to plan its distribution strategy.[16] The filmmakers grouped the shorts in a package called *dangan eiga*, or "bullet films," because they had "content that smashes into the enemy like a bullet." Referencing the famous Newsreel logo spelled out in animated machine gun fire, their screenings would be like "gun emplacements" wherever they went. No matter who they were showing the films to, they would make the screenings of these film bullets create new bullets, that is, new guerrillas. "These documentaries are, in the end, born from amidst the streets that open ourselves to understanding, the side that calls for struggle. As for the object photographed—the *taisho*—it is necessary to create a comrade-like union with it."[17] Judging from the group's distribution records, these were popular films and were often shown before one of the Ogawa Pro films over the next several years. One of the fliers produced by a high school group in Gunma Prefecture writes the following:

> They felt in their bodies the fear of their own police state. But what of Japan? The government is establishing American and Self-Defense Forces bases within a daily life that takes the appearance of calm. They utilize political power on the basis of a police state. Naturally, young people call out for resistance against the establishment, and recall Paris in May for freedom and the liberation of humanity. Then those flames spread to Haneda, Yokosuka, Sasebo, Sanrizuka. . . .[18]

The newsreels were meant to provoke such responses. Beyond the incendiary content, even Ogawa Pro's translations were designed for maximum agitation. They translated the titles quite liberally. *Black Panther* receives a direct translation, since the original subtitle was already pretty extreme: *Off the Pig*. However, *Les Cheminots (Railway Worker)* becomes *What Am I, a Robot? (Ore wa robotta kai?)*, and *Columbia Revolt* is rendered *Strike! Strike! Strike! (Sutoraiki! Sutoraiki! Sutoraiki!)*. The films received a most extraordinary dubbing. Ever on a shoestring, Ogawa Pro simply enlisted the help of friends from a radical theater troupe. Their voice-over makes no attempt to mimic the voices on the soundtrack. Rather, they *perform* their script with a full-throated theatricality. Even when the onscreen personas speak in a calm, even-handed manner, the Japanese voices seethe with barely controlled anger. Rather than pitching their performance against the original text—expressing a debt to the film and the people represented there—they seem to extrapolate to the subjectivities of the viewers. Their performance matches their spectators' presumed rage. Certainly, it incites it. What better way to prepare their audience of bullets—guerrillas for deployment?

Ogawa Pro benefited from these contacts with Western collectives in a variety of other ways. At a material level, it was finally able to acquire its

In September 1969, Ogawa Pro hosts two representatives of the Black Panthers: Elbert Howard (aka Big Man, the Minister of Propaganda) and Roberta Alexander. The banner in the background reads, "In one voice, there is discontent in Kanto"; it is signed by the collective.

own equipment. A French sympathizer smuggled a Beaulieu camera bought cheaply in Hong Kong into Japan using French diplomatic pouch. Ogawa Pro also used its French connection to deliver a Nagra donated by a French collective, a deck that was apparently used to shoot some of the May 1968 cine-tracts (or so it like to think). For Ogawa's own collective, the bullet films suggested a new possibility for documentary. While its productions had become increasingly labor and capital intensive, the newsreels demonstrated the virtues of being quick and dirty. Its next film would be modeled on the French and American newsreels, transmitting the latest news of Sanrizuka to the people as swiftly and efficiently as possible.

Sanrizuka—The Three Day War is a creditless, agit prop cine-tract shot over the course of three days. As the unilateral surveying of the construction site pushed into its final phase, the farmers and students undertook a massive attempt to obstruct its progress. This film records these days of combat between twenty-five hundred protestors and sixty-five hundred riot police. School had even been let out so children could participate in the action.

Ogawa Pro captured the events in an uncomplicated structure. The film starts with a simple title card bearing the famous calligraphy of its Sanrizuka logo and ends with another intertitle explaining only that the Kodan's week-long survey was cut short on the third day and called complete. There is no "The End," nor are there credits for the staff. Occasional subtitles keep things under minimal control. They put names to farmers' faces. They identify obscure objects like *funnyodan,* the bags of shit and urine they used as grenades ("We're used to this smell because we're farmers!" cries an old man, tolerance of the stench signifying cultural difference). Most helpfully, the subtitles inscribed with the date and time chart our progress through the three days of warfare.

The film focuses completely on the events unfolding immediately before the camera, with context left to viewers in the know. For example, Ogawa prominently shows a group of elderly protestors waving a large banner at a line of riot police. It shows a picture of police beating a man to his knees with batons and a quote from Tomura Issaku: "At the February 26 Incident, the riot police were told to 'kill' and I was attacked." This is a loaded reference to two historical events. The first is a near successful coup by militarists on February 26, 1936, which Tomura Issaku referred to in a speech at an early rally on February 26, 1968. The militants were uncomfortable with Tomura's ambivalent reference to fascism, but he continued to use it in subsequent speeches; clearly, it appealed to the older generation represented by the film's banner bearers. At the time of the 1968 protest, the most complicated crowd control tasks the local police had experienced were at horse races. They had only ten shields among them so when the protestors dismantled their placards and turned them into sticks, the police overreacted and turned to violence. The students started throwing stones, and 420 policemen were injured. In the melee that followed, Tomura—the featured speaker of the day—stopped to help someone get off the ground and found himself at the business end of many police batons. They had intended to arrest him, but were frightened off by the blood pouring from his head. In the end, he survived the beating with seven stitches; however, it became a decisive turning point in the Sanrizuka Struggle. It radicalized the farmers and encouraged them to accept the new militants from outside. Simultaneously, the police showed up to the next protests better armed, and more willing to use force. Apter and Sawa call the encounter "the event that precipitated what can be called the legitimization of violence," and is the historical context for the movement of power captured by Ogawa Pro cameras.[19] It is this kind of context that the films, curiously enough, rarely supply.

We are thrown into this violence in the first few minutes of the film. The first shot is a pan starting from a line of riot police in the distance, tilting up to a police helicopter in the sky, and back down to a loose group of farmers and students converging on a village. They cut to the Umezawas standing in their fields in the perfect picture of rage. Walking back and forth among their plants, they forcefully address the riot police, reporters, and plainclothes policemen invading their land. When a few step into his field, he chases them back to the road. Tomura Issaku tries to calm him down, but when he throws buckets of shit and urine on trespassing surveyors, the police finally arrest him. His wife then takes over the insults as the airport officials start measuring his fields. The circling helicopter finally drowns her shouts out.

After this confrontation, the bulk of the film consists of so many clashes between farmers and the police. Even with the subtitles, it becomes difficult to maintain cognitive control over the images, which are otherwise long sequences of writhing bodies—some clothed in *monpe* and straw hats, others in black armor and helmets.

Kitakoji and Ueno Koshi both discuss the style of Ogawa's cinema by this point in terms of breaking down distance between spectators and the action (although Kitakoji is suspicious that this is impossible in theoretical terms).[20] The viewer is confronted with a confusing situation, action fragmented with little explanation and no steady ground to stand on. This means that spectators must ultimately grope for some position on their own because the filmmakers are not providing them with one (as the previous documentary, particularly the news film and television documentary, are so wont to do). Conceived on the Newsreel model, *Sanrizuka—The Three Day War* is different enough that care must be taken not to generalize from this film to the entire series. Inextricable though it may be from the arc of the Sanrizuka Series, there are other ways to conceptualize the relationship between film and spectators that are more easily brought into focus with the next film of the Sanrizuka Series.

Ogawa Pro's next effort, *Sanrizuka: Peasants of the Second Fortress* (*Sanrizuka: Dai-ni toride no hitobito,* 1971) is the best known of the Sanrizuka films. It is also the most emotionally draining one. It records the first expropriation of land, which was only announced a week ahead of time and took place between February 22 and March 6, 1971. In January, the Hantai Domei anticipated the expropriation by digging tunnel networks in critical locations. Five fortresses scattered across the construction site protected the tunnels. Made of wood, scrap metal, logs, and barbed wire, the farmers fully expected the fortresses to be bulldozed and the tunnels turned into graves. You could call this film *The Seven Samurai* (*Shichinin no samurai,* 1954) of social protest documentaries for the epic scale of its depiction of farmers fending off invading "bandits," its moving commentary about power and human nature, as well as its revered place in the history of Japanese cinema.

By February 22, the Hantai Domei had amassed a reported twenty thousand protestors who faced off against thirty thousand police. The spectacle had grown to tremendous scale, turning into something far more than a "demonstration." In the open fields surrounding the fortresses, scrams of various units squared off with long rows of riot police. The Women's Action Brigade locked arms and marched up to the police to taunt them. The student sects attacked with rocks and long sticks.

A measure of their intensity is the fact that the riot police themselves were scared. On one research trip to Yamagata, I finished a long day of meetings and archival research at a bar near Magino. A group of drunken men were at the table next to me, celebrating their win at a *kendo* tournament. As often happens in such scenes far from the capital, the foreigner ended up drinking with the drunks. When they finally asked about my research project it was yet another cause for celebration, as their team captain was a veteran of the Sanrizuka Struggle. Now, he was the head of the region's early response police force; back then, he was one of the grunts in riot gear. We kept in touch over the years, and even went skiing together on Mt. Zao. However, he did not like to talk about Sanrizuka. One of the few things he told me had to do with the violence:

> As we prepared for a confrontation, we felt intense fear. Then when the guerrillas started hitting us or throwing Molotov cocktails at us, we naturally got angry. But we had to work to control our feelings and stick together. Go too

> far on your own—separate from your group—and they'd get you. It was serious. And it was really frightening.

This subject position inside the riot gear was never committed to film. The protests quickly became a regular feature in mainstream journalism, but always from a "critical" distance. The reporters may have been behind police lines—in every sense—but their commitment to the tenants of "balance" and "objectivity" basically devalued the humanity of the people fighting on both sides. In contrast, the riot police in Ogawa's films were anonymous, exoskeletal icons of state oppression, a measure of the degree to which his films were centered on the subjectivity of his *taisho*. Ogawa's crews traversed the barricades and fortress walls freely, literally diving into the thick of the ferocious clashes. Some of the scenes recorded by Tamura are absolutely heart wrenching, as when young women confront a long line of riot policemen who have constructed an ad hoc wall with their shields. The women grab the shields and peer over into the helmeted faces, crying, "Can't you see you're killing us?!? What would your mothers think!?!"

Peasants of the Second Fortress climaxes with the methodical invasion of the fortresses. The police attack with water cannons, but are repeatedly rebuffed by students lobbing Molotov cocktails and thrusting bamboo spears through holes in the fence. Upon their final assault, the riot police, the representatives of the state, storm the entrance and beat everyone in their path. They rip apart mothers and children who have chained themselves to trees. This film is like a mirror image of *Minamata Revolt,* the most memorable image of which is the calm face of the Chisso CEO surrounded by insurrection during a shareholders' meeting; activist Kawamoto Teruo sitting cross-legged on the conference table inches from the CEO's face, breaking down the executive's door with a battering ram of verbiage. In contrast, the real fortresses of Sanrizuka are brutally invaded. While the revolt in Minamata appears to be on the verge of some fleeting legal and moral victory, the Sanrizuka Struggle results in invasion, annihilation, and retreat. Upon watching *Peasants of the Second Fortress* at a government-sponsored symposium in the 1990s, even the president of the airport authority admitted, "As we just saw in that movie, what shall I say? Those were conditions we should properly call a war. We are now at a point when we have the sense that we don't want this to occur again."[21]

As in the previous films of the Sanrizuka Series, there are occasional moments when the action of the film grinds to a halt and people simply talk. While the students were once Ogawa's focus, they now haunt the background of the film. They appear only occasionally to clash with mobs of riot police. In their stead, the farmers take center stage, and in the most awkward of styles. Their speech is halting, filled with pauses and repetition. Where the typical filmmaker would search out the most articulate conversations and speakers (usually male leaders) and give them voice, Ogawa photographed unexceptional discussions and strategy sessions in exceptionally long takes. The breaks, silences, sidetracks, and repetitions were left untouched by editing. It is clear that as the farmers' comprehension of their situation deepened, so did Ogawa Pro's understanding of the farmers themselves. While this basic structure of discussion/interview alternating with chaotic action is familiar to anyone who had seen the previous films, there is an essential difference here. Ogawa Pro's approach had transformed in subtle but decisive ways.

This is particularly evident in one scene shot under the earth. As mentioned previously, one of the strategies of the farmers was to burrow underground—under *their ground*—and build catacombs of basements underneath their fortresses. Groups would rotate duty, living in the tunnels to make eviction and construction impossible. When the Ogawa Pro cameras tour the tunnels, their guide stops at a small hole designed for ventilation. After briefly describing how it works, the farmer holds a candle up to the aperture: "See, when I put the flame near the hole the fresh air nearly blows it out," and proceeds to repeat this action for several minutes. The point is clear the first time around, when the typical documentarist would cut to the next scene, but this ventilation hole is important to the farmers; it allows them to survive under the earth, and Ogawa refuses to interrupt the demonstration. When I asked farmers at Heta Village about this scene thirty years after the fact, they insisted it was not excessive. They rather liked the way it captured their neighbor's distinctive way of talking and the peculiar situation in the tunnels. This was, after all, the way they hoped to retain their land, by burrowing beneath it. And that little hole made it possible. This is paradigmatic of the attitude toward documentary forming within Ogawa Pro and becomes the predominant question in the rest of its work. How does one not simply stand on the side of the farmers but build their subjectivity into the very fabric of one's film? Writing in the mid-1970s, Noël Burch was one of the first foreign critics to recognize the real achievement of Ogawa Pro's films:

> Ogawa's and his cameramen's work had now come to *fit* the rhythms and patterns of the farmers' speech and behavior. [It] displays a remarkable *material* understanding of the concrete modes of behavior and discourse specific to those who work the land. The film's truly graphic sensitivity to cultural "otherness" has few precedents. It is not too much to say that the camera (or rather more precisely the editing) of the French master Jean Rouch is "condescending" by comparison.[22]

Significantly, this approach became generalized throughout the discourse on documentary, in part because everyone interested in the relationship between film and politics closely watched Ogawa Pro. For example, in 1969, a group of filmmakers including Oshima Nagisa, Wakamatsu Koji, Matsumoto Toshio, Matsuda Masao, and Adachi Masao helped bring back *Eiga Hihyo,* once an important forum for film theory in the era surrounding the previous ANPO. The writers of the new *Eiga Hihyo* attempted to theorize the contours of a "movement cinema" *(undo no eiga).* To this end, they resurrected the *shutaiseiron,* although with apparently little regard to the actual genealogy of the term.[23] In a typical debate from 1970, the writers discuss the complex relationship between the "conscious subject," "image," and "conditions." The image came to be perceived as a record stamped by the assertive hand of the filmmaker—that conscious, active subject—in the midst of the volatile "conditions" of the world. This "world" hid enemies and was structured by powerful institutions handed down from the past. As the new *Eiga Hihyo* group saw it, the quality of that relationship had implications for politicized aesthetics. In the next few years, the writing on Ogawa Pro and Tsuchimoto developed such ideas, focusing on the nature of *shutai/taisho* relations. It must be said that while we can certainly find continuity with earlier discourses on nonfiction filmmaking, the new discussions about *shutaisei* have none of the rigor or intertwining engagement typical of other moments in film theory—especially in other parts of the world. Writers seem to selectively appropriate, rather than rigorously contest and develop, previous arguments. The result is a protean *shutaiseiron,* the very vagueness of which may have made it more aesthetically productive in actual practice. For example, we sense only distant echoes of Matsumoto's *Eizo no Hakken* when Oshima Nagisa writes that Ogawa's method

> returns to the original intention of documentary, realizing the very principle of documentary. What are the principles and original intention of documentary? First it is a love toward the object documented, a strong admiration and attachment, and it is carrying this first principle over a long period of time. Nearly all the films considered masterpieces fulfill these two conditions.[24]

By the early 1970s, it was hard not to describe the films of Ogawa and Tsuchimoto, indeed most high-profile documentary filmmakers as well, in these rather vague terms. By *Peasants of the Second Fortress* these tendencies were in place, and in 1973, they arrived at their natural conclusion with Ogawa's *Heta Village.* This approach starts from the position of the filmed "object" and ends there, too. It is described variously as "letting the *taisho* enter the *shutai,*" "going with the *taisho,*" "betting on" or "depending on the *taisho,*" or becoming "wrapped up in the *taisho.*" Suzuki Shiroyasu, who will soon figure prominently into this developing story, described this approach in the following manner:

> I think that "symbiosis," *(kyoseikan)* as a goal or aim for the documentary, first came into parlance with Tsuchimoto . . . The filmmaker tries to take in and accept all the troubles, the conflicts, really the whole existence of the object being filmed. That's fundamentally different from the Western style of filmmaking. In the West, the object is never anything more than an element of the work, a particular work that is being made by a given filmmaker for him or herself. I think you can also see the effects of the Japanese attempts at a "symbiotic relationship" in the way the objects of the film are treated, or in the way the director refers to them. For example, Tsuchimoto doesn't call those suffering from Minamata disease simply *kanja* (victim), but he adds the polite suffix "-san": *Kanja-san* (victim-san). Ogawa refers to the farmers in his films with the honorific expression *"nomin no katagata."* They elevate the object of the film to their own level, or are treating the relationship with their objects and the objects themselves with a degree of respect.[25]

A reviewer for *Asahi Shinbun* puts it most simply in describing *Heta Village*:

> If we were to deepen the methodology that has the documentary camera facing two poles, between assimilation and othering, this film represents the move to the assimilation end. One could say the camera is one of the people appearing in the film.[26]

In contrast, Western theory since the post-structuralist intervention has theorized the documentary in terms of subject and representation, putting the referent *(taisho)* in brackets and only reticently discussing it. This is to say, Western documentary film theory focuses on the relationship of signified and signifier raked by the subjectivities of producer and spectators. Because these two groups approach the referent only through this signification system, the theory closes off extensive discussion of the profilmic world. The referent is used primarily to set the documentary apart from fiction film, as well as to lend documentary theory remarkable ethical resonance. The referent reminds us that, as Fredric Jameson puts it, "history hurts."[27] Less academically inclined discussions of documentary practice in the West are just as revealing in their own way. As noted previously, we generally refer to the *taisho* as "subject," strongly implying a desire to see the filmed human beings as acting and not acted upon, as free subjects rather than the objects they are in the context of cinematic representation. This is an artifact of earlier discourses of objectivity, forms of documentary realism that discount the subjective, creative force of the filmmaker.

Japanese theoretical and popular discourses do not suffer from this linguistic confusion between subject and object. In post-1960 film theory

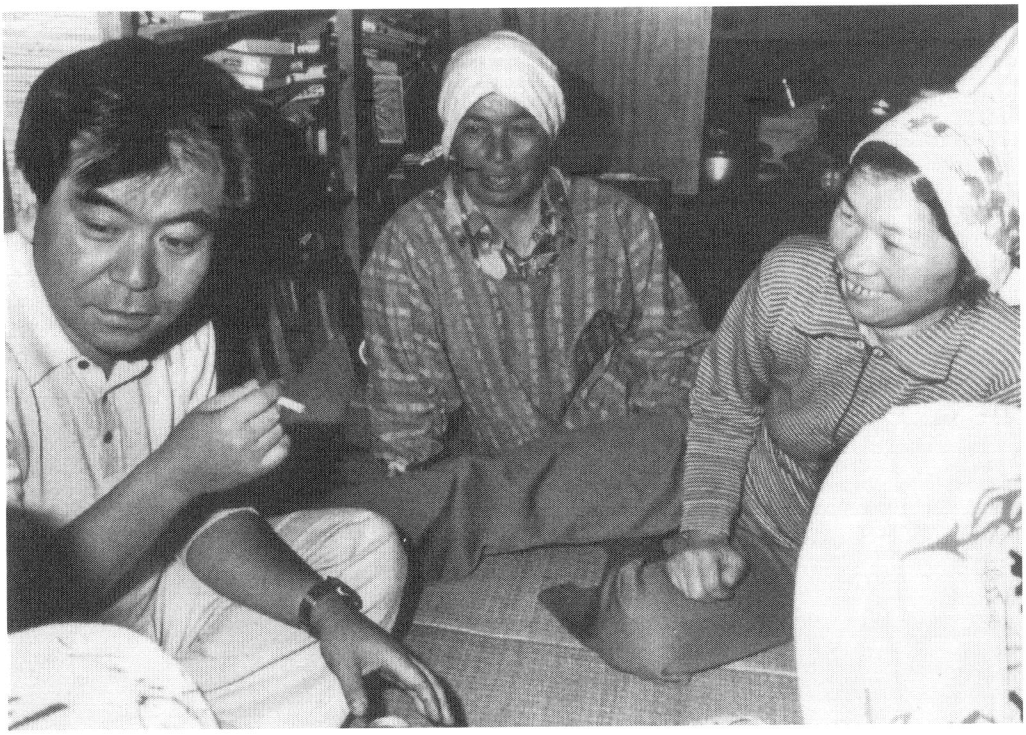

Ogawa chats with the neighbors in Heta.

and filmmaking, it is precisely the relationship between the subject and the referent that produces the sign. Where the American filmmaker creates a sign from a referent in the world, the Japanese filmmaker's intimate interaction with the referent leaves a signifying trace we call a documentary film. It is a subtle but decisive difference in emphasis that one can find in virtually every discussion of nonfiction film in Japan, a difference one would have difficulty articulating with the critical tools of contemporary documentary theory outside of Japan.

The discourse over the *taisho* is primarily concerned with the relationship of the filmmaker and *taisho* as it is represented in the cinema. Furthermore, it primarily attends to the quiet passages between the action sequences. What of the relationship between the filmmakers/*taisho*/film with the audience?

Simple, strong identification with the *taisho* is ultimately insufficient for a political film culture hell bent on social change, let alone revolution. The films had to *move* people. In one of the many surveys Ogawa Pro took at its screenings, a respondent succinctly frames the problem. This was from a survey for *Summer in Sanrizuka* and was written by a worker at the Nakano

Ward Office in Tokyo: "Will I support you? If all this means is screening films, then I'm against you. Basically, it's the problem of peddling humanism. If we can't provoke revolution, then making films that inspire sympathy is nonsense. The beginnings of struggle may start with sympathy (as long as it does not befall oneself). However, does not one need an after-film discussion that makes this sympathy your own problem?"[28] Someone from Ogawa Pro circled this comment in red pencil, so it must have struck a nerve. Perhaps it was Ogawa's scenes of alternating discussion and combat, the narrative stasis embedded in chaotic visual movement, that were problematic. Kitakoji and Ueno have discussed this feature, but Jane Gaines's theory of political mimesis in documentary is far more compelling and inspiring.

Gaines starts with the simple fact that despite the rhetoric of social action that always surrounds the political documentary, there is little evidence that they have actually "changed the world." There are no documentary blockbusters—few are seen beyond a handful of the already converted. It would seem the connection between sweeping social change and documentary might be mythical, buttressed mostly by anecdote and the flamboyant personalities of directors like Ivens, Eisenstein, and others. Gaines asks good, hard questions:

- What do we count as change?
- How do we know the effects a film has produced?
- How do we determine where consciousness ends and action begins?
- What *moves* people to act? What "moves them to do something rather than nothing in relation to the political situation onscreen"?[29]

These are some of the key questions I have been wrestling with as I watch the films, talk to former members of the collective and their audiences, and sift through the archive. The latter provides interesting, if obscure, clues.

First, there are surveys *(anketo)* for many of their films. Ogawa Pro conducted most of these, but some were sent in from sympathizers in other parts of Japan. Following are the tabulated results from the *Summer in Sanrizuka* screenings' surveys.[30]

Survey for Summer in Sanrizuka

We are working to create an independent screening organization in every ward and city to support the "guerrillas" of this self-styled film world from below. Thank you for cooperating in participating in this survey. Please join our organizing committee.

1. How did you hear about this film?
   Newspaper: 27
   Magazine: 32
   Poster: 89
   Union: 10
   Other (miscellaneous): 16
   Friend: 39
   Pamphlet: 5
   Sanrizuka: 1

2. Have you participated in the struggle to stop the Sanrizuka airport?
   No: 171
   Yes: 1 time, 15; 2 times, 56; 3 times, 6
   Total = 27

3. From now on do you want to participate in the obstruction struggle and farming support activities?
   I will participate: 98
   I cannot participate: 27
   I cannot judge: 60

4. Can you sympathize with the philosophy of the Sanrizuka Shibayama farmers' struggle?
   I sympathize: 166
   I don't sympathize: 6
   I cannot judge: 18

5. Do you support the idea of our independent screenings?
   I support: 189
   I can't support: 1

6. Do you feel like joining the organizing committee?
   I'll join: 29
   I won't join: 61
   I cannot judge: 82

Note the framing of the questions, which are written in an active voice asking for action, not just opinion. Inspiring people to participate and join the movement was the overarching goal, and judging from the answers perhaps they were successful. Many of the people who had not participated in the Sanrizuka Struggle expressed their intent to do so after seeing the film. This certainly suggests the film had the power to inspire action. From another perspective, the most lopsided result is in response to the fourth question. The vast majority of spectators "sympathized with the philosophy of the Sanrizuka-Shibayama farmer's struggle." This would appear to fail the challenge of that office worker from the Nakano Ward office.

The survey indicates Ogawa Pro's success in mobilizing people across Japan to join its screening movement as both spectators and organizers. Virtually all the respondents indicated they would continue to support the screenings, and this generally meant buying admission tickets and proffering donations. Another trace of the films' power to move people was the vast record of contributions flowing through the offices of Ogawa Pro. These ranged from massive grants to pocket change, duly recorded after every screening. The fundraising campaigns waged in the theaters were targeted at both the production of more films and the issues they were supporting.

Furthermore, nearly thirty people at this screening said they would help organize future events. When you discuss their film movement with former members of the collective, they automatically assume you are asking about the *distribution* and not production. Few filmmakers put as much energy into the exhibition of their work. Lacking the capital and infrastructure of conventional documentary and feature filmmaking, independent screenings demanded tremendous effort. One team of members worked full-time in Tokyo taking care of the constant flow of reservations and print traffic. Other individuals and teams spread out across the countryside, print in hand, finding supporters and setting up screenings with them. Halls had to be found, reserved, and rented; folding chairs had to be arranged. Projectors had to be prepared, often the persnickety Natco projectors from the Occupation with holey speaker cones. Bed sheets were strung up where movie screens were unavailable. When it was very crowded, some places would allow people to watch the film from behind the screen. Ogawa spoke of screenings where serendipity would turn the film into a "mysterious living creature." Wind would make the sheet=screen wave. Poor electricity would make the music waver. Hands would shoot up in the audience and make playful shadows over the image.

This last example points to another way the films moved people, which is also the most intriguing. It has to do with the gestures of the audience. Anyone who watched Ogawa's films back in the 1960s and 1970s can describe a scene of amazing participatory spectatorship. Audiences clapped, booed, chanted, and sang. When they saw something they liked, they would shout, *"Igi nashi!"* ("Right on!"); when the police arrived onscreen, they'd yell, "Nonsense!" Ogawa Pro sent their prints out with report forms, which would often come back with comments like the one from the death row inmate support club at a high school that showed *Peasants of the Second Fortress*: "First showing. 200 people. Shouts of 'Right on!' 'Nonsense!' Many people clapping. Scene of Youth Action Brigade crying had many people holding back tears. Participants mostly high school students. Principal (right winger) came. Smirking from start to finish."[31]

The most provocative part of Gaines's article suggests political documentary—with its spectacles of bloodied bodies, marches, clashes with police—is akin to what Linda Williams has called body genres. She begins where so many theorists locate their ethics of documentary: the body, here split between two locations, in the theater and on the screen. Above and beyond their efforts of "consciousness raising," political documentaries strive for mimesis, an embodied knowledge where representations of the world, energized and empowered by the world, make people move. Gaines writes, "There could sometimes be an aspect of the involuntary, an aspect that (kicks in) on top of politicized consciousness."[32] She suggests that filmmakers have historically used mimesis to both raise consciousness and make activists more active.

What makes Ogawa Pro's films a productive place to think through issues of political mimesis is that these two functions are boldly treated in separate and distinct styles, and also that these styles undergo certain transformations as the political landscape changes. The long sequences of discussions or interviews are stable and so lengthy they take on a sense of stasis. However, there is discursive movement that the action scenes lack, which is to say we learn things that affect our understanding of the historical events and, by extension, the scenes of violence that inevitably follow. At the same time, these discussions do not impart information in the manner we are accustomed to in the documentary. We really do not learn much about the circumstances of the Sanrizuka Struggle as the airport progresses toward completion. They are, rather, about what the combatants are thinking at a given moment. They are what allow us to come into that "sympathetic" or "symbiotic" relation with the films' *taisho*. They also locate the concerns of the filmmakers on larger issues, rather than on the morass of specifics of the Struggle's history and its mind-boggling complexity. They are also an important reason the films rise above their historical context and are as powerful today as they were when they were made.

As for the clashes, they are furious and chaotic. Visually they are exact opposites of the static shots of the discussions and interviews. The editing is largely accomplished in long takes, but the madness of the fighting, rendered as it is with jerky handheld camerawork, gives it the feel of rapid-fire editing. These scenes allow the spectators to experience the assault of the state's proxies directly, if from the safety of the theater. Their goal, stated over and over again, was twofold. First, they intended to stand firmly and unapologetically on the side of the oppressed and, second, they would use no hidden cameras and take whatever the riot police directed at them. One survey respondent called their approach to these scenes "cinematic *gebara*," using the German word for violence *(gewalt)* that had come to signify the positive use of violence by the student movement.[33]

These scenes are the basis for political mimesis. Gaines writes, "This idea of documentary as having the capacity to produce political mimesis assumes a faculty on the part of its audience that is only narrowly analytic. It assumes a capacity to respond to and to engage in sensuous struggle, in the visceral pleasure of political mimesis."[34] Gaines is unclear how this works exactly, but she suggests it has to do with the way documentary realism takes an event in history and aesthetically heightens it to create impact. However, the techniques she points to are only music and editing, which are certainly the likely starting points. What is interesting about Ogawa's films in this regard is that this is generally a long take aesthetic and uses music only sparingly.

Taking a cue from James Tobias, I would like to suggest that Ogawa's Sanrizuka Series is musical, that the visual movement in these films has musical qualities. Tobias' work stakes out new terrain for thinking about film and musicality (and not simply film music). He rejects the binary construction "music is affect/image is meaning," a structure that Gaines does not necessarily avoid by combining cutting with music in the affect column. Tobias asserts that *musicality* is the "performative discourse binding subjects and objects as collectivities."[35] He writes,

> Musicality comprises those effects of music as they may be performed or represented in other media: performances which only mime or otherwise do not produce music; qualities specific to music presented in visual terms. Musicality comprises those effects of music as they may be performed or represented in other than auditory media: performances which may only mime or otherwise do not produce audible music; or, qualities specific to music presented in visual terms. Musicality may inform visual lyricism in the mediated work even as it invites performative actions by audiences in response: foot tapping, head nodding, hand clapping, or even simply breathing. Musicality is what Eisenstein attempts to exploit in his plans for isomorphic movements between visual and sonic domains; musicality is what Eisler aims to enrich by means of a film music counterpointing the filmic image. And it's this same musicality in which Berkeley immerses the audience of the classical Hollywood musical with kaleidoscopic visual patterns set to music; which music video uses to advertise pop music; which television jingles implement to enhance the appeal of cars, cigarettes, or hygiene products; and on which film and television narrative draw to clarify for viewers ambiguously sequenced visual images.[36]

And I would add that this same musicality is what Ogawa uses in the Sanrizuka Series to make activists act. The films have a kinesthetic quality built out of a gestural "language" that is aesthetic *and* participatory. Through their own brand of sensuous lyricism, the films constituted their audiences through a complex of interaction: cat calls, booing, clapping, flinching, crying (even today spectators will produce the last two). Tobias is interested in musicality for the way it can account for interactivity of various sorts, from toe tapping to graphical user interfaces, and move from individual-oriented modes of being, such as agency, intentionality, and identification to think about creative audiences whose participation in making meaning reproduces gestures in the film. In the Sanrizuka Series, this means moving audiences far beyond a personalized sympathetic identification with the *taisho*, to constitute collectives ready to act once brought into relation with raw state power.

However, this is also a production of meaning by an audience that is historically situated and is not naturally equipped with faculties for political mimesis. An audience today, for example, will not show up wearing helmets, waving banners, and shouting "Nonsense!" They will, however, squirm and flinch, and some will cry; they will probably tap their toes at the drum beating and chanting on the soundtrack. Musicality is not a kind of film language or specific style; rather, it involves concrete experiences of the cinema grounded in the way people relate to the lived world.

The musicality of Ogawa's films is not restricted to the action scenes. The interview and discussion scenes have their own kind of lyricism, and at a macro level the constant alternation between these static scenes and the dynamic protest sequences are like the movements of a musical score. There is a rhythmic shifting back and forth that evokes Eisenstein's vertical montage, a "seismographic curve of anxious expectation giving way to the release of a pent-up sigh."[37] It is as natural as breathing.

The other reason Ogawa's Sanrizuka Series offers a kind of laboratory for thinking about political mimesis is that the films continue to follow the same people protesting the same government functionaries at the same construction site, but they start transforming quickly in the last films. Put simply, they demonstrate how the spectatorial faculty for political mimesis is cultivated and lost over time, as this change can be charted in Ogawa's approach to documentary.

There is a close connection to the political mimesis of the films, the participatory scene of the theaters, and the larger relation to history that Ogawa Pro envisioned for itself. Both Ogawa and Tsuchimoto brought as much creativity to their exhibition strategies as they did to the photography and editing of the films themselves. They worked to insert local struggles onto the national public stage. At the same time, they made attempts at negotiating a borderline between public and private spheres—territory generally mapped out by the state and by capital on their own terms. In the high growth economy after the occupation, public space increasingly became privatized and nationalized. In the film industry, a handful of heavily capitalized film studios controlled "mainstream" spaces for cinema production and exhibition. Thus, mainstream theaters—those deceptive places that pose as public places—would not touch the work of dissident filmmakers. As one kind of media, the movie theater could provide an arena for shaking the hegemony of the *keiretsu* system, as the short-lived New Wave attempted to do at Shochiku Studios. Significantly, these feature filmmakers went independent; many also made documentaries. Cultural critic Ikui Eiko points out that it is more appropriate to think of the cinema underground of the 1960s and early 1970s as functioning quite above ground. This is a measure for their success in carving out a space for public discourse, unmediated by state and capital—a place like a park, where strangers could meet and shake up each other's worlds. In the case of these filmmakers, this public exchange occurred within a dynamic between the local, regional, and national levels.

Since we usually consider this filmmaking in the context of a national cinema, our sense for these films' meanings is easily homogenized into the space of the nation-state. However, in some cases, the most politically effective interaction was local. As a compelling example, we can look to Tsuchimoto. While his films may have excited the national environmental movement and anyone suspicious of the collusion between government and business, back on the coast surrounding Minamata Tsuchimoto's films informed the families of fishermen of the mercury lacing their fish. In the face of government inaction and the chemical industry's denials, Tsuchimoto was saving the lives of people who did not know their food supply was dangerously polluted. This is not an exaggeration; the filmmakers were taking their films from village to village, informing the residents of the perils of eating their own catch.

Ogawa Pro was far more aggressive at constituting an alternative sphere for public discourse. Beginning with its independence from Iwanami, it was forced to distribute its films alone. The student movement provided a ready network. Upon Ogawa Pro's move to Sanrizuka, it sent projection teams across Japan, showing the print wherever the teams could set up a screening, in villages and cities alike. They also began to transform the spaces where they showed their films. Eventually, the teams codified their network into branch offices in Tohoku, Hokkaido, Kansai, and Kyushu. The public their ambitions envisioned was a collection of localities connected by cinema—not a homogenized national space based on a collective defense, an imperial symbol system, or a corporate network of production and consumption.

These local Ogawa Pro branches point to the scale of their ambitions and their weaknesses and contradictions as well. Their development was uneven and inconsistent, and differences between Tohoku Ogawa Pro and Kansai Ogawa Pro are revealing. Tohoku Ogawa Pro was originally a branch of Jieiso formed relatively independently by students at Tohoku National University in Sendai. It had an organic relationship to place. Because of this, it was by far the strongest of the branches. When Ogawa unilaterally folded Jieiso into Ogawa Pro, the conversion to the collective took place with relative ease. Aside from the distribution of the Ogawa Pro catalog, they published more elaborate newsletters than any of the other branches. Most important, Tohoku Ogawa Pro provided some of the most stalwart and enthusiastic staff members over the years, including Iizuka Toshio, Honma Shusuke, Yumoto Mareo, Iwasaki Seiji, and Tadokoro Naoki.

In contrast, the Kinki Jieiso branch in Osaka had a checkered relationship with Ogawa Pro. It shared an office with the Osaka Independent Film Center (Osaka Jisshu Eiga Sentaa). Jieiso handled distribution, and the Center devoted itself to production. Run by Korean resident director Ko Hiro, its most elaborate effort was *Osaka Encampment—The Face of War Opposition* (*Osaka no jin—Hansen no kao*, 1969), which documented the major demonstrations on international antiwar day (October 21, 1969) in Osaka. The Center also shot a film on taxi drivers and whiplash called *People Who Have Been Whipped* (*Muchi utareru mono*, 1970).

Kinki Jieiso, managed by Kitanoma Kan with Tamura Yae and Watanabe Hiroko, continued for a while after the establishment of Ogawa Pro, even after Ichiyama Ryuji arrived to create Kansai Ogawa Pro and produce Tsuchimoto's *Prehistory of the Partisans.* Both Kitanoma and Ichiyama were distributing *Summer in Sanrizuka,* and the latter was to continue the distribution of subsequent Ogawa Pro films. However, a number of factors led to the demise of this branch. While local sympathizers formed Tohoku Ogawa Pro, Ichiyama was sent to Osaka and told to stay there. As with all Ogawa Pro members who left, Ichiyama had plenty of reasons to quit that are best lost to history. However, one worth mentioning was Ogawa's acceptance of the Best New Director Award from Japan's Directors Guild in 1970. Ichiyama saw the award as disturbing evidence of Ogawa's embrace of the establishment. He and others wanted Ogawa to reject it, and this points to a deep contradiction in Ogawa Pro that would determine the choices it would make about its future when the "political season" ends several years later. While the young people Ogawa gathered around himself were all die-hard political activists, Ogawa was—first and foremost—a film fanatic. He came to film through *eiken*; his staff came to film through a desire to use the medium as a weapon for social change, not to mention the charismatic presence of Ogawa Shinsuke himself.

Thus, it is not surprising that Ogawa accepted the award and the stamp of approval it represented. This was an award from an organization whose past presidents included Murata Minoru, Mizoguchi Kenji, and Ozu Yasujiro. It implied his peers were other recipients like Oshima Nagisa, Hani Susumu, Urayama Kirio, and Kumai Kei. Ichiyama broke from Ogawa Pro, keeping his prints and establishing a new screening movement with the films under the banner of a new company they called Choseisha, after a famous Mao saying. Thanks to this situation, the Sanrizuka Series had extremely limited exposure in Japan's second largest urban area. Those who wanted to see the films had to order prints directly from Tokyo and organize their own screening. Longtime Ogawa Pro producer, Fuseya Hiro, half-joked that it was years before members of Ogawa Pro could step foot in Osaka.

Of all the Ogawa Pro branches, Kyushu was the most interesting and for a time promised to change the nature of the collective. After *Peasants of the Second Fortress,* Ogawa had already started contemplating a move from Sanrizuka to a new location. Ogawa and his staff were attracted to an area in the southwestern island of Kyushu known for the desperate poverty surrounding some coal mines. The workers from these mines were largely Burakumin and Koreans originally brought there for forced labor during World War II. Both groups were asserting their rights through organized efforts, this in addition to a movement opposing hazardous extraction practices. To all of these forces of organized political action add the legacies of colonialism, prejudices against race and class, and it was obvious the coal mines offered fertile ground for committed documentary filmmaking.

Acting on the invitation to make a film by local politicians in 1973, Ogawa sent Honma Shusuke and Mikado Sadatoshi to Nakama City to establish Kyushu Ogawa Pro. They set up shop in a *nagaya* near the mines, what was essentially a small one-room apartment in a rundown barracks. There, they met Hayashi Tetsuji, who joined Ogawa Pro. Having arrived with a cache of prints, the small group began organizing screenings from Hiroshima to Minamata.

Nakama itself was a rough town, and their living conditions were trying to say the least. Honma lived with his wife and three children in a six-tatami mat room. Despite their poverty, the proceeds from their local screenings of the Sanrizuka films were all funneled straight back to Tokyo, forcing them to live mostly off of the cram school run by Honma's wife.

Honma Shusuke recalls one New Year's Eve when the gas was shut off, followed shortly by the electricity and water. But they managed because they were confident someone would always help them in times of need. Sure enough, a supporter made the rounds of each utility and the supermarket, paying for everything and putting them back on track.

While struggling to survive and developing the Ogawa Pro screening movement in Kyushu and Wakayama, Honma, Mikado, and Hayashi conducted research into the history and politics of the coal mines. Their investigations were greatly facilitated by a body of writings emerging from a local "documentary literature" movement led by Ueno Hidenobu and Tanikawa Gan. Ueno was writing powerful nonfiction books about the desperate conditions surrounding the mines. Honma greatly admired the work of Ueno and aspired to make documentary films with the clarity and artfulness of Ueno's writing. He recalls showing several Sanrizuka films to the writer at his home: "Ueno sat there silently through the entire screening, watching with quiet intensity. To this day, no one has looked at Ogawa's films so incredibly closely. After it was over, he didn't say anything. It was rather disconcerting."

Honma spent several years in Kyushu, gathering information and paving the way for a film production. However, shortly after the collective moved to Yamagata, Ogawa sent Iizuka and others to visit Honma to break the news that it was not to be. After all this effort at paving the way for a film production, this was crushing news. He also found it mystifying. However, in the intervening years he suspects that Ogawa was terrified of Nakama. It was an extreme place that demanded a fortitude and bravery qualitatively different than Sanrizuka. After all, for all the problems faced by Sanrizuka farmers, they still had their land and homes; if they sold out to the Kodan, they had even bigger homes. The Burakumin and Koreans working the mines had nothing. Ueno's work was a challenge to Ogawa. He saw documentary (literature) as the giving and taking of life *(inochi no yaritori)*. Reflecting on Ogawa's decision not to document Nakama on film, Honma recalls the example of Ueno:

> After one of his publications, a coal worker broke into Ueno's home. He approached the author with a knife, plunging it into the floor and demanded to know why Ueno wrote what he did. Ueno defended his work rather than running away. In documentary, one must bet one's life. Ueno once wrote. "Don't be frugal with money; don't be frugal with time; don't be frugal with life." Only Ueno Hidenobu could do this. Ogawa Shinsuke didn't have the guts.

Certainly, Ogawa was never one to be parsimonious with time and money, but the decision to waste all the efforts of Kyushu Ogawa Pro to ensconce themselves away in the quiet mountains of Yamagata suggests that he was not prepared to bet his life on a film (one recalls that while his cameramen and assistant directors were confronting riot police, Ogawa stayed at home busying himself with producing and editing). Honma's associates in Kyushu did not want to give up their project, urging Honma to go independent and make his own documentaries on the coal mines and on Okinawa. He considered it until his wife told him to get a real job or get divorced. He chose marriage, and they both quit Ogawa Pro with a sour taste of betrayal. Mikado and Hayashi returned to Tokyo to rejoin the main collective. We can only imagine what Ogawa Pro would have become had they moved to Kyushu instead of Yamagata, assuming Ogawa would have survived the bet.

The Ogawa Pro branches were created as a practical way to extend their screening movement to the furthest reaches of the nation state and siphon much needed funds from periphery to center. At the same time, they constituted an ambitious attempt to create an alternative public sphere. Much as their effectiveness was hampered by structural contradictions, the

Ogawa's love of pipes infected all the men in the collective. From left to right: Iizuka Toshio, Ogawa Shinsuke, Okumura Yuji, Nosaka Haruo, Tadokoro Naoki. They are in the Shinjuku office in the Iwamoto building, January 1970.

activists of the branches appropriated a space historically managed by the forces of capital and state, carving out a place where people and political issues could be articulated into new relationships through the films' political mimesis. Ultimately, their project was a failure and the branches imploded one after the other; however, they did move people—physically and synergistically—positioning documentary as one of the sites where Japanese from all walks of life interacted, learned about the struggles suppressed from mainstream moving image media, and left inspired and committed to work toward making a better world.

Vertiginous Structures—The Construction of Iwayama Tower

The next film in the Sanrizuka Series is *Sanrizuka—The Construction of Iwayama Tower* (*Sanrizuka—Iwayama ni tetto ga dekita,* 1972). This is a deceptively simple documentary, and it is this simplicity that gives the film its charm. From *Forest of Oppression* to *Peasants of the Second Fortress,* we have seen a documentary approach in transformation; it slowly digs deeper and deeper into the historical scene, accomplishing in each new film what could not be imagined in the production of its predecessors. This is a reflexive brand of filmmaking—reflexive in the way leg muscles jerk upon a blow to the knee. No matter how thoughtful the production process was, these films represent Ogawa's automatic, or perhaps organic, response to the violent pressure encountered at the points of production. *The Construction of Iwayama Tower* still shares the mimetic impulse, but other qualities have also appeared. Considered in the broad view, these qualities appear less novel and more like something that had always been present in Ogawa's cinema, something that has been brought a noticeable degree towards the foreground. Why the change at this particular moment is a question we will try to address.

Nevertheless, one need only step back from *The Construction of Iwayama Tower* to see that its architecture is bared to view. There are two long sequences in the middle, book-ended by an introduction and conclusion. The confrontation with state power is condensed into the introductory pre-credits scene. The two main sequences have to do with, first, backstage responses to the new situation at the construction site, and second, the concrete preparations for the next stage in the battle. The conclusion provides some reflection upon the Sanrizuka Struggle as it enters this new phase.

The introduction details the fate of the Youth Action Brigade's hut. The film crew is invited into its underground fortress at the bottom of a large hole in the ground to investigate the conditions there and talk about the hut's imminent destruction. After the first expropriation struggle, the Hantai Domei strengthened its fortresses and tunnels with concrete. Unfortunately, rain filled many of them with water just before the second expropriation. This hut remained relatively dry. Flashlights are handed out to each person so crew members can illuminate their own faces for the camera. One of the adults, Ogawa Soichiro, acts as an intermediary and asks the assembled youth what the police are up to above. He reacts with a pep talk and leads them in a cheer—including Ogawa Pro in the string of *gambarimashos*. The riot police then crawl into the small entrance and expel the farmers, leading them away one by one. Outside, the elder Ogawa makes an impromptu speech, thanking everyone for their efforts: "They may have been expelled, but the police have not beaten their hearts." The image of Ogawa Soichiro being led away is replaced by the Sanrizuka logo.

After this introduction, the first of the two main sequences begins. It is one of those discussion scenes, but this is probably longer than any scene Ogawa Pro had attempted before. The topic at hand was the immediate political situation around the Sanrizuka Struggle and the possibility of derailing the construction project by building a tall tower. It could be situated on private land at the end of the runway. This first of two planned runways was nearly completed, and the pressure was on to do something about it. Situated at the very end of the runway, the tower they envisioned would actually be tall enough to prevent planes from taking off. It is hard to say if this was a stroke of genius or an act of desperation.

The story of this film begins slightly earlier, with the start of the second expropriation on September 16, 1971. Although it is hard to believe after seeing *Peasants of the Second Fortress*, this Kodan campaign was bloodier than the first. The main reason was the Toho Crossroads Incident. The crossroads are just up the hill from Heta Village, a stone's throw away from the present-day Terminal 2. On the morning of the expropriation, a group of 260 riot police from Kanagawa Prefecture found themselves under attack at the crossroads. The clash was particularly fierce, leaving one hundred police officers with serious injuries. Seven of their cars were reduced to smoking frames of iron, and when it was finally over, three policemen lay dead. A further shock hit the Hantai Domei shortly after this event when Sannomiya Fumio, a young man from Heta Village and one of the most beloved members of the Youth Action Brigade, scrawled an apologetic letter to his parents and then committed suicide.[38] His body was found hanging from a tree on the grounds of the local shrine.

Clearly the Sanrizuka Struggle was moving into a new phase, and the escalating level of violence was reverberating across the fields of Sanrizuka and through the entire New Left. These deaths were troubling developments.

The filmmakers in the Ogawa Pro's hut were no less affected, particularly by the tragic loss of their young neighbor. The death inspired a long passage in the production diary kept by Yumoto Mareo, who did the sound on this film. He begins by wondering what they've accomplished in the Sanrizuka films. There's something in the village, in the midst of all that turmoil, that they are trying to grasp, and when they do it won't be the end; it will only be the beginning. He continues:

> After *Peasants of the Second Fortress*, one thing our films discovered was space—probably only the people on this side of the fortress understand it. It was an attempt to deepen the root where the functional space falls. In the fortress for that month, the world that suddenly appeared there . . . it swelled with intense emotions. Further, at times, we found a softness like the winter sun and a creativity like that of children. . . . In the people left to carry on, there's no mistaking that we found a richness in the complete optimism of that country. Where does that richness come from? That world is the village in a valley surrounded by woods and solitude. A world that has continued to the present, day after day—or is there something else that has the same root?[39]

The last lines of the passage contemplate Sannomiya's suicide, speculating what kind of life he would have had had there been no airport. And it quotes an old man from the fortress: "Even if the fortresses are leveled they won't be able to destroy the fortresses in our hearts, so we will win."

One begins to wonder about the safety of those hearts in the long discussion at the center of *Construction of Iwayama Tower.* The bulk of the scene involves a meeting of the committee to build the tower. A member of the Youth Action Brigade suddenly takes the floor and submits the assembled villagers to an emotional tirade about the present state of affairs. Everyone listens on somberly, one friend attempting to calm him down. When he finally gives in to uncontrollable tears, Tomura walks over to comfort the youth. The sequence ends with a lawyer explaining the legal questions raised by the tower project, an abrupt end to a disquieting scene. For all the indelible images of anger, fear, and joy in the previous films, this was the first expression of deep, dark sadness, and it is difficult to bear.

The filmmakers suddenly shift gears for the film's second sequence, which describes in detail the construction of the tower. It sat on a square concrete base, which today lies in an uncultivated field, decorated by a small assemblage of iron bars. The filmmakers jump in at mid-construction. The tower is now high enough that their crane is of no use. They were encountering logistical problems in their attempts to leverage the three hundred kilogram struts of iron up to the top levels. "Logistical problems" and complicated processes were a subject matter of growing interest to Ogawa Pro. Here the filmmakers follow the construction in great detail.

The shots are quite long here, and so the structure of their relationships may not be immediately evident. However, there is an attention to visual form and space bordering on the symmetrical. When the team is constructing the fifth level, one fascinating sequence shot follows a construction worker mounting the base members and slowly climbing his way through the tangle of girders to the construction at the top; the camera angle is effectively disorienting, and lends the image an appropriately vertiginous feel as the (unhelmeted) man climbs into Narita's air space. An extreme telephoto shot follows, showing the work crew's tightrope struggle to nudge the frame into place.

Then, the perspective abruptly shifts to the top of the tower, looking down at the ground. A subtitle announces they have reached the seventh level, the height departing planes reach as they hit the position of the tower. We see two expansive views from this vantage point; one is the view of the airport runway construction, and the other is straight down at the impossibly small spectators looking up at the airy construction site. However, every shot after this is tight, simultaneously claustrophobic and acrophobic. It is some of Tamura's most impressive photography, filled with striking compositions of bodies balancing on beams and playful manipulations of space. It is an aestheticization of human labor Vertov would have appreciated—except for Ogawa's love of long takes.

The film concludes with an interview with a sect member back on the ground. The segue to this section is a shot of a Kodan jet flying a test run. Thanks to the tower, the plane is forced to veer sharply off to the side. In the final interview, the activist reflects on what they have accomplished and where he sees the struggle going from here. As he talks, his young child plays with his shoulder-length hair.

Ogawa always brought experimental touches to his films. One easily recalls the shocking freeze frames of *Summer in Sanrizuka* and *Report from Haneda,* even the ending of *Sea of Youth*. Despite being accused of throwing together "undigestable assemblages," all of Ogawa's films received painstakingly careful editing. A number of aspects of this film call for attention in this respect. The first is an *emphasis on process.* Ogawa Pro members were as thorough in their research as any scholar, an attribute easily traced back to the days of Jieiso. Their diaries and notes are filled with detailed descriptions of how things worked or how events unfolded. The close inscription of detail takes hold in their filmmaking with *Construction of Iwayama Tower* and becomes a dominant trait of the Magino Village Story.

Decorations inside the theaters showing *Heta Village* included these portraits of everyone in the village, with the filmmakers thoroughly mixed in with their *taisho*. From the screening movement for *Heta Village*.

More importantly, from the beginning of *Construction of Iwayama Tower* to its end, there is clearly an attention to the tools of cinematic expression, suggesting a growing maturity to the filmmaking. As is clear from the stark structuration of this film, the makers are giving more care to the artfulness of what they are doing. Starting with the traumatic and chaotic reality in their midst, they frame the world in delightfully new ways and give the whole of these images overt form. No wonder Aoyama Shinji put this film on his list of top ten Japanese films of all time.[40] From this perspective, we can see their next film, *Heta Village,* as something other than a stylistic break or anomaly in the Sanrizuka Series. Indeed, it is nothing other than the next logical step.

The Time of the Village—*Heta Village*

Sanrizuka: Heta Village represents the rich culmination of Ogawa Pro's efforts in Sanrizuka, which may seem odd considering the fact that the spectacle of the protests—those iconic images of struggle that everyone associates with Ogawa Pro—are completely missing. At the same time, *Heta Village* is thoroughly dependant on the memory of those images. Thus, rather than a culmination or a capstone film for the series, it would be most profitably seen as the keystone holding up the graceful arch of Ogawa's career. It brings the underlying transformation in their conception of documentary—that particular relationship to the *taisho*—into sharp focus. And just as this film would not have been possible without having lived and filmed in Heta for seven years, Ogawa's subsequent films draw fundamentally on the achievements represented by *Heta Village*. This is why, although remarkably powerful standing on its own, it should really be seen after watching the previous installments of the Sanrizuka series. And it should be understood as the crux of Ogawa's entire career and a crucial turning point in the postwar documentary scene as a whole. *Sanrizuka: Heta Village* is a masterpiece of the first order, a fine crystallization of the tendencies developing in the Japanese documentary for several decades.

As mentioned previously, the Sanrizuka Struggle had entered its darkest period at the beginning of the 1970s. Sannomiya Fumio committed suicide. Three policemen lost their lives at the Toho Crossroads Incident. The level of violence had pushed to new heights. In response, the plainclothes police began entering the villages scattered around the construction site, accompanied by squadrons of riot police. They arrested the youth in waves, keeping them in jails for interrogations for up to six weeks during the crucial harvest of watermelons. Arrests were nothing new, but now the warrants read "assault resulting in death." The stakes were considerably higher after the deaths of the policemen. The detectives also conducted a disinformation campaign through interviews of farmers in their homes. By feeding each family disparate stories, they hoped to sow distrust among the villagers.

Amidst all this turmoil, the oppressive inevitability of the airport construction weighed heavily on everyone's spirit. More farmers were joining the *joken-ha* and selling their land. One even sold the family graveyard containing the grave of one of the most respected leaders of the airport struggle, Ogawa Meiji. Not only that, but the sale was accomplished without informing the branch family in Heta, which had been so concerned about threats on Ogawa's grave that they had constructed a concrete fortress around it.

Ogawa Pro members were able to read Sannomiya's suicide note, and they noticed various notebooks the young man had kept on his desk. The notebooks recorded various aspects of the village, the kinds of local history and customs that are usually transmitted from generation to generation in an oral fashion. This would provide a key inspiration for the conceptualization of *Sanrizuka: Heta Village*. For their next film, the sixth of the series, they would look closely at the impact of the recent events on the villagers they lived with. They had always done this; however, this time it would be the center of the film. Their production notes leave traces of discussions about Tokyo as a "sphere of power" linked to modernity, and forced upon the villagers by the airport construction. This is what provoked the violence and chaotic change inside the village. In one of his production notebooks, assistant director Yumoto Mareo writes of the "need for a deeper politics": "Only the smoldering romance of the people's history has the power to rectify what politics has perpetrated. This is our home."[41] Yumoto's comment, filled with the earnest romanticism of youth, belies the complexity of their project. In the course of making their film, they would rethink history far beyond the invasion model mentioned previously. And to accomplish this, they would also need to rethink their media for writing that history, the documentary cinema.

The most striking change in their approach has to do with the absence of direct representations of violence. It is likely that their audiences were losing their faculties for engaging in political mimesis in these dark times as the passions fueling the student movement began to wane. This is to say that the musicality so central to their earlier films is no longer evident. In its place is something different, something that most have described simply as a long take style. However, Ogawa always used long takes. It would be more accurate to say that they developed a new aesthetic based on the long take, one in which time and duration were central questions.

This was their arrival at an aesthetic that was long in the making, a process involving some crucial technological determinants. Long after the fact, Fukuda gave a synoptic history of this process, one worth quoting at length because it raises a number of the themes that are highlighted next:

> In my memory the road from *Winter* to *Sanrizuka: Heta Village* pursued a consistent theme. What did we want to film? I think you could call it "village time." Making "time" the theme probably made us opt for the "waiting" method of diction and a style of editing that avoided montage techniques. Ogawa wrote . . . that when people say, "I'm here," "here" is the natural climate, and "am" is a form of dialogue. *Forest of Oppression* depicts an inherent dialogue of "hatred," but not a "here." When portraying the peculiarities of Sanrizuka, the larger theme of the village's own time, one held in conjunction with the natural climate came to the surface. After coming up with the theme of "time," the desire for synchronous sound recording equipment came up as a matter of course. . . .
>
> The Beaulieu [which we initially used] was equipped with a 200-foot magazine capable of nearly six minutes of filming. In order to grasp "time," we began experimenting with a "long take" shooting style combining the

> capture the Beaulieu and the EM-2. Our stance was to capture the leisurely drawl of the farmers during village meetings, so we mostly let go of the trigger when the talk ended. But by a strange coincidence we then discovered "village time." When we were doing a long take, the talk would sometimes end and there'd be less than a minute of film left, so we'd keep it running and not release the trigger. When viewing the rushes, we happened across such a scene. At a village meeting, one of the farmers finished having his say. Usually, we'd then close the shot, but this time we had kept it running. There, we were shown an unexpected mode of behavior. The farmer who had finished talking lightly scanned the other participants with his eyes as if to ascertain the degree to which his ideas had sunk in. The other farmers were fully aware of that glance and there played out with him a heated, but voiceless, dialogue.
>
> This was a find. That delicate flow of time was, I think, what Ogawa had in mind when he later said that, "There's something in village time that attracts me," or what Tamura was talking about when he said that, "I had the feeling I wanted to join the people there." For me as well, that time—a flow of time accustomed to circulating though that village—was something "nostalgic" located somewhere in my memory. Unfortunately, we subsequently discovered that putting the "village time" into images, given our equipment, was something we were unable to fulfill in *Winter.* Yet to develop the flow of time we experienced on screen was what we longed for. Our desire was finally fulfilled in *Heta Village* by getting a hold of a noiseless camera, the Eclair (which can film a lot longer than the Beaulieu: nearly 12 minutes), and a Nagra tape recorder, and using that combination to perfect the dual methods of synch sound and long take photography.[42]

This new technology, which offered the filmmakers longer shots, quieter photography, and synch sound, gave their images an immediacy that enabled a new kind of spectatorial engagement. In their previous films, the discrepancy between image and sound, with its jarring time lag, interfered with the viewers' ability and desire to immerse themselves in the world of Sanrizuka. This dissonance—between time and space, film and spectator—was the rift that musicality helped bridge.

The new equipment enabled Ogawa Pro to render a new representation of temporality that began with the photography and ended with sound editing.[43] Here, Tamura builds on the advances of his cinematography evident in *The Construction of Iwayama Tower.* In the group's discussions during principle photography, Ogawa meditated on the issue of space:

> In moments of drama, the coolness of the camera has an intensely focused eye that spreads and stretches across space. One takes in that drama, embracing it and creating it anew as an independent space. However, what do you do when there is no such drama? In such a time, if there is no effort on our part to do something about it, that coolness will create coldness and boredom. Let's move in when there is no drama. Let's pursue them in close-up.[44]

The stunning interview at the beginning of *Heta Village*, with Grandpa Tonojita telling Ogawa and Fukuda Katsuhiko about everything from rice farming to the brutal ostracizing of farmers who sold out.

This conception of space is evident from beginning to end. The first shot is for many a beloved moment in Ogawa's cinema. The director stands in the middle of Heta interviewing "Grandpa Tonojita," one of the oldest villagers and among the most vociferous protestors at the front. As Ogawa and Grandpa Tonojita dialogue, Tamura scans the surroundings. The scene, a sequence shot lasting eleven minutes, displays the key technical features typically found in long take aesthetics, no matter where they appear: pans, rack focus, reframings, the occasional zoom. However, while many long take aesthetics strive for the epic or operatic, this shot might appear amateurish. Seen with the sound off, it would seem randomly composed and chaotic. The stars of the show are the two men, but Grandpa Tonojita only occasionally comes into the frame and then in generally obtuse and partial views. Most of the time, Tamura scans across the rice paddies, pausing every once in a while on a home or a clump of trees or something even less distinct. This hints at the importance of sound. Tonojita is relating a rambling set of stories about his village. He is an inarticulate fount of knowledge, sating Ogawa's curiosity about village topography, custom, history, and whatever else might come up. The structure of his sprawling, jumbled monologue is something we explore later. Here, let us note the crucial way in which the human voice—in synch—breathes strange life into this "random" and "messy" image.

Watching the film, we gradually tune into the alternative logic at work, so that we are ready for the quietly thrilling sequence shot that exemplifies Tamura's photography in its purest form. Late in the film, as the villagers wait for the return of their jailed youth, the women take a rest from their collective efforts at the harvest (they are cultivating the land of those who sold out, Ogawa explains, as it was too painful to watch fields go fallow). They sit in a tight group in their broad straw hats and dyed work clothes, chatting. In the space of a nine-minute shot, Tamura scans the scene, gently panning from one face to the next and back, and often in tight close-up. The focus pulls in and out, drawing our attention along the axis of the lens. Between Tamura's searches for sharpness, the image softens with the lack of focus and becomes pure pattern, pure surface, before resolving once again into another human face engaged in conversation. The soundtrack features a polyphony of quiet chatter (an effect largely lost to those dependent upon subtitles). Here is a perfect and more profound synch of sound and image that has nothing to do with the motion of lips. Tamura tunes us into the vertiginous gossip, which flits from topic to topic just as his camera slides from face to face. While there remain elements of musicality here, there also is something else that invites us to experience other senses besides vision and aurality. Perhaps by directing us to the surface of the image, it appeals to our *sense of touch*. While not a strong quality in *Heta Village*, this will become a central feature of Ogawa's approach in the Magino Village Story.

In every historical case I can think of, the long take is associated with the image; however, Ogawa directs us to the crucial role of sound. Indeed, the bounds of Ogawa's long takes must be measured not by the in and out times of the shots, but with analogous points on the soundtrack. His is a long take aesthetic fundamentally based on continuous sound.

Consider the second scene of the film, directly after the conversation with Grandpa Tonojita and Ogawa's short voice-over introduction over a high-angle image of the village. Ogawa has just explained the grave events of the recent past and hinted at their political ramifications. In this second scene, the villagers hold a discussion about the Kodan's secret purchase of the grave of Ogawa Meiji, one of the most respected elders leading the airport struggle. A strong, steady rain falls, providing a background hiss that sets the sequence apart from those before and after. A representative from the Ogawa family relates their surprise and shock that the sale had been accomplished behind their backs, and then a convenient pause in the conversation enables Ogawa to insert intertitles providing background information about the situation at hand. However, the hiss of the rain continues in the background, and the image track returns to the discussion in time for the next speech. Tamura pans and zooms, but the image track remains basically unchanged—generic images of humans sitting, motionless and deep in thought, silently absorbing the thoughts of the speaker in what Fukuda called that "delicate flow of time" they found in these village meetings. This imagery continues over the next pause in the conversation, *which lasts a pregnant two minutes.* When the discussion picks up again, Ogawa cuts briefly away to an image of the graveyard, *once again without interrupting the soundtrack* and its aural backdrop of falling rain. The sequence ends several minutes later with a passionate speech by one of the young men in the Youth Action Brigade. While the scene contains a relatively heterogeneous image track, the sequence is measured—in every sense, temporally and experientially—by the soundtrack. Ogawa uses this technique of extended and multiple sound bridges throughout the film, and I will call these peculiar sonic long takes "sound shots."

The sound shot constituting this second scene in the film lasts a full seventeen minutes, and was culled from three hours of footage.[45] Remarkably, we are already half an hour into *Heta Village* by its end. Ogawa's new long take, established as a principle of organization starting with this film, demonstrates the contribution of technology (longer magazine, quieter camera, synch sound) to an aesthetic based on *continuous sound.* Time is constituted homogeneously, in long stretches, with occasional changes in the visual track bridged by sound, rendered something other than interruptions in time or shifts in space.

One's encounter with this film is punctuated by seemingly regular beats, moments to take a deep breath before entering the next stretch of time. The unprepared sometimes find the pacing "plodding," but that itself is revealing. There is a regular, if faint, *beat* that dimly lends structure to one's experience of the film's temporality. We can bear this underlying structure with a simple outline, a list of the lengthy scenes that make up the film. Should we exclude the short transitions between some scenes, it would look something like this:

1. Grandpa Tonojita describes the features and customs of the village, including an incident of *mura hachibu* (ostracization). [11:00 minutes; 1 shot, meaning a single uninterrupted image with synch sound]

2. Group meeting concerning the purchase of Ogawa Meiji's grave. [17:00; 1 sound shot, meaning one uninterrupted stretch of sound accompanied a number of images and/or intertitles]
3. Riot police enter village and arrest young men. [7:00, 2 sound shots]
4. Onnabisho: the construction of a phallic offering and the ceremony to the god that protects children. [13:00; 2 shots]
5. Grandma Hanzem poses for a funeral picture, telling many personal stories about village life. [15:30; 2 sound shots]
6. Police enter the village and arrest Haruo and Masahiko. [18:30; 2 shots]
7. One month later, a Parents Alliance meeting to discuss the imprisonments and their impact on the village. [22:00; 5 shots, 1 a sound shot]
8. One week later, a meeting to hear about a police visit to the home of the late Sannomiya Fumio. [10:00; 7 shots]
9. Women chatting in the fields. [9:00; 1 shot]
10. Haruo and Masahiko are released, and give speeches of thanks. [19:30; 4 shots]
11. Village women sing sutras in monthly prayer meeting. [4:00; 1 shot]

With this outline, we can see something extraordinary about *Heta Village*: the substance of this film is contained in eleven scenes of roughly equal length, most of which are only one or two sound shots.[46] I will admit to the necessarily arbitrary nature of such outlines. Indeed, I have ignored the film's introduction and a number of brief transitional scenes or shots. And my emphasis on the sound shot, while perhaps a welcome reversal of the supremacy of the visual, suppresses a degree of heterogeneity evident in the image track. My timings are rough, rounded up and down. However, by chancing charges of being "unscientific" or "sloppy," I hew closer to the logic of the film itself. In *Heta Village,* Ogawa has moved away from the political mimesis of his previous work to a different kind of cinema where time and duration are paramount. And because we are dealing with the documentary here, this temporality made manifest in sound and image inevitably has to do with the representation of history and of being, not the empty, homogenous time so aptly named by Walter Benjamin.

To explore Ogawa's new temporality for the documentary, a useful theory of representation may be found in the work of Dipesh Chakrabarty. We could say that Ogawa is treating the villagers of Heta as "peasants" in Chakrabarty's sense of the word, not merely as "farmers." When he uses the word *peasant,* Chakrabarty extends it far beyond its sociological meaning:

> The "peasant" acts here as a shorthand for all the seemingly nonmodern, rural, nonsecular relationships and life practices that constantly leave their imprint on the lives of even the elites in India and on their institutions of government. The peasant stands for all that is not bourgeois (in a European sense) in Indian capitalism and modernity.[47]

Inspired by another figure from subaltern studies, Ranajit Guha, Chakrabarty argues that the logic of European thought and liberal institutional frameworks is "braided" with another logic of older—but not archaic—relationships and practices that are not necessarily secular and are decidedly not bourgeois. He charts out a plural history of modern politics in the third world that steadfastly refuses the historicism that positions the political modernity of the subaltern, or "peasant," as incomplete or riddled with archaic practices and superstitions.

Ogawa's films from this point on are filled with these modern peasants. A scene from one of his last films centers on the marriage of the local mountain goddess to an ancient village god that takes the form of a large stone phallus. In the catalog for the film, Ogawa wrote about what impressed him about this story: "What I thought the most is that the gods in the village freely change depending on villagers' emotions or ways of thinking. Because of this freedom behind it, [that phallus] is not just a simple stone. It's vibrantly alive. The stone doesn't have an authoritarianism that orders people around. Actually, it's the opposite."[48] Ogawa uses the scene to introduce us to the sacred spaces of Magino, while confronting us with a different way of relating to both past and present.

Much of Chakrabarty's critique of historicism deals with time, which subtends narratives of development, industrialization, nationalism, and capitalism. In contrast to what Benjamin called the empty, homogenous time of modern history, Chakrabarty argues for a plural time for the subaltern. This is not something external to and displaced by the logic of capital, but rather "lives in intimate and plural relationships to capital, ranging from opposition to neutrality."[49] It is constitutive and supplemental in the Derridean sense.

In the hamlets of Sanrizuka, these two logics were at loggerheads. It would, however, be a mistake to simply see either side as separate, utterly opposed, or to think of the farmers as outside of the modernity represented by the government's massive construction project. *Heta Village* captures a moment when the villagers themselves lived the contradictions. The increasing scale of the violence was turning the villagers to this supplemental logic, tapping into the energies usually lying neutrally dormant there.

If we were to isolate a main theme in *Heta Village,* it would be the renewed importance of *ko,* or "associations," in village life. This idea is inserted into the film in Ogawa's voice-over early in the film, and repeated in their PR materials and in interviews the director gave to the print media at the time. For example, the text on several of their fliers reads,

> Lest the farm work of the families whose youth were taken away got behind, the other families breathed life into the idea of "*ko.*" These groups, called "Yui" ["ties that bind"] and "Straw Bag Friends," were for helping each other in times of need. The people of the village took turns working and didn't fall behind one bit. Even with the imprisoned youth, they took daily turns to visit the prison with gifts and mail. The village is, actually, full of life and keeping traditions of the past alive. With the fundamental optimism and long-sustained efforts of the village, they protect themselves. In this kind of real time *(tashika no jikan)* that circulates in the village, we recorded together with the camera.

Ko are forms of village associations with a history of more than a thousand years. Originally Buddhist in nature, they started taking many other forms in the middle ages. Some that pooled money for emergency support became banks in the postwar era, when *ko* proliferated into heterogeneous forms. When the central government encroached on their land and threatened their ways of life, the farmers in Sanrizuka drew on this traditional form of organization to combine their resources and marshal their collective energies for the fight.

Ogawa emphasizes the binding function of traditional practices, which often indicate that the modern political sphere is not bereft of ghosts, gods, and spirits. The last scene of the film shows a village that has returned to an uneasy peace, as symbolized by the monthly Buddhist ceremony that brings the old women of the village together. The second scene centers on a *ko* discussion provoked by the crisis at the graveyard. This is a serious issue, as the relationship to the people in that cemetery is much more akin to the ancestral graveyards of First Nations people like Native Americans and Hawaiians than that of European settlers. It is not simply a practical matter of moving the grave, but involves a complex mix of ethical, spiritual, and political problems. This scene ends with a passionate speech by a member of the Youth Action Brigade (yet another *ko*):

> On his gravestone is written, "After death the spirit still fights against evil." This was the last request of Ogawa Meiji, our vice-chairman. I believe his spirit remains with his family and with us in the Hantai Domei. In that sense, those that he left behind must respect the wishes of his spirit until the very end. With his spirit, we will oppose the airport.

In *Heta Village,* Tsubaki Taka shows the filmmakers how she turns a *daikon* radish, a handful of grass, and a couple of potatoes into a large phallus, introducing a little flair from her fishing village to Heta religious life.

The youth is speaking in a less than figurative manner. The villages are filled with spirits and gods. The fourth scene centers on the spiritual dimensions of another *ko,* the Koyasuko for protecting children. Just after the arrest of Haruo and Masayuki, Ogawa shows Tsubaki Taka, one of the stars of the Sanrizuka Series, giddily constructing a phallic offering out of a large *daikon* radish—completed to perfection with (grass) pubic hair and (potato) testicles. This offering is for a god that ensures safe births and childrearing. The Women's Action Brigade and the younger children gather to participate in the Onnabisho ceremony where the Tsubaki family hands the homemade phallus to the family responsible for next year's offering. Along with the phallus goes an ancient book recording every birth in the village. It is the inscription of one's name in this book that signifies one's belonging to the village. Ogawa is clearly using the Koyasuko and the Onnabisho rites for Tsubaki's cheerful optimism and as an example of the traditional mechanisms that bind human beings together in the village.

It is significant for another reason, as it helps show how these traditions are not frozen in time. Tsubaki, Ogawa explains, is from a village down on the nearby coast, and entered Heta through marriage. Before she came, the phallus the villagers made was relatively crude. When it was her turn to create the phallus, she used various embellishments typical of fishing villages, for example the hair and testicles. Ogawa is convinced of the importance of these traditional practices, but is careful not to essentialize them or pose them as archaic remnants of premodern rites untainted by modernity. Rather, it is through these creative and evolving life practices that the villagers network themselves and adapt to the flux of their modern lives. When the logic of the airport threatened their existence, it was the power of these networks and their constitutive activities that they tapped into, a reservoir of strength in their resistance.

It must also be pointed out that, as Ogawa avoids the essentialization of tradition, he also avoids its romanticization. The film's access to local practices, logics, and knowledge is predicated on the transmission from elders, as is asserted by the pre-credits interview with Grandpa Tonojita. He jumps abruptly from one topic to the next, very much on his own terms; Ogawa's questions are few and rarely leading, and the scene is offered in a single, unedited shot. However, Ogawa's intervention is still palpable in the way his one edit—eleven minutes in—makes a particularly terrifying story the climax of the scene. Turning from the topic of an old path across the village rice paddies, Grandpa Tonojita points out an empty house across the way. He explains that it used to belong to the Niya family, but when they joined the *joken-ha* the Heta villagers subjected them to the traditional practice of *mura hachibu,* or "village ostracization" (lovers of Japanese film might recall a famous example of *mura hachibu* from Imamura Shohei's *Ballad of Narayama* [*Narayama bushiko,* 1982], when an entire family is buried alive). What exactly this entailed in Heta goes unsaid, but Tonojita offers a chilling story that suggests that whatever happened was very unpleasant.[50] When the Niya family patriarch died and his body was brought back from the hospital, no villagers attended the funeral to help. Local custom was to bury the dead, but with no help to move the corpse and dig a hole, the Niyas were forced to drive the body to a crematorium. Just as Grandpa Tonojita's story appears to end, he fleshes it out with one more detail: the arrival of the body coincided with a police action, and someone started banging the oil drum that always called the villagers to action. The Niya family was terrified when they heard that drum beat; they thought the Heta villagers were coming to murder them. Grandpa Tonojita offers a somewhat sly smile and says, "We didn't mean for it to go that far." But Ogawa leaves us to wonder, cutting to the Sanrizuka Series logo and letting this unnerving anecdote haunt the film. For all his faith in local customs and ways of thought, Ogawa was careful to point to its potential for destructive violence as well.

As a serious and ambitious filmmaker, Ogawa was confronted with how to treat these ways of being in representation, precisely the challenge Chakrabarty is interested in for the historian. Chakrabarty writes,

> If real labor belongs to a world of heterogeneity whose various temporalities cannot be enclosed in the sign "history" . . . then it can find a place in a historical narrative of commodity production only as a Derridean trace of that which cannot be enclosed, an element that constantly challenges from within Capital's and commodity's—and by implication, history's—claims to unity and universality.[51]

The cinematic equivalent of this totalizing, universalist project would be the PR cinema of Iwanami Productions, especially after the departure of the Blue Group members. This was the anonymous representation of history on film, underpinned by a conception of time as empty as that of the 24 frames-per-second pace of the projector. Anathemic to any pretense to artistic expression, the PR film serves no master other than capital itself (and the documentary of television journalism is barely different). Unlike the television commercial, the purest form of the PR documentary—from which Ogawa himself emerged—resists the temptation to appeal to the pleasures and instinctual aspects of being that indicate the constituent presence of these other logics.

In contrast, *Heta Village* is, as Chakrabarty might put it, about "other ways of worlding." Through his unique deployment of the long take, Ogawa discovered a route to cinematically embrace the heterotemporality of the village. This is something the filmmakers were highly conscious of during the photography and editing process. For example, at one point in his production diary, Yumoto writes,

> During the village meeting the discussion did not develop along logical lines. But it's not that it was pointless or lacking direction. Rather, even in silence it's as if it is a time for communion, for deeply receiving another person's thoughts. That space is what the eye of the camera was able to wholly embrace and photograph. That kind of silent space deeply conveys the image of the living reality of human beings.[52]

The filmmakers always referred to what they called the *tashika no jikan*. Difficult to translate, it might be rendered as "real time." It indicates the compelling need for long takes that let events and conversations play out in whole and at their own pace, relatively untouched by editing. *Tashika no jikan* implies accuracy, authenticity, and sensibility—all temporalized. It is both present and imminent. It is on this basis that Ogawa Pro shifts the coordinates of the documentary from bimodal transmission between filmmaker and viewer, and reorients the film and filmmaker into an orbit around the *taisho*. Spectatorial and directorial desire and logic are bracketed, the interventional power of editing respectfully deferred. Ogawa Pro members sit amongst the silent listeners of the *ko* and are included in the speeches of thanks at the end of the film. The relationship between filmmaker and *taisho* approaches unification.

Ogawa Pro successfully reconfigures subject–object relations to an unprecedented degree in *Heta Village*. The conventional documentary filmmaker's relationship to his or her "subject" is essentially that of the historian's relationship with the evidence, a distant and lifeless past. That this book appears in an American series on documentary called *Visible Evidence* is suggestive in this regard. Although the documentary filmmaker's entire project is premised on an interaction, in the West this is disavowed through the rhetorical moves of the filmmaker in capture and editing. The autobiographical strain of documentary Michael Renov calls essayistic rarely escapes this logic. It may be premised on filmmaker–*taisho* interaction, but is firmly anchored in the subjectivity of the director/essayist. Renov's theorization reflects the positioning of these directors, who are mainly Euro-American or diasporic subjects living in the West.[53]

In contrast, Ogawa and his collective created a film that built the subjectivity of the *taisho* into its very fabric. Significantly, their audience knew what they were up to. Although I quoted this particular article earlier in this chapter, it is worth looking at a little more of the passage as this is from a *newspaper review,* not an academic journal:

> It is safe to say that as a methodology, this film represents a monumental achievement in the Japanese documentary. There is the powerfully grim synch sound that even captured the sigh of an old man at the village meeting. There are its long takes, with only 97 shots in its two and a half hours (there couldn't be more than 30 live action shots in the film). Put in affective words, it is the visualization of time. In documentary film, the camera faces the polar limits of assimilation and dissimilation. To deepen this methodology, this film indicates the outer limits of assimilation. In a sense, the camera becomes one of the players.[54]

Heta Village represents a climax to the Sanrizuka Series and a keystone to Ogawa's career because the director finally perfected the documentary aesthetic he had been searching for. Before this, he conducted his search—his practical experiments with all their theoretical implications—while necessarily tending to the practical and on-the-ground politics of the struggle. Only by staying with his *taisho* for so many years, by following their struggle *and* living with them as neighbors, did Ogawa reach the point where he could shuttle the spectacle and details of the political struggle to offscreen spaces without committing an unforgivable ethical compromise. Those years of living and filmmaking enabled the collective to see beyond the urgent contingencies of the confrontation with power and reach for a more profound understanding of the conflict that continued in the fields of Sanrizuka and the jails of Narita. As filmmakers, they built this new understanding into their cinema. *Sanrizuka: Heta Village* is ultimately about—and literally embodies—the diverse ways of being human.

[4] Segue: From "Sanrizuka Ogawa Pro" to "Documentary Cinema Ogawa Pro"

> The righteous divide and divide again, expending ten million words. What they've spoken then becomes their enemy, and finally unification becomes impossible. That is the law of the righteous. On this point, the wicked are quick. The wicked join forces and the righteous divide—this is social-scientific law. And yet, the righteous continue to think it is possible to achieve solidarity through words. . . .
>
> :: Tsurumi Shunsuke, *Chushingura and Yotsuya Kaidan—Japanese Communication*

Groping in the Dark

In the introduction, I wrote about the Groping in the Dark symposium at the 1997 Yamagata International Documentary Film Festival. This panel of directors was moderated by critic Yamane Sadao, who laid out a periodization of the postwar documentary borrowed from Ogawa Pro's Fukuda Katsuhiko. From the vantage point of the present, the assembled filmmakers agreed that something happened to the documentary in the mid-1970s. The passion and social commitment of the 1960s cinema seemed to give way to a new kind of documentary centered on the self. Significantly, this turning point from one epoch to another coincides with the release of *Heta Village* and Ogawa's resolution to leave Sanrizuka for the mountains of northern Japan, so it is tempting to see the decision as symptomatic of the contradictions of the historical moment. Before turning to the films of the Magino Village Story, we closely examine this issue of periodization and documentary's changing relationship to the politics of social action. We return to this issue in the concluding chapter. This chapter concentrates on this transitional moment in the mid-1970s and how Ogawa Pro reacted to the changes they only half-perceived. No one doubts that something happened; the question was what.

In the early 1970s, documentary was peaking. The National Film Center held major retrospectives of pre- and postwar documentary in 1973 and 1974. The leaders of documentary filmmaking were producing the finest films of their careers. Ogawa Pro released *Heta Village* in 1973. Tsuchimoto made *Minamata Revolt* in the same year. *Shiranui Sea (Shiranui-kai)* in 1975 was probably the finest film of his career. His interview techniques with the victims of Minamata disease were by this time refined into a powerful tool. He patiently listened to victims talk about their joys and anxieties, often with the sea—that source of life and harbinger of death—as sparkling backdrop. He revisited familiar personalities from previous films in the series and traveled to far-off islands where new victims were still being discovered. Few of his subsequent documentaries on the Minamata situation achieve the comprehensiveness and power of *Shiranui Sea*.

The exception is his astounding medical film, *Minamata Disease: A Trilogy* (*Igaku to shite no Minamata*, 1975), which he produced the same year. Harking back to his Iwanami days, he borrowed the conventions of the science film, politicizing it over a sprawling but meticulous three hours of cinema. The film is structured in three parts: progress of research, pathology and symptoms, and clinical field studies. Tsuchimoto painstakingly laid out the science of the disease, addressing medical practitioners and research scientists more than the general public. It was an extraordinary attempt to inventory the physiology of the disease and its human toll.

As Tsuchimoto and Ogawa were approaching the pinnacles of their careers, quite a few other filmmakers were also producing fine films: standouts include Adachi Masao and company's *Aka Serial Killer* (*Ryakusho: Renzoku shasatsuma*, 1969); Yamatani Tetsuo's *Living: Twenty-five Years after the Mass Suicide on Tokashiki Island, Okinawa* (*Ikiru: Okinawa Tokashikijima shudan jiketsu kara nijugo-nen*, 1971) and *Miyako* (1974); Hara Masato's *First Emperor* (*Hatsukuni Shirasumera no Mikoto*, 1973); the NDU collective's *Onikko: A Record of the Struggle of Youth Laborers* (*Onikko: Tatakau seinen rodosha no kiroku*, 1970) and *Motoshinkakurannu* (1971); Jonouchi Motoharu's *Going Down into Shinjuku Station* (*Chika ni oriru Shinjuku Suteshon*, 1974); Yamamura Nobuki's *Tokyo Chrome Desert* (*Tokyo kuromu sabaku*, 1978); and Haneda Sumiko's *My View of the Cherry Tree with Grey Blossoms* (*Usuzumi no sakura*, 1978). This is only a small sample.

It is, however, in retrospect that we see these filmmakers peaking because we know what followed. After the efflorescence of the late 1960s and early 1970s, the conditions of the documentary slumped, or at least the

Members were sent to the hinterlands to show the films, with a print under one arm and a one-way ticket. The Ogawa Pro name was their calling card, and people would help them set up screenings. Here, several members drive through a village announcing a screening of *Heta Village*.

conditions the filmmakers aspired to were slipping into the impossible. In the next few years, most of these filmmakers migrated to television and PR film or simply took up unrelated careers. Others settled into academia. Higashi and Kuroki basically became feature-film directors, apparently giving up on documentary, even though they continue to appear in public forums on the subject. The filmmakers who attempted to remain independent struggled and quickly lost their artistic and political edge while their audiences disappeared. While Tsuchimoto moved to smaller, less ambitious projects, he always engaged politically controversial subjects, such as Hiroshima, Afghanistan, nuclear energy, and a few other Minamata-related topics; but none of these films are quite as compelling or innovative as his previous work. Ogawa Pro began transforming during the production of *Heta Village*, as we saw in the previous chapter. In 1972, the Tohoku branch dissolved; then in rapid order, the Hokkaido and Kansai branches followed suit. The Kyushu branch survived until 1975, but by then Ogawa Pro had left Sanrizuka.

The filmmakers had finished *Heta Village* in April 1973 and initiated nationwide screenings in May, starting at Tokyo's Yujima Public Hall. Despite very favorable press, they felt they had to take a proactive approach to the distribution. Previously, they were circulating all the prints of all the films from their respective branches. This time, they divided the country into three regions, Tohoku, mid-Honshu, and Kyushu. For a month and a half, teams of five or six members borrowed places to stay, cooked for themselves, and organized a film viewing group (Eiga o Miru-kai) that sold tickets directly to viewers in a given area. They put enormous effort into the screenings of *Heta Village,* decorating the entrances of the theaters with bamboo, banners, and sculpture. Inside, lobbies were filled with photographs of every person in the village, drawings by Sanrizuka youth, even the equipment that had been used to make the film.

This personalized approach to screenings, which harks back to the prewar days of Prokino, was necessitated by a number of factors. Ogawa Pro had made a film that dealt with politics in only the most indirect of ways, which made it of less interest to the groups that had shown its films in the past. At the same time, those very groups were quickly becoming part of history. The student movement was winding down, and the passions that heated up the nation's political life were extinguished. Before, the films nearly distributed themselves. Now, Ogawa Pro had no choice but to become deeply involved in the distribution process. Something was clearly happening to Japanese documentary.

Amid the apparent dissolution of the support structures of the documentary world, two figures arrived on the scene to signal what would become a new direction, a path Japanese documentary has followed to the present day. Hara Kazuo and Suzuki Shiroyasu are the pioneers of what has come to be called "private film" ("*puraibeto firumu*" or "*kojin eiga*") in Japan, a new production mode based on the solitary work of a singular filmmaking subject. In this thoroughly artisanal mode, the lone filmmaker oversees the initial conceptualization, the photography, the editing, and even the distribution of his or her work. It is significant that the term *private film*—used as it is to signify a historical difference—implicitly posits the work of Ogawa and Tsuchimoto as public film. And once again, the *shutai/taisho* dyad maps this transformation.

Hara burst onto the documentary scene in 1974 with *Extreme Private Eros: Love Song 1974* (*Kyokushiteki erosu: koiuta ichikyunanayon,* 1974). The film lays the filmmaker's personal relationships out for the world to see. Having left his rather abusive wife (Takeda Miyuki) and taken up with a new woman (Kobayashi Sachiko, his present wife and producer), Hara decides to make a film to, as he explains in the opening voice-over, come to terms with his ex. With Kobayashi recording the sound, they follow his former wife around the country. Hara bares all: he includes the verbal abuse he takes from Takeda (some of it well-deserved), he runs his camera while making love with her, and he films her giving birth on the kitchen floor. This indulgence in the personal, this extremely public exposure of the private, proved earthshaking in the context of a documentary world whose values were formed by the Sanrizuka Series and the Minamata Series.

Hara's emergence was followed by the arrival of Suzuki, an NHK television cameraman and prominent poet. Considering this combination of vocations, it should not be surprising that the contradictions between producing corporate and personal representations proved stifling. Inspired by Jonas Mekas, Suzuki began producing diary films.[1] His *Impressions of a Sunset* (*Nichibotsu no insho,* 1974) and the 320-minute *Harvesting Shadows of Grass* (*Kusa no kage o karu,* 1977) recorded the mundane events of daily life, the details of the physical spaces he moved through, and his fetishistic fascination with the camera.

Thus, the early to mid-1970s seem to constitute a break, with new filmmakers rejecting the dominant conception of documentary practice in which films were produced within organizations of people, whether collectives, companies, political parties, or the military. However, to perceive this shift only as a break would conceal important continuities that can help us answer the question, "What happened?" Hara and Suzuki are the most important figures in this narrative for more than their timing. Both are simultaneously fascinated and repulsed by the collective approach to filmmaking represented by Ogawa and Tsuchimoto, yet they still locate themselves in that territory through their films, writings, lectures, and interviews. Indeed, they can hardly avoid doing so because they both have a strong historical consciousness, a sense of where they have come from or an identification with a long-running documentary heritage within the context of their own national cinema.

Hara had a close but ambivalent relationship with Ogawa Pro. Before making *Extreme Private Eros,* he flirted with the idea of joining the collective in Sanrizuka. He often tells a story about his decision to join the collective: he went to the Tokyo office intending to start work, but upon arrival he stood in the entranceway overwhelmed by the buzz of activity inside. He then discreetly backed out the door. Although that front door turned out to be a barrier, Hara constantly uses the older filmmakers as a filter through which to understand his own work.

Suzuki, for his part, has always haunted the fringes of the collective. In his 1980 film *15 Days (Jugonichi-kan)* he spends fifteen evenings in a largely empty room talking to the camera about whatever comes to mind; he constantly wonders about the legitimacy of locking himself away like this and waits for transformation, for change, for *something to happen*. Out of the blue, a bale of rice arrives from Ogawa Pro, a gift of the collective's recent harvest in Yamagata. More than anything, Suzuki has written extensively and quite provocatively on both eras of documentary in essays that have been collected in two books, which are among the most important works on Japanese nonfiction film.[2]

Most significantly, both Hara and Suzuki have continued to place their work within the discourse of *shutaisei*. We have already seen signs of this in a previous quote from Suzuki, but it is easy to find Hara speaking the same language. For example, in an interview with Laura Marks at the Flaherty Seminar, Hara described his approach in familiar terms that are difficult to gauge without contextualization in the Japanese postwar discourse on nonfiction filmmaking: "As a filmmaker I try to understand what I want to do, not so much by *confronting* my object, but by trying to become 'empty inside myself' and letting my object enter me. The object becomes my opponent and I become the receiver of the opponent's action and development."[3]

Readers unfamiliar with the previous discourses on subjectivity in documentary will key in on words like *confronting* and *opponent* (or possibly make vacuous comparisons to a Zen-like "emptying of the self"). However, Hara is actually staking out territory in relation to and within the theoretical heritage that has been handed down to him. This complex relationship to the past is also what sets Hara and Suzuki apart from the general turn to the individual that they helped create. If we use the *shutai/taisho* pair to sketch the shape of this shift, we could say that if the previous generation of documentarists strove to "go with" or "sympathize with" the *taisho*, the new generation of documentarists folded the *taisho* into the *shutai*. This is to say, the *shutai became the taisho*. The subject matter now centers on the self or the family and often with exceedingly personal concerns and obsessions. More often than not, the private film lacks any significant engagement with others outside the family and reveals a reticence to set out into the public world like the previous generation. Many of these young filmmakers, particularly those emerging in the 1990s, were students of Hara and Suzuki. While the two are often seen as epitomizing the private film, it is far better to see them as transitional figures with feet in both camps.

This change parallels developments in documentary in much of the world, where a combination of theory and practice interrogates the problem of subjectivity and representation through a kind of private film and video. However, it would be a mistake to conflate the Japanese and Euro-American approaches, just as the connections between Ogawa Pro and the

American Newsreel collectives are tenuous at best. The dangers of conflation are strikingly clear by comparison of the work itself. The current Euro-American documentary in particular is smart, sophisticated, and theoretically informed. It plays on the border between traditional notions of the avant-garde and documentary in ways that Matsumoto called for forty years ago in an entirely different context. Significantly, the conception of subjectivity in these films and tapes is inseparable from larger social and political problems, so that any close examination of the self raises issues as diverse as gender, colonialism, race, nationalism, and modernity. The Japanese counterpart of the 1990s is simplistic in comparison.

At their best, these Japanese documentarists who mine the self for subject matter can create moving portraits of emotional life. Kawase Naomi's *Embracing* (*Nitsutsumarete,* 1992) is an 8mm record of her traumatic search for a father who abandoned her; it is a beautifully crafted film that ends on a deeply moving note when she finally decides to phone her father. Kawase's work is exceptional, but most of these films and videos disappoint. On the opposite end of the spectrum of quality are the so-called self-nudes, which are produced exclusively by young women who turn the camera on their own bodies. Examples include Kamioka Fumie's *Sunday Evening* (*Nichiyobi no yugata,* 1992); Wada Junko's *Claustromania* (*Heisho shikosho,* 1993) and *Peach Baby Oil* (*Momoiro no bebii oiru,* 1995); and Utagawa Keiko's *Water in My Ears* (*Mimi no naka no mizu,* 1993). This form has been done in Western video art, but the Japanese variety has little of the self-conscious inquiry into problems of representation as does, for example, video art, such as *Birthday Suit: Complete with Scars and Defects* (1975) or *Tongues Untied* (1989).

Obitani Yuri's *Hair Opera* (*Mohatsu kageki,* 1992) is typical and among the most interesting films from this 1990s group. It follows the raucous relationship between the filmmaker and an artist whose current exhibit is a massive collection of pubic hair from all the men (and boys) she has slept with. The film is very much about social disconnection, perhaps unwittingly so, and personal obsession. The artist collects men; the filmmaker, in turn, attempts to collect the artist on celluloid, framing her in his own private world and fantasies. It is a very funny piece, but Obitani seems to be unaware of, or unable to deal with, any issues of gender; at least, the questions the film raises are not his own, an unfortunate tendency of the private film. The fact that Obitani's films—like a surprising number of these works—are fake documentaries is a significant index of his ambivalence about representing the public world and its inhabitants. Reality is where it hurts, and the filmmaker is as vulnerable as his or her object. It is far safer to stay home and shoot documentaries cut to the measure of the filmmaker's private desires. The difference between Ogawa joining the Sanrizuka farmers and filming one's own family is vast.

Indeed, there is something ironic about the moniker private film, considering that such a film is, by design, meant for public viewing. Probably anything named "private" implies a secularization of itself, as in Hara's *Extreme Private Eros*. However, quite unlike Hara, what we have here is a retreat from the world, leaving the moving image a singular conduit connecting the private self with a vague, inscrutable public. In the 1990s, the vector originally taken by Hara's and Suzuki's rejection of collective film practice intersected with the culture of the *otaku*. The stereotypical image of this 1990s icon is the dysfunctional cyborg youth, safely ensconced in the wired bedroom where all social communication becomes mediated through electronic gear, such as fax machines, computers, and phone networks. This turn inward is topologically equivalent to the artists of the private film who too often cut themselves off from social connection and interaction, that referential stuff of the documentary form. The *shutaiseiron* Matsumoto initiated cannot hope to account for the subjectivity of an *otaku,* a measure of the historical specificity of this theory and perhaps its philosophical poverty. In 1996, Matsumoto Toshio weighed in on the topic with some sharp observations:

> That's why, even though I do accord importance to these kinds of private diary films as a form of subjective documentary, I don't make them myself. One reason is the existence of the traditional "I-novel" or *"watakushi shosetsu"* in Japan and the danger that these films will connect with that kind of closed-off individuality. If they relate to it in a bad way, it will submerge them in a closed world lacking an Other similar to that of *otaku*. I wonder if this trend has not reached a limit. Certainly, individuality originally gained importance in the sense it opposed the "private" to the kind of coded and institutionalized "public" I just discussed. I support confronting this uniform public with individuality in order to destroy a homogenized public, but it disturbs me when this individuality becomes that of an *otaku*. That's one reason. The other reason relates to the "I" found in Descartes's "I think therefore I am," the "I" in a modernist cogito establishing an independent self through opposition with the world. Well, there are problems with an "I" which doesn't doubt its "self" and the so-called "I-films" *(watakushi eiga)* share those: they never put their "I" in question. Since they don't attempt to relativize themselves through a relationship with the external world, they gradually become self-complete—a pre-established harmony. Fidelity to this self-identical self is connected to something like the modern myth of individuality. In that sense, they are extremely over-optimistic. This trend itself stabilized years ago and has become just another system.[4]

Onstage at the Yamagata Film Festival, Ogawa Pro's Iizuka Toshio directed this very critique at Kawase Naomi, the de facto representative of the private film. She insisted vigorously that her films *did* have the *shakaisei* (sociality) Iizuka felt was missing. I have suggested this is probably the case; however, Iizuka does have a point. Private films are often creative works, but they nearly always disappoint in terms of conceptualization. The artists seem unable to articulate what they are doing or to comprehend the political and social implications of their work in representing the world. They present a politics of public exposure strikingly naive about the relationship between subjectivity and representation; theirs is a politics devoid of politics. Like Hara, they are standing at the front door of the public world bustling with countless people, issues, and ideas to engage; unlike Hara, who chooses to move through that public space as an individual, the private filmmakers retreat to the family rooms and bedrooms.

The first rumbles of this change may be traced back to the 1970 World Exposition in Osaka, which attracted (and distracted) independent artists of every stripe. The fair had enormous capital backing it and sponsored many moving-image media projects. It must have been difficult to turn down such luxurious offers after struggling with shoestring budgets. Perhaps Matsumoto Toshio provides the iconic example. Despite his fearless agitation through institutional reform, film production, and theorization, the 1970 Exposition seems to mark a turning point in his career. After politicizing the documentary in the late 1950s and 1960s, Matsumoto turned increasingly toward electronic technologies. For the Exhibition, he created a massive installation entitled *Space Projection Ako* (*Supesu purojenkushon Ako*, 1970) featuring a 27-meter-high dome with sculptures, ten 35mm projectors, and four screens. His next short was the Dadaesque *Metastasis* (1971), which used a newly invented medical device to create a beautiful solarization effect on the static image of a toilet. This work indicates a trend toward the structural film in the avant-garde. It came to dominate video art, which enjoyed the support of the exposition as its primary launching point.

Matsumoto throws himself into this vein of filmmaking, which explores the limits of the medium with little to no regard for its social embeddedness, through both production and pedagogy. It could be said that classic avant-garde films like *Spacey* (1981) would never have been made had Matsumoto not been teaching budding artists like Ito Takashi.[5] As for Matsumoto himself, he continues to make fascinating films, but they have less of the progressive and aggressive politics that were so important to so many people.

Not everyone was happy with the financial carrot the exposition dangled before hungry filmmakers. A small protest movement criticized the artists that accepted the money; they were criticized in turn for sour grapes.

Tsuchimoto considered participation a form of *tenko,* or ideological conversion that amounted to selling out to state power for the sake of money. Back in 1969 during the shooting of *Prehistory of the Partisans,* he took his camera to the International Peace Day rallies and caught the rioting at Osaka Station with a sign in the background counting the days down to the exposition. Later, during the production of *Minamata: The Victims and Their World* (*Minamata: Kanja-san to sono sekai,* 1971), Tsuchimoto got into a scuffle with riot police at the entrance to the exposition.

The results of the event were a watershed for avant-garde film and video, and an unfortunate episode for the independent documentary. Few of the celluloid-based works produced for the exposition are remembered. In many ways, this event marks the decline of the creative, independent documentary in the same way *Tokyo Olympiad* and *Exchange Student Chua Swee Lin* symbolize its beginnings back in 1965.

Since the 1970s, there has been no shortage of brilliant films available for inspiration. The best work from around the world is regularly shown at forums such as Image Forum, Scan Gallery, and various museums, festivals, and minitheaters across Japan. Unlike the 1950s and 1960s, filmmakers and audiences can also access the world's documentary through video tape, disk, festivals, personal travel, and study abroad. The generation that seemed to fall apart in the early 1970s did manage the occasional film.[6] The latter work of Ogawa Pro, Haneda Sumiko, and Hara Kazuo is particularly impressive. So why the sense of devolution? Why the need to "grope" at Yamagata near the end of the 1990s? Perhaps it is nothing more than a premature millennialism. In any case, panel members could not produce an adequate answer to Yamane's query, "What happened?"

I would like to hazard a guess . . . or two, to be precise: the factor of the women's movement and gender politics, and the unfortunate continuities between the Old and New Lefts. Before addressing these directly, we must acknowledge that these transformations in the film world were symptomatic of a wide range of political and economic forces. In a general historical sense, there is no question that the social space of the movement cinema was rapidly and radically changing in the early 1970s. The government had successfully driven the security treaty through passage, and the country was reeling from a series of crises relating to currency and oil. In August 1971, Nixon opened up relations between the United States and China (without informing Japan beforehand), throwing Japan's international standing as the primary Asian nation into doubt. When Japan followed suit shortly thereafter, it confused the ideological allegiances of the Communist Left. There were also new plans to protect the dollar and let the yen float.

After its failure to stop the security treaty, the student movement started losing steam. It was in a weak position to deal with a simultaneous escalation in violence, particularly that of the various factions of the Red Army. Starting on February 19, 1972, five members of the United Red Army (Rengo Sekigun) stood off police in the mountain cottage they had been hiding in deep in the mountains of Nagano. The siege ended on the February 28, when the police stormed the building, resulting in the deaths of two policemen and the arrest of the fugitives. Now prisoners, they made a shocking revelation. Over the past winter, while hiding from police, the group had tortured and murdered fourteen of their own for "ideological deviation." A few months later, the Japanese Red Army (Nihon Sekigun) claimed responsibility for a bloody attack at Tel Aviv airport that left twenty-four people dead and over eighty injured. At virtually the same time, the struggle at Sanrizuka reached its violent climax at Toho crossroads, forcing many supporters of the struggle to disillusionment with the movement as construction of the airport rapidly approached completion. So various contradictions in the Left emerged precisely when the high-growth economy ground to a halt.

We could also chalk the current situation up to the hyperconsumerism of late capitalism, which does encourage self-absorption and retreat from the social imperatives of the 1950s to the 1970s. However, do we not also find some form of that capitalism and consumerism in, for example, America? Perhaps it is an even more intense variety than Japan's in New York, San Francisco, Los Angeles, and other centers of the American personal documentary. Clearly, the most succinct response to Yamane's question is, "It's overdetermined." However, there are two places to suggest less obvious explanations for what happened. The first involves a comparison (while granting all the weaknesses of such an approach), and the second offers a telling example.

There has historically been a productive relationship between film criticism, theory, and practice, a relation traceable back to the 1910s. However, this relationship also seemed to unravel at the same time that documentary declined. Comparison to the U.S. situation is instructive. At the same time the independent film world in Japan experienced its shift, film theory and criticism in the West took a turn that would ultimately provide the theoretical ground for the Western work about subjectivity and identity politics. This is the innovation brought by feminist film theory. In the post-1968 scene, as semiotic and Marxist applications of nonfilmic theoretical discourse began to play out, feminism took the field prepared by the New Left—the collection of thinkers as diverse as Marx, Freud, Jacques Lacan, Ferdinand Saussure, Jacques Derrida, and Michel Foucault—and enabled a

Despite the vast number of photographs Ogawa Pro took of themselves, few seem to feature the women. Most show them at work in domestic spaces. Clockwise from upper left: Asahi Setsuko and Hatanaka Hiroko cooking in the Magino kitchen; Shiraishi Yoko shopping; Ogawa Shinsuke, Fuseya Hiro, Mikado Sadatoshi, and Iizuka Toshio in the Magino studio, with Shiraishi Yoko (standing) preparing food in its tiny one-person kitchen; Hatanaka Hiroko serving tea to everyone in the fields, with Fukuda Katsuhiko (standing), Kawada Yumiko (sitting), and Kimura Shigeko (far right).

new, poststructuralist synthesis that propelled film theory and practice in new directions. These developments coincided with our problematic moment in Japan. In 1972, the year Ogawa Pro's branch offices started closing, *Women and Film* began publishing, and major women's film festivals were held in New York and Edinburgh. Laura Mulvey presented "Visual Pleasure and Narrative Cinema" in 1973, the year *Heta Village* was released, and published it the year of *Shiranui Sea* (1975). Audiences were watching *Impressions of a Sunset* when the first issue of *Camera Obscura* came out in 1976. This feminist synthesis of poststructuralist theory has been remarkably productive for film theory and constitutes a complex, long-running debate continuing into the present and touching nearly all areas of inquiry. More recent explorations of identity politics, in both print and moving image, owe much to feminism if only because of its contribution to the shift from discussions about positive images/negative images to questions about the apparatus of representation itself.

In Japan, however, while Japanese feminism proved a potent agent for social reform and protest on many fronts, the discussions occurring in the film world did not respond to the feminist challenge. Although Japanese filmmakers and theorists paid close attention to Jean-Luc Godard's Dziga Vertov Group and the Third Cinema theories from Latin America of the same era, they basically ignored feminist criticism. One measure of this situation is that Mulvey's article remained untranslated until 1997; just as telling is that it was translated by Saito Ayako, a scholar of Hollywood cinema trained at UCLA. Japanese film semiotics was generally emptied of politics and never served as the petri dish for the cross-fertilization of diverse theories or for keeping theory socially and politically engaged.

Considering this, it should come as no surprise that self-consciously feminist film and video artists, such as Idemitsu Mako, always faced severe criticism in their struggle for legitimacy. Or that until recently, women feature-film directors were usually either famous actresses (like Tanaka Kinuyo and Hidari Sachiko), working hard in the pink film industry[7] (like Hamano Sachi), or coming out of television (like Yamazaki Hiroko). Or that the women in the Ogawa Pro collective were restricted to "supporting roles" like shopping and doing housework. Many of the most powerful women in the Japanese film world have been in programming and the distribution of primarily independent work (for example, Kawakita Kashiko of Towa, Nakano Rie of Pandora, Kamiyama Katsue of Image Forum, Takano Etsuko of the Iwanami Hall and the National Film Center, Araki Keiko of Pia Film Festival, and Ono Seiko and Fujioka Asako of the Yamagata International Documentary Film Festival). That a relatively small handful of women like Sakane Tazuko, Atsugi Taka, Tokieda Toshie, and Haneda Sumiko crafted significant careers makes the documentary seem like a paradise for aspiring women directors. However, they are exceptional for more than their talent; their presence hardly masks the fact that the film industry, from the feature film to the avant-garde, was largely a man's world. (It still is, even considering the veritable explosion of work by women filmmakers in the past two decades, thanks in part to inexpensive video, nonlinear editing, and art schools.)

We may find this issue condensed in the example of Ogawa Pro. First, Ogawa's sexual relationships with women are discomforting. As we learn from Barbara Hammer's film, Ogawa Pro itself was eminently sexless. However, Ogawa operated by different rules, leaving his first wife for Jieiso's Kobayashi Hideko, and then leaving her for Ogawa Pro's Shiraishi Yoko. The latter woman he married and lived with until his death. These relationships affected the tenor of the group in ways that are difficult to quantify. In our conversations over the years, Hara Kazuo always insisted that one cannot adequately explain Ogawa Pro without examining Ogawa's relationships with women. However, Ogawa left festering wounds I prefer not to aggravate here, although we will see how Shiraishi's role was "more equal" in comparison to roles of other members of the collective.

All the young people who joined Ogawa Pro did so because they were activists, not because they necessarily wanted to make films. In the Jieiso period, around half of the members were women, a ratio that would steadily decrease over the years. Furthermore, many of these Jieiso women served in positions of power and responsibility. Kobayashi Hideko, for example, not only acted in a leadership role but also was the producer for several of the first films. While this sounds refreshingly ideal, it does not necessarily mean that the consciousness of the typical Ogawa Pro member was devoid of "appropriate" gender-based roles. When I raised the issue in a conversation with Nosaka and Kobayashi, Nosaka jibed his friend, "You could be a producer because you're actually not a woman." Things changed in the course of the Sanrizuka Series, when women who joined the collective usually found themselves in the kitchen. This arrangement became far more problematic in Magino, where the group was attempting to live and work communally.

After the move to Magino, the cooking chores were assumed by Hatanaka Hiroko (Iizuka's wife) along with Kawada Yumiko (Fuseya's wife) and Asahi Setsuko. Kawada is a particularly interesting figure because she was taking care of two children in the Magino house. She was thrilled at the adventure promised by the idea of communal living, particularly since she would be living with her best friends. Little did she realize what difficulties lie in wait. For the first several years, most of the staff went back and forth between Magino and Yamagata, something like a month in the capital followed by a month and a half in Yamagata. When the staff was in Tokyo, Hatanaka remained in Magino with her children and Mikado. One of the most dramatic moments of Barbara Hammer's *Devotion* (2000) is during Hatanaka and Iizuka's interview. Hatanaka explains how little they saw of Iizuka, even when he was living in the busy Magino house. As evidence, she holds up a drawing of their family that teachers asked for at school; it featured mom and a whole gaggle of dads. Despite this skewed sense of family structure, it was heaven for the children. They had a big house to play in and all the adventures available to children growing up in a rural space. When the staff returned to Yamagata, things were different. The children had to learn to avoid their "uncles" when they were working, and they were suddenly restricted to certain areas of the house. During shooting, the kids had to be quiet as well, a tough task for youngsters.

In 1978, seven-year-old Iizuka Daisuke's teacher asked his class to draw pictures of their family. Daisuke's picture included the entire collective, encapsulating the complicated situation in the Magino house. Significantly, Ogawa is the smallest figure, and Daisuke's father, Iizuka Toshio, is simply missing. Drawing courtesy of the Iizuka family.

An enormous set of rules suddenly fell into place, only to be lifted when everyone left.

This movement between Tokyo and Yamagata forced Hatanaka to live by the same rhythm. Life was fun when no one was around except Mikado and the kids. However, when the staff filled the house, she worked extremely hard. With their ever limited resources, she had to turn menu planning to an art. The archives contain an extremely unusual, multivolume document from these days called the *Daidokoro Nikki (Kitchen Diary).* Handfuls of small note pads record every single meal eaten by Ogawa Pro for years on end. This was necessary because they had so little money to work with. All the meals were mapped out down to the gram, along with projected budgets. Only then would Hatanaka and other staff members venture out to the stores, where the shopkeepers were always thrilled to see them come because they bought in bulk. They would buy everything they needed while being extremely careful not to exceed their budget.

Back at the house, Ogawa demanded real meals for at least lunch and dinner. He disliked fish and vegetables so the meals centered on cheap meats and heavy sauces. If it was oily, Ogawa loved it; everyone else craved the more simple pleasures of fermented soybeans and dried fish, but Ogawa decided the menu according to his narrow tastes, predilections that probably killed him in the end. If he did not get what he craved, someone would be criticized. Hatanaka recalls serving curry without a proper accoutrement, and Ogawa made the entire staff wait a couple of hours—their meals getting cold under their noses—while he chewed her out. Above and beyond Ogawa's stringent demands, it was a considerable feat to cook for seventeen people day in and day out. By the time they had finished cleaning up for one meal, it was time to prepare the next one. Even when the staff returned to Tokyo, the women had to make *bento* lunches for everyone because Ogawa hated roadside food.

The most difficult time for the women was rice-planting season. As part of Ogawa Pro's attempt to study and reproduce the lifestyle of the village, the collective's women performed the traditional women's work. This meant some fun activities like learning how to make the pickled vegetables Tohoku is famous for—by the vat. But it also included the difficult task of picking and bundling sprouts for planting the following day. It was backbreaking labor that started first thing in the morning and lasted all day; the Ogawa Pro women still had to make meals for seventeen while doing this kind of work. During the planting itself, they also had to prepare and serve tea for the breaks. Neighbor Kimura Shigeko—who taught them everything about making local foods and the common sense of village life—told Hatanaka, "Now you can see how tough women have it." She performed her work with ease, while the Ogawa Pro women struggled to catch up. It was a strange and friendly kind of competition, seasoned village woman versus green city girls, and the latter were on their own. When Iizuka attempted to help his wife take care of things, Ogawa criticized him. As Hatanaka sees it, she was Ogawa Pro's *oyome-san* (bride); Shiraishi was her *shutome* (mother-in-law), and her own husband Iizuka was the *kojuto* (one's husband's brother). Ogawa's role goes unnamed.

Things changed when Hatanaka left after nearly seven years of this lifestyle. First, Shiraishi took over the *Kitchen Diary,* but she simultaneously played the role of the faithful and protective wife. More significant were the new female members, Mitsumori Yoko and Hirose Satomi. They represented a new breed. Up to this point, all the women of Ogawa Pro were activists first, and filmmakers second if at all. These new women were fresh graduates of art schools, which were opening up film and video production courses across Japan. Mitsumori, for example, came from

Musashino Art University. She made an excellent 8mm documentary about her father's role in World War II, an experience he declines to discuss (so perhaps it should not be surprising that she chose to enter Ogawa Pro). These women aspired to become filmmakers through Ogawa Pro, and plainly refused to be restricted to the kitchen. It was evidence of a new era when women could potentially speak their minds and pursue their interests more aggressively. Mitsumori and Hirose are also examples of an emerging generation of female documentarists exemplified by Kawase Naomi. They graduated from art universities and typically chose the personal film as their mode of expression.

Nearly the only time that the women are mentioned in Ogawa Pro's newsletters is January 26, 1975, when they performed the Onnabisho ceremony, the women's celebration they learned during the production of *Heta Village*. *Ogawa News #5* makes special note of this, leaving the impression that the only time that the women are given voice is when it has something specifically to do with their gender. The women do not write articles and are not mentioned in the production notes or the blow-by-blow accounts of the production process in *Ogawa Pro News*. Working through the archival records of the collective, there are moments when this division of labor jumps out from the pages. For example, in one of the many notebooks of the directing unit, an anonymous author notes a visit from Tsuchimoto Noriaki on Christmas 1976 and transcribes Ogawa's comments after the director left; Ogawa felt everyone's fatigue and need for energizing, and his description separates Ogawa Pro into three sections: the directing unit, the production unit, and the women *(onna no hitotachi)* who are obviously excluded from the previous two categories. Sensitive to this issue, Regina Ulwer focused on the role of women in her film about Ogawa Pro entitled *Hare to Ke* (*Hare to ke—Das besondere und der Alltag,* 1988). The director's questions of Shiraishi Yoko draw the admission that her job is cooking, making her visibly uncomfortable. According to the farmers in both Heta Village and Furuyashiki Village, the women rarely came to the shoots. In Furuyashiki, they only got to know Shiraishi after Ogawa's death. Few of the films make the women's role clear. *Construction of Iwayama Tower* credits Nakano Chihiro and Shiraishi for *kaji* ("housework"). Elsewhere, they get credits like *shinko* ("logistics") when they're lucky to be acknowledged at all.

Fuseya notes that after Hatanaka and (his wife) Kawada left the collective for independent lives, they basically ended up paying for their husband's careers because Ogawa Pro could not provide adequate financial support for all the work they put into filmmaking. Yumoto's wife stirred up a firestorm in her *Hare to Ke* interview by comparing Ogawa Pro members to "corporate warriors" (*kigyo senshi*) that are so wrapped up in work that they neglect their families and ignore their wives and children. This comment infuriated many of the former and contemporary members of Ogawa Pro upon the film's release. What could be more insulting than the equation of the filmmakers' social, political, and artistic commitment to the mindless march of capital's machine? How could one reduce their artistic achievement to the production of consumer items?

Ulwer's criticism did begin sensitizing members to the sexual politics of their organizational structure, but it failed to penetrate to the far larger issues that this sexism is symptomatic of. To use a word like *failed* might, to some, indicate that I imperiously suggest that feminism was a necessary or natural—and thus missing—stage in the development of Japanese film (although the film world's imperviousness to it has had material implications for any women interested in careers in film). Furthermore, it lets Western filmmakers off the hook, as if collectives like the American Newsreels treated women much better (they didn't).

Rather, what this comparison between the roles of women and gender politics in Japan and U.S. film worlds reveals is a deep, dogged authoritarianism that carried over from the Old to the New Left. Reflecting on his generation's deep antagonism for the older independent filmmakers, Tamura Masaki suggests, "You don't attack someone so harshly unless you are very close. Why else would you care? How else would you establish your difference?" In retrospect, it would appear that the critiques of the Old Left were an honest attempt to renovate the relationship between art and politics but without substantially rethinking social politics. Indeed, looking at the way Ogawa Pro actually functioned, it was obviously an autarchy. For all the rhetoric about collective production, there was a crystal clear hierarchy with Ogawa in the unquestioned seat of power. The structure was relatively faint during the Sanrizuka Series, but after 1975 and the move to Magino, the isolation amplified the hierarchical roles. Those who could not keep up with the debate were swiftly purged. This structure may also be seen as an analog of the nation-state itself. The authoritarianism that all these factors point to may have left Japanese critical theory and documentary filmmaking of the early 1970s an inflexible discourse incapable of meeting the challenges of a social world undergoing massive change.

This is precisely what is suggested by the extraordinary Adachi Masao, whose example offers a second and final perspective on the apparent end of social movement documentary. As a student in the film studies department of the arts faculty of Nihon University, Adachi met a number of other budding filmmakers interested in breaking the rules of convention. Along with Jonouchi Motoharu, Hirano Katsumi, and others, Adachi formed the Film

Research Group, an *eiken* that played a key role in the postwar avant-garde. After an impressive set of shorts, such as *A Wooden Bowl* (*Wan,* 1961) and *Shadow Chains* (*Sain,* 1963), Adachi entered Wakamatsu Productions, the production company infamous for its ultra-low budget, often ultra-radical pink films. Adachi wrote the screenplays for Wakamatsu Koji's most important films, including *The Embryo Hunts in Secret* (*Taiji ga mitsuryo suru toki,* 1966), *Go, Go You Who Are a Virgin for the Second Time* (*Yuke, yuke nidome no shojo,* 1969), *Sex Jack* (*Seizoku—sekkusu jakku,* 1970) and *Ecstasy of Angels* (*Tenchi no kokotsu,* aka *Angelic Orgasm,* 1972). In addition to directing his own feature films under the Wakamatsu banner, he provided the screenplays for Oshima's *Three Resurrected Drunkards* (*Kaette kita yopparai,* 1968) and *Diary of a Shinjuku Thief* (*Shinjuku dorobo nikki,* 1969), and had an acting role in *Death By Hanging* (*Koshikei,* 1968). (As assistant director he also directed the amazing trailer for *Death by Hanging,* which features a passionate speech by Oshima Nagisa while choking on a noose.) When the firing of Nikkatsu director Suzuki Seijun led to a movement by fans and intellectuals to reinstate him, Adachi helped organize the protest movement. The intensifying politicization of Adachi's activities led him to spearhead the rejuvenation of the film journal *Eiga Hihyo* from 1969 to 1973. His contributions were among the most radical film criticism of the period.

One of the frequent visitors to the editorial offices of *Eiga Hihyo* was Shigenobu Fusaku, a leader of the Japanese Red Army, whose own offices happened to be in the neighborhood. Adachi became interested in the politics and activism of the Japanese Red Army and began entertaining the idea of making a film through their auspices. This would be a chance to put his theoretical writings to the test. The film would be a laboratory for testing his hypothesis about a "movement cinema" *("undo no eiga")* opposing both a cinema of corporations and a cinema of auteurs. So when Oshima Nagisa used his cultural capital in Europe to get Wakamatsu and Adachi invited to the Cannes International Film Festival in 1970, they brought along a camera and a plan. Oshima was showing *The Ceremony* (*Gishiki,* 1971) and *The Secret Tale of Tokyo Before and After the War* (*Tokyo senso sengo hiwa,* 1970), and Wakamatsu and Adachi screened their *Sexjack* and *Raped in White* (*Okasareta hakui,* 1967). On their way back to Japan, they dropped by Palestine to visit Shigenobu and make a documentary. Wakamatsu describes the tenor of the production:

> When I tried to get permission from them to film from the inside, they asked me if there were an emergency, would I pick up a gun or a camera. I said I'd grab a gun. After that, I was training to be a guerrilla every day. Dressed in guerrilla gear, drawing water, digging ditches, learning how to use and take

apart a gun—all guerrilla training. They didn't let me film at all. Then one day they finally let me film, that day only, so I had to do everything, filming and interviewing, in the space of a day.[8]

The result was entitled *The Red Army/PFLP: Declaration of World War* (*Sekigun/PFLP: Sekai senso sengen*, 1971).[9] As the production company finished the film, Adachi paved the way for its release through constant writing in the pages of *Eiga Hihyo* and other publications. He tried to codify the structure of a movement cinema produced independently, exhibited independently, and designed to dismantle the industrial structure of the cinema and its ideological underpinnings. The company called this its "news film," which sent the world a declaration of war. It is an odd film that seems to miss the lessons Ogawa was teaching in Sanrizuka. Adachi called for radical films to attend to *fukei* (scenery, a view), to explore the organic connections between humans and the land that one can photograph, the very land that people inhabit and spill blood for. Curiously, in his film, this call becomes manifest as many dull scenes of guerrilla training and long takes shot from the windows of traveling cars, interspersed with slight interviews with members of the Red Army and the Popular Front for the Liberation of Palestine.[10] The Red Army drove the film print around Japan in what was called the "Red Bus," setting up screenings wherever it went.

Adachi made a number of additional trips back to Palestine after the production of *Red Army/PFLP: Declaration of World War*. On one of them he was even arrested and deported.[11] It seems Adachi was also beginning to undergo some serious self-reflection about what he was doing. There are hints of this in the film itself, which is partly structured as a dialectic between two declarative theses. The PFLP exclaimed that "The best form of propaganda is armed revolt." This slogan is stated in bold characters in the film's intertitles and is intercut with footage of a bomb exploding in a parked aircraft. At the same time, the film itself—along with all the articles and *zadankai* surrounding its reception and production—was created under the supposition that the best form of propaganda was cinema! The film does not overtly resolve this collision of claims; however, in a sequence of intertitles inciting armed resistance, the intertitle for "muzzle" is printed backwards, hinting that the Palestinian strategy of taking up arms may backfire in the context of Japan. This would seem to leave filmmaking and other strategies the upper hand.

Not long after the release of *Red Army/PFLP: Declaration of World War*, Adachi appeared at a rally for an interview, subsequently published in the Red Army's newsletter. It suggests an artist in crisis, doubting the political efficacy of his art:

> In Japan it is the problem of, "What are we fighting for?" We're nothing but filmmakers, nothing but Shinjuku drunkards. But then, (Palestinians) have nothing other than a fight for life or death. No matter how far you take it, the distance between us is vast. Or say we are in their midst. Even if we can physically or morally become guerrillas, it is different. . . .[12]

In that critical moment at the early 1970s, Adachi began publicly doubting the success of Japan's movement cinema, seemingly asking Yamane's question, but posing it in the present tense. In a 1974 article entitled "The Last Gasp of Film Movement," Adachi summarizes what they had tried to accomplish, which was nothing other than a reorganization of Japanese cinema. However, in the end, he comes to a stark conclusion:

> Oshima aptly announces, "I in no way believe in any 'Cinema of Movement.' In other words, it is a 'Cinema of Auteurs.' Cinema increasingly moves toward individual expression, to the exclusion of all else. This 'Cinema of Movement' does not have a chance."[13] These regulations for the "Cinema of Auteurs" being pronounced by Oshima actualize the last gasp of a "Cinema of Movement." This pessimistic view regresses the film = movement circuit to "Movement = Auteur = Corporation" and is the flipside of Solanas' optimism.[14]

Shortly after the publication of "The Last Gasp of a Film Movement," just as Ogawa moved to Yamagata and Hara and Suzuki appeared on the scene, Adachi appeared to demonstrate his answer to the unresolved dialectical clash structuring his *Declaration of World War*. The Shinjuku drunkard decided what to fight for.

Adachi Masao gave up his art and became a guerrilla.

He joined the Red Army and went to the Middle East never to return. His whereabouts were unknown except to close friends until 1997, when a group of Red Army members was arrested in Lebanon and Adachi was among them. That he has been unbending in his beliefs was evidenced—while he sat in a Lebanese jail awaiting extradition—by his response to an *Eiga Geijutsu* poll concerning Elia Kazan's Oscar for lifetime achievement. The question was, "When you evaluate a film director or scenario writer, what determines your evaluation: 'works and achievements' or 'way of life'? And why?" The older directors who have figured into this history of Ogawa Pro, such as Kuroki Kazuo, predictably refused to separate the two. However, there was a distinct tendency for the younger generation to evaluate Kazan only by his work; in an accompanying roundtable, one of the editors suggested this revealed the prevalence of the text-centric approach to cinema associated with Hasumi Shigehiko.[15] In contrast, the last response in the poll was Adachi's, sent from his prison cell:

> Regarding Kazan's award, I would not applaud it. Moreover, I cannot forgive his attitude and position. This is not just as an informant, but I cannot forgive his attitude towards those people that remained. . . . Kazan has no regret or remorse, and even asked for our forgiveness. What a disgrace! In the case of Chaplin, he was wise and sought shelter in Europe.
>
> At the same time, I too was a fan of Kazan's films in my youth. Recently, compared to the greatest crime of the twentieth century, the one perpetrated by Gorbechev, can we not forgive all of the sins, all of the informers, and all of liars? This is what I think.[16]

After his extradition to Japan and trial for passport fraud, Adachi has told the story of all those years in Palestine.[17] He was living in Beirut and hardly hiding. More significantly, he revealed that he did not go to Lebanon intending to quit filmmaking. He took a circuitous route to the Middle East, traveling through North Africa to watch and compare strategies for political filmmaking. Once among the Palestinians, he actually began filming a sequel to *Declaration of World War,* and basically got stuck there as the political situation there deteriorated and his home country made it clear he was to be arrested and imprisoned. Unable to return home, he continued to film the Palestinian situation and help the struggle in various capacities as an intellectual and filmmaker. Unfortunately, his footage for the sequel was destroyed in an Israeli bombing. Thus, while it appeared that Adachi was probably the only filmmaker anywhere in the world to actually reject political filmmaking for armed resistance, the story is quite a bit more complex.

Nevertheless, in Adachi's absence, his example was repeated to the extent that it achieved mythic proportions: Adachi was the brave warrior that put down his camera and picked up a real weapon. Recall Wakamatsu's story, where the PFLP asked him whether he could pick up a gun or a camera in an emergency. This is a perfect example of the discourse Adachi's profile became iconic for. Something was going on in the Japanese political film world in the early 1970s, and it demanded a choice. Regardless of the reality of his situation, the myth of Adachi's choice seems to be paradigmatic for the decision facing all political documentary filmmakers at that moment—give up politics for art or abandon art for politics.

The Adachi meme, his apparent decision that the best form of propaganda was indeed armed struggle, must also be considered in the context of the self-annihilation of the Red Army in the Asama Cottage Incident and its reverberations throughout the New Left.[18] The shock of this incident, along with the continuing terrorism of the Red Army in the Middle East, cannot be underestimated for the way it contributed to the alienation of the New Left from movement politics. Ogawa himself appears to have, in retrospect, considered the Asama Cottage Incident and other terrorist acts the end point of the passion of the student movement, seeing it in terms of inevitable failure while resolving not to minimize the value of the earlier activism.[19] Performance artist Hori Kosai, who was an avid fan of Ogawa Pro, recalls that after the Asama Cottage Incident the participatory atmosphere in the theaters died away. The thought of shouting at the screen in a chorus of catcalls and cheers became embarrassing, and the representations of reality the screen offered became opaque.

At the very same time, the Asama Cottage Incident marks an important turning point for televisual documentary. During the entire ten-day siege, all the television networks broadcast the standoff live. Nihon Television, TBS, Fuji, and Net (now TV Asahi), each stayed live for around nine hours, deploying some 340 television people behind the barricades with the police. Before this, there were only occasional live reports.[20] On the final day, NHK set a record for live television in Japan with ten hours and twenty minutes of nonstop broadcast from Nagano, starting at 9:40 in the morning until 8:00 at night. The ratings combining all networks showed an astounding 98.2 percent viewership (as compared to only 54.7 percent for the biggest event of the Sapporo Olympics). In other words, it is no exaggeration to say that the entire nation was watching. Spectators were glued to their sets, nervously awaiting the next turn of events and watching the remarkably static, artless images of live television.

This puts the stylistic transformation of *The Construction of Iwayama Tower* and *Heta Village* into a new perspective. We could see these changing conditions creating a radically new relationship to the screen, where television offered new experiences of the moving image, and the mechanisms of political mimesis no longer functioned. To draw on old analogies in a new manner, audiences and artists now found the independent screen transforming from a window on the collective world to a canvas for the individual artist.

Historiographic Caveat

I have dramatized the generational differences represented onstage at Yamagata by Iizuka and Kawase Naomi. However, it is crucial not to neglect the fact that there were two other filmmakers on that stage, Ise Shin'ichi and Kanai Katsu. Ise makes very fine, very conventional documentaries;[21] Kanai is known for his wildly experimental films that also have a documentary touch.[22] As the other two filmmakers argued over Yamane's provocation about the generational split on group versus individual, Ise and Kanai looked on, slightly puzzled, wondering what it had to do with them. They said as much.[23] Their existence cannot be accounted for in this topology of self and other. They represent two large areas of practice, the conventional documentary, often made for television, and the avant-garde, that are largely excluded from the Japanese historiography of postwar nonfiction film in Japan. What we have here in these discourses surrounding *shutaisei* is a historical narration that suppresses vast areas of practice while offering a powerful explanation for others with more prestige.

For these reasons, I must offer the following historiographic caveat: I am presenting the strong version of postwar Japanese documentary history, but this rhetorical strength is precisely what makes it useful for present-day observers. If such tropes of discourse thin out our sense of history, they are also unavoidable because they attained such cogent powers of explanation *and affect*. Produced here by the pressures of postwar politics, they provide a measure for the filmmaking identity. The artists who emerged in the late 1950s and 1960s transformed their art in reaction to the authoritarianism of both the war and the high-growth economy. They searched for a form of representation that did not involve an imperial or technocratic signification that overpowered and dominated the referential world. In theory, and especially in practice, they accomplished what appears to be a radical democratization of the relationship between *shutai* and *taisho*. Often inserting an equal sign between the words *film* and *movement*, they started with the assumption that such a public art form—so easily reproduced and presented to masses of strangers—was so rooted in the world that it could not but affect the world. Clearly, it possessed the power to complicate a public sphere.

The Invitation

Nineteen seventy-five was a busy year for Ogawa Pro. The filmmakers finished the shooting, editing, and initial screenings of *Dokkoi! Song of the Bottom* (*Dokkoi! Ningenbushi*, 1975). They borrowed a work shed in Magino, reformed the interior, upped its amperage to handle the filmmaking activities, and built a bathhouse in back. They also borrowed a 100 by 24 meter rice paddy and started learning the skills of farmers. They moved their Shinjuku office to a small apartment in Ogikubo, where they reconstructed a postproduction studio by adding walls for an editing room, office, screening/sound mixing room, and projection booth. Finally, they also shot and completed their first film in Yamagata.

As noted previously, Ogawa Pro had no choice but to become deeply involved in the distribution process, in contrast to a time when the films very nearly distributed themselves. Ogawa himself ran the Tohoku screenings, from the Sendai showings in July 1974 until those in Iwate Hanamaki at the end of the year. In the course of these screenings, the subject of representing farmers and their worldview repeatedly arose, and the collective began to think about moving its home base. Ogawa wanted to try entering a new village, perhaps one where nothing particularly unusual was happening—the exact opposite of Ogawa Pro's current situation in Sanrizuka. He once glibly mentioned the possibility of a house in nearby Saitama owned by Shiraishi's father, an idea squashed immediately by Shiraishi's silent frown. Ultimately, she was saved by events surrounding the showings in Kaminoyama City in Yamagata Prefecture, where the audiences were particularly large and quite vocal. One of the things that made Kaminoyama special was a literary and culture movement with roots in the prewar period. For the Yamagata screenings, the collective enlisted the help of a group called Groundwater (Chikasui), a relationship that changed everything for Ogawa Pro. Groundwater's driving force was Makabe Jin, a renowned farmer poet who had spearheaded culture and education movements in Yamagata since before the war (when Makabe studied with Ozaki Kihachi and Takamura Kotaro and wrote from an antimilitarist, anarchist stance). Groundwater published its own journal and organized activities that celebrated their local culture.

Groundwater helped Ogawa Pro borrow what was once an old bar to live and work out of. For more than a month before the screenings, the filmmakers collaborated with local youth—mostly farmers—in putting out the word and selling tickets. Thanks to Groundwater, the Kaminoyama screenings of *Heta Village* in Yamagata Prefecture were unusually large and enthusiastic. At the same time, audiences were surprisingly harsh on Ogawa's exclusion of the labor involved in farming. They wanted to know why he didn't show the work. That was the true face of farmers, the only honest way to understand their world. Although Ogawa Pro filmmakers had shot an enormous amount of footage about plowing, planting, and harvesting, everything that constituted life and work in Sanrizuka, it was true that they did not include much of this material in the final films. This was about to change.

During preparations for the Kaminoyama event, Ogawa struck up a friendship with Groundwater's Kimura Michio, a farmer and garbage collector (it was increasingly difficult to survive exclusively on agriculture by the 1970s). Kimura lived in a small village down the road from Kaminoyama City and was deeply impressed by *Heta Village*. He was a sympathizer of the farmers at Sanrizuka and had regularly offered donations over the years. However, to this point he had never seen an Ogawa Pro film; he recalls seeing a poster for *Summer in Sanrizuka* at a soba shop in the next village, but did not care at the time. However, after the *Heta Village* screenings, Ogawa stayed in Kaminoyama for a few weeks to mop up operations, collecting money from presold tickets and the like. Every once in a while, he would accompany Kimura on his morning rounds, sitting shotgun in the garbage truck. On one such day, Kimura told Ogawa that he thought that *Heta Village* was the sum of their experiences in Sanrizuka and that they had nowhere else to go. Why not come to his village, Magino? He threw out the suggestion half-jokingly. Little did he know that Ogawa already had his staff thinking about new places to move to, from the possibility of a food co-op in Kyushu with Yumoto to other sites like Osaka and Hokkaido.

Much to the surprise of Kimura Michio, Ogawa Pro accepted his offer and moved to Yamagata in 1975 to make rice and films.

Magino is a small village of ninety-nine households—227 men and 259 women in 1975—and is tucked between the high mountains and Kaminoyama City, a hot springs resort town. There is a fire tower and shrine on one side of Magino and a few other monuments and smaller shrines scattered around the rest of the village. Walk 50 to 100 yards in any direction, and you are surrounded by rice fields. On one side, an expansive valley opens across a river and views of distant peaks. On the other side rises the hulking massif of Mount Zao, an old volcano and one of Japan's larger mountains at 1,841 meters above sea level. This was a huge move. Picture the New York Newsreel collective moving to rural Montana. In the mid-1990s, a bullet train was completed from Tokyo to Yamagata City, and it stopped at Kaminoyama hot springs. This made the journey from the capital a manageable three and a half hours. However, in 1975, that same trip required a long day of train rides or an exhausting eight-hour drive on narrow, serpentine roads. Makabe and city councilor Sato Shozo supported the invitation, recommending Magino by suggesting its strengths were what it lacked. It had lots of nothing in particular: no protests, no student movement sects, no riot police, no field hospitals. On the contrary, what it did enjoy was a generous supply of conservative Liberal Democratic Party supporters. It was an extraordinary decision.

The staff that agreed to the move and stayed on included Ogawa, Shiraishi, Fuseya, Kawada, Asahi, Mikado, Nosaka, Iizuka, Kikuchi, Hara, Hayashi, Watanabe, Yoshida, Takahashi, Kawaguchi, Hatanaka, and Yumoto—as well as Iizuka and Hatanaka's two children, Daisuke and Shusuke. Seventeen adults, give or take a head or two, lived in that tiny house in the first few years. Yoshida had left Ogawa Pro earlier and moved to Minamata, where he spent an extended period of time collecting oral histories. He returned to Ogawa Pro with a thick manuscript under his arm, which would eventually be published in an Oya Soichi Prize–winning book based on his research. It was particularly controversial for the way it publicly dealt with the Minamata victims' feelings about their own sexuality. He returned to Ogawa Pro with the manuscript and two of the researchers that assisted him in Minamata, Takahashi Shinji and his wife Kawaguchi.

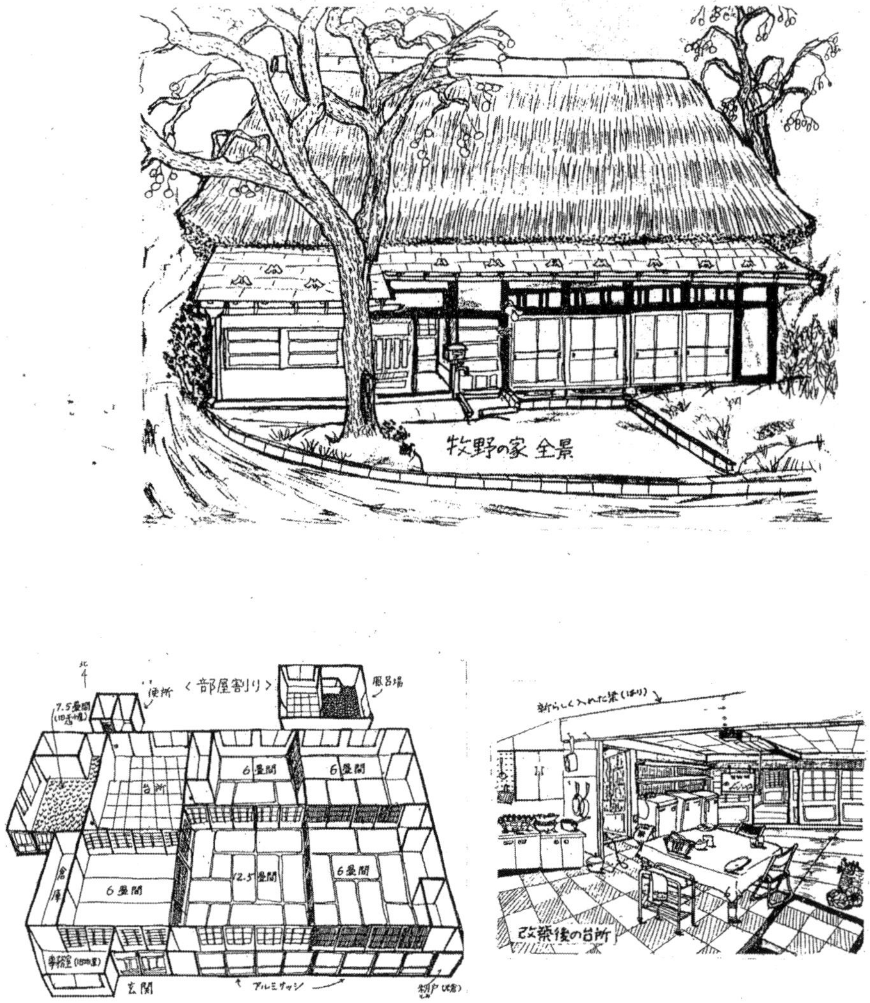

Mikado Sadatoshi's drawings of the Magino house from Ogawa Pro's newsletter. One entered in the lower left and either turned right into the living/working space or proceeded straight into the kitchen. The two buildings out back are the toilet and bath. At night, people slept everywhere. The drawing at lower right shows the kitchen.

The house they borrowed was a century-old barn. It actually belonged to a neighbor that had planned on destroying it and selling the land. Kimura bought the building, thinking that it could be used for something at a later date, and offered it to Ogawa for the time being. The house was not in move-in condition. It had recently been used as a workshop for raising silkworms, and a 7.5-mat room on one side was a horse stall. Borrowing and buying new materials, and drawing on the expertise of various supporters with electrical and other skill sets, they renovated the barn and transformed it into a home for living and filmmaking. The house basically had seven rooms. At the entranceway was a common room with a large closet they turned into the office. Behind this room was the kitchen, which they completely renovated, and the adjacent horse stall, which they converted into a bedroom. In the back of the house were two 6-mat bedrooms, one with three refrigerators. To the right of the common room was a 12.5-mat room with a coal-burning *kotatsu,* and next to that a mini-studio for shooting, editing, and projecting films. They had to construct a bathhouse in back, next to the outhouse. At night, every room necessarily transformed into a bedroom, since anywhere from ten to twenty-five men, women, and children slept there.

Life was difficult. The quarters were cramped, and entire families were living and working together. Farming is tiring work anywhere in the world, and these people were new to the profession. Like other farmers in the region, they had to hold second jobs to survive, and even then they were as impoverished as ever. To add to the challenge, Yamagata is notoriously cold in the winter. I vividly recall a January visit to the Magino house, sleeping under a foot's worth of futons in an unheated room, and taking a scalding bath in such freezing temperatures that water spilling onto the cement floor quickly turned into a sheet of ice.

It was difficult for Kimura Michio as well. First, he failed to properly consult his family about the invitation extended to Ogawa Pro. It was one thing to invite them to Yamagata, but quite another to put so many people in an adjoining house. He heard from other quarters as well. The villagers in Magino were hardly the farmer-soldiers of Sanrizuka. Most were loyal supporters of the Liberal Democratic Party and were alarmed at the "Trotskyites" suddenly appearing in their midst.

Kimura tells a great story about all the people concerned about the new neighbors.[24] One day, he was called to the home of Kaminoyama's mayor, Suzuki Keizo. He inquired, "Kimura-kun, there's a rumor flying around that some red birds from Sanrizuka swooped into Kaminoyama. Everything's okay, right?" Kimura answered, "Mr. Mayor, we'll never be trouble for you. If we do something bad I will offer you my head, even though my head's not worth anything." A few years later, Kimura received a call from Okuyama Shigeo, the number-two man at city hall. "Kimura-kun, there's a peace officer sitting in my office that says he wants to meet you. You'll come won't you?" Kimura went and found Okuyama and the detective. After exchanging greetings, the detective said, "On the ○ of ○ you are holding a meeting in the break lounge of such and such an office."

The detective knew a lot.

"By all means hold it as planned." And then he proceeded to ask Kimura to take careful note of who attended and who sat next to whom.

Kimura responded, "Iya, iya, I stopped organizing that kind of political meeting."

The detective continued, "And wouldn't you send me all the newsletters and pamphlets you're getting from student agitators and activist groups?"

"I'm so busy with farming and collecting trash in the city, I don't open or read any of it. I'm using it in the bathroom."

"What a waste. You know it's pretty difficult for us to get a hold of that kind of material. Please don't use it for the toilet. Give it to us."

Kimura sat without answering.

"Of course, we'll pay your real expenses."

In other words, the man was asking Kimura to be a spy. He sat thinking, this detective is pressuring me, but didn't say it out loud.

Okuyama interjected, "Kimura-kun isn't that kind of man."

"Well, would it be okay if I came out to your house once a month from now on?"

Kimura demurred, but starting with the planting season the detective showed up every month. He'd sit in front of the house all afternoon until Kimura returned from the fields. Kimura's mother—who loved meeting people and would become famous for her monologue at the end of *The Sundial Carved with a Thousand Years of Notches*—would tell him, "A guest has been waiting all day for you. I fed him some soba." His mother was kindhearted and loved everybody.

Kimura would always tell the detective, "There's nothing much to talk about."

"Okay. See you next month," and he would leave without protest. Then the next month, he would show up and ask, "I suppose nothing has changed, right?"

"Nothing happens in this village. Of course, there's nothing to talk about."

The detective would respond, "I notice that next door, Ogawa Shinsuke's not in. I suppose he's in Tokyo, right?" or "At the moment, there's only twelve people next door, including the kids. But there were seventeen of them when they came to this village, right?" or "Iizuka and Nosaka are in Iwate and Hokkaido for the screening movement, aren't they? Today is Mikado out helping someone in the fields?"

They knew everyone's name and where they were at a given time. After half a year had passed, the detective stopped coming. Instead, a local policeman stopped by the house once or twice a month.

"I suppose nothing has changed, right?" he'd ask, just like the previous detective.

"Iyaa, this is such a quiet, sleepy village. Nothing's changed," said Kimura's wife, Shigeko . . . he got sick of the bother and had her take over. Sometimes he'd listen in on the conversation, which reminded him of a comedy routine.

"No one in the village has died of illness? No one's done something terrible to stray cats?" he'd ask.

And she'd reply, "This is such a healthy village. No one's died lately. And I haven't heard any stories about dogs getting hit by cars, or stray cats being attacked."

This went on for quite some time. There were two probable reasons. First, in those days Ogawa Pro was seen less as a film production company than one of the many sects that participated in the anti-airport protests. They're a Trotskyist group, so you better watch out, thought most of the village. When the collective built a shed next to the house and filled it with beakers, microscopes, and bottles filled with various chemicals, the villagers noticed these materials through the window. These were actually being used for conducting the group's studies of rice agriculture, but the villagers figured they were making bombs. It was no wonder the police also thought they were terrorists, or an activist group out to agitate the farmers of Magino just as they did in Sanrizuka. The thought is laughable if you imagine this small village in the middle of the northern mountains. The monthly surveillance of Ogawa Pro did not stop until *"Nippon": Furuyashiki Village* (*"Nippon koku": Furuyashiki-mura,* 1983) won the FIPRESCI Prize at the Berlin International Film Festival, some ten years after Ogawa Pro moved to Magino from Sanrizuka.

Actually, the police were not the only ones concerned about the film collective. Although Groundwater was instrumental in the success of the Yamagata screenings of *Heta Village,* some in the group were critical of Ogawa Pro. When these Groundwater members heard about Kimura's invitation to move to Magino, they came down on the farmer poet. Most of them were faithful members of the Communist Party, and for all practical purposes considered the film collective a Trotskyist group of terrorists. Enduring severe protest, Kimura ignored them and refused to rescind his invitation.

Furthermore, at about the same time he was called into the city hall to meet the detective, Kimura was visited by the famous proletarian novelist Kurahara Korehito, then the head of the culture section of the Communist Party's national office in Tokyo. Kurahara asked Kimura to rethink what he was doing and prevent Ogawa Pro from moving. Kimura refused. Kurahara tried another tactic:

"Well then, how about if you keep an eye on them? Keep a daily log, note the names of people at screenings, and that kind of thing?"

Kimura refused this familiar offer, although Kurahara subsequently came to his Magino home once more to ask the same questions. Kimura never told the filmmakers about these attempts at surveillance until long after Ogawa's death.

Ogawa's decision to move from Sanrizuka, the political hot spot that Ogawa Pro was so deeply associated with, to the quiet village of Magino has puzzled many people over the years. Many thought—and still think—that Ogawa Pro was turning its collective backs on the movement in a latter-day version of *tenko* (the ideological apostasy of the prewar era). Some accused the group of *hiyorimi,* or fence-sitting opportunism.[25] Athénée Français' Matsumoto Masamichi—one of the people who eventually bought the rights to the Ogawa Pro catalog—recalls holding a film screening/talk show in the late 1970s during which a Sanrizuka activist grabbed Ogawa in the hallway and demanded to know why he threw away Sanrizuka and left for Yamagata.[26] Within Ogawa Pro itself, a vigorous debate ensued before the final determination was made. And when the decision was in favor of moving, quite a few members quit.

In retrospect, some people think that Ogawa saw something others failed to recognize—that "something" that happened in the 1970s—and it was time to move on. Others emphasize that Ogawa could imagine leaving the fight in Sanrizuka because he had a different relationship to politics, that he was from the very beginning more interested in movies than politics, or even that he was fundamentally apolitical at heart. Looking at the films and the proclamations that Ogawa left behind, the latter explanation is difficult to accept. Iizuka suggests,

> There was a politics to it, and it was connected to the assertion that you can't simply think about rice. You have to *do* it in order to talk about it. Living communally, these values displace profit and personal gain. This was the time of the Cultural Revolution and this was the way people in urban centers were reading Mao. A favorite Maoism from the time went "Lots of Talk/Empty

> Hands." Our generation grew up with the high growth economy, but was not as happy and hopeful as our parents were. We were all talk with empty hands. So joining Ogawa Pro was a way of *living*. Going to Yamagata to farm represented a continuation of this spirit. My grandparents were making their own food and clothing, and now I would be, too!

Kimura Michio offers the most interesting explanation. Kimura basically tendered the invitation to move to Yamagata for selfish reasons: he was bored. Magino was an incredibly quiet, dull place. He likened it to a swamp where all the vegetable matter was in the process of putrefaction. Bringing the filmmakers of the Sanrizuka Series to Magino would be like draining the water from the swamp and turning it into productive soil. It promised to make life interesting. Reflecting back on his life shortly after being diagnosed with stomach cancer, Kimura felt that despite all the hassles and problems they had with Ogawa Pro over the years, the collective's stay in his village was the most exciting experience in his life. Ogawa brought a strange excitement and an electric energy to sleepy Magino.

Ironically, Kimura felt Ogawa desired a life in Magino precisely because it *was* swampy. At Sanrizuka he had experienced "the limits of politics" and now wanted to experience the *seimeiryoku* of farmers, their life force and vitality. This came out strong in *Heta Village* in their turn from the riots to plunge into the farmers' daily lives. Magino was a quiet place. For someone living in Tokyo, Yamagata had a remote feel—a sense that only intensified as one moved from the cities and train stations into the mountain villages. It was just the kind of swamp that Ogawa was looking for, a place where he could think about village Japan without the political struggles that increasingly felt like diminishing distractions.

Despite the quiet surface, villages like Magino were undergoing sweeping structural changes, transformations whose politics Ogawa studiously avoided in his films. For example, starting in 1960, farming in Japan became increasingly mechanized, especially after tractors appeared on the scene in the 1970s. The government helped stimulate this process with legislation passed in 1961, shortly after passing the U.S. Security Treaty. Magino lagged somewhat behind the typical village because the fields were smaller, and most planting was done by hand when Ogawa Pro arrived on the scene. To get the machines, the farmers would work as *dekasegi,* spending the winter months in large cities like Tokyo to make and save money. As the machines cut down on the amount of time needed to farm, people started taking weekday factory jobs and tending fields on weekends, a phenomenon known as *kengyo*. Of the households surrounding the Ogawa house in Magino, only two were able to support themselves entirely through farming. The most radical changes started with the government policy of *Gentan* in

1970, a large-scale directive to decrease rice production; the orders were top-down from the central government, just as in Sanrizuka. There was a grassroots protest movement against these policies—Kimura Michio even wrote a novel in support of the movement[27]—for fear that it would rip apart the fabric of the village economy and culture.

There were other forces heralding massive change, such as Japan's Comprehensive Development Plan (Shinzenkoku Sogo Kaihatsu Keikaku), the central government's plan to change the landscape of the rural areas through the construction of factories, freeways, bullet trains, and airports (Narita should be seen as part of this). Although he worked in the midst of this massive transformation, Ogawa made the curious decision to turn his back on that reality of village life. *Seishin kokkaku hokai* ("collapse of the spiritual infrastructure") became the theme they pursued, says Iizuka, because they saw the backbone breaking in Sanrizuka. They focused on less gritty subjects, such as history and hard science, and the films became more like salvage anthropology attempting to rescue a disappearing culture.

Kimura's sense that Ogawa had experienced the "limits of politics" suggests an overdetermination of reasons converging on Ogawa Pro's decision-making process. In *Ogawa Pro News,* the collective offered an array of logical, practical reasons for abandoning Sanrizuka. Up to this point, it accrued a significant amount of debt. Starting with *Song of the Bottom* and *Interview at Clean Center* (*Kuriin Sentaa homonki,* 1975), Ogawa Pro tried to make films on budgets that remained in the black. Sponsors, tickets, and rentals would pay for the production in the end. However, up to this point the budgets had to support the lives of all the members at the same time. They received no salaries to speak of, money for meals only when they didn't eat as a group, a pittance for clothing and transportation, the rent for the several apartments they lived in, and that was about it. The move to Yamagata was an attempt to separate the budget lines for life and filmmaking. A budget from one of the meeting agendas reveals they were actually spending more on screenings than on life support! With the move to Yamagata, the films would be on their own track of income and expense. Meanwhile, rents would not be necessary since everyone was living communally, and everyone would support the cost of living through farming and side jobs.

For example, there were curious plans that came up after the move—selling coffee to the farmers in the fields who had no time to make their own, or marketing the famous Ogawa Pro curried rice in Kaminoyama (neither of which ever materialized). Ogawa, Nosaka, and Iizuka even visited Kyushu Ogawa Pro, where Honma introduced them to people running food co-ops (although an ulterior motive appears to have been for Ogawa to finally nix Honma's idea for a film on the mines in Kyushu). Once they found out how capital intensive and complicated a co-op was to establish, they decided against attempting one in Kaminoyama. Instead, they took odd jobs like driving one of Kimura Michio's garbage trucks, a position they took turns at.

There were other factors converging on this move to Yamagata, the most significant being that the filmmakers were getting older. It was becoming difficult to maintain such a low-budget lifestyle as they entered their thirties. It is one thing to live frugally in one's youth, and quite another upon getting married and having children. At least two of the key members were now married, and others were considering it. During the production of the Sanrizuka films, these couples had to live apart, but in Yamagata they could live together, albeit in a communal situation. And even if they had no money, at least they would have food in Yamagata. From the perspective of the postwar social landscape, their decision clearly participated in the larger phenomenon of the emerging environmental movement and the retreat of activists to communes in the mountain ranges of the hinterlands. These *chiiki paruchizan* (local partisans) often took up organic farming. For Ogawa Pro, the point was not precisely to make a commune, but rather to live communally to make movies organically—live close to the earth so that you could know it intimately enough to film it.

Furthermore, the move was a way to deal with the sense of crisis in movement politics. Essentially, there was a felt need for a sure footing, a reliable home base. We can find an expression of the same feeling of crisis in the centers of the independent screening movement. While the weak points gave in and disappeared, the most committed groups ensured their survival by building their own permanent theaters. Thus, Nakajima Yo in Hokkaido established Cinema Kino. Kuramoto Toru created the Nagoya Cinématheque, and Nagasawa Yuji built the Forum Theater in Yamagata City. These independent theaters constitute a structural legacy of the 1960s screening movements Jieiso and Ogawa Pro forged, and at the same time were the precursors to the mini-theater boom in the 1990s.

Finally, the filmmakers themselves saw the move as an expression of their desire to pursue their filmmaking without necessarily being tied to political movements. The title of a 1974 meeting agenda for a debate about whether or not to leave Sanrizuka is significant: "From Sanrizuka Ogawa Pro to Documentary Cinema Ogawa Pro."[28] When photography started on their first rice film in May 1978, Iizuka remembers being scolded by Ogawa and Tamura: "Iizuka, you haven't changed your attitude from '*gakusei*' to '*eiga-ya*.'" Thus, the ethos of Ogawa Pro was changing from "student" to "professional," from "activism" to "filmmaking." In Sanrizuka, they did have a Directing Unit *(enshutsu-bu),* but there was an effort to get rid of the hierarchical structure of the Japanese studio system. They were consciously attempting to avoid the reproduction of authoritarian structures; the challenging task at hand was to create nothing less than a new human being. However, in Yamagata they took the form of a production company for all practical purposes—a production company that happened to be living communally. And when they got to Magino, they found roles (not freedom), poverty (not politics), and this in addition to a total loss of privacy. Ironically enough, they had gone back to their old way of making films in a number of substantive aspects. Having joined Ogawa Pro as student activists and never fully leaving that identity behind, many of the members found themselves shocked by these developments.

In contrast, when cameraman Tamura looks back at his career with Ogawa, he senses the films became more interesting to shoot. In the early part of the Sanrizuka Series, they were mostly concerned with capturing the most spectacular confrontations between power and the powerless. He is fond of comparing it to sports. I must admit this took me aback the first time I heard it, at a 1999 event devoted to Tamura's career at the University of Chicago. Curious about their reaction, I recently relayed this comparison to sports to some of the Sanrizuka farmers. They laughed heartily, saying it sounded like something Tamura would say. After thinking about it, they wholeheartedly agreed. In Sanrizuka, it was sports and politics; in Magino, they could be filmmakers and artists. In the course of Tamura's relationship with Ogawa, he gradually found himself able to concentrate on the photography itself. By the Magino Village Story, he felt he was able to put his soul into the images.

Songs from the Bottom

The all-new Ogawa Pro that members imagined would be a flexible organization running on a number of fronts. Instead of offices out in different parts of Japan, they would have units that could operate anywhere. In their production diaries from the time, for example, the people in Yamagata were called the "Magino Unit." They kept the Tokyo office as the base of production matters and fundraising. So there were two poles, Magino and Tokyo, with teams working in other areas on other problems. For several years, they managed to reach this ambitious goal with simultaneous productions in Magino, Sanrizuka, and Yokohama's Kotobukicho.

Kotobukicho is one of Japan's three major neighborhoods for temporary workers from the rural areas *(dekasegi),* the elderly working class, and the impoverished. The other two areas are Osaka's Kamigasaki and Tokyo's Sanya. They are often called slums, but this is a poor description. Kotobukicho took its present form during the Occupation, when it housed the many workers building the nearby American naval base. It is a relatively compact area that looks so similar to the rest of the urban core that unwitting visitors could probably pass through without noting much difference to the surrounding neighborhoods. Despite being only 250 meters on a side, this small district was home to about ninety flophouses with 5,300 rooms at the time of production. There were also about fifty restaurants and forty bars. The total population was between 5,600 and 6,100, which broke down to 200 children, 400 married couples, and 4,000 to 4,500 single men.[29] Most of these men competed for short-term jobs at Yokohama's harbor. There are plenty of people, however, for whom a place like Kotobukicho is the last stop for a down-and-out life. Their problems range from familial to medical to alcoholic. Homelessness is endemic. Violence is intimately woven into the fabric of daily life.

Dokkoi! Songs from the Bottom (1975). From left to right: Watanabe Takaaki on sound, Okumura Yuji on camera, and Yumoto Mareo.

It is easy to imagine what attracted Ogawa Pro to Kotobukicho for its first film after the Sanrizuka Series. At the same time, it was a decision with some weightiness. Medical support institutions were minimal and underfunded. The police were not in complete control of the area, and were popular with no one. Organized crime basically ran the daily work system. This was one of those places one was supposed to avoid. As a measure of the very real dangers for filmmakers, one need only consider the slightly later production of *Yama—Attack to Attack* (*Sanya—Yararetara yarikaese,* 1985). The initial director, Sato Mitsuo, was actually murdered during filmmaking. It was completed by Yamaoka Kyoichi, who was then shot to death on the eve of the film's premiere. The film continues to be shown by an independent screening group to this day. However, Ogawa Pro's film remains a vastly superior effort.

This is actually rather surprising, considering the miserable conditions of the shoot and the string of personnel crises that erupted along the way. The Kotobuki film was to be Yumoto Mareo's debut as director. Yumoto was Ogawa's assistant director toward the end of the Sanrizuka Series. Although Ogawa Pro was consciously trying to avoid replicating the structures of the mainstream film industry, boosting his assistant director into the director's chair was obviously a tradition Ogawa made an exception for. As Ogawa Pro's newsletter explains,

> [In January after the screening movement for *Heta Village* calmed down] assistant director Yumoto told us something he had resolved to attempt. He wanted to become a director, so how would it be if he tried to make his debut film? This made us realize it had been a year since we had shot a film, and at the same time we were moved by his determination to shoulder that responsibility. In the course of some staff meetings, the Kotobuki Unit was born. It was the smallest sized team, consisting of a location staff of four people (Yumoto, Watanabe, Hara, and Okumura) and a three person production staff (Fuseya, Shiraishi, and Asahi). We set out expecting to finish the film within the year.[30]

The process was far more difficult than Ogawa Pro expected, and it took much longer as well. The allocated budget was entirely too small, so the filmmakers shot much of the film on the ends of rolls left over from Sanrizuka. They bought a cheap Canon Scopic camera and an even cheaper tape recorder for the sound. Because the staff was still inexperienced, Ogawa teamed them up with Okumura, an older professional cameraman Ogawa knew from his *eiken* days and the cinematographer of *Sea of Youth* and other student movement films.

They rented a room in one of the flophouses of Kotobukicho, continuing the Ogawa Pro ethic of living with one's *taisho*. This aspect is actually addressed in the film itself. At the beginning, the film shows a still photograph of the crew as if to provide visual evidence that they were living like the people they were photographing. This kind of visual evidence is no longer necessary, however, when the filmmakers start telling the stories of Kotobukicho's inhabitants. It is overwhelmingly clear that they had become very close to their neighbors. The narration speaks what is usually left unsaid by documentaries on the urban poor: "At first, no one would talk to them except their neighbor Tanaka. As the crew struck more friendships, they were told, 'Many people come and take pictures. They get what they want and then leave. They use us. Don't be like them.'"

The location shooting turned out to be rocky, something the production diaries make thoroughly clear. There were a wide variety of reasons, but the main one centered on Yumoto. He was not taking charge of the production as his directorial role demanded, and there was great discomfort among the staff concerning the way the shooting was proceeding. Ogawa tried to keep his distance, literally, by going only as far as a coffee shop at a nearby train station to hunker down with Yumoto. The production diaries are sprinkled with entries that express the discontent. For example, on January 10, 1975, Yumoto writes,

> Now what we have to sincerely think about are the things that people are keeping secret in their hearts in Ogawa Pro. . . . No one is going to throw away "egoism." However, for that reason, we have to endeavor to separate from the place we ourselves are at. Then through relationships with others, we can gauge our own roles—it's got to start with "egoism."[31]

Traces of the problems are left in the film as well. The black intertitles that interrupt Acid Seven's folk song cover a mistake the editing unit found. When watching the rushes they discovered the sound and image parting ways midway through the song, thanks to low batteries in the camera. The record of the collective's daily life in *Ogawa Pro News* #5 makes note of this incident,[32] but the production unit's diary contains a word-by-word account of Ogawa dressing down Yumoto and Watanabe:

> Ogawa scolded everyone: "Don't you know how much we're concerned about this kind of thing every day?! Didn't we test and prep this equipment over and over again?! We did all this because we wanted to be true to the fact that you only have that 'one-instant' to shoot. You can't retake in documentary film! We have to understand this profoundly! The location is the best studio. If the sound you record on location is bad, there's nothing you can do."[33]

Seven refused to shoot the scene a second time, but they managed to rescue the song with some creative editing and even won an award for sound recording from the Japanese Association for Film and Television Technology (Nihon Eiga Terebi Gijutsu Kyokai). By this point in postproduction,

Ogawa had actually taken over the film's structuring and editing process, effectively demoting Yumoto to his assistant. This was understandably a major blow to Yumoto, who was left emotionally and physically weak from the trying location shoot. Always referring to himself in the third person, Yumoto's production notes grow increasingly dark, although they dwell on his relationship to and conversations with Ogawa—at one point he throws a glass of sake at the senior director—one senses a collective pressure bearing down on Yumoto as well. In the end, the film's credits do not even list a director. It had to be devastating to Yumoto. He helped Fukuda with the film's distribution but abruptly went missing. Much to his colleagues' distress no one knows where he is to this day.

The film they finished is a set of moving portraits of the friends they made, interspersed with poignant moments in the everyday street life of Kotobukicho's inhabitants. The main vignettes include people like Takahashi Sueji. Our first view of Takahashi is a close-up of his face on the floor, drunkenly singing a song. A victim of muscular dystrophy, he was raised by his sister when his parents died; when she died he ended up in Kotobukicho, where he circulated between the hateful hospital filled with apathetic doctors and the street where all his friends were. Takahashi provides one of the film's strongest moments—this in a film chock full of unforgettable scenes. In a single shot, a close-up that tracks across his tortured body, Takahashi slowly speaks of worker solidarity and his dream of a Japan that commits to communism. He won't live to see the day, but he is sure it is coming. He speaks with such conviction; these are not idle, fashionable words for him.

From scenes like this we come to see Kotobukicho as a place seething with anger, a by-product of the struggle to live. In a brilliant bit of camerawork, one man on New Year's Eve leans almost playfully into the lens and explains that there are no jobs, and he has had to rely on charity for the first time in his life to avoid starving and freezing to death on the street. He blames Prime Minister Tanaka for the job situation, where only the rich can hope to survive. The poor have to stick together, he proclaims, as unemployed men saunter aimlessly in the background. Just then, the camera tilts down to the man's feet, revealing more men huddling around a campfire in the street. Another man, quite drunk, speaks up: he has been in Kotobukicho for twenty years, but there is no work now; he criticizes Mayor Asukada for saying he is a socialist, yet all the while ignoring the workers. The mayor got a huge salary, he bitterly jokes, and should use a little of it to buy them noodles.

As these two examples suggest, when the film encounters a politicized anger, it checks the impulse to idealize it. One story from the editing diary describes the staff watching five hours of rushes from the wintering season and noticing the gap between the dreams and real lives of the men of Kotobukicho. They described this as a gap between thinking "This is the way I'd like to live my life" and the reality of "However, in reality this is all that's possible." Bringing out what lurked in that crack was their task.[34] Where the Sanrizuka Series featured a cast of poised heroes and heroines, the people Ogawa Pro encountered in Kotobukicho were literally struggling to stay alive. They may be class conscious and see their exploitation as systemic; however, their energies are funneled not toward organized resistance or revolution. Instead, they just aim at survival.

This is no idle exaggeration. The pall of death hangs over *Songs from the Bottom*. The very first scene shows a woman wrapped in a blanket, like a piece of luggage, dying on the sidewalk. This is followed by photographs of all the people who have expired on the streets in the previous year. The narration notes that while the crew was shooting, people kept asking them to shoot their portraits. When asked why, they explained that they wanted nice photographs for their funerals because they never knew when they would die. One old man at a hospital tells the crew a story about how he got drunk on New Year's Eve and someone stole his money and even his clothes, leaving him for dead: "They say that this is a town of robbers, but they all come from Tokyo or Osaka. Here, they'll kill you to rob you." The screen goes black, with an intertitle emphasizing his last sentence: "I'll never forget this debt."

In another encounter, a man named Kuma complains about his general health, abdominal pain, weight loss, lack of appetite, and constant vomiting. His liver is failing, and so the doctor and nurse both tell him that he has to stop drinking. As he closes the door, an intertitle cuts in and announces, "While we were in the midst of editing, Kuma-san (age 46) died in Kotobukicho. We pray for his soul." A conventional documentary would only have announced his death to make a point. This film establishes a far different relationship to its *taisho*.

In the production diary from the editing, there were many discussions about life and the ethics of filming people who are facing death. For example, on January 2, 1975, there was such a conversation between Tamura and Ogawa. The cinematographer wonders, "For example, say someone knows he's going to die soon. How would you shoot it? In the end, we wouldn't shoot, would we?"

Ogawa replies, "If he's trying hard to live, we can film that."

"There's only one way we can shoot someone who knows he's going to die," responded Tamura, "That's when he says, 'Please shoot me.'"[35]

Several weeks later, someone wrote,

> People do everything they can to live. Even when it's difficult, they've got to live. That's why no one can be disinterested in death. Furthermore, when there are meaningless deaths one after another—the anger also runs deep. Regret. Resentment. Understanding "death" means the same as understanding "life." "That's why we have to live!" We want our camera to evidence this.[36]

In the end, their film does give evidence to the drive to life, beginning with its title. It was originally entitled simply *Kotobuki,* which ironically happens to be the character for "happiness." However, they came up with *Dokkoi! Ningenbushi* during the editing. *Dokkoi!* is a call, something on the order of "Oof!" People utter it when they summon all their energies for something requiring great *physical* effort. *Ningenbushi* would translate along the lines of "Song(s) for Humanity," the word *bushi* being a Japanese suffix used for songs over the past millennium.[37]

This presents the film's string of stories as a collection of songs—*Songs from the Bottom,* as the considerably less eloquent English title puts it. However, this musical analogy is literalized with two songs in the tale of their next-door neighbor and first friend, Tanaka Yutaka. He sings a song about Manchuria, where he grew up as a child. After his song, he narrates his life story for the crew. After the war, he was an orphan in Tokyo. In 1948, when he was eight years old, he escaped from his school and went to Ueno but got caught. He successfully escaped at age ten, and stayed with a Korean man who made moonshine. After being arrested in 1953 for stealing military raincoats, he ended up in reformatory, followed by prison. Upon release he ended up in Kotobukicho, working, until he lost his leg. During filming, Tanaka collapsed on the street and died of a brain hemorrhage. However, no one knew this until long after the fact because the police left his body unidentified for most of a week. Reflecting on these events, his friends at the dorm state precisely what the film argues implicitly: "That's Kotobukicho. That's the police. We are all Japanese, but they don't even treat us like humans." The day they heard about Tanaka's fate, two other workers died—one was drunk and drowned at the docks, and the other died in a fight.

In Tanaka's room, they found a sheath of papers upon which he had recently scrawled a kind of story. In the course of editing, the filmmakers resolved to put this to music as a tribute to their friend. The editing staff recalled a folk singer from Kotobukicho named Acid Seven and asked him to put Tanaka's words to song. Yumoto recorded the song, and it was so powerful they decided to shoot Seven singing the song on the roof of their dorm. Seven sings Tanaka's last words in a cramped close-up that struggles to keep him in frame. The lyrics begin by narrating his miserable, violent life but then suddenly tell a story about a small boy he meets at a park. He finds a wallet in a park and then meets this boy in raggedy clothes. They talk about baseball, and then he offers the boy some money from the purse. The boy is delighted. "As he hopped away, I felt the child was mine," wrote Tanaka, "I have a child! I have a child! In my mind, I thought he called me 'Father' instead of 'Old Man.'" The song continues, describing one more encounter before the boy disappeared from his life: "We never met again. How old was he? I didn't ask his age. As I look back, thanks to him, my heart found the right path. My heart found peace."

Although Seven's folk music feels dated, Tanaka's last words are powerfully poignant and elegant in their own way. This is the theme song for Ogawa Pro's "Songs for Humanity." At the same time, every portrait included in the film, long or short, represents one of those poems. This is to say, we are not witness to sober transmissions of the filmmakers' encounters in Kotobukicho. The poetry of the lyrics is rendered in the photography, in the arrangement in the editing, and most particularly in the newly sophisticated use of two basic cinematic tools: voice-over narration and intertitles reminiscent of the silent cinema. These two techniques would become the hallmarks of the upcoming Magino Village Story.

Ironically enough, these innovations came from unlikely sources. In the middle of editing, the filmmakers decided to use a combination of subtitles, intertitles, and narration throughout the film. And in many cases, these elements would occur simultaneously, one repeating the information imparted in the other. There was the danger that spectators would find them redundant, but there were two main reasons for the decision. The first was that they wanted to give the sense that this was the Kotobukicho that they witnessed firsthand, so the narration itself would be informal, discarding the polished standards of television gloss. Their critique of slick narration could be leveled at the Sanrizuka Series as well. With the exception of *Heta Village,* those films used professional voice actors, although the text they read is slyly subversive of the norm—agitation delivered by the voice of God.

The second reason, curiously enough, had to do with the reception context of their films. They knew from experience that their films were rarely shown in ideal conditions. One had to expect dim lamps, rotten speakers, barely functioning projectors, and ancient screens (when they weren't using white sheets). The audio-visual doubling of information would ensure that the film would not lose its impact if one channel was less than ideal. And if both were bad, there was always the staff member to pick up the pieces in discussions.[38]

But this reasoning is hardly suggestive of the layer of narrative complexity the intertitles add to the documentary. The most powerful are hybrid intertitles and subtitles. For example, at Tanaka's wake, the ceremony that most men dying in Kotobukicho never get, two of his friends are before the shrine talking, one determined to blame himself for Tanaka's death and the other trying to convince him it is not his fault. At the end of the conversation, the image goes to black and subtitles emphasize the words passing forth: "No matter how tough life is, you have to live. I'll live, but when a man died like this, what can I say? What's my life? Is it worth living?" And the scene ends on a close-up of Tanaka's face on the wall of portraits of the dead.

Another scene *begins* with this style of hybrid intertitle-subtitles. By this point, the technique has become associated with the most dramatic pronouncements of the film. It is a kind of graphic exclamation point: "They beat and bullied me. On the break, they said Koreans are dirty and told me to get out of there. That time I bit my tongue and tried to be patient, but I hated it. Humans bullying other humans, I hated it." When the image returns, it is an extreme close-up of the man who had been talking, with a wild look on his face. A superimposed title explains that at the free dorm for wintering, a worker of Korean descent suddenly exclaimed that all violence was wrong, starting the following conversation. The man, who had started working at Sanya and Chigasaki, continues describing the abuse he has suffered at the hands of racist Japanese, about the way his father was brought to Japan from Korea by force and called names. Pointing out how many people are murdered in Kotobukicho, he calls for a reciprocal violence of revenge. Others disagree and try to calm him down.

Dokkoi! Songs from the Bottom is an unblinking portrait of a space repressed from the Japan of the high-growth economy and is one of the collective's most powerful films. This was a place that breaks human beings. The songs Ogawa Pro committed to film testify to the resilience of the men and women inhabiting Kotobukicho. But their sheer will to live is suspended in the precarious delicacy of their bodies. And most of these bodies are sick, old, abused, or damaged, as the film's premiere exemplifies.

The film had its Kotobukicho premiere on May 25, 1975, in the local park. When Hara and Yumoto arrived to show the film, they found a very tense situation. The night before, a worker had died on the street. When the nearby police box was informed, it took over twenty minutes for an officer to arrive. All he did was manhandle the corpse into a body bag like luggage, with no investigation into the cause of death. When his friends asked the police to treat the body with more respect, the policeman left, only to return twenty minutes later with over twenty riot police. They summarily dragged the body away, and this time protests were met with violence. At dawn, the workers of Kotobukicho had formed scram lines of solidarity in protest, and the riot police reacted by surrounding Kotobukicho, attacking anyone who tried to enter or leave the area. This was the situation in which the film had its Kotobukicho premiere. During the film, the workers cheered and clapped and called out to the screen, particularly when they saw the images of people who had already passed away. After the screening, the protest against the riot police reignited, and the filmmakers were led to a quiet corner of Kotobukicho. There, the friends of the deceased held an all-night vigil with incense burning in an empty food can.

The Smoky Skies of Yamagata and the Brilliant Blue Skies of Narita

While the Kotobukicho unit was busy with *Dokkoi! Songs from the Bottom,* other members were up north in Yamagata settling into their new Magino home and shooting the first film of the Magino Village Story, *Interview at Clean Center*. At one point, a third production unit started up under Fukuda back in Sanrizuka as well. Like *Dokkoi!, Interview at Clean Center* may also be seen as a transition to the distinctive approach they used in their later films. For example, the documentaries of the Magino Village Story are thoroughly self-referential. In the Sanrizuka series, the farmers would often refer to the filmmakers, and there are those strong moments when the crews confront the police directly; however, these are fleeting references to the film under production. *Dokkoi!* and *Interview at Clean Center* are pitched firmly in the first person, foregrounding the encounter with their *taisho*.

The latter film takes a further step into self-referentiality with Ogawa's first significant on-screen appearance. A subtitle nominates him "the interviewer." Iizuka also appears as "the reporter." The film is as much about the crew as the Clean Center. There is an ulterior reason for this. *Interview at Clean Center* was Kimura Michio's idea. In February 1975, while Iizuka was traveling between Tokyo and Magino to prepare the way for the move, Kimura approached them about making a PR film for Kaminoyama City. Like most farmers in Japan, Kimura had to hold a second job to survive. When he wasn't farming, he collected garbage. Around this time, Kaminoyama had just started a new facility to dispose of garbage, and Kimura suggested that making a film could introduce the new facility while simultaneously reminding people of the importance of separating their garbage. For the filmmakers, it might not be an exciting project, but it would be a way to introduce themselves to people in the area. It was difficult for people to imagine what Ogawa Pro was up to in its move to Yamagata, so this would be its new calling card.

As in Sanrizuka, the filmmakers performed richly detailed analyses of their subject before loading the camera. *Interview at Clean Center* is very much about *process,* a theme that would come to dominate many of the later films. It is a glimpse of their new method in action. Each stage of trash collection—sorting, burning, and disposal—is conscientiously covered, along with the problems caused by people who ignore rules to sort out nonburnable and toxic materials. They kept remarkably detailed notebooks about this process, notebooks that appear in the final film. It may sound terribly boring, but Ogawa and staff bring a new political twist to their approach to the PR film, harkening back to the scripts Ogawa wrote after quitting Iwanami. Two aspects of the finished film did not make its sponsors happy.

The first had to do with the portrayal of the people operating the machines. The collective watched PR films on trash borrowed from Tokyo, and none of the documentaries paid attention to the workers. They were films simply about trash, and little more. Ogawa brings the people behind the process to the foreground, starting with the first shot: a pan over the faces of all the workers. Later in the film, this scene is reprised with Iizuka interviewing each worker. While the typical PR film erases the people running the machines to dryly explain processes and procedures, Ogawa inverts this structure. He interviews the men and women operating all the trucks and machinery. The interviews cover the basic functions of their jobs, but Ogawa includes questions that are never asked in the PR documentary: How do you like this kind of work? What do you find interesting about this machine? How about your job? What's the most difficult thing about your job? Do you find yourself the object of discrimination because you haul trash? The answers are fascinating. For example, to the last question, a worker reveals that parents discourage their daughters from marrying men in their occupation. Needless to say, this comment did not enhance the film's PR value.

The sponsor's second point of contention was that the film takes note of the city's struggle to control the smoke emitted by the facility, and there were concerns over pollution. Indeed, an ulterior motive for having the film produced was that the facility was originally to have been built in another area, but a not-in-my-backyard citizen movement stood up to stop it. The same pattern occurred in two other places before they settled on its present location. This was one of the first of the so-called "clean centers" in northern Japan, and the company that constructed it hoped to use the film to allay fears and nip future protest movements in the bud. Unfortunately for the sponsor, the pollution problem lent itself to the kind of data collection the filmmakers had taken a fancy to, and they rigorously studied the amount of smoke, the effects of wind direction, and the potential health problems.

While the city was apparently happy with the film, the company filed a protest, and they were forced to add a subtitle to the ending—an image of the smoke drifting from the stack into the mountain air—a subtitle that claimed the smoke problem was cleared up in the following months. Combined with the focus on workers and the discrimination they face by citizens, there were too many forces working against the PR value of the film. It was, for all practical purposes, shelved. Kimura was told that he had been tricked by Ogawa, but the discrimination and the smoke were indisputable, documented facts. In *Interview at Clean Center,* Ogawa finally realized the PR documentary that he had conceptualized on paper at the beginning of his career.

This was precisely the field of documentary Ogawa fled and studiously avoided. He and his collective had little to say about the film one way or another. However, in the midst of its editing, an anonymous writer entered this telling entry in the collective's production log: "*Trash* PR film. It makes no difference if it's seen or not. Inspires no feelings at all. Utterly ordinary. It probably has no PR value."[39]

In April 1975, with *Interview at Clean Center* in production and *Dokkoi! Songs from the Bottom* nearing completion, Ogawa spread the staff out even thinner by sending Fukuda back to Sanrizuka to direct what would be the final film of the Sanrizuka Series, *Sanrizuka—The Skies of May, the Road to the Village* (*Sanrizuka—Satsuki no sora sato no kayoji,* 1975). Riot police were pouring into the construction site from all corners of Japan and building an encampment at the border adjacent to the Hantai Domei's tower. Both sides were preparing for a showdown, performing drills within sight of the other. The situation was tense.

Despite the volatile conditions around the tower, the filmmakers spent considerable time looking at the periphery, documenting what was at stake in the tower's defense. This is evident from the precredits sequence, always a key moment for Ogawa's films. Here, Fukuda conducts a long interview with Old Man Yanagi at Heta's local shrine. Yanagi explains that the shrine and the forest that surrounds it once belonged to the state, but they were granted to the people of Heta Village with postwar legal reforms in 1951. He opens the doors to reveal a ceramic *haniwa*. Ancient objects like this are always turning up in the fields; nearby is a burial mound built a millennium ago or more. As if to make the message clear, the soundtrack features the roar of aircraft, signaling the fate of this shrine and its rich history, along with the people that worship the god it houses.

Having moved to Yamagata to become farmers themselves, Ogawa and his crew had come to see Sanrizuka a little differently. Their attention to village history, both recent and ancient, was an ongoing concern. This film, however, displays a newfound respect for farming. Immediately after

Ogawa Shinsuke (left) and Fukuda Katsuhiko (right) conduct an interview at the base of the tower in *Sanrizuka—The Skies of May, the Road to the Village* (1977).

the title calligraphy, Ogawa and Fukuda strike up a conversation with Yanagawa Hatsue in her field amidst a dust storm. Yanagawa is one of the most familiar faces of the Sanrizuka Series, starting with her passionate speech at the end of *Summer in Sanrizuka*. After exchanging warm greetings, Ogawa and Fukuda immediately quiz her about the wind that carries her fertilizer away. She offers a story about her honeymoon, spending five days putting in a field of wheat only to see one of the spring winds whisk the seeds away. "They call this good land, but with this wind it's hell," she explains cheerily. "Our ancestors have been doing this, and so we just carry on. But the weeds cling to the soil like the hair on your head." The scene ends with a close-up of a single leaf breaking through a plain of dirt and a superimposed title: "It's a wonderful thing: the power of the soil."

Ogawa's conversations with the villagers—for while they are "interviews" in the strictest sense, the tone is of best friends reunited—revolve around the work of agriculture. In a charming scene where Ogawa chats it up with the women, he pumps them for information on planting. They describe the way the political tensions take them away from their fields at precisely the critical window within which they must sow seeds to ensure a successful crop. The scene has a somewhat different feel from all the other Sanrizuka films. While it is another example of locating the concerns of the film around the world of the *taisho,* it is also an opportunity for Ogawa to show that he's been studying farming. He is edging into that village world himself in a new way. The experience of research and data collection back in Yamagata makes itself felt.

Ogawa drives his point home in a couple of rambling conversations with a farmer named Iwasaki , who lives and works in a small valley just below the new runway. His village is now a ghost town, but he refuses to move. It takes a decade just to learn the particularities of a field, he explains, and he knows this field intimately. He cannot bear to start over. The filmmakers demonstrate how a lush forest covering the surrounding hills was denuded by the construction. With the trees gone and the topsoil stripped, nothing prevents the rain from streaming into Iwasaki's fields and flooding the rows of plants. Rice agriculture involves careful regulation of water levels depending on the stage of growth, something that takes decades to master. The construction is rendering all of Iwasaki's accumulated experience, this *knowledge,* useless. It is precisely the kind of knowledge Ogawa Pro was busy learning up in Yamagata.

The original plan for *Sanrizuka—The Skies of May, the Road to the Village* was to foreground the farming completely, focusing on the process of planting, nurturing, and harvesting crops in great detail. This plan would have to wait, because the events of May quickly overwhelmed the production. On May 6 at 3:00 in the morning, 2,100 riot police invaded the tower and the cement hut it was propped upon. Squads of policemen blocked all routes to the tower, forcing all the farmers and student supporters to watch from nearby hills. The filmmakers had to shoot from the same vantage point, re-creating the early morning clashes from still photographs. The images show road blocks, lines of riot police cutting off shortcuts through the fields, and the chaos that ensued when police shot water cannons and tear gas into the Hantai Domei crowds without warning.

The crew did capture the late morning toppling of the tower. In a long shot, it jerks and tilts at an impossible angle. Imagine the Eiffel Tower leaning to one side and then whipping to the ground. The words of farmer Tsubaki Kiyokatsu are superimposed over the image: "When we rushed back, the tower was felled by an evil ploy." These few poetic lines assign the farmers' subjectivity to this straightforward, if spectacular, image.

After registering the farmers' shock and humiliation at this surprise attack, the filmmakers turn to a staging ground for a large demonstration two days later. The police gather to prevent people from reaching the protest. Ogawa suddenly cuts to the point where the demonstration breaks into chaos. People flee the riot police, who pour into the frame. The camera crew is positioned right at their lines and records one of the policemen loading a tear-gas gun, peeking around the shield of another policeman, leveling the gun horizontal to the ground and firing. A pan reveals his target: a large, densely packed group of demonstrators—frighteningly close.

The tear gas canister tore into the crowd, hitting student Higashiyama Kaoru in the head. He was not wearing a helmet. Higashiyama instantly lost consciousness and was declared brain dead at the hospital. He died fifty-nine hours later.

Two trials ensued for what became known as the Higashiyama Incident, one for pinning responsibility on the police (which was lost) and the other for damages. Tamura's shot of a riot policeman firing horizontally into a crowd of Hantai Domei protesters was entered as evidence. The first court decision turned down the suit, citing the possibility that a protestor's rock could have killed him. The appeal overturned the decision and

The moment before Higashiyama Kaoru's death: this frame blowup from *Sanrizuka—The Skies of May, the Road to the Village* captures a riot policeman aiming his tear-gas gun horizontally at a group of protesters.

awarded Higashiyama's parents ¥40,000,000, thirteen long years after their son's murder.

In a scene reminiscent of *Report from Haneda,* the filmmakers interview a field hospital doctor about tear gas. They dissect grenades to explain exactly how the weapons function. The doctor describes the physical effects of the chemicals on human eyes, eyelids, throat, and lungs. He talks about what people must do if they are exposed, how they must wash and protect their health. Then, they show the kind of plastic shell grenade that killed Higashiyama, a new type that seems to have been developed just for the tower attack. Hit with one of these directly, even the armor worn by the riot police would not prevent serious injury. Finally, they visit a cornfield to show how the gas kills plants when stray grenades fall into the fields.

The final sequences of the film report the funeral of Higashiyama Kaoru. In a long shot of the procession, with flags and banners waving in the skies of May, a speech from the boy's father scrolls across the screen:

> When Kaoru was born the leaves were green and the sky was serene. Today is the same kind of day, with serene skies and full of green. That sky sees many tragedies in the world of the humans. A heart as broad and pure as this sky is the finest tribute to my son.

This scene brings the film to its end. The title of the film, *Sanrizuka—The Skies of May, the Road to the Village,* refers to this lovely and tragic speech. It reflects an attempt to heighten their chronicling of the month with poetic intertitles, most of which were written by farmer poet Tsubaki Kiyokatsu. The poems are rendered through subtitles and intertitles and half-written *haiku.* For this reason, I have substituted the English release title with a direct translation. However, I must admit that the work of some anonymous subtitles translator—*The Events of May*—is not entirely inappropriate. The filmmakers' effort at creating documentary poetry is ultimately undermined by the strict chronological structure they chose. Each scene starts with the tick of the clock, a subtitle marking the date as they progress through the month. While the film is filled with memorable scenes, and some moments of real pathos, it feels as though it was pulled in too many directions at once: to the farming, to Ogawa and Fukuda's relationship to the farmers, to the tower attack, and finally to Higashiyama's death. Compared to the achievements of *Heta Village* and *Dokkoi! Songs from the Bottom,* the film disappoints. Perhaps one explanation is that in this production Ogawa once again pulled the director's chair out from under his pupil in mid-production, completing the film himself. Yet another explanation could be that Ogawa Pro was just entering an unusually unproductive and sickly phase in its long history.

[5] The Magino Village Story

"A Mountain Pass Demands a Decision of Us"[1]

Dokkoi! Songs from the Bottom and *Sanrizuka—The Skies of May, the Road to the Village* were major accomplishments, and the former was particularly well received. They would appear to have successfully launched a new organizational structure for Ogawa Pro, with the new home base in Magino, a Tokyo office, and flexible units that could go anywhere to film new documentaries. However, this activity swiftly ground to a halt in 1976, as the collective entered a period of transition characterized by inaction, even stagnation. Within a couple years of the move to Yamagata, most of the staff from the Sanrizuka Series had left for new lives. Some were disappointed with the apparent apolitical turn the move had spelled. Others could not bear the stress and demands of communal living. Yet others were bored with the lack of filmmaking. In the Ogawa filmography, the late 1970s are a blank spot on the map.

During this period, Ogawa had his production team work hard at transforming into farmers. His choice of method was unusual to say the least. Ogawa told them not to read books but to learn by doing instead. Along the way, they created reams of elaborate notebooks about the intricacies of rice production. These notebooks, which make brief appearances in *Interview at Clean Center* and Regina Ulwer's *Hare to Ke*, are actually shocking in their detail. Handwritten in careful script by people like Yumoto, Fukuda, and Yoshida, they cover the biology, culture, and human labor involved in Japanese rice farming. The neat rows of text wrap around still photographs, hand-drawn charts on growth patterns and temperature, and elaborate line drawings. Paging through these notebooks today, one is struck by the sheer volume of the data collection going on in the years following Ogawa Pro's move to Magino.

While the Ogawa filmmakers had always carefully studied their subject before shooting, nothing at this level of detail and comprehensiveness was going on in Sanrizuka. It was a new turn in the collective's production method, and it palpably signals something gone awry. This was more than the product of bored filmmakers with too much time on their hands. Ogawa was in the midst of a confidence crisis. His personal chaos reverberated through the group, whose living circumstances now put them closer than ever before. The overwhelming detail of the notebooks registers their attempt to manage Ogawa's insecurity and bring their increasingly isolated world under steady control.

Some members look back at this period and suspect that Ogawa's nervousness was initially triggered by anxieties that, with *Dokkoi! Songs from the Bottom,* his staff may have produced a film better than he. This would also explain why he overran the production so late in the game. Whatever the cause, there was no denying that something was very wrong. Ogawa finally saw a doctor and was diagnosed with a form of depression, a kind of midlife crisis the doctor called *fuan shinkeibyo* (anxiety neurosis). Ogawa spent less time in the nighttime discussions he so loved. He

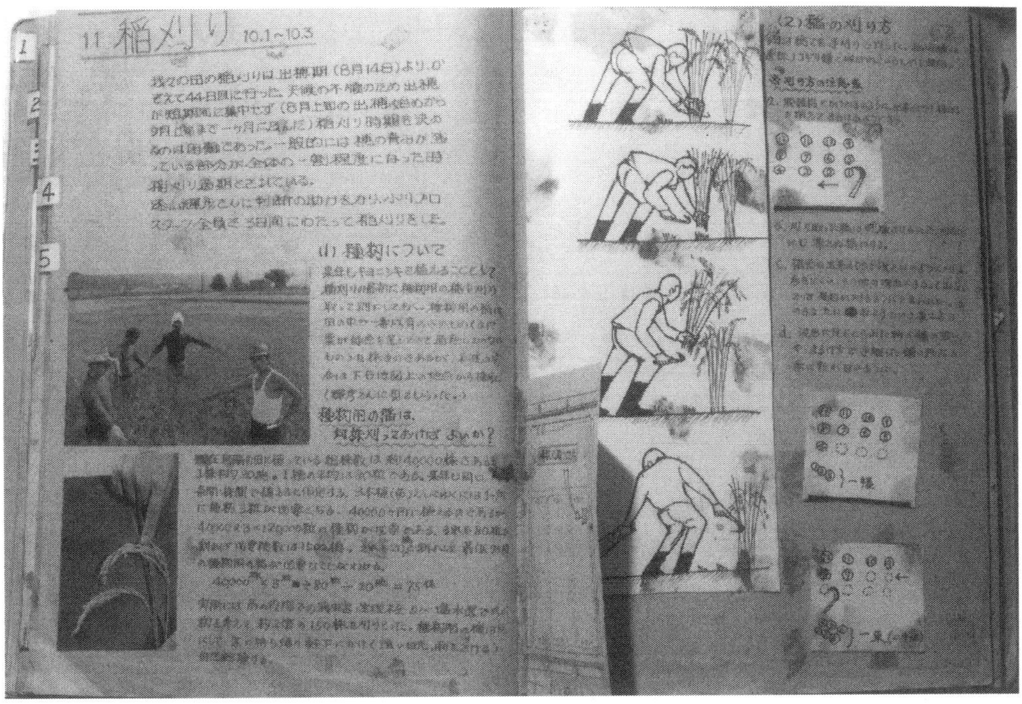

After the move to Yamagata, the collective's production notebooks became remarkably elaborate. Scrapbooks included beautiful drawings, photographs, and handwritten text describing every aspect of farming life. This page shows how they learned to harvest rice by hand. The overwhelming detail of the notebooks seems to register their attempt to manage Ogawa's insecurities and bring the collective's increasingly isolated world under steady control.

increasingly depended on his wife, Shiraishi, as the most passionate staff members from the Sanrizuka days disappeared one by one.

The fervent and careful research and data collection was Ogawa's way of managing the chaos of his world, and the way it overwhelmed the collective is obvious from the newsletters the members published. For example, during the Sanrizuka era, their *Joei Undo no Kiroku* (*Record of the Screening Movement,* September 1970 to March 1971) was filled with short essays about the sociopolitical significance of their films and the events portrayed within them. The same was true for the newsletters, pamphlets, and catalogs published by the outlying branches of Ogawa Pro, as well as the allied publications by sympathizers showing its films across Japan. After a period of silence, the collective started an ambitious newsletter called *Ogawa Pro Seisaku Nyusu (Ogawa Productions Filmmaking News)* in June 1974. It followed the production of *Dokkoi! Songs from the Bottom* in much the same manner as previous publications. However, once Ogawa became sick and the collective turned into data miners, it changed the newsletter's name to *Ogawa Pro Nyusu (Ogawa Productions News),* significantly dropping the *seisaku/production* part of the title at about the same time it stopped making films. Beginning with the April 1976 issue, it is mostly data in the form of a diary.

In *Ogawa Pro News #8* (January 1, 1977), the actual data collection makes its full-blown, public appearance. Instead of the usual diary of events that filled previous issues, the members wrote in extraordinary detail about what they learned about farming, including comparisons of their own field with their neighbors' fields. They show the results of their first macrophotographic footage of stamens popping out of slowly opening rice buds. The newsletter has the air of a grand back-to-the-earth experiment in living. This tendency peaked with the tenth newsletter in July 1977, when Ogawa withdrew from the group and threw himself into the issue's astonishing detail on silkworm farming. It has almost nothing on filmmaking.

In actuality, they were making a film on the subject: *The Magino Village Story—Raising Silkworms* (*Magino Monogatari—Yosan-hen: Eiga no tame no eiga,* 1977). It was originally meant to be a loose collection of visual notes on 8-mm film, a moving image supplement to their elaborate scrapbooks. Along the way, they could train members to operate the camera and learn other aspects of film production. However, Ogawa thought the footage was good enough to convert into a documentary. They edited the footage together, blew it up to 16mm, and it eventually became what they refer to as the Magino Village Story's *Silkworm Chapter,* or *Yosan-hen.*

Silkworms entered the village economy in Magino as late as the 1950s; however, the filmmakers mostly ignore the economic materiality of silkworm farming for *process* (a telling counterexample to this approach is Ogawa's posthumously released *Red Persimmons* [*Manzan Benigaki,* 2001], which I discuss in depth later). Silkworm farming was primarily women's work. The men would only occasionally lend a hand, which is why their film prominently features Ogawa's wife, Shiraishi Yoko, as she learns the ins and outs of silkworms from neighbor Kimura Hatsu. The film describes every step of the process. This is interesting enough, but amounts to little more than the kind of education film Ogawa rejected nearly two decades earlier. In the end, it feels too much like the data-driven notebooks they continued to create. Indeed, for this little 8mm documentary, Ogawa and Shiraishi poured enormous energies into a beautiful catalog containing the script for the film. Quite a few members resented the attention this catalog got and saw it as a self-indulgent waste of precious resources. Indeed, boxes of the catalog remain untouched in the Furuyashiki Village archive, but perhaps this is because it was actually serving a different purpose. Nosaka suggests it best to consider the film, along with the elaborate catalog and special issue of *Ogawa Pro News,* Ogawa's lasting tribute to his wife.

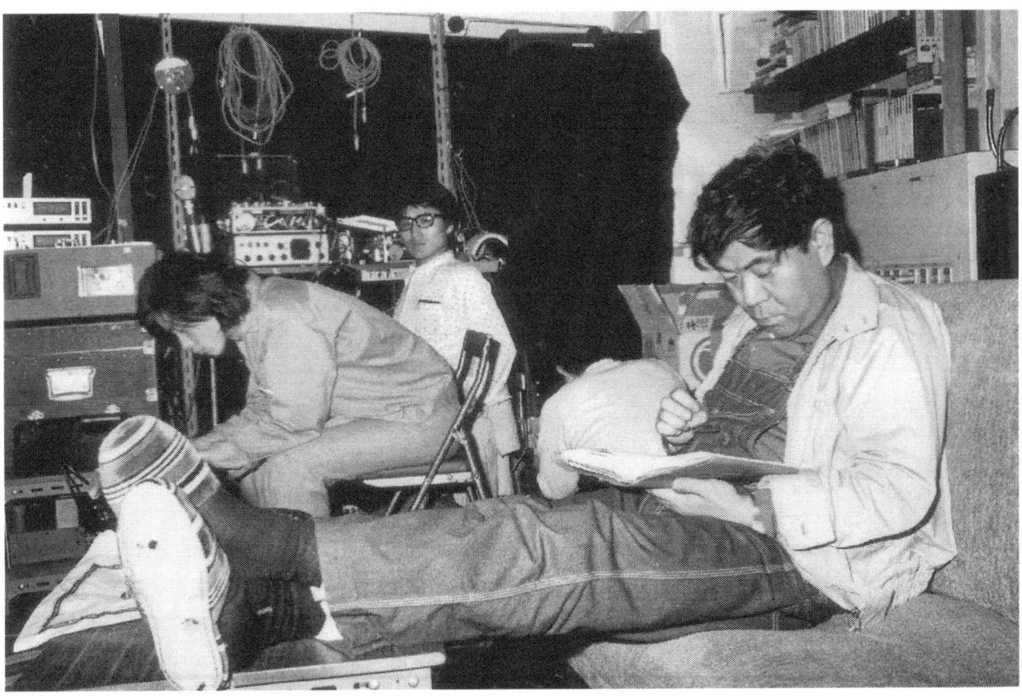

Ogawa Pro operated under the banner of collective production but was raked by hierarchy. Ogawa Shinsuke (foreground) sat at the undisputed seat of power, with members like Nosaka Haruo (background) at the bottom and Ogawa's spouse, Shiraishi Yoko, somewhere in the middle. Photograph courtesy of Shiraishi Yoko and Athénée Français Cultural Center.

Fukuda Katsuhiko felt that they should never have made the *Silkworm Chapter* because of one particular scene. While the film is overwhelmingly focused on the process of silk farming, the ending features a neighbor pulling out an old document charting the lineage of his family. The ostensible purpose for this diversion is to point to the tradition of farming that runs through this family, but Fukuda noted that it also makes a display of the family's pedigree. Only a wealthy family would have such a document. Until World War II, class was highly codified in village Japan, and while the American Occupation attempted to destroy it, such things persistently continue in people's minds and social relations. This class-consciousness weakened starting in the 1960s along with the structural transformations of the village economy, particularly *kengyo*. However, Fukuda worried that such a film could reinvoke that class-consciousness, an opinion with which Kimura Michio tended to agree.

Ultimately, the collective's fervent data collection cannot be reduced to a simple expression of anxieties flowing from Ogawa through his staff. It was also inspired by the work of Minakata Kumagusu, an ethnographer who did work on bacteria in rice in Wakayama (and also lived down the street from my home in Ann Arbor back in the late 1800s). Unlike Yanagita Kunio, whose famous studies of local folklore partly motivated Ogawa's turn to fiction in the last installment of the Magino Village Story, Minakata was a data collector, a number cruncher under the spell of enlightenment thinking. Iizuka calls his work a kind of bacteria mania and recalls how impressed Ogawa found these studies. From the beginning of his career, Ogawa was interested in the recording properties of cinema. Much more than a document of *what* happened, Ogawa was also committed to the power of showing *how* things happened. In the past, this meant the occasional investigation of, for example, a baton blow to the skull; Minakata's work provided Ogawa a footing to indulge in the very public collection of mundane minutiae.

Ogawa Pro began this new emphasis on process in the notebooks from *Interview at Clean Center*. And when the filmmakers finally started shooting in the late 1970s, they attempted to do the same thing on film, essentially treating the notebooks as storyboards. Somewhere in the Ogawa archives is an hour-long reel called *Rice Straw (Ine no wara)*. It shows the various uses of straw—for tatami, shoes, and the like—in microscopic detail. We may find a glimpse of what this film would have been like in a scene from *The Magino Village Story—Pass* (*Magino Monogatari sono 2 Toge—Zao to Makabe Jin—*, 1977), in which a farmer demonstrates how his family turned rice straw into winter shoes. After putting on the shoes, he dons a straw hat, straw cape, bag, and elaborate rigging of fiber rope to keep it all attached to his body for a trip up Mount Zao. In *Pass,* this lovely scene demonstrates a material relationship to the mountain, a relationship the locals had turned their backs on after crossing the pass into postwar modernity. However, Ogawa's rough cut of *Rice Straw* also included an overwhelming amount of detail about the biology of the straw and the role of bacteria in its development. They screened it for a curious professor in Tokyo, who was left speechless. "You could show this at an academic conference," he said, and they immediately shelved the film. No one, they realized, would want to watch this! They may have committed the reel to obscurity, but the spirit of data mining survived in the sequences on rice in the two masterpieces of the Magino Village Story, *"Nippon": Furuyashiki Village* and *The Sundial Carved with a Thousand Years of Notches.*

The only other Magino film Ogawa Pro was able to make during this period was another short, *The Magino Village Story—Pass,* which takes its name from the famous poem by Makabe Jin (1907–1984). This second installment of the Magino Village Story was the collective's tribute to the poet that enabled the members' new life in Yamagata. Shot upon the dedication of a monument for the author on his seventieth birthday, *Pass* indicates the direction Ogawa Pro's filmmaking would take in the coming decade. In the broadest terms, it uses Makabe to consider the importance of water to life on the slopes of Mount Zao. The film starts with an old woman explaining the geography of the region hand-in-hand with its spiritual significance and couched in the language of the folklore she grew up with. Then, up above the tree line and literally in the clouds, Makabe describes the way weather slides off continental China and slams into massive Mount Zao. Standing in a meadow, he gestures to the pioneering grasses that transform the volcanic lava into soil that can support other, less hearty plants—a story easily taken as a metaphor for his own forbearers—and then points to the drainage that collects the rain and snow falling on Zao and sends it toward his village. At the dedication to the new monument, Makabe tells his audience about living with Zao. He drinks the water it sends, makes rice with it, cooks with it. The water gave us life, he explains to the audience. Without the mountain there would be no life, so he climbs it often to show it respect and reverence.

After this scene, Ogawa interviews an eighty-five-year-old man who lives at the gateway to the mountain. He reiterates Makabe's reverence for the peak and explains how the water drains down a valley from the highlands where the film began. He describes how an ancient ditch diverts some of the water across the flanks of Zao to feed the fields of his own village. Then, the conversation takes a surprising turn. Ogawa asks about water wars. The old man responds that he heard about many in the past, but had personally experienced only one back in the early 1950s. The problem was that the ditch diverts water that would otherwise flow straight down to another village. Over the centuries, the two villages would feud over water rights. The old man stresses that without water, there is no life, and so back in that 1950s water war, he worked hard to mediate between the obstinate old people of each village and finally reached a peaceful settlement.

As in *Heta Village,* Ogawa turns to the past and uncovers an earthy mix of beauty, humor, and violence. In this case, Ogawa's approach to history is deeply inflected by the Makabe poem that gives the film its title. Makabe recites the short poem twice: once in that foggy meadow up on Zao and again at the end of the film. Written in 1947, "A Mountain Pass" ("Toge") is one of a handful of famous poems that mark the beginning of postwar poetry in Japan:

"A Mountain Pass"

By Makabe Jin

Passes are places of decision.
The familiar melancholy of parting drifts at passes.
Squeezing the mountain road
the ridges loom over your exposed body
and before long you put them behind you.
Two views are woven together there.
Without losing one world,
you cannot enter the other, separate one.
Only by enduring a great loss
does a new world unfold.
When standing on a pass
the path you've passed is a charming memory
and the path unfolding below is pleasing.
Paths do not answer.
Paths do nothing but invite.
The sky above the pass is as sweet as a dream.
Even if you know the route
there
you must abandon one world.
To hide such feelings
the traveler stops to pee
pick some flowers
enjoy a cigarette
and take in the view as far as the eye can see.

Makabe wrote this poem in the wake of World War II. Even the life of a farmer deep in the mountains of Yamagata was touched by the war's turbulent violence. Makabe saw family and friends migrate to Manchuria or leave for the front. Many never returned. After his first reading of the poem, Makabe sits in a study where his family used to raise silkworms and reminisces about its writing. The war left him dumbfounded, wondering what to do and where to go from there. The poem arose from his experience of that time, and the process of thinking about moving from a tumultuous era of warfare into a new and uncertain world. "A Mountain Pass" shares a number of qualities with Ogawa's cinema—its deep-rooted connection to the rural, its earthy humor, and its fundamentally optimistic voice.

The Magino Village Story—Pass clearly indicates the landscape Ogawa Pro had entered, literally and figuratively. For such a short film (a mere forty minutes), one learns a remarkable amount about life on the slopes above Magino Village. The film maps out the area's geography and climate, broaches its rich history and folklore, and introduces both its traditional crafts and modern literature. It features all the elements of Ogawa's coming films: storytelling, cheerful interviews with old folks, endearing voice-overs by Ogawa, religious ritual, traditional craft, obsession with weather, poetry, spirits, biography, war memory, and the impact of modernity on this remote corner of Japan and its inhabitants. Ogawa's subsequent films would combine this medley of elements with a substantial dose of data collection, although rendered in aesthetically pleasing and self-consciously ironic ways (in stark comparison to the *Silkworm Chapter*). Significantly, Makabe's disciple, Kimura Michio, felt that making this film helped Ogawa pull out of his depression, lead a more normal life, and start pursuing a "real" film. From this perspective, *The Magino Village Story—Pass* itself represents a number of passes: from World War II to the postwar, from Sanrizuka to Magino, and from sickness into health.

The Heart of Science

Entering the 1980s Ogawa emerged from his depression, and the collective embarked on a two-part film it intended to call *The Magino Village Story.* However, the filmmakers were swiftly sidetracked by unusually cold weather during the spring and summer of 1980. The season's average temperature had plunged, and this was worrying the farming communities. Such cool weather could spell serious crop damage by harvest time.

Ogawa decided to investigate the impact this weather would have on local farmers, particularly those at higher elevations. The crew scouted various surrounding villages to use as locations and finally settled on one called Furuyashiki—much to the consternation of some people in Magino, who could not understand why Ogawa Pro didn't make a film on the place it called home first. This tiny village of eight families was upstream from Magino, nestled high in the mountains. There, Ogawa Pro found a microcosm of Japan and the subject of its next film, *"Nippon": Furuyashiki Village.*

Before the filmmakers could shoot a foot of film, they had to ingratiate themselves to the villagers. Still in the midst of their problems entering Magino itself, they fully realized the difficulty of their task. The collective members—sans Ogawa, who mostly stayed at home—spent an enormous amount of time up in Furuyashiki helping people with the most difficult parts of farming, silkworm raising and charcoal burning. It was an attempt to make their prospective *taisho* understand their seriousness through hard manual labor.

The villagers of Fukuyashiki responded to the sincerity of the Ogawa Pro members, and soon they began studying the environment of the village and shooting their first reels of film. Once again their method relied on studious research borrowing the tools of hard science and the careful recording of their findings in elaborate scrapbooks. This clearly affected the course of the production: the first half of the finished film is a scientific investigation of the cool weather's effect on that year's crops.

They discovered the existence of what villagers call a *shirominami,* which might be translated as "White Souther." This was a weather pattern specific to Furuyashiki's valley, where particularly cold air would spill over a nearby ridge and course down the narrow valley. The White Souther brought a white mist and very cold temperatures. It was enough to affect the crops and, by extension, the culture of the valley's inhabitants. Ogawa Pro members illustrated something as abstract as the movement of cold air by constructing a large three-dimensional map of Mount Zao and its slopes. The villagers thought they were crazy but were won over by the results. Using dry ice, they replicated the air flow of the White Souther on their three-dimensional map. More importantly, they demonstrated how the position of trees and paddies in relation to air flow affected crop production.

Many people dislike this first part and easily imagine the film without it. It is probably the reason that the film made both the top ten and worst ten lists in the film journal *Eiga Geijutsu.* But thinking twice, the critics who condemned it to their worst films lists would probably admit that without the science scenes, the film would look uncomfortably close to NHK television documentaries. In fact, NHK's educational channel has broadcasted the film several times, but it was shunted to the wee hours of

The Sundial Carved with a Thousand Years of Notches (1986) has long sequences on the science of rice farming, the urban collective's prime route into the world of the village. From left to right: Mikado Sadatoshi, Tamura Masaki, Yoshida Tsukasa, and Ogawa Shinsuke.

the morning thanks to its quirkiness. Many aspects of the collective's new style were far from the typical nonfiction fare of television, starting with language. The film mixes the thick dialect of the Yamagata region with the "standard" Japanese of the staff members and Ogawa's own narration. The director's narration is, at the same time, quite unconventional for its affable informality. Ogawa's narration rejects the smoothness of the typical documentary's voice of God; his speech proceeds in jerks and halts, using informal sentence final particles like *ne* and *yo,* which address the spectators as intimates, cordially inviting them into the world of Furuyashiki Village.

The film also sets itself apart from the usual NHK-style documentary through its structure. Thanks to its sheer length—the film weighs in at over three and one-half hours—it ranges patiently over the breadth of the village's history, geography, and human work. It is a heterogeneous mulch of material broaching many areas of Furuyashiki's existence, ambitious in its scope and patient in its procession. The interviews by Iizuka and Ogawa are casual conversations between friends. When people pause to think, so does the film. They refuse to cut away. This is one of the liberating aspects of the long-form documentary, and the filmmakers make great use of that freedom in letting people speak where most filmmakers would stop the camera to save expensive film or cut for fear of alienating their audience.

What gives the second half's more ethnographic sections their uncommon power is their thorough grounding in what the filmmakers constantly referred to as "the life and language of rice," as embodied by the film's first half. It is Ogawa's attempt at something like an organic history writing. Their investigation into the mystery of the White Southers culminates in the careful excavation of a local rice paddy and the discovery of a rich layer of red iron embedded deep under its surface. This was evidence of a White Souther's impact on the village ages ago. One realizes that Furuyashiki's history is actually inscribed in the earth. Looking at Hanaya Yoshio's face brighten up with the realization of what makes the White Souther work, one can see that the long passages of scientific investigation into rice farming are absolutely essential to the film *because we understand the complex thoughts that light up Hanaya's face*. The science transports the viewer to Furuyashiki as something more than a tourist or an anthropologist. In terms of structure, the first half's unrelentingly scientific gaze builds an almost oppressive pressure, and the subsequent turn to the human history of the village delivers an immensely pleasurable release. Throughout this second half, Ogawa weaves the stories of the villagers' histories with the work that they perform, whether it be the burning of charcoal or the raising of silkworms. And these histories range from the retelling of personal experience to the discovery of fossilized sea shells that point to the village's prehistoric past.

The film also points to an organic continuity in village life that is endangered by outside powers riding the tides of modernity. Ogawa hints subtly at the trajectory of the film in the opening scene, which starts with a title that suggests the beginning of a story, "Long ago—in a village in the countryside. . . ." The first image is of a woman in her mid-eighties sitting on tatami in a splash of light and directly addressing the camera. She speaks in remarkably thick Yamagata dialect, so dense that most Japanese would have no idea what she said were it not for the Japanese subtitles Ogawa kindly supplied:

> Well, it's, you know, a story I heard from m'grandmother. 'Bout 100 years back, or 200 years back, don't exactly know. When she came up to the mountains to become a bride, my family's gramma. The feudal lord took taxes, so they say she came up from her hometown, from the valleys, to where life was comfortable. Back at her hometown taxes were high. Life's miserable, 'cause they'd take one bottle of sake per window. But then, if she came up to the

> mountains, there're no taxes. No taxin'. Go to the mountains as a bride, there's no tax 'n you could live comfortably, so she left. So she came, but the peppers didn't turn red . . . she'd grow peppers, but they wouldn't turn red. "A place're peppers don't turn red's nowhere to live," they [her parents] said. But she tried comin' as a bride anyhow. Gradually, more people came, I think, lots, the number of people grew, and for some reason it got warmer. Maybe 'cause they're cuttin' the trees. An' the peppers got red. Everybody started livin' well. That's that.

This delightful tale brings us into the world of Furuyashiki, and the story's traces remain in our memory for the subsequent three hours, marking the scientific investigations that punctuate the film. Through the evocation of a communal, familial past in the retelling of an old story, this grandmother points to the primary concerns of Ogawa: the struggle to establish a comfortable and good life in a remote space and the threat to that life by powerful forces from without. These are remarkable tales of families and lineages, of farming and burning charcoal, of entering and leaving the mountain village and not necessarily by choice. It is impossible to reduce *"Nippon": Furuyashiki Village* to any one of these elements, so perhaps it is best to take Kitakoji Takashi's lead and call it a film about multiple modernities.

Kitakoji wants to call the work of Ogawa Pro a kind of visual ethnography, drawing on the critique of anthropology led by people like George Marcus and James Clifford. This critique has drawn fruitful comparisons between travelers' accounts and the writings of ethnographers for the way they both describe meetings with other, beautiful cultures, and for the way they often highlight arrival scenes.

For their part, Japanese ethnographic filmmakers' conception of ethnographic documentary is strongly rooted in the salvage mode. For example, the work of Japan's most celebrated ethnographic filmmaker, Himeda Tadayoshi, is primarily a form of data collection of materials in danger of oblivion. It is clear that in most of his documentaries, Himeda's use of people is uncomfortably close to the first half of *"Nippon": Furuyashiki Village*. Too often he converts people into data for storage in the cinematic museum, and in this sense he subjects his *taisho* to the powerful gaze of the human sciences. This is reflected in the very style of his approach, which is conventionally homogeneous and emphasizes the recording properties of the cinema. Significantly, in his collaborations with Kayano Shigeru, Himeda did not teach any of his Ainu collaborators how to film themselves. They sincerely speak of a deep and respectful friendship, but the professional collaboration never substantially strays from the confines of the conventional ethnographic film. Finally, Himeda generally attempts to avoid interjecting his presence in both the profilmic scene, to say nothing of the camerawork and editing.

In contrast, Ogawa's relationship to the people in his films serves ends that are both ambitious and ambiguous in comparison to Himeda's work, and he never hesitates to play and experiment with the tools of cinema. One can cite the simple example of the monuments collected in one corner of Furuyashiki. In a typical ethnographic film, they would be ends in and of themselves. The filmmaker would record the meanings they memorialize before those villagers with memories pass away themselves. Ogawa shares this desire to record, but after the production of the *Silkworms Chapter,* he became far less concerned about the value of collecting in and of itself. At some level, he salvages the fading village history, but only in order to embed it in larger networks of meaning circulating in the film. Thus, while Furuyashiki's monument to bear hunters is dutifully recorded for posterity, the delightful manner of its telling—Hiroshi sitting on the hillside with a bemused look on his face talking about the bears that haunted his ancestor who erected the stone—has all the simple and powerful pleasures of storytelling. Simultaneously, it serves as a transition between scenes that also sort out the complicated family lineages of the villagers, and explore the various ways modernity affected such a remote village.

Kitakoji compellingly reads the Ogawa filmography as an ethnography that does not constitute an asymmetrical meeting that posits the filmmaker—and by extension the spectator—as civilized and the villagers as primitive. It is not a Hegelian meeting between the modern and nonmodern. Instead, he sees a film like *"Nippon": Furuyashiki Village* as an ethnography that records the fact of multiple modernities. The mountains of Yamagata provide a field for this work.

The film is sprinkled with stories that point to this uneven development of modernity during the historical transformation of the village. I have already noted that those fleeing the oppressive, centralized power of the feudal system formed the village itself. Many of the sequences on farming are framed by discussions of economic survival. No single industry could support a family, especially since the climate and soil of Furuyashiki did not lend themselves to productive rice farming. In the beautiful sequence on making charcoal, with its blazing flames amidst the snow and soot, Ogawa's narration points out that the custom started in order to survive the brutal winters. Sericulture was one family's strategy to supplement income from rice and charcoal, and within a couple of years, every farmer was replacing cedar forests with mulberry trees and cultivating worms. Some families struggled to purchase land in the lower valley, which they could loan out in exchange for rice, only to lose the land in Douglas MacArthur's land reforms. As one elderly woman explains, "MacArthur stole that land from us for a measly 3,000 yen. It wasn't even enough for 60 kilos of rice." Watching Hiroshi making a door to his charcoal kiln, Ogawa notes that he spent some time laying track for the bullet train into Yamagata; he quit and returned to Furuyashiki because he hated being used by other people: "If you're going to be used by humans, you might as well be used by charcoal." Finally, there is the fact, haunting the entire film, that young people are fleeing the village for the cities. Halfway through the film, Hanaya Kumazo bitterly complains that everyone expected the completion of the paved road to make their lives better, but it only made it that much easier for the youth to leave.

This shift in the village demography plays against the strongest set of stories in the film, those of World War II. These begin abruptly when Ogawa shifts his attention from Hiroshi's charcoal kiln to his mother and her precious photographs of the two sons she lost to the war. Both were killed in the final stages, one in Saipan and the other in the Philippines. She answers to Ogawa's patient, round-about line of questioning. In the long silences, they shuffle through all that remains of her sons' presence: some letters from the front, locks of hair, death notices, and dreams. At the end of the scene, Ogawa notes, "You still have Hiroshi." To which she replies, "But he wants to leave."

Of the original eighteen families pioneering the village when peppers failed to turn red, only eight remained by the China War in 1937. From these families, nine young men were called to the war and three never returned. The third killed in action was annihilated with his entire Yamagata garrison on Attu Island in the Aleutians. His sister-in-law displays the ¥1,650 in war bonds that the government exchanged for his life. When the emperor surrendered in 1945, they became worth only the price of the paper they were printed on, but she keeps them in the family altar all the same.

Ogawa allows the survivors to tell their tales, and each has a different relationship to the war. Suzuki Tokuo was a bugler who survived malaria, beri beri, bombings, and starvation of New Guinea. After years of struggling against the cruelty of officers to the rank of sergeant, the war's end leveled the military's hierarchies. Devastated, only his bugle allowed him to regain his spirit. He proudly plays it for the camera in his old uniform.

Hanaya Kumazo, the only veteran to live to see the new millennium, joined the army in 1932 mainly to see Manchuria with his own eyes. He returned to Furuyashiki in 1934, farmed for a season, then decided to rejoin the army strictly for the pension. Aside from marrying into the Hanaya family in 1938 by becoming Hanaya Sayo's husband, Kumazo devoted a full sixteen years of his life to Japan's wars. After a tour in China, he found himself in the Kuriles at surrender. However, he was taken prisoner and spent the next three years at hard labor in Siberia. He was thirty-six when he returned to Japan. Displaying his medals for the camera, he mutters, "They're junk." Upon returning home, he never left Furuyashiki Village.

Hanaya Kiichiro, of the bear hunters family, tells the last war story. Drafted in March 1945 at the age of thirty-six, he bitterly describes constant beatings by the officers. "Everyone whispered complaints. Someone gained something from that war, but it wasn't us. We got no food. No pay. I lost so much money by being away from my fields. No pension. I hate war! I'll hate war until I die. Longer!" It is a diatribe made profound by our knowledge of the place and life that he was dragged from.

Scenes like these, scattered throughout the expanse of this powerful documentary like precious narrative jewels, do not pose the villagers as endangered purities from the past in need of salvage or salvation. Instead, they stand as representatives of local instances of modernity, spread thick and thin across the globe. As Kitakoji suggests, this is what links this film to the Sanrizuka Series. In the airport struggle, Ogawa introduces us to the small, traditional collectivities (*kyodotai*) fostered by the farmers in their little corner of modernity. These collectivities are being upset by brute, centralized, rationalized force—by a national power wielding cash in one hand and a club in the other. Kitakoji writes, "Their resistance and their noise revealed the violence of modernity and strengthened the collectivities of their existence, whether at the family or village level. However, this is not a matter of returning to the nonmodern, but forging the possibilities of 'another modernity,' of a subaltern subjectivity within multiple modernities."[2]

The title of Ogawa Pro's documentary encourages spectators to produce Kitakoji's reading. The characters *"Nippon-Koku"* appended before "Furuyashiki Village" literally read "Japan-Nation." However matter-of-fact this sounds, its manner of inscription provokes surprised contemplation before anyone enters the theater. *Koku*/nation is written using the conventional Chinese character; however, for *Nippon*/Japan, Ogawa uses *katakana,* the domestic syllabary reserved for foreign loan words. Thus, they denaturalize the nation, urging spectators to search for an alternative vision of Japan in tiny Furuyashiki. (This is why I put the name of the nation-state in quotation marks in my translation of the title.)

During the screenings of *"Nippon": Furuyashiki Village,* Ogawa Pro handed out postcards to spectators, who could return them with the thoughts the film provoked. These were so fascinating that the journal *Shiso no Kagaku* (*Science of Thought*) considered collecting them in a book. Quite a few people read the film as the portrait of a microcosm. One of the more quirky examples came from a twenty-six-year-old woman from Tokyo:

> Fu fu fu fu. . . . .
> Within outer space—Furuyashiki Village
> Within that a puny
> "*Nippon*" Koku.
>
> Ha ha ha ha. . . . .
> Lots of, well, fighting and fighting
> So much sprinkling piss, no?
> "*Nippon*" Koku.
>
> Humans are amazing, no?
> Trees and flowers and beasts in the snow
> They can't live properly.
> The time when words are abandoned is coming.
> —Twenty-six-year-old woman, Tokyo[3]

This was a new audience for Ogawa Pro. This kind of young viewer began appearing with the screening movement for *Dokkoi! Songs from the Bottom,* where showings in Yokohama drew significant numbers of teenagers. Before this era, groups of high school or college students would go to great lengths to orchestrate screenings of the Sanrizuka Series on their own dime, doing their best to top off the rental fee with donations they collected from spectators above and beyond the ticket price;[4] now the young people asked about student discounts! Starting with *Heta Village,* Ogawa Pro had to spearhead its own screenings. It also sold larger numbers of same-day tickets, as opposed to presold tickets purchased from friends or directly from Ogawa Pro, further evidence that spectators were increasingly seeing an Ogawa Pro film for the first time in their lives. For this reason, *Furuyashiki's* release was deeply dependant upon the prestige of international film festivals, good press, and high-profile venues in Tokyo. One hates to imagine the fate of Ogawa Pro had it not won the FIPRESCI film critics' prize at the Berlin Film Festival for this film. That probably would have been the end.

Ogawa Pro still had its old audience, but judging from the postcards viewers sent in, the new Ogawa Pro did not necessarily impress them. The following response on a Furuyashiki survey card was typical:

Rice Porno: Ogawa watching rice flowers bloom through his Bolex, August 16, 1979. Tamura used macro lenses and time lapse photography to capture the moment of fertilization. His astonishing images of rice fields and natural settings in Yanagimachi Mitsuo's *Farewell to the Land* (*Saraba itoshiki daichi*, 1982) and *Himatsuri* (1985) are the fruits of his cinematic experiments in Yamagata.

> Ten-odd years since *Sanrizuka* I've come to the age where I bring my children. It doesn't matter if I bring them [to this film, as opposed to the disturbingly violent Sanrizuka Series]. Now as for the film at hand. Despite this being the information age, I came knowing nothing about the film. Just from the papers that Ogawa Pro's staff moved to Kaminoyama, and that they were making rice in Kaminoyama . . . the stage of opening people's hearts. That's why it's just fine to be able to bring one's kids. It's a good education film, and I think there's nothing wrong with that. However, outside of nature and earth and songs, I want power. I saw *Partisan* and *Kotobukicho* [sic]. Emphasize the "spectators" who still have no human power. That's what I'd ask of you.[5]

Another important audience lived in the village of Furuyashiki. The villagers were reportedly split between those that did not care for the film and those that did—a distinction that had everything to do with whether or not they appeared in the film!

Today Furuyashiki is very nearly dead. The only people who live there are Hanaya Kumazo and Sayo, and they stay only part time to grow their vegetables. They recently bought a condominium in Kaminoyama City; aside from the difficulty of living in the freezing mountains, they had completely lost their community. Everyone had either moved out or passed away.

However, the village is no ghost town, thanks to a rather startling development in the 1990s. The owner of one of the largest hot springs resorts in Kaminoyama purchased most of the land and buildings in the village and turned Furuyashiki into a museum, capitalizing on the village's beautiful, old architecture, its lovely mountain setting, and its relative fame thanks to Ogawa's film (advertisements and signs for the museum feature the film's title, calligraphy and all). In a supreme stroke of irony, Furuyashiki has finally been salvaged to package the past for future generations. Even the Chinese characters of the name *Furuyashiki* feel as though they were chosen by the marketing department: they literally signify "old residence."

While researching this book, I frequented Furuyashiki because the Magino-era archive sits within the ancient barn where Hanaya Sayo once raised her silkworms. I remember leafing through the boxes of notebooks, production diaries, and other records of the filmmakers' life in Yamagata as busloads of tourists disembarked for a trip to their (imagined) collective past. They would stroll through the maze-like collection of thatched farmhouses as the tour guide spouted the same tired jokes: "Welcome to Furuyashiki's Ginza-dori!"[6] Occasionally, the stray tourist would peek inside Hanaya's dark shed, only to be shocked by the ghostly historian in their midst.

One evening after a long day in the archive for me and an afternoon of hanging *daikon* to dry for the Hanaya's, we all retreated to their *kotatsu* table for *tsukemono* and the sumo tournament. I asked them if they liked Ogawa's film, and they said they had just seen it recently. The Yamagata Documentary Film Festival had shown it to guests in the old community center across the stream. Sayo said, "It was so wonderful! You know, I met my mother that evening. . . . All the dead people. . . ." When I pressed them to name their favorite scene, they agreed on the ending. I wasn't surprised, as it features Sayo's mother, the old woman telling a story about red peppers and power at the film's outset. In its dénouement, the very same woman hobbles toward us down Furuyashiki's empty "Ginza-dori" on a blustery day. She repeatedly stops, peers up at the camera, and asks Tamura if she should keep walking. On the soundtrack, Kimura Michio reads a poem he wrote, which leaps the length and breadth of the documentary, collecting a bundle of strong images that sum up the last several hours' immersion in Furuyashiki's past and present. One of the best works by Ogawa's poet host, I would like to offer it in its entirety.

Village of Spearheads, Village of Shells

By Kimura Michio

The hill overlooking the red riverbed
An earthenware shard with Jomon designs
Shattered by a spearhead
Came from the barren field
Sparks fall in the dirt
I stopped plowing
Placed on my palm
It was a flint spearhead
My sister and I
Cried in surprise
I slipped it in my sleeve soaked with sweat
My sister blushed
With hands covered with dirt
She brushed her breast
Back then, I was just a boy
From a charcoal kiln
A shell fossil came
In my village
No one made charcoal
In the villages near the mountains
Charcoal was a way of life
The shells turned to stone
Must have lived back
20,000,000 years   30,000,000 years
No, much older
Shells on the seafloor
Near a deep trench
Surrounded by forests of seaweed
Okhotsk's seasonal current
Cold water flowing south from far, far away
Never dreaming of dying out
It survived
Flowing down the mountain valley
Once the deep sea trench
The White Souther
Like wind
But not wind
Not cloud, nor fog

In silence, ridges disappear
Enveloping all without limit
A hidden existence in-between
Together with the flying birds
Humans pierce through
Boars Bears Blue boars
The White Souther
The day our village was created
Is fresh in our memory
The day the White Souther cleared
People plowed the land
Burned trees
Hoed with stone spades
Sowed chestnuts, barley, wheat
They nourished life
Carrying quivers
And drawing arrows
They also entered the mountains
They lived with the beasts
Lives intertwined and overlapped
Blood Flowed thickly
Through the village It ran
Humans live
Beasts become human
Beasts live
Humans become beasts
Like the mountain face
The skin of the villagers endured the cold winds
Humans speak the language of beasts

The film ends with a view of Furuyashiki Village and the tips of distant mountains broached by clouds and a superimposed title: "July 3, 1981, 4:00 PM. A White Souther descended." With its curt precision inscribed on such a lovely image, the ending is a final nod to the heart of science, which has come to mean so much more than data.

History Writing as the Carving of Notches on a Sundial

Like *"Nippon": Furuyashiki Village,* Ogawa's next effort was a hefty documentary ages removed from the frenetic immediacy of their social movement films. It is also a masterpiece that would have been unimaginable without the accumulated knowledge and intimate friendships built up over years of interaction with their neighbors. *The Sundial Carved with a Thousand Years of Notches: The Magino Village Story* is a compendium of everything they had learned in Magino and a coalescence of the various documentary approaches they had developed—creative intertitles, informal and cheerful voice-over narration, the long form, a thoroughgoing self-reflexivity, and a centering of the film's site of enunciation in the subjectivity of their *taisho*. The resulting film is among the most complex of documentaries. Along with *Heta Village,* it is one of those achievements that will never be replicated, partly because of massive transformations in Japanese society, but primarily thanks to the circumstances of its production. This film was completed in Ogawa Pro's thirteenth year in Magino and after two decades of collective filmmaking. *Sundial* represents the sum of the collective's experience as artists, farmers, and progressive intellectuals.

The opening maps out the heterogeneous territory of the village we are about to enter. The first shot resonates strongly against the film's title: it is an astounding *time-lapse pan* (!) following the sun as it rises from behind a

Shooting inside the Magino house. The panels on the table were used in *The Sundial Carved with a Thousand Years of Notches* to describe groundwater levels. From left to right: Ogawa Shinsuke, Nosaka Haruo, and Tamura Masaki.

distant mountain and arcs across the sky. This is an extraordinary technical achievement above and beyond its undeniable visual impact, and the first of many manipulations of time.[7] In the next shot, Tamura and the film crew work in a field of rice, an introduction to the film's meticulous self-reflexivity. Ogawa inserts the fruits of these working filmmakers, spectacular time-lapse photography collapsing both time and space. They capture and compress the forty-minute process of a rice flower opening, starting with the stamen projecting out of its husk, followed by pollen attaching and finally cells transforming with fertilization. The sequence moves powerfully from macrophotographic close-ups to the almost abstract images of photomicroscopy. Intercut with time-lapse images of a gathering storm, a single flower begins its transformation into a head of rice. Cut to a high school band (the village's human inhabitants), then to the dark, stormy clouds. Lightning flashes illuminate a shrine's stone *dosojin,* and then the title of the film slowly emerges out of the muck of a dark rice paddy.

This opening sequence hints at where the film is taking its spectators, and we can extract three broad discourses from the mix: farming, scientific investigation, and storytelling about both the mundane and sacred aspects of village life. These discourses are woven imaginatively into one of the most complex documentaries I have encountered. This is Ogawa at the height of his powers as a director, and unfortunately it would be his last film.

Ogawa front-loads his documentary with a portrait of rice farming, the first of those three discourses built into the architecture of the film. After the opening title sequence, Iizuka and Mikado run through their own paddy in Magino counting the bails of their 1978 harvest. This scene initiates a long sequence about the efficiency of their farming since their first attempts in 1975. As in *"Nippon": Furuyashiki Village,* the graphs, colorful diagrams, and density of data threaten to convert the film into a mind-numbing education film for science pedagogy. They demonstrate that certain areas of their field collect too much water, and by improving drainage, they were able to increase their harvest. This scene takes up nearly the entire first hour of the film, and many spectators find it akin to a hoop one must jump through for the prize on the other side.

However, as with *"Nippon": Furuyashiki Village* before it, there is an inscrutable fascination to be found here as well. The filmmakers treatment of the graphs and diagrams has that curious informality they perfected over the years, with explanations and narrations ornamented with halts, "you knows," and rough self-corrections. Their confident curiosity about the workings of rice is infectious, and certainly a big part of the reason is Tamura's photography. His camera alternately speeds up and slows down

Shooting in the fields for *The Sundial Carved with a Thousand Years of Notches.*

time, moving from spectacular scenery of huge mountains to focus in on single cells of rice. His time-lapse photography of pollination is simply breathtaking. It took years of failures before they got it right; after all, they were attempting to capture the very moment a single rice blossom opens, and had only one chance before they would have had to wait another year for the next spring.

This wonderful photography and unique informality of presentation act as the medium through which the discourses of farming and science interact. At one level, they probably represent the differing perspectives of Ogawa Pro and the farmers in Magino. For the latter, rice farming has a materiality one feels in the mucky close-ups of planting and in the radio broadcasts of storm warnings; farming is about hard-won knowledge and the mundane cycles of daily life. As urban wannabes of a sort, Ogawa Pro did not arrive on the scene with the common sense handed down through generations of farmers. The members had to learn everything from scratch, and the entry point they chose was the data-driven approach of hard science. This is, however, a "soft" hard science, even a fictive biology. They enhanced and amplified their discovery with a creativity of presentation one rarely finds in the educational film, but they also complicate science itself with the integration of "history writing" and "archeology" into the "biology" of rice. Amidst the scientific explanations of rice biology are equally rigorous and dispassionate investigations into the historical record and an actual archeological dig.

This is to say, *The Sundial Carved with a Thousand Years of Notches* exhibits the hallmarks of what Laura Marks has called an "intercultural cinema." Marks's prototypical examples all come from the ephemeral world of experimental documentary and video art, especially by diasporic artists of the late 1980s and early 1990s. However, she is attracted to these works for the way their autobiographic practice works out the epistemological problems of people living between ways of thinking and being. It should not be surprising that her description of intercultural cinema evokes both the thought of Chakrabarty and the cinema of Ogawa:

> Intercultural cinema by definition operates at the intersections of two or more cultural regimes of knowledge. These films and videos must deal with the issue of where meaningful knowledge is located, in the awareness that it is between cultures and so can never be fully verified in the terms of one regime or the other. Yet the relationships between cultures are also mediated by power, so that the dominant regime—in the following examples some configuration of the historical Euro-American hegemony—sets the terms of what counts as knowledge. Other knowledges cannot be expressed in its terms. . . . Intercultural cinema turns to a variety of sources to come up with the new conditions of knowledge: written history, sometimes; the audiovisual archive; collective and personal memory; fiction; and the very lack of images or memories, itself a meaningful record of what can be expressed. Cultural knowledges are lost, found, and created anew in the temporal movement of history and in the spatial movement between places.[8]

Marks is interested in the way intercultural films appeal to senses other than sight—auditory, olfactory, kinesthetic, and especially tactile senses—to develop an epistemology that rejects distance for touch, domination for a yielding-into-knowledge. In *The Skin of the Film* and *Touch,* she offers a provocative and complex synthesis of theorists, notably Henri Bergson (on memory and the senses), Walter Benjamin (on mimesis and aura), and Gilles Deleuze (especially his cinematic philosophy of the time-image). Artists who resist the objectification of their *taisho,* who innovate with the audio-visual tools of film and video to render a sensuous knowledge, produce intercultural films. Marks calls these innovations haptic, or having to do with touch. Whereas enlightenment thinking conceives of knowledge as something attained through distance, vision, and objectification, Marks emphasizes physical contact. "Haptic identification is predicated on closeness, rather than the distance that allows the beholder to imaginatively project onto the object," she writes, "The haptic is a form of visuality that muddies intersubjective boundaries.[9] While most forms of documentary are constructed out of symbolic representation demanding clear-cut division between subject and object, tactile epistemologies rely on mimesis. Following Adorno and Horkheimer, she asserts that "Mimesis . . . is a form of yielding to one's environment, rather than dominating it, and, thus, offers a radical alternative to the controlling distance from the environment so well served by vision."[10] Marks elaborates her position by navigating between the mimeticism of Benjamin, Susan Buck-Morss, Michael Taussig, Alois Reigl, and Deleuze and Guattari.

Haptic visuality forces us to "touch a film with our eyes" by emphasizing the surface of images and interfering with our tendency to expect illusionistic depth. Haptic images play with focus, exposure, and grain. They move close to the surface of things to render texture. In this way, they provoke a multisensory exploration on the part of the spectator.

There are parallels here to Ogawa's earlier aesthetics of political mimesis. Indeed, Gaines and Marks draw on many of the same theories of mimesis. They both describe a body-first approach to knowledge. However, the former is driven by political imperatives and describes a faculty that spectators seem to possess in urgent situations of sociopolitical stress. In contrast, Marks suggests that the faculties necessary for engaging haptic visuality are learnable or cultured (a move that allows her to avoid the prelapsarian tendencies of many theories of mimesis). They tend to arise in situations when filmmakers are forced to the limits of representation and must develop other representational and spectatorial possibilities. This search is precisely what has driven the innovations of Ogawa from the very beginning. Over the course of many years, his intersubjective stance first led him to an aesthetic of political mimesis, and the changes in political and social landscape in which he worked led him to haptics and mimetic strategies.

The most prominent haptic images of *Sundial* are in the rice fields. One enduring bit of imagery every spectator takes from this film puts us right down in the muck. Tamura attached a miniature camera to a long pole to make pans down the rows of the paddy. Hovering only centimeters above the water of the rice paddy, he captures enormous rubber boots sloshing through the muck and giant hands plunking down delicate shoots of rice plants just inches before the lens. This was Tamura unleashed and at his most creative and playful, but its forcefulness is audio-visual. The scenes achieve a tactile quality from the combination of the impossible angle and the vast sucking sounds of feet pulling out of deep mud.

These long takes, wallowing in the paddies, punctuate the entire breadth of the film. They bring us into contact with the sensorium of Magino Village, appealing to the shared structures of our senses. A conventional scene of *taue*, the hand-planting of rice sprouts, would objectify the process. The cameraman would shoot the process from the dry banks of the paddies. The farmers would have symbolic value available for interpretation and guided by the narration of the film. However, Ogawa's approach here draws on the process of sensing itself to bring us into contact with Magino, to unify us through touch, blurring intersubjective boundaries between us and them.

One of the other muscularly haptic qualities of the film comes from the soundtrack with its percussive music. As Marks points out, the haptic does not necessarily have to be visual: "Sound does come into play insofar as it is experienced kinesthetically; for example, the booming in the chest caused by deep bass tones, or the complex effects of rhythm on the body."[11] Although the study of film music is enjoying a surge in productive research programs, it has historically been one of the most overlooked areas of cinema. As most scholarship inevitably seems to point out, an important factor in this neglect is the nature of film music itself, which is generally

Tamura Masaki attached a miniature camera to a pole to shoot planting at mud level. From this perspective, enormous rubber boots slosh through the paddies, and giant hands plunge delicate rice shoots into the muck. It gave this mundane chore a startling, tactile quality that brings us into contact with the sensorium of Magino Village, appealing to the shared structures of our senses.

characterized by what Claudia Gorbman has called its "inaudibility." While she is primarily referring to the feature film's score, which subordinates itself to dialogue, visuals, and narrative, her terms apply equally well to the documentary. And as Neil Lerner has pointed out, in one of the first studies of documentary music, the ideological and ethical aspects of music take on a new dimension in this medium that makes claims for representing the real. Lerner writes,

> [Music's] mere presence, threaded throughout the cinematic narrative, creates a sense of flow and directionality. It acts as an agent of manipulation and change within the discourse of the film. And its raw power to alter the perceived visual landscape drastically has caused it to be subjected to a number of artificial constraints and conventions. An attempt to interpret, and thus control, film music involves the harnessing of forces that normally travel freely, if not passively, across the audiences' consciousness; if engineered properly, this harnessing generates interpretive energy.[12]

Throughout his career, Ogawa used music sparingly. The lush, symphonic score of *Winter in Sanrizuka* was an exception springing from serendipitous circumstance (budget, willing composer, and proactive sound editor); however, in this film he was also trying to *say* something. To say the last word on Sanrizuka. The attempt failed. What worked were films that used music sparingly, that built a kind of musicality into the fabric of the film. This use of "music" as musicality rendered the Sanrizuka Series a medium through which spectators were hailed to mime the resistance of the farmers and fight political oppression in their own lives. Put in Lerner's language, the musicality gave the film a directionality—from the local profilmic to the filmic and ultimately back to the dispersed public extrafilmic. It harnessed the film's forces to effect an interpretive energy involving both the raising of consciousness and the inspiring of social and political action.

When Ogawa did use nondiegetic music it was locally restricted and strategically deployed. For *Summer in Sanrizuka,* Ogawa Pro brought in Beethoven for the finale. Arriving at the symphony's tympanic climax, this high-brow music clashes with its subject matter like so many charging riot police. In *Dokkoi! Song from the Bottom,* a young man strums a guitar on a rooftop. The passion with which he sings, the content of the lyrics, the folk mode in which the lyrics are rendered, all locate the film in the nexus of politics and music within early 1970s youth culture. The filmmakers began using soundtracks designed for the entirety of the film precisely when the mimetic properties of their filmmaking fell away in the early 1970s. In *"Nippon": Furuyashiki Village,* Ogawa Pro used traditional instruments for a delicate soundtrack evoking an earlier era. Music was needed to fill silences and flesh out and direct meaning. The film required transitions and a level of "professional" filmmaking Ogawa Pro's previous audiences cared little about and/or forgave. Thus, music became a crucial element of its filmmaking in Magino.

However, these previous uses of music were largely symbolic deployments designed to shape meaning in quite specific ways. With *Sundial,* Ogawa turns to an entirely percussive sound that signals an avant-garde sensibility. The music was by Togashi Masahiko, a child prodigy on the violin who later became a professional drummer. In the reflexive spirit of the film, Ogawa shows him performing behind the end credits. The musician is surrounded by drums of every size and sort. In the film, the rolling storm clouds, bursting rice flowers, mushing galoshes, Jomon figurines—even the professional scientists—were accompanied by the staccato stabs of drum beats. They tumble in and out of the soundtrack, evoking the inexplicable, seemingly referencing nothing quite specific. Being modernist music, it suggests the filmmaker was thinking less about the symbolized, instrumental possibilities of music than its powerful physical affect. The pounding beats are the aural counterpart of the title: *The Sundial Carved with a Thousand Years of Notches*. It feels as if each drum thump carves a notch in the sundial, making the film a portal to the Magino sensorium.

One might be tempted to accuse Ogawa of a prelapsarian nostalgia here, of a romanticization of a rural way of life that is being tainted by Western influence. When I first visited Ogawa Pro in Magino back in the 1980s, I was struck by an advertising campaign in the railway stations that prominently featured my destination of Yamagata. The posters were everywhere, with beautiful photographs of the northern mountains and the legend, "Sono sakki no Nihon e" ("Toward that Japan from Before"). Marilyn Ivy has identified this very campaign as one of many postwar "discourses of the vanishing."[13] Ivy would challenge us to think of Ogawa—and all the other directors of his generation that made similar turns to the rural, most notably Imamura—as part of a celebration of folklore provoked by anxieties over national identity. Folklore studies by scholars like Ogawa's hero Yanagida, advertising campaigns like the railway posters, local preservation efforts like Furuyashiki's outdoor museum, are attempts to give permanence to nostalgic sites of authenticity. They provide a sense of continuity in a modern era filled with anxiety over the fragmenting of identity.

Ogawa's films were available for appropriation by (urban) spectators ill at ease with the regimented modern life, but the films themselves are much more than elegiac spectacles of loss, recovery, and preservation. This is largely attributable to Ogawa's elaborate conception of history, and we can look specifically at this treatment of folklore to tease out his position.

Just when the hard science seems about to take over the entire film, an intertitle suddenly announces, "In the village, a wealth of folklore has been handed down about the water of rice paddies." Villager Satake Kiyoshi stands on a hill overlooking Magino and relates a thousand-year-old story he heard from his grandmother, all in a wonderfully thick Yamagata dialect. After nearly an hour of intense consideration of rice, we greet his story with intense relief. Sitting in the forest, he explains how his ancestors tried unsuccessfully to draw water for their fields from an adjacent watershed on Mount Zao. Without more water, rice would be difficult to grow, and farming would be unfeasible. All their schemes to direct water to their feeder streams failed. However, Satake explains how one day a beautiful woman and a band of unshaven men offered to help by constructing a dam.

Suddenly, an elderly historian appears—literally jumping out of the bushes—interrupting Satake's wonderful story. The historian addresses Satake (in standard Japanese): "Oh, a young woman suddenly appears, you say?" He then stands next to the bush he emerged from and gives the professional historian's take on this old Magino tale. Noting that young girls appearing out of nowhere are a typical feature of Japanese folklore, he suggests the story has something to do with fertility. At the same time, he offers archeological evidence of a large community in the region a millennium ago. Digs at the site uncovered the skeleton of a woman in an important burial site. The historian suggests that it is likely that this woman helped spread rice cultivation in the Magino area. In tribute, memory of her gift has been preserved in the tale told by Satake, who turns from the historian's interruption with a bemused grin to complete his story for the camera.

A typical ethnographic film would have placed the senior historian's explanation in a position of textual power. Everyone knows these strategies. They usually involve a voice-over narration vested with explanatory authority or a head-and-shoulders interview in a university office decorated with books. The professional filmmaker or professional historian would have introduced the story, and then summarily explained it away with whatever anthropological paradigm was dominant at the time. However, Ogawa levels such distinctions by making the historian's discourse *an interruption,* as opposed to an authoritative book-ending that regulates the knowledge of the story and the status of its teller. Ogawa further calls the academic's position of authority into question by having the historian emerge from the woods—Satake's territory—in such a comical manner. The historian from Tokyo is the new standard bearer for the opening discourse on distanced, objectifying ways of knowledge, now of the social scientific variety. He may also be seen as a surrogate for the filmmakers themselves. However, Ogawa tempers it with humor and surrealism. At one level, the historian is mocked and rendered absurd. At another, it is clear that Ogawa cannot and will not dispense with this epistemological route to the village. It is through these ironizing moves that Ogawa puts these two regimes of knowledge into contact, demonstrating that the villagers are hardly untouched by Enlightenment epistemologies. Neither is complete; each holds a supplemental relationship to the other.

This stance is rearticulated in a sequence that brings in archeology as a route to village history, taking us back to the very beginnings of human history in Magino Village. The farmers in the area often find artifacts in their fields, usually shards of pottery. Judging from their patterns, they date from the Jomon Period. This is the furthest back archeologists have taken human habitation of the Japanese islands, dating from 1,000 to 10,000 BC. In an almost serendipitous fashion, Ogawa decides the collective members will dig in a corner of a field near their house and see what they can find. In the previous scenes, they played agronomists, biologists, historians, and anthropologists; now they take on the role of archeologists. Although it was the dead of winter, the film crew shoveled away the snow and started scraping away the earth. With small scoops and brushes they carefully penetrated the soil of Magino, layer by layer, and actually discovered some artifacts. First, a few mysterious-looking figurines emerged from the dirt. Then, they noticed the stones of an ancient hearth. They call in an archeologist from a university to help them interpret their discoveries.

What is ultimately interesting about this archeological sequence is what it tells us about Ogawa's use of science in general. It is evident that Ogawa doesn't really care all that much about the things professional scientists devote their lives to; it is a different kind of knowledge production. Looking at the arrangement of the hearth in relation to the distant mountains and the inexplicable patterns in the figurines, Ogawa almost gleefully concludes it must be some kind of shrine. This quick conclusion—"This means that!"—is less scientific deduction than one more novel fiction spun from the fertile imagination of Ogawa. This is science as style, an approach that questions the authority of scientific discourses while deploying them in rich, new directions.

What Ogawa is ultimately attempting is the forging of one more creative route into the world of Magino. Upon "discovering" the religious value of the objects the collective brought to light, the members immediately bind that significance to present-day village life. Kimura's wife, Shigeko, suggests they had better have a local priest hold a ceremony to make sure that the local gods are not upset by the older gods Ogawa Pro unearthed. This fluid movement between the past and the present is a structure repeated through nearly every scene of the film.

I can think of few films that complicate the notion of history to such a degree; we see the competing knowledge produced by story and social science, the written records of the village heritage, the oral tales handed down through the generations, as well as fragments of history left from the furthest reaches of human experience. All of this is marked by that arcing of the sun across the heavens and the cycles of the rice harvest that have governed people's lives through the ages. What is truly extraordinary is the sense it gives for a conception of history that may not make much sense in Tokyo or Ann Arbor or Berlin, a sense of history that is not so much a thing resurrected from the past, but palpably alive in the present.

The most powerful tool Ogawa uses to this end is performance and mimetic reenactment. While this became a common feature of world documentary in the 1990s, Ogawa Pro arrived at it early. Along with its intense documentary scrutiny of rice and archeology are short, episodic narratives that often pair professional actors with the villagers taking the roles of their own ancestors. In this way, embodied knowledge of these villagers is rendered visible; personal and collective memories are given material form. This mimetic approach constitutes yet another innovative yielding into knowledge. These are the stories that have circulated among the members of this tiny village throughout its history and are anywhere from one generation to several centuries old. Furthermore, the treatment of time *within* these narratives is exceedingly complex and often relies on auratic objects to enable sudden time slips.

For example, one scene tells the story of an ancient stone god that sits next to the god of the mountains in a Magino shrine, a tale originally related to Ogawa by his neighbor Inoue. Ogawa has the farmer reenact the story of his deceased father digging up the ancient god—a large stone phallus, to be specific—shortly after World War II. Embarrassed, he apologized to the god and promptly returned it to the earth of their field. As Inoue, playing the role of his father, fills up the hole, Ogawa's bemused narration explains that when the father returned home, he couldn't stop laughing and wouldn't tell anyone why. Curious about what the father could have found out in that field, the young Inoue struck out with his wife to dig it up. Now Inoue and his wife play themselves as a young couple several decades in the past. They dig in the hole surrounded by mulberry bushes, giggling in their self-consciousness before the camera. Finally, they strike something hard with their shovels. Pulling out the big phallus from the earth, they embellish their reenactment as they would any good story: "Wow, take a look at this. It's spectacular!" says Inoue to his wife, "Hmmm, anatomically correct. Here, grab a hold!" He unexpectedly changes his tone and adds, "We

In *The Sundial Carved with a Thousand Years of Notches,* Ogawa handles the ancient phallic god unearthed in Magino, discussing its betrothal to the mountain goddess with a local priest. In the background, Tamura Masaki on camera, Kikuchi Nobuyuki on sound, and Iizuka Toshio enjoying the conversation. Photograph by Naito Masatoshi.

better pray." He sets it proudly upright at the lip of the hole and they offer their apologies to the god in prayer, and then Ogawa reverts to traditional storytelling methods. Inoue explains how his father did not want to show the phallus to his children, but he was also hesitant to return it to the earth after being buried for thousands of years—that would be rude! So his father hid the phallic god under the house. Then returning to reenactment, Inoue once again takes the role of his father and performs the conclusion of the story. He and another villager tie a sacred straw rope around the stout shaft of the phallus and marry the god to the goddess of the mountain. The two sit side-by-side in her shrine to this very day.

This is just one of the stories that provide the present-day scenes in Magino a powerful resonance with village history. Although there is absolutely nothing extraordinary about Magino, Ogawa impresses upon us the extra behind the veil of the ordinary. After seeing this film, one never looks at a Japanese village in quite the same way. One assumes that every stone monument and shrine, no matter how small or neglected, hides a wondrous history. Every village must have as rich a past as Magino, a history that ties all the people inhabiting the houses and working the fields to all the people and all the gods in their collective past.

Ogawa recreates two other stories that effectively politicize that link between past and present, while pushing the limits of documentary reenactment. The first of these comes after Satake's story about the digging of the dam and its ditch a thousand years past. Satake's traditional mode of storytelling segues to the reenactment of a tale circulating in the village that taps on changes in the village economy and the postwar flight to urban metropolises. The story is centered on a shrine next to the sluice, where the beautiful young woman who helped divert the water is worshipped as a mountain goddess. Her image sits in the shrine, carved from a stone pulled from the ditch. Ogawa relates the story of her shrine, a tale that places four generations of a single family against the backdrop of modern Japanese history.

Simply told, at the very beginning of Japan's modern era in the mid-nineteenth century, a man named Yonosuke was one of the first in the area to defy convention by refusing to make charcoal. He grew cedar trees as a cash crop instead. By planting the trees, he made the land his possession, this at a time when Japan was opening up to the world and transforming itself into a modern power integrated into the nation-state system and capitalist conceptions of private property. Yonosuke's grandson cut the cedar in the 1890s when wood was in great demand in the burgeoning cities and used the profit to introduce silkworms to the village economy. The village cash crop suddenly went from a thirty-year to one-year cycle. However, Yonosuke squandered the family fortune for *sake,* women, and gambling; his son, Yoki, took after his father's unfortunate vices. By the mid-1930s, the family fortune was depleted, and Yoki's wife left him. He went insane and started living in the shrine next to the sluice, taking care of the mountain goddess for the rest of his life. By 1965, their village was dead. No one lives there anymore, and what buildings are left are pathetic ruins.

This sequence has a remarkably complex structure. At one fundamental level, Ogawa himself is telling the story; aside from directing and editing the film, his voice-over narration and intertitles fill gaps, propel the story along, and keep all the heterogeneous elements in synch. At a secondary level, Kikuchi Masao,[14] a popular performer in Yamagata who is something like a folk comedian, sits in the actual ruins of Yoki's village. He relates Yoki's family history in thick Yamagata dialect ornamented with all the color of local storytelling and song. Finally, the story itself is reenacted in a fictional diegesis by an ensemble of villagers and professional actors. The fact that this is documentary allowed the filmmakers to break rules that usually reign in creative treatment of time and space in the fiction film, and this they do with a brilliant flourish. As the three upper levels of narration—Ogawa's filmmaking, his persona on the soundtrack, and Sato's storytelling—tell this tale, the images flit from Yoki's mother to his sister. Both are played by the same actor, Miyashita Junko, while the role of Yoki is performed by Hijikata. This was my first Ogawa Pro film; I recall watching it shortly after its completion, not knowing I was watching professional actors in these scenes, oblivious to the fact that Ogawa playfully references the star personas of both. In one sequence, Miyashita, the most famous of the Nikkatsu Roman Porno stars, sensuously wipes her chest down beneath her kimono. Hijikata, one of the inventors of *butoh,* delivers a strange performance as the mad Yoki that is more dance than acting.

Without understanding Hijikata's place in the history of modern performance, his scenes, with their bodily embellishment of the narrative, were absolutely mystifying to watch. For example, when Yoki's sister visits him at the shrine, the siblings appear as if in two different realities. The sister is in a real-time, relatively normal (conventional cinematic) space. Yoki watches her spread a picnic before the shrine from a dark space that

Ogawa directs Nikkatsu Roman Porno star Miyashita Junko, with Shiraishi Yoko assisting in the background. Shot in May 1985 for *The Sundial Carved with a Thousand Years of Notches.*

approximates his contorted frame of mind. However, when Yoki pulls his mother's hair pin from his wild hair and inserts it into his sister's coif in a perfect shot-reverse shot, from his darkness to her realm of sunlight, we realize that the two worlds are contiguous. After this scene, the narrative completely shuts down while Hijikata performs a baffling dance in the darkness, twirling wildly in the dirt and swinging off the trees. This is documentary on the edge, where language utterly fails. He picks up the large, stone icon of the mountain goddess and stumbles down a mountain road. In a stunningly beautiful shot, Yoki falls into the sluice, breaks the icon into pieces, and continues down the stream, disappearing from this world. Upon watching this film, one of Hijikata's disciples, *butoh* dancer Yamada Etsuko, was left breathless, "I couldn't believe this performance. Especially the way he dumped himself right into that stream. I went away thinking he had arrived at a new level. He went beyond dance. He simply was." During the filming, no one knew that Hijikata had a secret. He was swiftly dying, and the performance committed to Ogawa's celluloid was to be one of his last.

While Yoki's story points us to the complex of connections between modernization and the plight of village Japan, the other reenactment I wish to highlight turns us back to Sanrizuka. As one enters Magino Village from Kaminoyama City, Itsutsudomoe Shrine is a prominent structure on the left-hand side of the road. Mount Zao rises to the sky above, and a row of nearly identical bodhisattva sculptures are lined up alongside the shrine. These sculptures represent the villagers who stood up to the oppressive taxes of the local ruler. They led a revolt that was eventually put down, its five leaders executed.

The shrine commemorates their sacrifice, which ensured the continuity of Magino to the present day. Every New Year's Eve, the villagers open up the shrine, and enter its inner sanctum where the ashes of the martyrs are preserved. Each villager makes a visit that evening, offering a prayer, and partaking in some sake. Ogawa was impressed by the way this space served as a site for binding the villagers to each other and their collective past. He saw how the media for this "binding" involved a combination of ritual and storytelling, and he recognized that what this shrine represented was the link between sleepy, swampy Magino and the uprising at Sanrizuka. This shrine revealed what Ogawa Pro was missing during the Sanrizuka Series. Thus, in their most elaborate reenactment for *Sundial,* the filmmakers staged the trial of the martyrs using the shrine as their location. An on-screen narrator reads from an old scroll explaining the incident. Veteran *jidaigeki* stars brought in from Tokyo, including Ishibashi Choichiro, Kawarazaki Renji, and Shimada Shogo, play the local officials. The vil-

The crew stands before the statues commemorating the sacrifice of farmers who gave their lives for the sake of the village hundreds of years ago. Their descendants reenact the trial for the last scene of *The Sundial Carved with a Thousand Years of Notches.* Photograph by Naito Masatoshi.

lagers staging the revolt, however, were played by their real descendants. In a preface to the sequence's scenario, Ogawa writes,

> The documentary we have been shooting for the last seven or eight years hopes to recreate the natural features—rice, earth, water—and recreate the stories sleeping in the hearts of the villagers. *Itsutsudomoe Jinja Daihokai* is, in this film, what could be called a (as if it were a) film within a film. I use the word "theater," but on this stage where everyone participates and there is not a single spectator, we consider it a vivid ceremony that exceeds the framework of simple drama. With our camera, we want to shoot Itsutsudomoe Shrine—the drama that will unfold there—as a space where souls come into contact.[15]

To this end, they used a special writing method that brought the villagers into the process. These were stories they had heard many times over the years. A typical documentarists would simply sit a villager in front of the camera for an interview: "So tell us about the time you pulled a penis out of the ground." Ogawa told Regula König what they would do instead:

> We started the discussion saying: "Yasu-san, we think it would be interesting to film that story, but where do you think would be the best place to start

from?" So Yasu said, "Well now . . ." and began to think seriously about the plot and the lines that would best express his own feelings. All of the scenes where the farmers played themselves were done that way. We and the villagers would come up with an idea together, discuss it, plan it together, and make it together. We didn't want to reenact the story so much as we wanted to document the soul of the person telling the story.[16]

The villagers took their task seriously. They helped construct the scenarios. They showed Ogawa Pro the actual spots where each story took place, taking props and old clothes from their barns that had taken part in the events being represented. For example, villagers whose mothers or grandmothers knew Miyashita Junko's character lent the actress clothes and shoes that had been handed down to them from the time. They helped with the hairdo and even hid objects in her sash that never made it on screen. In the Itsutsudomoe Shrine scene, the document that the judge (a professional actor) shows to the rebel leader (a Magino villager) proving his guilt was actually signed by the original rebel leader and used in his trial. Many years later, Kimura Michio wrote about the importance of the Itsutsudomoe Shrine scene for the people of Magino:

> The film shoot was amazing. What exactly was amazing is difficult to express. But any rate, within the village, it had been some 240 years—since that insurrection itself (Enkyo Era 4)—since the people of the village came together as one like that, since they felt the possibility of unity, the capability of united action, or the assembly of great power. We embraced these feelings to the degree that everyone felt like they had participated in a rising. The villager actors that played the five leaders naturally felt that way, as did the ones with bit parts. But those whose faces did not appear onscreen—the housewives' association, which provided the food, the young wives' association, the volunteer firemen who directed traffic, the men who cut and hauled the firewood used for campfires, the people who made torches—there wasn't a single person from Magino Village who wasn't caught up in the film production in one form or another. The Buddhist song group featured at the end of the rising scene involved over 60 people. This orchestra—with everyone from graceless, gossipy housewives in their 40s to graceful old women in their 70s—was a bit self-indulgent, but it was the best part. Because of this the entire village, young and old, male and female, participated in the filming. Wartime programs like "patriotic cooperation" (*hokoku itchi*) are pale shadows of this kind of village esprit de corps.[17]

Ogawa Pro was not isolated from the changes that were transforming Japanese documentary from a collective spirit to the private film. And neither were the farming communities isolated from the urban filmmaking centers. Indeed, these sweeping changes in Japanese society deeply affected the filmmaking of Ogawa Pro's Magino period. Iizuka Toshio recalls showing the Sanrizuka films across northern Japan, and everywhere he went, the work was greeted with passionate, sympathetic responses. The young people of the village watched the plight of Sanrizuka carefully in those documentaries, and the films sparked honest discussions about their own local situations. They deeply identified with the Sanrizuka farmers and were inspired to think through ways of protecting their own village and its way of life. By the time Iizuka carried *The Sundial Carved with a Thousand Years of Notches* to the same villages, those young people were now in their forties and had installed themselves in the seats of village power. While the Sanrizuka Series went straight to their hearts, their response to *Sundial* was, "Huh, so Ogawa Pro could make that kind of film."

The Sanrizuka Series was deeply in tune with its era, but by the time Ogawa Pro made *Sundial,* there was a slippage between its cinema and both its *taisho* and its audience, especially its rural segment. The filmmakers brought many of their working assumptions about village Japan from Sanrizuka to Magino. Farmers, like workers, were always among the poorest groups in Japan, so the question was how to liberate and empower them. In Yamagata, there were no riot police to fight, but there was this incredible collectivity with an untapped wealth of power. Set it aflame and who knows how Japan would transform.

There is an interesting moment in their last film, *A Movie Capital* (*Eiga no miyako,* 1991), when American filmmaker Jon Jost follows a bitter critique of America with an optimistic, slightly jealous observation that he could feel a collectivity in Japan. Iizuka was shocked upon hearing this: "Ah, there's still a possibility here!" He now realizes he was mistaken. Someone like Jost had devoted decades to the problem of individual and group and bringing people together. However, this was only Jost's dream meeting Iizuka's dream.

This was, after all, precisely the time of Japan's bubble economy and farmers were quite well off (especially in contrast to the hard case poverty of Ogawa Pro). Farmers were enjoying a measure of prosperity, a participation in the fruits of modernity to a degree never experienced in the past. The Magino Village they portrayed on film was primarily one of Ogawa's own prodigious imagination. The film was widely criticized for this, especially in the hinterlands. *The Sundial Carved with a Thousand Years of Notches* was made at the end of an era; it is a film that could never be made today. As Iizuka Toshio points out, the people that really loved the film were—like Ogawa himself—lovers of the cinema, not the village.

If Ogawa's first films and the Sanrizuka Series structurally represent an arc from the self-obsessed concerns of the student movement (students making films about students) to a collective effort at understanding the collective way of life of the village, then the Magino Village Story displays a similar arcing movement away from the collective toward the powerful individual expression of Ogawa. It was a conception and hope for documentary cinema pitched at a scale unprecedented in the world of independent documentary, as Ogawa Pro's next film adequately demonstrates; it was also simultaneously out of synch with its era.

The Theater of a Thousand Years

Upon completion of its four-hour opus, Ogawa Pro was confronted with the problem that had become perennial in its Magino era: it had no place to show the film. The student movement era audience had moved on to more mundane lives. The elaborate network of sympathizers the filmmakers had pioneered as Jieiso and cultivated during the Sanrizuka Struggle had largely disintegrated. Nothing had really taken its place, with the exception of a few "mini-theaters" dedicated to art film. These were reliable distribution points. Sympathizers who had been showing their films for decades ran most of them. But there were not enough mini-theaters to ensure wide distribution, let alone adequate box-office receipts. As usual, Ogawa Pro members were going to have to distribute the film themselves.

Sundial was a work of documentary art so intimately tied to the *place* of its creation—its space and time, its sights and smells—how could one bear watching it in a dilapidated civic hall or high school gymnasium? For a while, the filmmakers seriously considered holding the screenings at the Budokan, the famous sports arena where most major rock concerts were held. What better way to start their screening movement than with an attractive splash sure to attract the press? The idea was to mount a three-screen extravaganza. *Sundial* would be shown on the middle screen, and they would project their hours and hours of rushes featuring rice and Yamagata scenery on either side. Tests using slides on the side screens did not work out very well, so they decided against that idea. Instead, they moved on a proposal from their fans in Osaka, where the readers of *Eiga Shinbun (Film Newspaper)* had been tracking the film's progress. The idea was to borrow an empty lot and build a theater from scratch. This way, they could create a space tailored to the film and the world it represented.

The fruit of their efforts was the Theater of a Thousand Years (Sennen shiataa), a traditional structure made of dirt, logs, tatami, and thatch, which the filmmakers and their fans brought from the mountains to an empty construction site in Kyoto. Built specifically for this single film, this ephemeral theater was partly an experiment in exhibition, partly a last-ditch response to a fast-changing film culture. A publicity flier for the The-

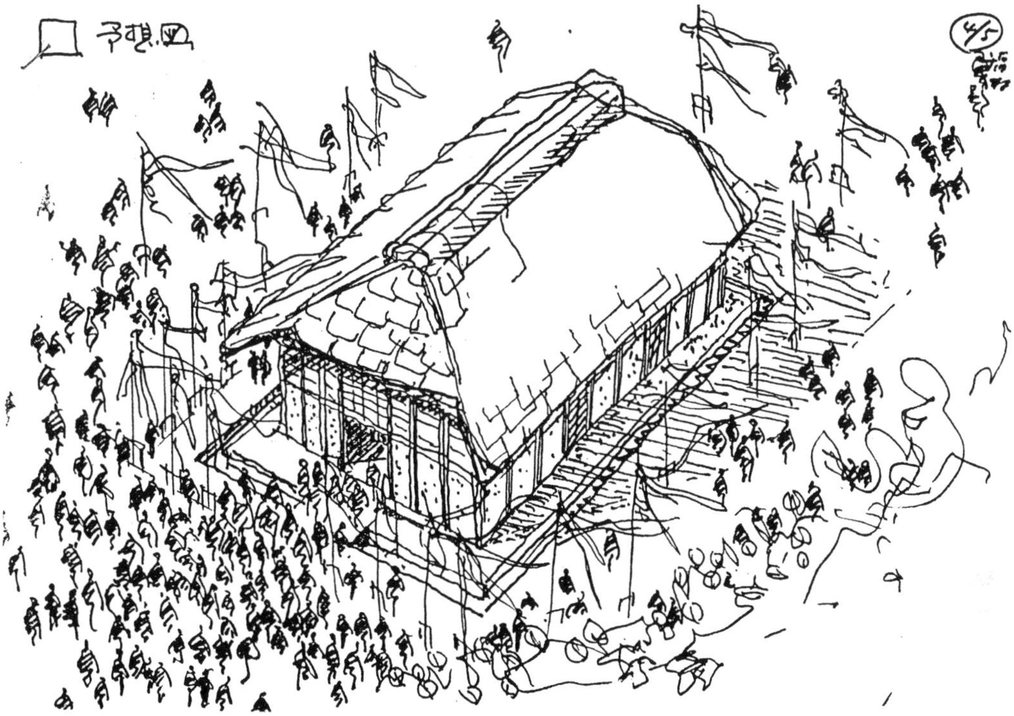

Architectural sketch for the Theater of a Thousand Years.

ater of a Thousand Years describes the motives behind building a temporary exhibition space for a single film:

> Welcome to the Theater of a Thousand Years! Considering the freedom of cinema, should not the places cinema is shown enjoy that freedom as well? This is the conception of The Theater of a Thousand Years. From the end of production to the screening of the film, most filmmakers entrust their films to the hands of other people, but here this activity is being handled from the filmmaker's side . . . It is the romance of cinephiles that a theater could be devoted to a single film. The Theater of a Thousand Years is the first embodiment of what cinephiles have long dreamed of. To be specific, it could be said that this film is utterly wrapped up in the world of Magino Village in Yamagata Prefecture. The space of this theater is surely the same, and the embodiment of that dream entirely sweeps away one's feelings toward the movie theaters of today.

This "embodiment" involved an enormous amount of sweat (all volunteered, of course). Through the efforts of Kageyama Satoshi and other members of *Eiga Shinbun's* staff, the filmmakers borrowed the construction site in Kyoto. On the same plot of land, the famous *butoh* dance troupe Dairakudakan erected their own temporary theater—one with a modern, industrial design—and held dance performances throughout the run of the film. Surrounding this was a fair modeled on the traditional *matsuri,* which they called the Demon's Market (Oni Ichiba). From ancient times, Kyoto has had its own peculiar directions, and the theater was positioned in the direction known as *Onimon* (demon gate), where bad things happen. They thought this actually might be a good thing, although they still performed a ceremony to keep any demons away. If one did visit, they thought it actually might be interesting. A highlighted phrase in the announcements put out by Ogawa Pro and Dairakudakan played with an old saying: "Will a demon come out or a snake come out? Keep watching the Demon's Market to find out what comes." In other words, demons, snakes, whatever happens it won't be good!

A young architecture student helped plan the building, using traditional designs and methods of construction. Seven hundred logs were used for the framework. Three thousand bundles of grass were brought in from the countryside for the thatched roof, along with fifty tons of mud for the walls. Ringing the outside of the theater were the tents and tarps of a local *matsuri,* or fair, featuring plenty of food and trinkets from the countryside. Occasionally, singers and acoustic bands entertained the audience arriving for the screenings. Among them was Kikuchi Masao, the folk storyteller that appeared in the film. Rows of tall, traditional banners—as used for *sumo* and *kabuki*—lined the perimeter. At the theater entrance, spectators could browse through photographs of the production, examine some of the props from the film, and buy fried noodles and home cooking from Yamagata in lieu of popcorn. The theater itself held 140 spectators, all of whom sat on pillows on the floor. Before the large screen was a hole in the ground with the ancient Jomon pottery unearthed in the film placed as though they had come once more to light. The theater was air-conditioned, but it seemed as though the cool air was rising from the "archeological dig." With the blessing of a Shinto priest, the screenings were underway.

This is, perhaps, the ultimate instance of independent film distribution. Ogawa Pro's theme was *darkness (yami)*, because new theaters are quite bright with emergency exit signs. Making it a very dark theater would transform the exhibition space into a different world. Photographer Naito Masatoshi, a long-time supporter of Ogawa Pro who had been photographing the collective for many years, was conducting research into darkness and the way it was historically used as a metaphoric space for people in society who don't fit into paradigms acceptable to power. Thus, Naito's own black-and-white still photography for Ogawa and his own projects have some of the deepest blacks imaginable. This was one more way in which Ogawa Pro meant the Theater of a Thousand Years to constitute a critique of the traditional movie going experience.

However, the most significant departure had to do with the aesthetic sensibility of the film projected in that space. As pointed out previously, Ogawa fills the film with haptic imagery. When the farmers plant their fields, we accompany them, hovering inches above the rice paddies as they slosh through the mud. When Ogawa's neighbors create a sacred straw rope for a local god, we are close enough to the twisting straw that we can virtually feel it. Our sense of time warps, becoming newly sensitized through time-lapse photography. Rice blossoms crack open like magic. The sun races across the Yamagata sky. *Sundial* removes us from whatever world we begin the film in, and transports us to the sensorium of Magino Village. Theater of a Thousand Years completed that process, literalizing the haptics of the film. Surrounded by those mud walls and thatched roof, one could actually *smell* the movie. Many of the after-film surveys expressed gratitude for this experience. A typical response ends,

> While watching the film, my eye suddenly wanders away from the screen. It was pleasing to find that this did not destroy the experience. A regular theater is different. There is only the image projected on a large screen, a world floating mysteriously in the dark. However, in Theater of a Thousand Years—with its logs, mud walls, and thatched roof—the screen and I are fully embraced in the flow of time. I look around. A man sits cross-legged on the dirt. Children lie sleeping. Everyone enjoys the film freely, in their own way. This is also nice. What is a theater? And what does it mean to show a movie? I thought this place forces you to ask such questions through *experience*. It was wonderful.[18]

The Theater of a Thousand Years may have created a unique and moving experience for those lucky enough to attend; however, Ogawa Pro's effort to confront the new difficulties of showing an independent film was as ephemeral as the structure itself. Occasionally, independent filmmakers attempt to circumvent the seemingly insurmountable problems of the exhibition situation by building their own theaters. Suzuki Seijun showed his *Yumeji* (1991) in a bubble-like tent supported by air pressure. Yamamoto Masashi borrowed an empty lot amidst the love hotels of Tokyo's Shibuya district and constructed a theater out of fluorescent-painted junk and scrap metal for *Tenamonya Connection* (*Tenamonya konekushon*, 1991). I even built a theater out of pipes and colorfully painted canvas for a First Nations documentary program at the Yamagata Film Festival in 1993. However, these are only temporary, tactical solutions to the difficult problems the Japanese film world faces.

The problem is that while Ogawa Pro became dependent on the traditional exhibition route (film festivals, critical praise in prestigious mass media periodicals, runs at mainstream movie theaters, etc.), the Japanese film industry's infrastructure was deteriorating rapidly through massive, systemic problems. As Japanese land prices skyrocketed throughout the 1980s, the number of movie theaters dropped precipitously. The year Ogawa began his filmmaking career—the year Kurosawa's *Yojimbo* (1961) smashed all the Japanese box office records—there were over seven thousand theaters in the country. By the late 1980s there were only two thousand as attendance dropped precipitously. Many of these theaters were part of chains vertically integrated into the studio system and did not pick up documentaries for distribution. There were only a couple small distributors interested in documentaries and the avant-garde, but they generally bought prestigious Western work. This left independent filmmakers—documentary and fiction filmmakers alike—distributing their own films and videos, as much out of the inertia of tradition as for lack of alternatives. After the supreme effort necessary to finish a film, the filmmakers themselves had to put equal energy into hand-carrying their film around the country. Little has changed in the intervening years, although there is some hope for change with the (small) popularity in so-called mini-theaters (art theaters) and new laws supporting the creation of nonprofit organizations.

In retrospect, Theater of a Thousand Years was yet another interesting experiment by Ogawa Pro and further proof of the boundless enthusiasm of its sympathizers in the audience. During the screenings, Ogawa shot *Kyoto Demon Market: Theater of a Thousand Years* (*Kyoto oni ichiba: Sennen Shiataa,* 1987). It is a simple record of this ephemeral event. As one of the handouts states, a month later "there was nothing left but the wind." And in some ways, we could almost say the same of Ogawa Productions.

[6] After Ogawa

Ogawa Shinsuke and the Asian Documentary

When *The Sundial Carved with a Thousand Years of Notches* was being distributed, Ogawa and Iizuka started thinking about moving the collective out of Magino and at the same time allowing Iizuka to start directing on his own. He and another member, Abe Hiroko, went to a village in southern Yamagata called Tamanoi and began working with the local people and generally researching the area. Based on this investigation, Iizuka produced a script he wished to direct. Over several sessions of "open discussions" with the entire collective, which was now down to five or six members, Ogawa harshly criticized this scenario. Revisions did not satisfy him either, and Ogawa eventually ended up bringing Abe back under his wing and returning Iizuka to Magino to think about where to go from there. As an alternative, Iizuka was put in the director's seat for a film about the 1989 Yamagata International Documentary Film Festival (YIDFF).

The idea for this festival emerged during preparations for a celebration for the one-hundredth anniversary of the founding of Yamagata City. Organized and paid for by city hall, it is hard to separate this project from the rhetoric of "*machi okoshi*" and "*kokusaika*," which was popular throughout Japan in the 1980s. Japan had to rejuvenate its rural areas and internationalize its insular population. One of the strategies local governments used was the creation of film festivals. Around the time of the first Yamagata festival—and shortly afterward in the wake of its success—film festivals popped up all across Japan. However, Yamagata set itself apart by the global reach of its ambitions and its unusual choice to focus entirely on documentary.

The decision to focus on documentary had much to do with Ogawa's presence in Yamagata but was originally the proposal of Tanaka Satoshi.

He was a leader in the local media who devoted endless energy to culture-related organizations (and whose daughter Nobuko, amazingly enough, worked in Jieiso and Ogawa Pro and married Nosaka Haruo). Tanaka proposed a documentary film festival to the city as part of its one-hundredth anniversary celebration in 1989. He went to Ogawa for advice, and on Ogawa's suggestion they enlisted critic Sato Tadao. Both Sato and Ogawa encouraged the city to specialize. It was excellent advice because it enabled the city to stage what would, as the first documentary film festival in Asia, become a significant site in the Asian independent film sector. By bringing directors from all over the world to the event, Ogawa impressed upon the organizers the meaning it would have for the filmmakers themselves, for Asian artists, for Japanese film lovers, and ultimately for the ordinary citizens of Yamagata. Always nervous about using tax money, the city hired consultants from Dentsu, the largest PR firm in Japan. Not surprisingly, they hated the idea, describing it as "dark, depressing, and dangerous." For some time, the organizers wavered, uncomfortable that so many of the films would be antiestablishment by default and implicitly critical of any form of organized power, both governmental and industrial. But as a testament to their intelli-

A Movie Capital (1991). Shooting the Asian visitors at the first Yamagata International Documentary Film Festival in 1989. From left to right: Kato Takanobu, Otsu Koshiro, Korean screenwriter Hong Ki-Seong, Asanuma Yukikazu, and Filipino critic Teddie Co. Photograph courtesy of the Yamagata International Documentary Film Festival.

gence and bravery, qualities one rarely expects from Japanese bureaucrats, they put themselves on the line and gave the go-ahead.

Ogawa affected the shape of the YIDFF in a number of ways. Since most people thought of NHK television programs when they heard the word *documentary,* Ogawa taught them what a rich tradition of filmmaking this actually was. He showed the city bureaucrats and potential volunteers works by Flaherty, Ivens, and Ogawa Pro and taught them about nonfiction filmmaking. He impressed upon the bureaucrats the meaning such an event would have for the city, for the bureaucracy, and for the world; he gave them the confidence they needed to proceed. Ogawa also gave the festival its special Asian focus, and Yamagata immediately became the most important space for independent Asian documentarists to meet and see each other's work. At the same time, he supported and energized the young volunteers that formed the film festival's "Network," empowering them while fighting for them.

The meaningfulness of the Network's role cannot be underplayed. Because of the decline of the Japanese film industry and the way film culture is centralized primarily in Tokyo, it has largely been up to the spectators to nurture their film culture. Universities, local governments, museums, and the film industry have been remarkably poor at cultivating a film culture outside of the major film chains, routes devoted primarily to Hollywood product flow. This fell to small independent theaters in urban centers. For example, the Forum Theater in Yamagata City was a legacy of the screening movement that showed the Sanrizuka Series and other independent films. It was run by Nagasawa Yuji, who began organizing Ogawa Pro screenings back in his university days. In the late 1980s, Ogawa inspired a new generation of film fans in Yamagata to take matters into their own hands. These younger people were looking for "something," and here Ogawa appeared and plugged them into the entire planet. And that world Ogawa connected them to was in turmoil in 1989. Amidst the planning stages of the festival, filmmakers like South Korea's Hong Ki-Seong and China's Tian Zhuang-zhuang were forbidden to attend by their governments for political reasons. For the Network, this was more than simply a dead-end in some of their plans; it palpably implicated these local volunteers into the martial law of Korea and the oppressive measures taken by the Chinese government in the wake of the Tiananmen Massacre. Masuya Shuichi, the long-time head of the Network, recalls the typical scene: "Ogawa basically thought anything was possible. He would tell someone, 'You, do this!' And they'd think, 'Eh?! You can do *that* in Yamagata?!?!' But his enthusiasm always won out."

In 1989, the fruits of their labors resulted in the assembly of world-renown filmmakers like Nestor Almendros, Teshigawara Hiroshi, Richard Leacock, Marceline Loridan, Jon Jost, Tsuchimoto Noriaki, Kidlat Tahimik, and many others. After the festival, the network continued to invite filmmakers, Japanese and foreign, to their events year-round. They even participated in the selection of the competition films for every festival, something extremely unusual and perhaps unique on the international film festival circuit. Thanks to the fires Ogawa set, they functioned more like staff members than volunteers during the festivals. Even back then, according to volunteer Sendo Takashi, these young people spoke of a quasi-religious "Ogawaism" (Ogawa-kyo); today they offer comparisons of their Network to Aum Shinrikyo, the cult responsible for the sarin gas attacks in Tokyo.

Before this, it was impossible to imagine such an impressive gathering in the northern mountains of Japan. Ogawa told me about the impending 1989 YIDFF when I met him at the 1988 Hawai'i International Festival, which served as one of the centers for introducing Asian cinema to the West in the 1980s. He breathlessly described their plans, and while being impressed by his enthusiasm, I remember thinking, "A documentary festival in rural Japan. Huh. You can do *that* in Yamagata?" Little did I know I would be working for them a couple years later, newly converted to Ogawaism. I arrived in the midst of postproduction for *A Movie Capital,* a PR film about the 1989 festival financed by the city. I even ended up translating the subtitles for the film.

Being in the vicinity of the postproduction, I recall watching Ogawa slowly edging into the editing process and finally overwhelming it. For some of this period, I lived in the Ogawa Pro apartment with Iizuka Toshio. During long conversations at the public bath and talking over beers before bed, Iizuka was careful and polite about what was going on. He said that Ogawa was "helping him with some tough parts," but what was really happening was much more trying. Ogawa disliked Iizuka's film but couldn't step back and let it go. While Iizuka was put in charge of the production, it is ultimately impossible to say whose film this really was. Iizuka started it, but along the way Ogawa had much to say about how things were proceeding. As with *Dokkoi! Song from the Bottom* and *Sanrizuka—The Skies of May, the Road to the Village,* Ogawa ended up taking over. Thus, it is not exactly Ogawa's film, and it is certainly not Iizuka's film.

A Movie Capital weaves three strings together, albeit in an uneven warp. First, it functions as PR for the city of Yamagata and has cheery scenes that remind one of *Sundial:* Network volunteers scurry around town, the high school band practices, and a local artist forges the bronze

Ogawa Shinsuke and his assistant director, Iizuka Toshio, shooting an interview in 1986. In Ogawa Pro, no one got to shoot their *ippon*, their chance to direct a film and establish a career as an independent director. Photograph by Naito Masatoshi; courtesy of Shiraishi Yoko and the Athénée Français Cultural Center.

trophies for the top prizes. Second, it emphasizes the international backdrop of the festival, starting with the death of Joris Ivens—who had planned to attend—and ending with the events of 1989 in Beijing and Berlin. Finally, there are extensive interviews with the visiting filmmakers and generous clips of their films. The most important of these interviews, positioned at the end of *A Movie Capital*, celebrate the new connections forged between Asian filmmakers visiting the festival. This was one of the first indications of a massive shift in the geographic imagination of the Japanese film world, from a primarily Euro-American bilateral conception of international film flow to a strong identification with other Asian filmmaking centers. The Japanese were beginning to reconfigure their neighbors as *fellow* Asian filmmakers.

Ogawa arrived at his interest in Asia through a number of routes. First, Shiraishi was born in colonial Manchuria, where her father was a middle-class bureaucrat in the 1930s and early 1940s. Ogawa found himself fascinated by their stories tinged by nostalgia for a long-lost, foreign home. Undoubtedly, it was just the kind of spectacular family history he found himself lacking. Above and beyond this, he was simply concerned about the legacy of the twentieth-century wars and Japan's imperial past. When Ogawa traveled abroad for the first time in his life, it was to accompany *"Nippon": Furuyashiki Village* to the Berlin International Film Festival. This was also the stage for his first encounter with fellow filmmakers from Asia. He had the same experience with the screenings of *Sundial* at the Berlin and Hawai'i festivals. The latter was known at the time for introducing new, noncanonical Asian works to the West, and he found many new friends there. This being the very early stages of video tape distribution, Ogawa was jealous of the access Americans and Europeans had to the latest Asian cinema thanks to their many film festivals. Indeed, despite their close geographical proximity, nothing was known about the state of documentary in the rest of Asia. However, Ogawa was struck by the fact that there were virtually no documentaries in the film festivals outside Japan, and not a single Asian nonfiction work made the Yamagata competition in 1989. These are the reasons he poured his energies into the Asia Program of the YIDFF. Something had to be done.

The Asia Program of the first YIDFF in 1989 included Ogawa as moderator and Tsuchimoto Noriaki, Stephen Teo (Malaysia), Nick Deocampo (Philippines), Teddie Co (Philippines), Zarul Albakri (Malaysia), (Peggy) Chiao Hsiung-ping (Taiwan), Kong Su-Chang (South Korea), Manop Udomdej (Thailand), Kidlat Tahimik (Philippines). Hong Ki-Seong (South Korea) and Tian Zhuang-zhuang (mainland China) were unable to attend for political reasons. They held a panel at which each filmmaker explained the state of documentary in his or her respective country.

Their reports painted a picture of artists restricted by the censorship of oppressive regimes and entrenched poverty. The bleakness of the current situation was underscored by the fact that not a single Asian film made it into the competition of Asia's first documentary film festival. There were glimmers of hope, however, with the rise of democracy movements in places like Taiwan, China, Korea, and the Philippines, where camcorder activism was taking root thanks to the falling prices of video equipment. The filmmakers ended their meeting at YIDFF by signing a manifesto declaring a new age of cooperation among Asian artists.

This manifesto is long forgotten in Asia, including Japan, so it never had the impact of Spain's Salamanca Convention or the Oberhausen Manifesto. However, these documentarists did set the stage for the remarkable explosion of documentary in Asia. The Asia Program at YIDFF became the place where all of Asia's documentary film and video makers met to network and see each other's work. Asian documentaries became regular features of the competition starting with the next festival in 1991. An Asian film finally won the top Robert and Frances Flaherty Prize in 2003 (Wang Bing's *Tie Xi Qu: West of the Tracks* [*Tiexi Qu,* China]). Programmers from European festivals left the YIDFF with Asian documentaries for their own events. Finally, documentary film festivals modeled after the YIDFF sprouted up in Bombay, Taipei, Jeonju, and elsewhere. Ogawa sat at the nexus of all these activities. Even memories of his commitment continued this work long after his death. Ogawa stimulated people across Asia with his boundless energy that answered a hearty "Yes!" to the question, "You can do *that* in Asia?!?!"

At the same time, Ogawa's Asia was a rarefied one, an Asia very much spun from his own interests and creative obsessions. He was happily oblivious to the complicated public and private politics that Asian documentary was emerging from. Instead, he enthusiastically threw his energy into a new network of relationships with colleagues across Asia. He died before these friendships had a chance to mature; however, his impact on many of the leaders of documentary was undeniable, particularly those in the Philippines, China, Korea, and Taiwan. It is to the stories of their encounters with Ogawa that I will devote the last pages of this book. One of the original signers of the 1989 manifesto was Stephen Teo. He was brought on to that year's festival as a coordinator, lending his English writing skills and scholarly expertise to the fledgling festival. Teo was also a director, and the semidocumentary qualities of his *Bejalai* (1986) deeply impressed Ogawa. Teo was encouraged to attempt documentary by his friendship with the Japanese director, however, the conditions for independent production in his native Malaysia or his adopted Hong Kong, among other factors, led him to a life in the academy.[1]

Ogawa's legacy is particularly strong in China. One of the first documentarists to pioneer independence outside of the People's Republic of China's official system was Wu Weng-guang. He surfaced out of nowhere with *Bumming in Beijing (Liulang Beijing)* in 1988 and struck up a friendship with Ogawa Pro and the YIDFF. Ogawa and Fuseya worked hard to help with distribution deals in Japan, press attention, as well as visits to Tokyo for study, screenings, and work. Today, Wu and other PRC directors will quickly exclaim that Ogawa is their hero. However, as Asian cinema scholar Ishizaka Kenji wryly notes, "Of all the Asian filmmakers, the Chinese have by far been the most profoundly influenced by Ogawa Shinsuke . . . even though they have never seen the films!" I once pressed Wu on which films he admired, and he admitted with a smile that he never made it through any of them.[2] It was Ogawa's charisma, infectious optimism, and his cheerleading for Asian documentarists that Wu found inspiring.

We can see that the relationships Ogawa struck with other directors in

Asia are similar in quality, although there is a clear spectrum, from simple engagement in the spectacle of Ogawa's charisma to honest debate over the most complex issues about documentary filmmaking.

The 1989 festival was also where Ogawa met Filipino critic Teddy Co and filmmakers Nick Deocampo and Kidlat Tahimik. Deocampo was flush with excitement over a new career in film studies, as he had just returned from America where he studied with Annette Michelson at New York University (NYU). He was already well-known for his Super-8 experimental shorts and documentaries, especially *Oliver* (1983), a nonfiction portrait of a male dancer. However, his heady experience at NYU inspired him to give up filmmaking and attempt to rewrite the history of Filipino filmmakers from a more theoretically informed position.[3] It was simply too difficult to make nonfiction films back home. This was a radically expensive art form for the context of the Philippines. Furthermore, the taste for popular American cinema and its Filipino analog was too overwhelming for a filmmaker with ambitions for the documentary. Thus, he arrived as a guest of the 1989 Asia Symposium ready to quit filmmaking and become a historian and theorist. He even went so far as to announce his frustrations and his intent to give up hope for an independent Asian documentary on the festival platform.

However, the very next day, he saw competition films that he couldn't believe were considered documentary. Their use of fictional narration and the tools of film style were so inventive he found himself embarrassed about his proclamations of the previous day, and he determined to return to the YIDFF in two years with an Asian documentary for the competition. And he did so with his 16-mm documentary feature entitled, *Ynang Bayan: To Be a Woman Is to Live in a Time of War* (1991). He has continued his filmmaking to the present, all the while heading up the Mowelfund Film Institute, writing history and theory, and releasing his first feature film. While he only remembers being inspired by Ogawa's awesome passion as the chair of the Asia Symposium, Deocampo provides the ultimate example of Ogawa's dream for the YIDFF—the way he returned to filmmaking after giving up all hope.

In contrast, Ogawa cultivated a deep friendship with Kidlat Tahimik. The director of the celebrated *Perfumed Nightmare* (*Mababangong bangungot,* 1977), Tahimik was one of the few (non-Japanese) Asian independents to achieve widespread recognition in the West before the 1990s. Kidlat was "completing" his finest film to date, *I Am Furious Yellow* (*Bakit Dilaw Ang Gitna Ng Bahag-Hari*? 1981–?), when he met Ogawa at Yamagata. I put "completing" in quotes because Kidlat rejected the concept of *ending* for this film, which followed the development of his sons against that of the nation. Over the course of the 1990s, he regularly brought back new, longer versions to Japan, allowing spectators to watch his family grow with the traumatic and spectacular backdrop of the Aquino assassination, the Yellow Revolution that ousted Marcos, and the terrible eruption of Mount Pinatubo. Along the way, Kidlat teaches his children about Magellan, Spanish and American colonization, and the imperial qualities of Hollywood cinema.

Throughout the 1990s, Kidlat came back to Japan to screen the film with a new ending, which inevitably involved a performance using a hodgepodge of props, including wooden Indian busts, reels of film, and "Third World projectors" constructed out of junk. After Ogawa's death, the new endings often included tributes to Ogawa summoning up his spirit for the sake of Asian cinema. As the ending lengthened through constant fiddling, these tributes became integrated into the (current) ending of *I Am Furious Yellow.*

One spring, Kidlat and I visited Magino together to visit Ogawa. We sat around the *kotatsu* eating, as always around Ogawa Pro, great food, soaking in nearby hot springs, and pounding rice into *mochi.* We both had a wonderful time talking to Ogawa and what was left of the collective. In retrospect, however, we both have come to recognize how superficial our communication was. None of the people at Ogawa Pro, including Ogawa himself, had a strong command of English. Kidlat had no Japanese, and my speaking abilities were still rudimentary. Communication was anything but transparent. In a recent conversation, we reminisced about that trip and realized together that our relationship to Ogawa relied to a striking degree on the spectacle of his charisma and the power of his films. As guests from far away places, unable to engage Ogawa at a critical level and oblivious to the many contradictions and controversies swirling around the man, we could hardly fail to be impressed.

Beyond the power of Ogawa's personal presence, Tahimik felt extraordinarily deep connections to Ogawa. He had seen a sampling of the Sanrizuka films, and was impressed by Tamura's camerawork. However, the two major films of the Magino era fit snugly into Tahimik's own fascination with rural cultures in the Philippines, and the deep importance of rice in many Asian cultures. They were roughly the same age. They both liked making and watching long films. And Ogawa's late turn to Asia coincided ideologically with Tahimik's ongoing project of attacking the imperialism of Western powers in Asia and the need for a pan-Asian solidarity among film artists in the face of Hollywood's awesome power.

However, now that over a decade has passed since Ogawa's death, the emotional trauma of the loss has worn away. It is possible to look back at

The obligatory commemorative photograph in front of the Magino house, on the occasion of a visit by Filipino director Kidlat Tahimik and me in 1990. We later realized that our relationship to Ogawa relied to a striking degree on the spectacle of his charisma and the power of his films.

that time and recognize that their relationship was mediated by watching each others' films, by play, and by unavoidably slow conversations in simple (if ecstatic) English. Tahimik has recently moved out of Bagio and into a small village of indigenous peoples in an experiment in living (he is taking video cameras along to teach the people he's living with). Japanese critics pointed out the parallels to Ogawa Pro's move from Sanrizuka to Magino. But for Kidlat Tahimik, it is not the expression of influence or homage, just more evidence of the fact that he and Ogawa seemed to (to put it in language Tahimik himself might use) "live in parallel cosmos."

Of all the Asian connections he cultivated, Ogawa was most interested in the Korean situation and its possibilities. I remember him talking with some agitation about the similarities between Korea of the 1980s and Japan of the 1960s. He spent considerable time with the Korean delegation to the 1989 YIDFF, which included Kong Su-Chang, and two feature filmmakers, Bae Chang-ho (whom he met in Hawai'i the previous year) and Lee Myung-se. However, the visitors to the 1991 festival have a far more interesting relationship to Ogawa.

Nineteen ninety-one was a historical turning point for Korean documentary, because fifteen aspiring filmmakers visited Yamagata where they had their first chance to see foreign documentaries. Before this, they could read about documentary history in the standard histories by Barnouw and Barsam, but the only films they had access to were government propaganda or network television. Travel was also restricted, so they had only their imaginations before the YIDFF, which was no different for other filmmakers across Asia. In 1991, the two most profoundly influenced filmmakers were Kim Dong-won and Byun Young-joo. This pair was in the process of starting a film collective themselves, so their timing in meeting Ogawa couldn't have been better.

Kim Dong-won had already made his first film, *The Sang Kye-dong Olympics* (*Sang Kyedong Olympics,* 1988). This was a searing exposé of the evictions of impoverished citizens of Seoul on the eve of the Olympics. The government's pretext was to clean up the dirty, unsightly parts of the city, but it, in effect, forced already poor people into homelessness. Kim accompanied the film to the 1991 YIDFF where he heard that Ogawa wanted to meet Korean directors. Unfortunately, Ogawa's cancer was metastasizing, and he was unable to attend the festival that year. Kim visited Ogawa's hospital to meet the director, who looked pale and thin: "We met for about half an hour before the nurse kicked us out," recalls Kim, "In that time, I was able to speak only two sentences: 'Hello, I am Kim. Pleased to meet you.' And after that Ogawa did all the talking. He spent about eight minutes sharing his thoughts about Korea and twenty minutes complaining about Japanese documentary filmmakers." During his eight-minute monologue on the state of Korean film, Ogawa told him that the number of Japanese directors interested in nonfiction was decreasing so he had great hopes for the future of Korean documentary. He complimented Kim on *The Sang Kye-dong Olympics,* and offered advice on editing. He suggested that Korean directors should cooperate and network, and ended by promising his support—even the possibility of lending his camera to projects.

During the previous week in Yamagata, Kim, Byun Young-joo, and two other filmmakers visited the house in Magino as well, where they saw the names of the 1989 visitors from Korea on a screen. There, Kim learned about Ogawa's life and was particularly fascinated by the collective's move to Yamagata and the long period of farming without regularly producing films. Kim's understanding is a simplified version of the history that focuses on the decision to move north to leave the ongoing struggle at Sanrizuka. At the time, the Koreans had just fought ferociously in the 1980s student movement, were still very militant, and had doubts about Ogawa's decision to move. "Was this the best choice he could make?" they wondered. Kim did not think so. If they had to move, then it would have been better to stay in a city and not the countryside. Today, Kim understands the decision better, probably because the political conditions of Korea have changed so radically ("something is happening" in South Korea). The student movement all but died in the mid 1990s, and their situation at the turn of the century holds striking parallels to Japan in the late 1970s or early 1980s. Aside from becoming more democratic, young people lost a sense of purpose with the end of the student movement and the collapse of the Soviet Union. Now, the political climate is far more complex, as is managing daily affairs. From this perspective, the more simple life Ogawa chose in Yamagata looks quite attractive to Kim today.

Kim Dong-won sees a lot of himself in Ogawa Shinsuke. They had both similar concerns and changes over the course of their lives. Ogawa began his career with the evictions of peasants for an airport; Kim's first film covered the evictions of poor people for the Olympics. Ogawa ended his career in a community movement in a local area; Kim has been making films about and with the urban poor and the activists fighting for them. Such change is inevitable, particularly for those engaged in social movements. When the struggle weakens, we must change. Thus, the Korean names scrawled on the Magino screens are all people who chose to migrate to the feature film or publishing.

In contrast, Kim formed a group with Byun Young-joo and others. The project came out of their frustrations with the simple choice between independence (and poverty) and television documentary (and the money and compromises that come with it). They left their meetings with Ogawa inspired by his passion and with the confidence that working in a group would be the most effective and satisfying way to make documentaries. They formed PURN Productions in December 1991. Before leaving Japan, Fuseya had given them video tapes of *Peasants of the Second Fortress*, *"Nippon": Furuyashiki Village*, and *Sundial*. PURN's relationship to Ogawa was cemented by these tapes, which they watched carefully together and discussed. They were particularly shocked by the shooting style of the Sanrizuka Series. In such a chaotic situation—something they were quite familiar with themselves—how could they manage to capture what was happening with little or no narration? Up to this point, they were accustomed to the expository mode of government films. They had heard of *verité* and direct cinema, but were surprised and delighted to see it deployed to such militant ends. Having accumulated enough equipment to complete productions on their own, they also provide a space where anyone can make their own tapes. For example, when I visited their offices in

2000, a primary school class was editing an animated short on bullying in their school. After nearly a decade behind them, PURN has over 250 members.

Over the years, PURN produced a wide variety of progressive documentaries on political prisoners, the urban poor, and local social movements. Kim released a major documentary in 2003 entitled *Repatriation* (*Songhwan*), a film Ogawa would have deeply admired. For over a decade, Kim had been shooting the plight of unrepentant political prisoners languishing in Korean prisons. These were North Korean spies who, after having been captured, imprisoned, and tortured, refused to undergo an ideological apostasy. After the end of the dictatorships, the South began freeing them while blocking their return to the North. Over the years, Kim followed their struggle to return home, exploring their steadfast commitment to Communism while documenting their hardships in the capitalist South. The film was shown at YIDFF and won an award at the Sundance Film Festival.

The other major figure at PURN was Byun Young-joo, who met Ogawa slightly before Kim. She visited Japan in the summer of 1991, thanks to bad information that it was the place to quench her thirst for world documentary (this is no longer the case thanks to the ever-growing library of the YIDFF). She was able to see only few films, but did go to the Ogawa Pro office in Ogikubo and talked with the director for five hours. Like all the Asian filmmakers lucky enough to meet Ogawa, she left inspired and returned with the Korean delegation to Yamagata in October. In December, she participated in the formation of PURN. Her contact with Ogawa left her motivated to strike out on her own, but she still could not understand his approach to cinema in 1991. Basically, she was just impressed by Ogawa's physical presence and the power of his films.

After her first PURN production, *A Woman Being in Asia* (1993), she felt she understood Ogawa better, but it made her want to quit filmmaking. She decided that her documentary amounted to nothing but a compilation of lies because all she cared about was the subject matter—the institution of prostitution across Asia—and not the relationships with the people she was shooting. She left PURN shortly after this, primarily over her desire to shoot 16mm when PURN was increasingly dedicated to low-budget video activism and a looser, more artisanal group structure. To make the transition to film, she actually borrowed Ogawa's camera and Nagra, the very tape recorder used for the French cinétracts. And one of her strongest sources of financial support was Japan's Pandora Films and its president, Nakano Rie, herself a long-time supporter of Ogawa Pro.

Byun's next project was a documentary on a house occupied by former comfort women, the women who were used as sexual slaves by the Japanese military during World War II. She consciously attempted to shoot her film in the way she thought Ogawa did. Her camera would be a participant in the scene. Its position would be *close*, spiritually, politically, and physically.

Actually, she was most like Ogawa in ways she didn't even realize. This film took nearly two years to make. More than half of this time was spent in preproduction, which amounted mostly to Byun's visits to the women's home. No one would talk to her, so in a manner strikingly similar to Honma and the old man from Komaino, she just sat quietly in the home and let them get used to her. After months of waiting, one old woman spoke to her, and after that she gradually became friends with everyone in the house. Only after that did they start shooting. There was an easier way to go about this. Some of the women regularly performed interviews with television crews, as long as they paid cash and listened to the same few stories. Byun had no money, but she did have time and spent it on a long approach that Ogawa would have been proud of. The finished film is entitled *The Murmuring* (1995).

Byun had no intent to make another film on comfort women, but the women themselves asked her to continue on. By this time, Byun had seen all of Ogawa's films at various festivals, and for her second film about the former comfort women, she aspired to make a Korean version of *Heta Village*. She had worked her way far enough inside to secure the total trust of her *taisho*. This was her opportunity to attempt a portrayal of comfort women with a depth that no one had achieved before. The resulting film, *Habitual Sadness* (1997), is even more impressive than her first.

However, in the process of production she realized the ultimate impossibility of following in Ogawa's steps. She offers three reasons. First, their *taisho* are so different. In Sanrizuka, the farmers are important for their present-day lives and the struggle to protect land and livelihood, and in Yamagata the farmers readily talk about their past. Comfort women, however, are important precisely for their past, traumatic times they would just as soon forget. Furthermore, Ogawa became a farmer, but Byun could never become a comfort woman; this was an unbridgeable distance between filmmaker and *taisho*. Second, Ogawa was making his greatest films in the 1960s and 1970s, but she felt 1990s Korea was far more complicated because she was now facing the prospect of producing social movement documentary in the absence of mass movements (ironically, she is oblivious to the similarity of her situation to the post-Asama Cottage Incident Japan). Third, Ogawa was influenced by world film, but by virtue of living in Korea, Byun had only Ogawa.[4] Upon completing her list, she cocked her head and added one more item: "Also, I don't have Tamura."

Byun made one more film about these women, this time as a memorial to those who had died in the intervening years. She called it her "answer to Ogawa," in the sense that she tried to make it without referencing the Japanese director in her approach or in her mind. She came to realize that Ogawa was special and so was the era in which he worked. She notes that both she and Ogawa started their careers in a highly realist mode driven by the passions of social movements. They were activist cinemas that demanded a directness that documentary traditionally lends itself to. However, times had changed in both countries, and the direction Ogawa seemed to be heading in echoed the trends appearing in Korea. With the first Jeonju Film Festival in 2000, filmmakers and spectators expressed a strong interest in nonfiction forms that tampered with style, films that emphasized the material qualities of the media they worked in. Thus, the artists who left the most profound impression at that festival were Jon Jost and John Akomfra. Byun is now trying to go in as different a direction from Ogawa as possible . . . as Tamura would point out, this means she is still as close to Ogawa as ever.

Undoubtedly, Ogawa had the most impact on Taiwan, which remains the only country that has published a translation of Ogawa's writing.[5] This activity centers on Wu Yii-feng, who actually looks a little bit like Ogawa and certainly possesses the same charisma and passion.

At the Golden Horse Awards in Taipei, Ogawa saw Wu's *Moon Children* (1990), and Wu saw Ogawa's *The Sundial Carved with a Thousand Years of Notches*. Ogawa contacted the Taiwanese filmmaker and arranged a meeting. He later showed other Ogawa Pro works to Wu at the Ogikubo Ogawa Pro office, and they visited Magino together. Over a series of very long talks, they each discovered a strong sense of sympathy and connection with the other. In many ways, they were so completely dissimilar, coming especially from such different generations, but they felt they had the same fate. Wu and Ogawa were making similar films about local communities and had much to share about their respective approaches and techniques. On this trip, Wu conducted what was to be Ogawa's last public interview, which was eventually published in *Eiga Shinbun*.[6]

Wu returned to Taiwan energized and, in retrospect, sees this encounter as a turning point in his life. At that moment in the late 1980s, he saw two possible routes extending before him. He was either going to start making personal documentaries and organizing his life around his own concerns or he would funnel his considerable passion and enthusiasm toward others and become an educator. He went to Japan confused, but left filled with resolve and upon his return made the decision. He created the collective Full Shot and has since raised a new generation of Taiwanese documentarists.

In the course of their conversations, Wu recognized that Ogawa was not giving his all in nurturing new filmmakers. Part of his decision to return to film was a determination *not* to be like Ogawa. He says that Ogawa recognized this problem as well, and asked the Taiwanese documentarist how they could work together to bring up new filmmakers in Asia. They laid out a plan for a coproduction.

Ogawa would travel to Taiwan in two to three months to make a film on aboriginals who were fighting Japanese during the colonial period. In the process, they would train new filmmakers. However, on the third day of the Chinese New Year, Wu received the call from Shiraishi informing him of Ogawa's death. He stayed at home for a week, depressed and thinking hard, and in that week, he made the biggest decision of his life: he gathered the entire membership of Full Shot and asked them a question: "If I died today will I have brought up a new generation of filmmakers or done everything for myself?" He renewed his commitment to spearheading a documentary movement, and this happily coincided with the lifting of martial law. Ogawa's death provoked him to reevaluate his life and commit his energies to bringing new ideals and people to the representation of local issues: aboriginal, handicapped, class, gay, anything.

Wu was sitting in the audience at the opening screening of the 1999 YIDFF when Iizuka related some of the pain that working within Ogawa Pro entailed. Afterwards, Wu said he still felt Ogawa's spirit within Iizuka, concluding, "We only met over a single afternoon, but I felt we were of the same people, from the same country, the country called 'documentary.' He had the strong feeling of a father figure. While watching *Sundial,* it occurred to me that it wasn't really a documentary. I was amazed at the subtlety of representation of people, earth, and culture. I dislike Ogawa for some aspects of his personality or whatever, but I respect Ogawa for being a human daring to speak to the human race."

The question remains why Ogawa was turning to Asia at this moment. Once again, his private obsessions seem to have arrived at the cusp of larger movements. A read through of the transcript of Ogawa's 1988 workshop at Nagoya leaves the overpowering impression that Ogawa had lost both his group and his sense of direction after the completion of *The Sundial Carved with a Thousand Years of Notches*. The first half of the workshop was filled with precious discussions of the collective and its method of filmmaking, but by the end, his talk devolved into storytelling. He described one entertaining incident after another, while his collective disappears from view. It feels like a structured absence. The major collection of Ogawa's writing edited by Yamane Sadao is largely the same. Few people can seize on a tidbit from reality and spin it into a story with such flair. But by the end, it is Ogawa's exclusive show; while he is filled with ideas, it is unclear if he knows how to accomplish them—at least on his own.

More than once in Nagoya, Ogawa mentions the fact (the problem?) that his staff members are now in their forties. This workshop was held at precisely the period when Iizuka was up in Tamanoi scouting a location and a new role for himself. At the same time, the underlying motive of the workshop seems to be to agitate the young people attending, and perhaps inspire a few to join Ogawa Pro. In like manner, his enthusiasm for Asia explicitly involved the creation of a new group, a new collective that was transnational and filled with the vibrancy of youth and multiple cultures. In the final interview with Wu Yii-feng, Ogawa brims with enthusiasm for the possibilities he sees in other parts of Asia: "If there is no staff that can make a documentary film, then I want to raise and nurture that kind of staff. . . . I really want to gather a young staff and have workshops together, and the actual work of making their own films will be like their film school. . . . I want lots of documentaries to emerge from all the southeast Asian countries. I think amazing films will come out."[7] The sad fact is, however, that at the height of Ogawa's artistic powers, Ogawa Pro was no longer collective in any true sense; before he had a chance to make his visions of a renovated (pan-Asian) Ogawa Pro a reality, he passed away at the youthful age of fifty-five.

The End

In 1991, Ogawa Shinsuke finished *A Movie Capital* and was preparing to turn to new projects after that fall's film festival in Yamagata; however, pains in his gut became enough of a nuisance to visit the doctor. Test results revealed that the aches were symptoms of an advanced cancer. His fatty diet was killing him. He was scheduled to organize the Asia Symposium with Stephen Teo. Instead, he scaled back his participation to an advisory role. By the time of the October festival, he was in the hospital recovering from surgery. He seemed basically healthy and happy when everyone visited him in the hospital, but we all assumed it must have been serious if he had to miss the film festival.

By the time Ogawa knew of his imminent death, there was too little time to reflect on his own career or attempt to construct an authorized spin to his legacy through autobiography. However, the last project of his life serves as an interesting substitute. Ogawa spent the last productive months of his life translating Frances Flaherty's biography of her husband, Robert. If there was anyone Ogawa would have compared himself to, it would probably have been an awkward confabulation of Joris Ivens and Robert Flaherty, the former for his politics and the latter for this approach to documentary. And Ogawa was probably audacious enough to attempt the comparison. A retrospective of Flaherty's work at the first YIDFF reminded Ogawa of the way his first viewing of *Nanook of the North* (1922) as a student taught him the potentiality of the form and was one of the factors leading him to a life in documentary. Flaherty's daughter, Monica, accompanied the films to Yamagata, and Ogawa took this opportunity to interview her.

Although the interview begins with Monica's rather insulting demand that her father's films are "motion pictures" and that we should forget this word *documentary*, the two seemed to develop a rapport over the course of the conversation. Monica described her father's approach to filmmaking, which often involved extensive periods of preparation at the shooting location, little scripting, miles of footage, and lots of careful editing. In turn, Ogawa reflected on this method in terms of his own career: "This was the first time I've seen Flaherty's films in a long time. What I felt the strongest was that the staff shooting the film and the people being shot had an honestly good relationship. I think what clearly comes out on screen in documentary cinema is the relationship between the humans shooting and the humans being shot. That is where an amazing drama emerges."[8] By the end of the interview, Monica invites Ogawa to her home and says she feels like he's the son she never had. Ogawa was so touched by the experience that he undertook a translation of Francis Flaherty's autobiography.

There were other reasons for this translation, beginning with the fact that, thanks to his illness and extended hospitalization, he had a lot of time on his hands. He also was newly enamored with a recently purchased personal computer, fascinated by its large screen and word processing program (today, he is probably up there editing rushes of rice footage on his Mac). According to Shiraishi, Ogawa was like a little boy with a new bike; he was having so much fun word processing that he freely added and heightened Flaherty's story.

He may not have written a book about his career, but as a translator he produced a text that came close to autobiography. As previously noted, the director's command of English was roughly conversational, but hardly up to the task of translation. Despite heavy editing by a Japanese film scholar, the final result is as much Ogawa as Flaherty. Where he did not completely comprehend the original text, Ogawa projected his own understanding of filmmaking and Flaherty into the Japanese.

Its rough draft was completed by the time Ogawa was spending most of his time in the hospital. I remember being asked to contact Monica to clear the publication rights. Something strange had happened in the intervening year, and I was surprised to be on one end of a rant along the lines of, "How dare that Red translate my mother's book. He's a suspicious type, that one. Of course, you can't publish that book." Not knowing whether the book could actually be published, the publishers at *Eiga Shinbun* put together a mock-up and showed it to Ogawa on his deathbed. By then, Ogawa was losing his grip on reality, but he was able to see what would be his last work on earth.

Ogawa could only dream of future films. There was the idea of another Sanrizuka documentary that would exploit their vast visual record of the airport struggle, an idea still being tossed around by former members. He talked about a film examining the human relationships in a hospital, something he was becoming intimately familiar with. There was also a roughly edited reel on persimmons that he dropped from *Sundial*, and he always wanted to return to that to finish it off.

Another idea he revealed at his 1988 seminar in Nagoya was about a village called Hiraba on the slopes of Mount Zao, the volcano towering above Yamagata City. The little village was between five hundred and six hundred meters above sea level. In March 1945, a B-29 dropped onto the slopes of the mountain because of extreme turbulence. The entire crew perished. According to the lore of the area, the people in the villages nearby could not reach the plane until the heavy snows had melted. When they did, they looted whatever they could find. A car dealer Ogawa knew hauled a small mountain of gelatin back to his house. Others took watches, or broke off the fingers of the crew to win their rings. The radios and other small machines were also valuable at that late date in the war. Then one night in April or May, people living in neighboring villages saw Hiraba suddenly shine in the deep mountain night. These mountain villages were still far from getting electricity from the city below, so one can imagine what a mysterious sight this must have been. The explanation was simple: the Hiraba villagers plundered the electric generator of the plane and converted it to hydropower.[9] Naturally, Ogawa found this kind of subject matter richly appealing.

There were two projects that Ogawa had actually embarked on before his death. The first was a film on kimchee. He was fascinated by the amazing kimchee made by a woman in the Furuyashiki area. Why? Because during World War II her son went to China and married a Korean woman. He was forced to return alone and made kimchee for the rest of his life. Ogawa's interest in the story was probably related to a larger project entitled *Mountains as Culture (Bunka to shite no yama)*. They planned a bit of this during the production of Furuyashiki, but never completed it. This was, however, one reason Iizuka was in Yonezawa picking vegetables at the end of the 1980s. The project got little further than Ogawa's dream of an homage to Kamei Fumio's *Tragedy of Japan*: a dissolve between a rice flower and the emperor. Knowing what he accomplished with *Sundial,* one can imagine what the final documentary would have been like.

The last project was well into preproduction when Ogawa succumbed to his cancer. He had become interested in a place called Okura Village at Hijiori Hot Springs, where he sensed there were many new stories to be told. The first he wanted to adapt to film centered on Mori Shigeya, a local bureaucrat who was also a *butoh* dancer on the side. He was a *deshi* of Hijikata, which is how Ogawa met him. In Yamagata in general, and this village in particular, there were many single men in their thirties who took Southeast Asian brides, especially from the Philippines. Mori worked in the city hall, and arranged many of these marriages. The film would creatively combine both of Mori's activities, arranging marriages and dancing. In January 1990, they shot some footage at night in the middle of an intense snowstorm. Hijiori Hot Springs is known for accumulating a couple meters of snow on the ground. The cinematographer was Kato Takanobu, the last Ogawa Pro member. Ogawa also took Abe Hiroko and Kuribayashi Masashi for their training. He did some slight editing of this material as a kind of sample reel, but the project was initially sidelined by the demands of *A Movie Capital,* and then by his illness after that.[10]

Ogawa had left the hospital several weeks after the 1991 YIDFF, and spent the rest of the year recuperating and translating the Flaherty book. His condition suddenly deteriorated, and he checked back into the hospital. The cancer had metastasized and he was dying. In the new year, he entered a new state of consciousness as well, drawing invisible lengths of film between his hands and looking at them in the light, just as he had edited at the flatbed his entire life. Other times, he watched rushes on the blank wall before his bed.

On February 7, 1992, his friends gathered for what appeared to be his last night. We took shifts over his bed where he was wheezing with such labor that we expected every breath to be his last. Fuseya and others began preparations for the wake and funeral. Tsuchimoto gathered information to write his obituary. Feeling useless, Kato Takanobu and I finally retreated to the Ogawa Pro office in Ogikubo. Minutes after we arrived, the phone rang.

Ogawa Criticism

Ogawa's wake was held several days later at a temple in Ogikubo. It was attended by friends, filmmakers, and former members of the collective that bore his name. Some people who had been active in the collective were notably absent. After people paid their last respects, they filed into the next room to eat, drink, and talk about old times. At one memorable moment, a former member of the collective suddenly stood up and started airing old grievances in a drunken tirade. Friends finally calmed him down, and he returned to his glass to sulk.

This was the first eruption of what would come to be known as Ogawa *hihan*, or Ogawa critique. This was something that had circulated backstage since the formation of Ogawa Pro, but after Ogawa's death it would become increasingly public. The Ogawa critique culminated in the release of Barbara Hammer's *Devotion* (2000).

I suppose one must see Regina Ulwer's *Hare to Ke* (*Hare to Ke: Das Besondere und der Alltag*, 1988) as a precursor, but the first rumbles occurred the night of Ogawa's death. Someone had to write the obituary, and the responsibility fell on the shoulders of Tsuchimoto Noriaki. Talking about Ogawa's career and reputation was no problem, but the facts were complicated by the need to get dates and details right. But as he compiled them, there were inconsistencies and things that escaped the memories of those gathered at the hospital. Tsuchimoto called Ogawa's father to ensure the facts were straight. What he learned was disturbing. The standard biography that Ogawa had circulated—the one I began this book with—was riddled with inaccuracies. As I mentioned in the Introduction, Ogawa was born in central Tokyo, not rural Gifu. Although he celebrated his own rural roots, he went to Gifu only in his first year of primary school to flee the bombings of civilians at the end of World War II. He did spend some time in Nagano, but then returned to Gifu and eventually to the capital once again. Ogawa went to conservative Kokugakuin University, the school favored by the imperial family. He bragged about being kicked out of school for his activism and never graduating. Actually, he not only received his diploma but lied about his major as well. Rather than literature, a hotbed of student radicalism on most campuses, Ogawa studied economics—

"because it seemed like a safer career," according to his father. Most egregiously, Ogawa was born on June 25, 1936, not 1935. This last piece of information was a blow to some of his oldest and closest friends because it made Ogawa their "*senpai*"; in Japan, age counts. Defenders of Ogawa's petty avarice argue that this creative treatment of autobiographical actuality was precisely what made him a great documentary filmmaker. Others find Ogawa's vanity difficult to forgive. Tsuchimoto puts the counterargument most succinctly: "It was power, this profile. It helped make films, grease wheels. I feel a complicated anger."

Another key criticism of Ogawa is directed at the measures he took to secure funding for his extravagantly long films and extended shoots. Ogawa had three conditions for making good films. Common sense holds that filmmaking costs money and takes time, but Ogawa's conditions state these in a more active, direct fashion: first, the relationship with the *taisho*—the love for the people one is shooting—is extremely important; second, to make films you have to use money; and third, to make films you have to take time. The Ogawa Pro approach used whatever time and money necessary to develop the relationships that are the precondition of a successful documentary so their films could only be shot over the long term.[11] This was easy for Ogawa to say, because he never became involved in the nitty-gritty process of gathering cash. According to his long-time producer, Ogawa never really knew or cared how much he owed people. This issue of money is worth a careful look, as it is the most controversial aspect of Ogawa Pro.

The student movement films forged a method of production that created budgets through campaigns to raise donations from student groups, unions, and from individuals. We can see some of this activity onscreen in *Sea of Youth*. At the end of this first production, the Jishu Joei Soshiki no Kai had spent ¥1,705,556. However, it had only collected ¥774,760 in its fundraising campaign. The balance had to be raised through other means. The group borrowed most of it but also went so far as selling blood to the blood bank—one visit roughly equaled a roll a film. Okumura sold his personal book collection to used bookstores to pay for film stock. In the end, the group's efforts at distribution did not recover the cost of the film, and the Jieiso members took whatever jobs they could find to repay their debt. Whether Ogawa did as well is unclear, but it is unlikely, knowing what we do about his relationship to money for the rest of his career.

For the production of *Forest of Oppression,* "director" was one of the few positions specified with a line item in the budget, although as director he received no more than the other three paid positions (cameraman, assistant director, and sound recordist). Jieiso's growing network of contacts produced a substantial sum, with contributions from the student governments of twelve universities, five labor unions, and twenty-seven student newspapers.[12] Its printed appeals for donations included a list of all these organizations, along with the singling out of three high-profile individuals who offered their names along with monetary gifts: Hani Goro, Hoshino Ansaburo, and Odasetsu Hideo. Internal Jieiso memoranda chart the steady increases in their budget. On December 12, 1967, the budget totaled ¥2,373,000; weeks later a revised budget came to ¥2,440,622 with ¥819,000 in outstanding debt. According to meeting agendas at the end of 1967, the budget for *Forest of Oppression* amounted to ¥2,850,000, and it had raised ¥2,195,000 in loans and donations. Altogether, its loans and unpaid bills amounted to ¥968,000. In the end, this debt was no problem thanks to the rousing success of the film. It apparently turned enough of a profit to float the production of *Report from Haneda,* which was a miserable failure in terms of receipts.

The money situation changed with the inauguration of the Sanrizuka Series. Spending a year on preproduction and establishing the new Ogawa Pro offices in Shinjuku and Sanrizuka was extremely expensive. From this film on, Ogawa Pro steadily accrued an ever-growing debt. A big part of the reason was the unlimited budget line Ogawa devoted to production; as producer Kobayashi Hideko put it, "Ogawa started using film stock like drafting paper."

Fuseya Hiro—chief producer for the Yamagata era films—joined Ogawa Pro in the midst of preparations for *Summer in Sanrizuka* in early 1968. He recalls that a little footage had already been shot at the March protests by the camera unit, which consisted of cameraman Otsu Koshiro, Matsumoto Takeaki, Nosaka Haruo, Jin Kohei, and Yoshida Tsukasa. Fuseya had just finished school, and Ogawa was searching for recruits for his newly formed production company. Fuseya loved films but had never considered making it his profession. However, Ogawa was irresistible, and Fuseya found himself in the production unit such as it was. At the time, it amounted to only two other persons, Kobayashi and Ichiyama Ryuji. The day he arrived at the office—a one-room apartment with a table and a phone—nothing happened. There was nothing to do, and no one asked anything of him. He spent a month of idle waiting, with hardly a phone call. Then Kobayashi abruptly came to Fuseya and revealed that, actually, they had no money. Wouldn't he go find some? He was flabbergasted, as this was exactly the opposite of the common-sense way of making films; you simply don't start a movie until the budget is in place.

Fuseya made the rounds to various universities. He made appointments with the leaders of the newspapers, student governments, and clubs.

Thanks to the success of *Forest of Oppression,* most of them had heard of Ogawa. Many were willing to offer donations, as he was one of the only filmmakers they knew of whom they felt was making films that engaged their sensibilities and understood their world. *Sanrizuka in Summer* eventually cost ¥7,000,000, roughly 30 percent of which was unpaid by the film's completion.[13]

The production unit also borrowed money. Bank loans were out of the question so members borrowed money from sympathizers, people in labor unions, teachers, and the like. Whenever they found someone supportive of their project, they would pump them for new contacts. When someone set up a screening, they would often ask the organizers, "Actually, we need money as soon as possible; won't you send the rental fee before the screening?" One last strategy was selling presold tickets. These were printed tickets, quite elaborate ones for the later films, and were sold for something like ¥500 to ¥700. They would allow entry for the film whenever it was completed. Occasionally, they would also send out mass mailings to their list of sympathizers, calling for direct donations to support the latest film project. This method remained largely in place throughout Ogawa's career, with the exception of their sponsored films like *Clean Center* and *A Movie Capital.*

It worked—to the extent that they made films while compiling an enormous debt—partly because of the nature of the collective and the era. First and foremost, the collective was at least partly a commune as well. In the Sanrizuka era and especially in Yamagata, the filmmakers mainly lived together. In the early days, members were offered minimal salaries. Basically, they were asked the minimal amount needed for survival. For someone whose parents lived in Tokyo, it amounted to a pittance. Those with rents to pay, or girlfriends, were given more. Fuseya recalls being promised ¥200,000 when he joined and receiving only half that on his first payday. However, it was an era when someone short on cash could always crash at a friend's place. It was a time when pursuing a lifelong job in a stable company was tantamount to supporting the conservative status quo, while joining a politicized film collective was something someone could boast of, and still boast of to this day with obvious nostalgia for the simpler days of youth. Nosaka Haruo clearly enjoys recalling visits to the tax office to submit his forms to incredulous tax officials. "A yearly income of 20,000 yen?" they would inevitably ask, "Are you nuts? How do you survive!?!"

Upon moving to Yamagata in 1975, everyone was truly living communally. They grew much of their food. There was no rent to pay. Fuseya covered the rent of the Tokyo office and apartment, so that when members traveled to the capital they only needed ¥1,200 a day to pay for trains, food, and cigarettes. At the very same time, the producing unit ended its more or less collective style, and Fuseya was asked to become the sole "producer." It remains unclear what motivated this change, even to Fuseya himself, but he was taken aback by the request. He knew about the collective's massive debt and was unsure he wanted to shoulder this responsibility. However, Ogawa assured him that the debt was ultimately the director's responsibility.

This assurance must be seen as disingenuous, and this is one of the points where my admiration for the accomplishments of Ogawa Shinsuke runs head-to-head with deep doubts about the ethics of his production method. While on the one hand, Ogawa took a high moral stand in defense of his *taisho,* he had his other hand out to anyone who might give him money. To be specific, he had his staff's hands out, not his. Ogawa never seriously dealt with the financial end of his work. Despite public shows of anxiety over the financial and emotional debt he owed to all the people who supported the collective's filmmaking over the years, Ogawa himself never did the dirty work. He had his staff hit on people instead. And despite rhetoric about engaging in social movements and consciousness-raising in the hinterlands, the ultimate purpose of the branches was to funnel money to Tokyo. When someone signed his or her name to a positive postfilm survey, he or she soon received a phone call asking for donations. Kimura recalls experimental filmmaker/critic Suzuki Shiroyasu saying that everyone in Tokyo said, "When you visit Ogawa Pro in Yamagata you'll feast." They did eat well, but visitors never realized that before those feasts Iizuka would drop by Kimura's house asking for money for groceries.

After *Summer in Sanrizuka,* it was an ongoing race to keep up with Ogawa Pro's debt, which only grew. We know the budget for the student movement films and a number of the Sanrizuka films because it was an era of openness. However, this ethic of openness ended in the 1970s, and the extent of Ogawa Pro's ever-expanding debt remained unknown until after Ogawa's death.

During production of the Sanrizuka series there was a fairly healthy flow of revenue thanks to donations and the constant circulation of prints. Even so, the collective racked up some ¥50,000,000 in debt by the time it moved to Yamagata. Upon Ogawa's death, it owed upwards of ¥100,000,000[14] to various individuals, organizations, and companies. Each loan is recorded in a stack of notebooks nearly two feet thick.[15] Paging through these yellowing pages, it is obvious that few of the forms are stamped "returned." Toward the end, loans were implicitly donations. People started lending money not knowing if they'd ever see it again; the staff member hitting on people knew there was little chance of Ogawa Pro returning what it borrowed. More disturbing is the fact that some donors recall payback dates passing into oblivion without even a phoned apology or explanation.

At the end of *A Visit to Ogawa Productions* (*Ogawa Puro homonki,* 1981/1999) Ogawa displays remarkable hubris when Oshima Nagisa asks him about the money that supported their lifestyle. Ogawa told Oshima that they only asked people for financial help when they were completely sure about their project, and because of that confidence the donors had no business getting involved in how they were using their money. Chuckling, he admitted he knew he was going to hell for all this, but it was far better to be in heaven while you're still alive.

People from all walks of life supported Ogawa's heaven on earth. One of the most ironic and symbolic examples I came across in my research was the donation from an activist group that posted bail for political prisoners; the collective never returned the money, which means some poor soul languished in jail longer than he should have for the sake of an Ogawa Pro film.

Many of the staff remain uncomfortable with the massive debt accrued over the years, most of it attributable to the kindness and political commitment of sympathizers and friends. One member admitted to me that whenever he hears someone saying how great the Ogawa Pro films are, he silently cringes inside because they were made with the sacrifice of so many people. All donors whom I spoke to, however, refused to see themselves as victims. Most have the attitude of Hara Kazuo: "There are two sides to Ogawa Pro's money situation. On the one hand, they borrowed all this money without returning it, and it is difficult to forgive. On the other hand, it was a movement and they were the vanguard; supporting them financially was a way of participating and seeing oneself in their films. To this day, we can't help but have these two conflicting tendencies within us." In other words, Hara argues a rush to judgment is unfair because the debt cannot be extracted from the context of movement politics—no one got rich at Ogawa Pro. No one got salaries, either.

At the same time, there is an air of dishonesty about Ogawa's work ethic that leaves me uncomfortable. If we are to take Ogawa at his word, the words recorded at various public events, he also felt pain at the sacrifice of his supporters. However, the words ring hollow because his deeds speak a different story. He faithfully lived out his own creed—you *have* to spend money—making films of such ambitious scale in Yamagata that could *only* be imagined free of the constraints of budgets. Ogawa never made PR films or television commercials, although he had the perfect film unit to produce such lucrative work considering they had all the equipment and talent in-house. By way of contrast, Tsuchimoto Noriaki made around twenty such

PR works, some of which won major prizes and few of which appear in his filmography. These were expressly made to support his staff for the Minamata Series and other independent films.

Just as important, it seems Ogawa never asked anyone for money, making his staff do the face-to-face dirty work of raising funds. According to Fuseya, Ogawa never new how much his films cost, let alone how much he owed. He never asked, or seemed to care for that matter. There was a ridiculously careless attitude underlying the time-consuming method of Ogawa Pro, yet another reason its accomplishments will probably never be reduplicated. Ogawa's approach to documentary made the location in which the camera moves a highly charged, ethical space; ironically enough, the economics of Ogawa's approach was remarkably—even unforgivably—irresponsible. However, in death he transferred that legacy to the staff members who bore the original burden of collecting the debt. After Ogawa's death, the little income the films brought in was mismanaged by Fuseya and never reached the original lenders, but to focus on this problem deflects attention from decades of red ink and the site of ultimate accountability. As the leader of the group, Ogawa bears the responsibility for the massive debt accrued by the company bearing his name. After all, according to Tsuchimoto, this was why he called it "Ogawa Productions" in the first place, because he wanted to take responsibility.

When Kim Dong Won found out about Ogawa's million-dollar debt, he was circumspect about its significance: "It's a symbol of his passion," and after a beat Kim continued, "In Korea, debt *is* property!"

Fukuda Katsuhiko and the "Ippon" Problem

The final criticism often directed at Ogawa is in some ways the most disheartening. As I have insisted from the beginning, this was no conventional production company, and the relationship between the charismatic director and his staff was highly unusual, even mystifying. Former members are fond of comparisons to Asahara and Aum Shinrikyo, but the analogy is more provocative than helpful.

At the same time, they replicated certain structures and traditions from the mainstream film industry. One that was certainly worth embracing was the training of assistants and honest attempts to ease them into their own careers as filmmakers. Years of backbreaking, thankless work are repaid through independence and the satisfaction and prestige that come from taking responsibility for one's work. While Ogawa seems to have made that attempt with Yumoto's *Dokkoi! A Song from the Bottom,*

Fukuda's *Sanrizuka—The Skies of May, the Road to the Village,* and Iizuka's *A Movie Capital,* we saw how Ogawa stepped in and took control of each of these films. This intervention by their mentor was very hard on these budding filmmakers, as Yumoto's disappearance seems to suggest.

Signs were good for Yumoto's *Dokkoi! A Song from the Bottom.* The reviews were extremely complimentary. Requests for screenings were far more forthcoming than they were for *Heta Village.* However, instead of exploiting this movement and nurturing the distribution of the film, Ogawa swiftly moved everyone but Fuseya to Magino.

A wide distribution of *Dokkoi!* was far more than a one-man job, and it left Fuseya puzzled. In retrospect, he suspects it had something to do with Ogawa's unusual relationship with his assistant directors. He was jealous that his staff might produce a more successful film than he. In an interview with critic Matsuda Masao, Ogawa made a revealing comment about *Dokkoi!:* "In the end, it was the side being shot rather than the side shooting. I think the directors of this film are the people of Kotobukicho. They themselves directed their actions. They themselves did everything for us. At any rate, the young staff members basically did their best to hold the microphones in front of their mouths and determine if it's recording at the right level—and that's about it."[16] Comments like this could be read as a tribute to the *taisho* or a diminishment of his young staff members' considerable accomplishment.

The sad fact is that no staff members were truly nourished in Ogawa Pro. It was only after they departed the collective that they could establish their own careers and roles of increased and independent responsibility. All their examples provide effective fodder for the Ogawa criticism, but I would like to focus on the story of Fukuda Katsuhiko. He is the most interesting exemplar for the way his post-Ogawa career resonates against some of the larger historical trends. When Ogawa Pro moved to Yamagata, Fukuda chose to leave the group and remain in Sanrizuka. There, he established himself as an independent filmmaker and writer.[17] He published books and made PR films and various documentaries. Most importantly, he established his own film series on the airport struggle entitled Sanrizuka Notes.

The most powerful film of this series is *A Grasscutter's Tale* (*Kusa tori soshi,* 1985). It explores the life history of an eighty-four-year-old woman through her current daily life. Someya Katsu grew up in the Sanrizuka area before marrying a barber in the 1930s and moving to Tokyo. There, she was treated poorly for being from the country, and she moved back to Sanrizuka. Her husband eventually followed, and over the years she gave birth to eleven children, six of whom perished from sickness or war. She lived with the oldest son until the airport struggles, when he sold their property to the airport authorities without consulting her. Since that time, she lived alone, farming a plot of land and working at the pickled onion factory that still obstructs airport construction. There is almost no mention of the Sanrizuka Struggle. Rather, most of the imagery is Someya patiently working in the midst of her shockingly green plants. The structure relies on short vignettes separated by wonderful calligraphic intertitles. She meditates about life and living alone. In the larger scheme of things, there is a curious symmetry to this situation. When Fukuda made movies in Sanrizuka as a member of Ogawa Pro, he learned to operate as part of a group filming another group; returning to Sanrizuka, he shoots a single individual as a lone artist. Significantly, it is a film largely about forging a meaningful and happy life all alone.

Perhaps the most important film Fukuda made reveals volumes about the tensions inherent in any collaborative artistic venture. It is called *Filmmaking and the Way to the Village* (*Eiga-zukuri to mura e no michi,* 1973), and was largely forgotten until after Fukuda's youthful death from a brain aneurysm in 1998. This is an Ogawa Pro film about Ogawa Pro. Up to this

Ogawa eclipses Fukuda Katsuhiko on location with Yanagawa Hatsue, who explains how the winds kick up horrible dust. Snapped on May 1, 1977, during the troubled production of *Sanrizuka—The Skies of May, the Road to the Village.*

point, Fukuda had been Ogawa's assistant director, which meant that one of his greatest responsibilities was sound recording. On the production of *Heta Village,* Ogawa replaced him with Yumoto and assigned Fukuda to direct a documentary that would show the unique method of production they had developed in Sanrizuka. But despite having commissioned this film himself, Ogawa never showed it to anyone, nor even hinted at its existence.

What does it take for a film to deserve being shelved for eternity? Now that we can see the film, the question is even more perplexing because—far from being a failure—Fukuda Katsuhiko's *Filmmaking and the Way to the Village* is actually quite good. Indeed, in the context of "films about filmmaking," which have become all the more popular with the advent of DVDs and cable television's appetite for synergetic advertising for the film industry, Fukuda's film is a masterwork of the genre. That being the case, what could Ogawa possibly have found so offensive? What does the film tell us about Ogawa and Ogawa Pro?

Certainly, the film gives us a glimpse at the inner workings of Ogawa Pro at the most interesting point in its twenty-five-year history. Fukuda made *Filmmaking and the Way to the Village* after the group had completed five films at Sanrizuka. It shows the members' activities during the filming of *Heta Village.* By this point, Ogawa Pro had established its reputation as an innovative film collective and touchstone for the radical Left.

In the midst of this massive change in the early 1970s, Ogawa Pro was completely reconceptualizing its approach to film for the production of *Heta Village,* shuttling the Sanrizuka Struggle to the margins and concentrating on the life and history of the village and its inhabitants. At the same time, the group was undergoing a transformation, leaving its roots as a makeshift group of activists that used film as a weapon of social struggle and turning into a professional filmmaking group that happened to live and work communally (and as we have seen, the question of where politics and social struggle fit into this new identity is an exceptionally difficult question). It is fascinating that the filmmakers would decide to make a film about themselves at precisely this moment in history, for this scene of transformation is what Fukuda Katsuhiko captures in *Filmmaking and the Way to the Village.* Former members often minimize its importance by saying, "It was only a study film," or a practice film. However, a film is a film nonetheless. It is a significant investment in time and money. Furthermore, this "study film" could have been about anything, but they significantly chose to "study" themselves. So what does Fukuda tell us about Ogawa Pro?

Filmmaking and the Way to the Village is deceptively simple. It shows most steps in Ogawa Pro's innovative production process: fundraising, filming, evaluating rushes, distribution, and preparations of one sort or another. What is most striking is the attention Fukuda gives to discussion, something crystal clear when compared to the cable-television style approaches to "genius directors." While the latter focuses on the spectacle of a master director crafting his singular vision from the raw materials of human beings, costumes, and special effects, *Filmmaking and the Way to the Village* zeros in on the very human activity of interpersonal interchange before and behind the camera.

One of the few scenes of location photography features the wonderful scene of Grandpa Tonojita telling that story from the opening of *Heta Village*. Many other scenes focus on human interchange between the members of Ogawa Pro. Nosaka Haruo and Fuseya Hiro discuss plans over the phone with members in the hinterlands. Iizuka Toshio relates anecdotes about a recent trip to Tohoku for screenings. In other scenes, members plot out the next step in filming.

One of the most thrilling scenes Fukuda captures centers on a discussion taking place after reviewing rushes. Ogawa and other key members sit around a small table, drinking and talking about what they had just watched. What they actually say is less important than the quality of the interchange. There is a palpable exhilaration among the participants, even those who sit silently. The level of seriousness with which the smallest details are hashed out is impressive. The passion is undeniable. It is more than a little seductive, being the kind of intensely pleasurable conversation about cinema we all crave but only rarely experience. However, while most of us have only the pleasure of discussing films after the fact, the members of Ogawa Pro were joyfully digging into the minutiae of their sounds and images in the midst of their creation. This true give-and-take is a scene one never sees in the typical "making-of" films, which dwell excessively on the technical apparatuses that "genius" directors deploy as a vehicle for their supposedly personal vision.

Simply put, Fukuda gives us a glimpse of what people often call the *shudansei*, or "groupness," of Ogawa Pro, and what exactly it meant to be producing cinema as a collective. Ogawa's rhetoric about collective filmmaking reached fever pitch with the making of *Heta Village*. Traces of this may be seen in the style of the film's credits, which list the names of members without specifying their roles. The reality, however, was a bit more tangled than this. There are traces left of this complexity in Fukuda's film. For example, while the film *Heta Village* projects itself as a collective work—and by extension the product of a radical politics—fliers for the film duly note that Ogawa was director and Tamura was his cinematographer (the other members are left anonymous). The importance of the Tamura–Ogawa relationship is strikingly documented by the after-rush discussion described previously; the discussion is primarily between these two, while all the others sit quietly listening.[18]

Another way of thinking through the problem of *shudansei* is to ask whose film this is in the first place, this *Filmmaking and the Way to the Village*. The easy answer is that it belongs to Fukuda. After all, he was director and, judging from the other members assigned to the project, Fukuda had a remarkable degree of independence from the rest of the production company . . . at least until Ogawa decided it should be shelved. To supplement this argument, we could note—as does Iizuka Toshio—that the film's approach shows all the evenhandedness, sensitivity, and balance of attention that was so typical of Fukuda's personality. In terms of tone it sports a strong resemblance to the films Fukuda completed after leaving Ogawa Pro in 1977, particularly his Sanrizuka Notes. We also have the knowledge that Ogawa resolutely rejected the film, while Fukuda finally embraced it before his untimely passing.

From another perspective we could see *Filmmaking and the Way to the Village* as a late addition to the massive Sanrizuka Series, particularly if we were to wrest the series' authorship from director Ogawa and grant it collectively to Ogawa Pro. After all, the film was made with money donated to Ogawa Pro and was completed with direct collaboration from people like Nakano, Yumoto, Asanuma, and Iizuka. Having been made at the behest of Ogawa, *Filmmaking and the Way to the Village* is qualitatively different than Oshige Jun'ichiro's *A Visit to Ogawa Productions* (*Ogawa Pro Homonki,* 1981/1991) or Regina Ulwer's *Hare to Ke*. Indeed, the film was enough of an Ogawa Pro production to have been locked away in the Magino house under Ogawa's leadership. Finally, while this is the only "making-of" film the collective attempted, nearly all of Ogawa Pro's films are to one degree or another *about* Ogawa Pro and how it made films. Indeed, this ultimately constitutes the theoretical core of Ogawa Pro's work, perhaps making *Filmmaking and the Way to the Village* among its most important films.

Ultimately, we can never answer the question of whose film this is—Fukuda's, Ogawa's, or Ogawa Pro's—because this question runs up against the contradictory heart of Ogawa Pro and its rhetoric of *shudansei*. Ogawa went down in history as one of the great independent filmmakers who challenged filmmaking-as-usual, and one of the ways he did this was by projecting the *shudan*/group as the subjectivity behind the film; and to a significant extent, that *shudan* included the film's *taisho* as well. These were films by Ogawa Pro, not simply Ogawa. It rejected the studio system with its rigid process that enslaved new talent to old, authoritarian structures. It wanted to forge a new way of filmmaking, and in the process a new human being as well.

By the production of *Heta Village,* it had succeeded in this to a remarkable degree; however, along the way it reproduced some of those older structures, sometimes in not so subtle ways. Despite the rhetoric about group production, Ogawa Pro was hardly an amorphous mass of filmmaking talent. With only a small shift in our position we can see a very different Ogawa Pro, just like the slight turn of a holograph produces a new image.

To make this shift, we might treat *Filmmaking and the Way to the Village* as such a holograph and reconsider the film in light of one of its most curious scenes. Standing out in one of Heta's fields, Ogawa interviews Tamura and Yumoto about their equipment renovations. The way they adapted the camera and tape recorder to fit their physique and withstand the heat of the Sanrizuka battles is absolutely captivating. Ogawa is also fascinating. As he interviews Tamura, he allows the cameraman to describe his equipment and its jury-rigging relatively freely, at his own leisurely pace and in his own way. Tamura was a colleague of Ogawa's from the Iwanami days and never a member of Ogawa Pro. When Ogawa turns to Assistant Director Yumoto, the two men proceed to struggle over the plumber's pipe-cum-microphone boom. Their contest lasts only a moment, an instant of ballet-like gestures that would usually end on the editor's floor, but the image condenses Ogawa's relationship to Ogawa Pro. This might be a group effort, but in the end there is no mistaking who is in charge.

There are plenty of other traces of the hierarchy that stratified Ogawa Pro, beginning with the name. At the time of its formation, there were relatively few production companies sporting the name of a director at the center. Just the fact that *Filmmaking and the Way to the Village* was called a "study film" indicates it was operating under rules similar to a typical production company, where an assistant director must prove himself and put in his dues before "graduating" to independence. This is why, to this day, most of those involved with Ogawa Pro insist on drawing a line between "professionals" and "amateurs." The former were people who came out of places like Iwanami and belonged to organizations, such as the Documentary Producer's Association, people like Ogawa, Otsu, Tamura, Kubota, and Asanuma. The "amateurs" refer to the vast majority of the one-hundred-odd people involved in Ogawa Pro, those members who often assert their identity as activists and downplay their lives as film artists.

However, the fact remains that this group of "activist amateurs" produced an amazing number of powerful documentaries that can compete with the "professionalism" of any documentary filmmaker at any time in history, at any place across the globe. One can also remember that rank amateurs accomplished many of the great documentaries in film history. The need to differentiate "amateur" from "professional" speaks less to the talent of the members of Ogawa Pro and more to the fact that a rigid, industrial hierarchy underlay the group, with Ogawa at its apex.

Fukuda's *Filmmaking and the Way to the Village* is a fascinating and well-made film created in these conditions. However, when Fukuda screened a work print for the group, Ogawa hated it. The people who were there to hear Ogawa's criticism do not remember specifics, only the gist: that it was a failure too embarrassing to show publicly. (That no one can remember the specifics suggests the reasons were trivial.) It was shelved and forgotten until after Ogawa's death.

After Ogawa's death, a small group of former members were sorting through the Magino house. Fukuda found *Filmmaking and the Way to the Village* among the mountainous pile of prints and outtakes. He said to his friends, "Ah, this is mine; does anyone mind if I take it home?" Since Fukuda had directed the film and Ogawa had disowned the project, no one saw a problem with Fukuda's request. Before his own youthful death, Fukuda was quietly making plans to do something with the film, having transferred it to video and shown it to at least the soundman for the film, Asanuma Keiji. However, what his plans were we will never know—except that he did not intend to return it to the ad hoc committee managing the Ogawa Pro legacy.

Without Fukuda's guidance, *Filmmaking and the Way to the Village* was restored posthumously and received its public premiere at the 1999 YIDFF. Now the film has been shown publicly, and no one has considered it a failure. It has its rough edges; on the other hand, in some respects, it is far more polished than many of Ogawa's pre-1974 films. Whatever Ogawa's problem was with the film, we can assume there was more to the issue than the critical comments he made to the group. Knowing Ogawa, it is difficult to imagine him shelving the film because of modesty, as if making an autobiographic film would be arrogant and immodest. Was the project only a way of shuffling his staff around? Or in this period of incredible transition—as a nation, as a generation, as a group—did he greet this diamond-in-the-rough self-image of the new *kiroku eiga no Ogawa Pro* with self-loathing? *Filmmaking and the Way to the Village* is one of those precious films that inspire those after-film discussions we all love and crave.

In Ogawa Pro, no one got to shoot their *ippon*—their chance to direct a film and establish a career as an independent director. Ogawa made only gestures in that direction. When Ogawa granted this opportunity, he either nipped it in the bud, overran the production at the last minute, or shelved the film in the spirit of "self-criticism." There were no noisy movements to have the films shown, as in the case of Kuroki's *Silence Has No Wings,* Oshima's *Night and Fog in Japan* (*Nihon no yoru to kiri,* 1960) or the Suzuki Seijun Problem. The simple fact is that no staff members were ever truly nurtured in Ogawa Pro. The people who stuck with him to the end have had to struggle to regain their professional composure, having been left without the tools to deal with a style of production other than the group coziness of Ogawa Pro. The world of independent cinema had changed radically, but Ogawa had not. It is a discomforting commentary on Ogawa's relationship to his staff and retrospectively casts a shadow of absolutism over the history of Ogawa Pro. It makes that scene of Ogawa struggling to control the mike boom almost heartrending.

Japanese Documentary at the Turn of the Century

In one way or another, Ogawa (and Tsuchimoto) set the terms for evaluating documentary in Japan. The reason Ogawa grips the imaginations of historians and filmmakers more than Tsuchimoto has to do with the power and politics of this issue of group versus individual production. It is now obvious that the rhetoric of the collective compellingly veiled the centrality of Ogawa's position in the collective. This contradiction is secreted away in the very name of the collective: Ogawa Productions. One cannot conceive of it without the charismatic presence of Ogawa and the concomitant abbreviation of the rest of the staff, who remain silently watching the conversation and largely anonymous.

There is something terribly ironic about this from a historiographic perspective since the big picture in which we must place Ogawa Pro changed drastically at the very time they left Sanrizuka for Magino. This is always perceived as a shift from the group ethos of the social movement films to the individual effort and focus on the self of the private film. Ogawa Pro has been absolutely necessary in providing the ideal example of the group approach to cinema. It is the mode of production to either strive for or avoid, the conception of cinema used to measure filmmakers no matter the persuasion. However, from a richer sense for the nature of Ogawa Pro, we can see even them shifting to a thoroughly "private film," that of Ogawa's. What is the Magino Village Story but the personal vision of its director-narrator?

By the turn of the century, the private film had become the norm for documentary, and yet more people were becoming aware of its problems. One reason is probably the vibrant discussion of Ogawa Pro in print, symposia, and film schools. Memories of the Ogawa films remained fresh thanks to regular showings at retrospectives, festivals, seminars, and schools. Finally, the YIDFF exposed Japan to the newest and oldest offerings of world documentary and published scholarly level catalogs and translations. The possibilities of the documentary form were boundless, making this manifestation of the private film seem impoverished in comparison.

At the same time, the group approach was under reevaluation. Much of this discourse centered on Sato Makoto and the production of *Living on the River Agano* (*Aga ni ikiru,* 1992). When Sato first contemplated a career in filmmaking, Tsuchimoto and Ogawa dominated the documentary scene. While the student movement was a thing of the past when he went to school in the late 1970s, the films made him interested in the continuing struggles at Sanrizuka and Minamata. He became a member of the collective that shot *The Innocent Sea* (with Kakesu Shuichi, Katori Naotaka, Shiraki Yoshihiro, Sugita Kazuo and Higuchi Shiro, *Muko naru umi,* 1983). This was a Minamata film, and he drew on the national networks of Ogawa Pro and Tsuchimoto's Seirinsha for distribution. In 1988, he and a crew of seven went to Niigata to make a documentary on the other area where Minamata disease had affected people living along the Agano River. They wanted to work in the mode Ogawa Pro epitomized, living collectively in Niigata with the same farmers and fishermen for an extended period of time. At the same time, they wanted to avoid some of the problems they perceived in Ogawa Pro. On a roundtable featuring Fukuda Katsuhiko among others, Sato recalls,

> The system of actually living and working somewhere no longer existed, but we were taken by the idea that we had found an opening that no one else had. We were very clear that the messages in our films should be different. We didn't want to convey the whole of Minamata, but rather to film its daily life. We thought that our films should be personal, that we should try somehow to break down social problems and focus on how lives can be lived and on the individual. Our way of filming was very 70s in that we worked in groups, but we absolutely did not want collaborative work to be a hard and fast rule as it had been at Ogawa Productions. There, it was a matter of hierarchy and poverty. We decided not to give the director all the power, and not to exhaust crewmembers without giving them any reward. We were determined to pay them at least something. We were trying to create some kind of community, but after three years, we found that we were just like a miniature Ogawa Productions. I don't think that this kind of thing will really succeed.[19]

The film that resulted from this collaboration, *Living on the River Agano* (*Aga ni ikiru,* 1992), was one of the high points of 1990s documentary. However, the production proved rocky, highlighting the problems of the collective approach. In retrospect, it appears like something of an experiment, to test whether the prestigious method represented by the example of Ogawa Pro was viable in the age of private film. Perhaps not. Sato's comments were provoked by something Fukuda said: "Film units have gotten smaller, with all the main filmmakers, like Kawase Naomi, working either alone or as a couple. Documentary filmmakers no longer get a film crew together to shoot movies. So it is not only the film subjects, but also the way people make films, that has shifted from the group to the individual. I have the feeling that Sato's *Living on the River Agano* will be the last collective film in this sense."[20] Indeed, Sato has gone on to direct documentaries in a conventional setting.[21]

We can sum up the state of Japanese documentary at the turn of the century with a look at four filmmakers who presented work at the 1999 YIDFF. These are prominent filmmakers of various predispositions and generations. They include Matsue Tetsuaki (b. 1977), Tsuchimoto Noriaki (b. 1928), Hara Kazuo (b. 1945), and Tsuchiya Yutaka (b. 1966).

Matsue Tetsuaki brought a delightful little film to the festival's Asia Program called *Annyong Kimchi* (*Annyon kimuchi*, 1999). Matsue was a film student and employee at Box Higashi Nakano mini-theater. During the Yamagata festival, he pamphleted all the parties, fearlessly asking people to attend his screening. Thanks to these tireless individual efforts, he managed to pack the house. The documentary is about Koreans living in Japan and fits into the rubric of personal films about one's family. This almost turned me away from the film, but I admired Matsue's spirit.

Clearly, what made this film about resident Koreans special was that Matsue is third-generation Korean. He possessed a very different relationship to both Korea and Japan than any of the other filmmakers that had dealt with the subject before. The energy driving the filmmaking is Matsue's guilt for not being a good grandson to his first-generation grandfather. He makes the film to make up with his grandfather, and along the way, he charts the different generations' identities vis-à-vis "home." His aunt in America has left Korea and Japan behind. The affinities of his other aunts seem split between Korea and Japan. His grandmother thoroughly identifies with Korea, and he and his sister basically consider themselves Japanese. But what of his grandfather? He remains a cipher who pushes the film along because he seemed to suppress his Korean heritage all the way to the grave, which has the Japanese name *Matsue* carved in stone.

Matsue's film is quite funny, and his "characters" are charming. In the survey he passed out at screenings, many respondents loved his sister and joked that they wanted to be introduced. Some even compared her to Sakura in the Tora-san series. I guess that makes Matsue himself Tora-san.

While talking to Matsue that first night, I pushed him to express what he thought he was doing in this documentary. He provoked this line of questioning by asserting that his film had no *poli* (policy) because he was third generation. What he really meant is that he did not perceive his film as political and reveals a second layer of generational difference: that of today's youth versus the Ogawa Pro generation. Like most people his age, Matsue wants to avoid politics at all costs, which is certainly one factor driving him and other young documentarists inward to the self, family, and friends. Hara Kazuo, who was at Yamagata for another event, told me it is like an allergic reaction. By all measures, Matsue's film is profoundly political. It ranges across subjects, such as generation gaps, North versus South Korea, World War II, slave labor, racial discrimination, imperialism, national and racial identity, immigration, and exile. That he cannot acknowledge the politicization of his own doing points to the biggest problem with the private film's manifestation in Japan.[22]

The screening of Tsuchimoto Noriaki's *Memories of Kawamoto Teruo—Minamata: the Person Who Dug the Well* (*Kaiso—Kawamoto Teruo~Minamata—Ido o hotta hito,* 1999) was my most powerful experience of the 1999 YIDFF. This was Tsuchimoto's first documentary on Minamata in thirteen years. He was provoked to take camera in hand from the traumatizing death of friend Kawamoto Teruo, who was one of the key activists in the fight against the Chisso chemical company and the central government to get official recognition and reparations for the mercury poisoning in Minamata. Originally, there were just a handful of recognized victims, but thanks in part to Kawamoto's efforts, this number went into the thousands. Kawamoto died in February 1999, and this film is Tsuchimoto's tribute to him. It was also an expression of frustration with the people of Minamata and by extension with Japan itself.

This was the first time Tsuchimoto recognized the virtues of video, having shot and edited the film entirely on his own. He sheepishly called *Memories* his "home video version" because of its rough production values. It looks this way because it wasn't meant for public showing. He originally wanted to make a 16mm film, but for various reasons, the plan fell apart. Because of the subject matter, however, he felt compelled to *do something*. In a matter of months, he edited this documentary from his 8mm video home movies. Tsuchimoto originally meant to send tapes to those who asked for one. He showed it at Yamagata at the request of Video Act!, which was programming an event on video activism that fall. However, the film was not made with public exhibition in mind. In this sense, it could be thrown into the genre of private films to interesting effect because, unlike the typical *kojin eiga,* Tsuchimoto's film was not meant to be a public exposure of the private and yet it is passionately engaged and deeply political.

The tape is framed by the New Year's cards that Tsuchimoto received from Kawamoto in the years preceding his death, with a long middle section featuring Kawamoto's greatest hits clips from the Minamata Series. We see some breathtaking shots of, for example, Kawamoto sitting cross-legged on a luxurious conference table; his face is just inches away from the face of Chisso's CEO who maintains a rock-solid expression in the face of Kawamoto's harangue. I understand why Tsuchimoto hesitated to show *Memories* publicly. It's rough and simple. But his talk afterwards was intricate and heartrending. Kawamoto's last New Year's card, sent just months before his death, had a handwritten scrawl that he wrote only on Tsuchimoto's greeting: "Those who dug the well have been forgotten." This shook Tsuchimoto to the foundations of his soul, and after the festival screening, he was on the verge of breaking down throughout his talk.

For all of Kawamoto and Tsuchimoto's work, no one seemed to appreciate their lifelong efforts. The people of Minamata turned their collective backs on them. For example, Kawamoto kept running for public office but lost even though a vote from every victim would have meant certain victory (he won the last election but only by default). In survey after survey, Minamata citizens have expressed their desire to strike the name of their city from the term for the disease. Activists' efforts to preserve the chemical factory via the UN's historical sites list—as has been done with Auschwitz and Hiroshima—have gone nowhere. Everyone wondered why Tsuchimoto was not producing more films on Minamata, and this is his answer. He felt silenced by Minamata's own efforts to suppress this history. Ultimately, Tsuchimoto placed the blame on Japan. He left the audience with the depressing sense that he had come to a roadblock, immense and insurmountable. No doubt this has something to do with Matsue's conflation of "policy" and "politics" and his fervent desire to avoid looking "political." However, Tsuchimoto impresses because whatever old paradigms from the past stand in his way, he still made this documentary and sent it out into the world.

That there are lessons to be learned that are concealed in Tsuchimoto's story is Hara Kazuo's sense as well. In the mid-1990s, he signaled a turn away from the private film by forming a nascent collective of his own. His office bustled with the energy of young people who have gathered around him. Together they conducted mini-seminars Hara called *Cinema Juku* (which could be translated as "cinema cram schools"). These were short courses held in various parts of Japan to investigate historical and aesthetic questions like the ones raised in this book. Visitors included famous directors, cinematographers and actors. They constituted an impressive body of research into Japanese film and some of its neglected areas, including television documentary. One of the projects Hara has considered is a long-term study and book project on Ogawa Pro, which haunts the background of Cinema Juku in the deepest of ways. By the 1999 YIDFF, they had even made a 16mm film in the collective mode: *My Mishima* (*Watakushi no Mishima,* 1999).

Hara was a fan of every genre of feature film, but it wasn't until he moved to Tokyo in the late 1960s that he paid serious attention to the documentary. It was probably impossible to miss at the time, considering the excitement over the films of Tsuchimoto, Ogawa, and many others. Like most young people interested in politics, Hara looked forward to every new film from Ogawa Pro:

> I was deeply attracted to Ogawa Pro, the collective itself. . . . Actually, I never went, but did think about it. Still, jumping into the middle of that kind of thing, I just couldn't imagine myself in that kind of collective. . . . Those people were, after all, from the sixties, one generation earlier. Since we were from the seventies . . . there's the question of who exactly is that self that's participating in the struggle. Oneself . . . who are you? We'd face that individual, our self, and ask that question. . . . Who are you, this individual that wants to express something? That's how we thought. For example, even if I entered Ogawa Pro, in the end it is my self that's wrapped up inside there. While I kept thinking that creating things in a collective was incredibly attractive, in the end those Ogawa Pro people were already doing it. So I might as well try and do it from this place called the individual.[23]

What intrigued Hara were the television documentaries at the time. They were also experiencing a radical shift in style, one that was undoubtedly related to the larger discourses swirling around Matsumoto and the others. At the very moment when the massive Sanrizuka protests became iconic for drawing a contrast between the styles of television news reportage and Ogawa Pro—between styles that *take sides* with either the powerful or the powerless—there were certain spaces in television available for experimentation that blurred the very same boundaries. This is why, when Hara moved into moving image documentary, he chose television as his entry point.[24]

However, Ogawa never left his sights, and the collective nature of Cinema Juku, bringing young people under his wing in an attempt to nurture them and, thus, invigorate Japanese documentary, was probably impossible for him to conceptualize without reference to the prototype provided by Ogawa Pro. But the world had changed. At one level, the young people joined Hara's group for radically different reasons than Jieiso and Ogawa

Pro members. They were film fans that want to become filmmakers. It could be that quite a few wanted to ride Hara's coattails for career purposes. By the time they made their first documentary in 1999, only three of the original members remained.

The example of *My Mishima* raises other issues of striking similarity to those left swirling around the legacy of Ogawa. For example, the tension between individual and group agency remains unresolved here. The credit for the film reads "Hara Kazuo + Cinema Juku," effectively singling out Hara's lead while collapsing the group into anonymity. Apparently, Hara also asserted his directorial powers when he didn't like the way things were going, although with none of the dictatorial flair of Ogawa. *My Mishima* was made through the auspices of Hagi City, which sponsored many Cinema Juku through their own local film festival. The idea was to bring in a bunch of young people, in almost a kind of summer-camp situation, and make a 16mm film about Hagi's Mishima Island. After sessions on filmmaking skills, the students went out to the island to do research. Like Jieiso before them, they came back with written reports, and Hara would determine if the material was usable for the film. They then shot and edited the film together.

Hara showed *My Mishima* in one of the most interesting events at the 1999 YIDFF, the encounter between Cinema Juku and Full Shot.[25] The latter is the group Taiwanese director Wu Yii-feng organized after Ogawa's death and is quite a lively crowd of young filmmakers. Much of the discussion at this event centered on a comparison of their respective situations. They discussed their material conditions of production, their historical circumstances, and their sociopolitical contexts. The comparisons were quite revealing, and it seemed to leave Hara both jealous and frustrated. During the discussion, the story behind the "collectivity" and "togetherness" started coming into focus, mostly because of surprisingly harsh criticism from the Taiwanese side. Hara and his Cinema Juku people appeared taken aback by the candor of their Taiwanese counterparts.

One sounding board for the comparison was *My Mishima* itself, which had none of the edge Hara's films are famous for. In this sense, the film was inscribed by the desires and influences of the younger people working with him. They wanted a film that dealt with issues they felt many Japanese could identify with, such as leaving one's hometown and mother behind for a new life in faraway cities. There are interesting scenes where ten to twenty young people express, in a single shot, their dreams for the future (which usually have to do with leaving Mishima) and their relationship to their hometown. However, as the Taiwanese pointed out, the film is weakened because it doesn't explain *why* people are leaving. A representative from the Hagi Film

Festival attempted to be helpful by explaining some of the structural reasons, like taxes and public funding, that make life on the island unattractive. This simply added fuel to the Taiwanese fire. Put simply, the Full Shot youth were demanding the Cinema Juku youth be cognizant of the complex politics that underlay their subject matter, and this is exactly what the young Japanese filmmakers were trying to avoid.

Hara and Cinema Juku members tried to defend themselves, but kept falling back on the issue of *generational difference*. Hara revealed how he always criticized the young people that attend Cinema Juku, trying to provoke them and tease them out of complacency and silence. But his students keep quitting, making continuity difficult, and making the generation gap seem insurmountable. The Taiwanese berated Hara for criticizing his own students like that, but they seemed incapable of appreciating how problematic the relationship is between Japanese youth and the world—a paralyzing situation for anyone aspiring to create documentaries. There was almost a feeling of despair on the Cinema Juku side, in strong contrast to the energy and optimism of Full Shot. That night, everybody made up in a party that lasted until breakfast, and it gave me a chance to talk to everyone at length.

In the end, my sense was that the generational difference that weighed down Hara and Cinema Juku has a second historical dimension—that of major transitions in aesthetics and politics. Hara is dealing with the legacy of the early 1970s, when the New Left crumbled. However, many of the attitudes and values embodied by those days of public passion continued to the present day without adequately transforming to meet historical changes. This is provocatively suggested by the structure Hara chose for Cinema Juku and *My Mishima*. It was conceived as a return to the collective mode of filmmaking best exemplified by Ogawa Pro. Turning away from what he called the Super Hero-ism (*supaa hiiro-shugi*) of his previous films—his former wife, veteran Okazaki Kenzo, novelist Inoue Mitsuharu—this would be a group effort (Cinema Juku + Hara Kazuo) concerning another group (the Mishima islanders). It was as if Hara could not think beyond the earlier paradigm. By contrast, the sociopolitical upheaval Full Shot was dealing with was far more recent: the lifting of martial law in 1987, the collapse of the USSR, and the subsequent reevaluation of Marxism. But for reasons that were not entirely clear, the Taiwanese filmmakers were dealing with the transition in far more interesting ways. The documentaries they showed were about issues like aboriginal people and the deaf (by a deaf woman, with no sound!). And while there might be a generation gap between Wu and his students, it is not silencing them. I sensed Hara's jealousy regarding the way Full Shot works together. Here is what Hara wrote in the festival's main catalog:

> Taiwan's history of documentary film is not as long as Japan's; it is still in its nascent period. Because of that, however, its films are full of a youthful energy of which I am envious. By contrast, when I think about documentary film in Japan, I am full of bitter doubts over whether we have passed our prime and lost our energy. . . . I have the fortune this year to come to the magnet that is Yamagata. I have made a promise with director Wu Yii-feng to do our best in dialogue. Both Hara and Tsuchimoto are at a loss about what to do from here on out. How do you invigorate Japanese documentary without transforming Japan itself?

Hara senses that the future for artists of the documentary lies in the interstices between the individual and the collective, between fiction and documentary, between the extremely private and the extremely public. It remains to be seen whether Cinema Juku productively navigates these contradictions.

At the turn of the century, the closest thing to a movement in the Japanese cinema world was Video Act! The structure of this organization bears out the era's atomization of passion. It is a loose confederation of groups, connected more by a catalog and an Internet site than anything else. One of the prime movers behind Video Act! was Tsuchiya Yutaka, who showed one of the finest films at YIDFF in 1999. It was entitled *The New God* (*Atarashii kamisama,* 1999), and is undoubtedly among the most important Japanese documentaries of the decade. Depending on the course of Japanese documentary in the twenty-first century, it could eventually be seen as a turning point coming at the end of the century.

Before this, Tsuchiya's most interesting work was the controversial *What Do You Think about the War Responsibility of Emperor Hirohito?* (*Anata wa tenno no senso sekinin ni tsuite do omoimasu ka?* [96.8.15 Yasukuni-hen], 1997). In this fine example of video activism, Tsuchiya and a friend go to the Yasukuni Shrine on the anniversary of the war's end to ask old people the question of the title. There are many impressive things about this project, both politically and formally. However, it is significant that these young filmmakers stepped into the Yasukuni Shrine in the first place, let alone asking such a provocative question. This indicated a precious flexibility and an unwillingness to paint the right wing in broad strokes in order to dismiss it.

For *The New God,* Tsuchiya capitalized on his flexibility and eagerness to engage people across the entire political spectrum. Its premise was simply startling: Tsuchiya, the progressive video activist, hooked up with an ultranationalist punk band, and each tried to figure the other out. He gave the lead singer, Amamiya Karin, a video camera, and both she and Tsuchiya recorded the development of their unlikely encounter from their own perspectives. They treat the video camera as a kind of intimate, confessing their deepest thoughts. At one point, Tsuchiya arranged for Amamiya to visit the Red Army members who hijacked a plane to North Korea back in 1970, and the visit forces her to think hard about her own life. As the deep similarities between the extreme Left and extreme Right become clear to her—including the intolerance of their politics and their untenable idealism—Tsuchiya and Amamiya find themselves drawing closer together, perhaps politically and certainly emotionally. By the end *The New God,* they enter a romantic relationship, she quit her affiliation with an ultranationalist organization to rethink her musical activism, and we will have to see if they live happily ever after.

The New God fit uncomfortably into the rubric of the private film, that genre that so dominated the 1990s Japanese documentary. It constantly threatened to devolve into a love story, but Tsuchiya was too smart and too dedicated to an engaged documentary to let that happen. It started out looking like a somewhat conventional documentary until he handed a camera to Amamiya and her guitarist Ito Hidehito. From that point on, they became collaborators, something quite novel to the personal film as it was construed in Japan. In addition to the footage each shot, all three offered their own voice-over commentary on the soundtrack. Tsuchiya makes great use of the confessional mode that seems so specific to video as a medium. When they turned the camera on their own bodies, they constantly reflected on the latest twists and turns of their encounter. It became a mutual self-reflection, energized by the fact that each speculated on the motives and emotions of the other. Some audience members complained of a sense of performance during these private sessions with the camera, but that is only a matter of course. All documentary involves performance, but it also provokes what never would have happened without the presence of the machine.

To focus on these matters of style would be to limit *The New God* to the confines of the private film. What generated this phenomenon was precisely a refusal to enter the world, camera in hand. It was a dismissal of the political and the engaged, and a concomitant retreat to the safety of the self, the family, and the friend (or even the aesthetic). Our study of Ogawa Pro suggests that "something happened" in the 1970s, and conceptions of progressive politics in the film world fell into a kind of stasis in the 1970s. It is as if no one took account of the mid-decade crises, when the student movement boiled down, when the vanguard of the Red Army exposed a corruption within the Left by killing its own, when the oil shock hit hard, when the advances of Third-World and feminist filmmaking and theory were passed by, and when the airport was completed. Stuck with a conception of the political defined decades in the past, young filmmakers became quick to dismiss any affiliation with it. Tsuchiya cites their constant consumption of the newest of the new as a deflection of the emptiness this causes, a way of engaging something safe, or creating a seemingly solid place to stand. He suggests the other safe haven is the personal. This situation helps explain why Tsuchimoto felt silenced, why Hara could not escape the paradigm of *Heta Village's* Ogawa Pro, why Matsue made a complex film about identity in spite of himself, and why most young filmmakers seemed unwilling to take their cameras into that troubling world out there.

Tsuchiya's use of the private film constituted a critique from within because instead of using the genre to confirm one's identity and worth through public screening of the private sphere, he used it to engage the public arena with a resolute and refreshing passion. Bringing in the Red Army was a brilliant move and reminds us of that other Red Army revolutionary=artist, Adachi Masao, who seemed to pose the choice in the early 1970s as one between politics and art. But like the reality of Adachi's position, Tsuchiya was dedicated to avoiding these kinds of either-or choices and traps. His commitment to escape the closed circuit of consumption and dedicate oneself to something larger was also a refusal to become dead-ended in the vestiges of Old Left party politics or New Left revolutionary politics. In 1999, I was not the only one who left the theater feeling like I had *finally* seen a committed, passionate, engaged documentary by someone from my own generation, that someone from the younger generation had finally arrived. While the film broke down easy oppositions of Right and Left, new and old, private and public, it left everyone on shaky ground. This is why, ultimately, *The New God* will either be seen as one of the most interesting films of the 1990s, or it will mark a turning point.

Postscript

Devotion

At the close of the century, two filmmakers undertook films about Ogawa Pro. They came from very different parts of the world, from very different perspectives, and they entertained very different relationships to Ogawa Shinsuke. One is American experimental filmmaker Barbara Hammer, and the other is Chinese feature film director Peng Xiao-lian.

Hammer came late to Ogawa Pro. As a guest to the YIDFF in the 1990s, she encountered the films of Ogawa Pro and met Shiraishi Yoko—former member and Ogawa's wife. She was taken by the passion of the films, the unusual story behind their production, and by the role of women within that history. After long discussions with Shiraishi, she decided to embark on a project exploring Ogawa's widow and the women of the collective. However, in the course of the long production, it became a very different kind of documentary that is sure to produce long and involved debate.

There are a number of fundamental reasons for the transformation in Hammer's trajectory. One is simply that as she conducted research and performed interviews, her perspective on that history naturally matured, and she was able to take more educated and complex perspectives on that past. She was working with a subject that looked fairly straightforward on the outside. However, as anyone who has thought about Ogawa Pro knows all too well, this was a very unusual and complicated group. Ogawa Pro was something of a phenomenon. It defies easy explanation.

Another reason for the change in Hammer's approach was the resistance she discovered from many of the former members. She arrived in the midst of a difficult period several years after Ogawa's passing. There were various contradictions and tensions emerging within the committee in charge of the fate of Ogawa's material legacy, which centered on film prints, rushes, their rights, the thousands of still photographs, notebooks, fliers, manifestos, catalogs, letters, postcards, after-film surveys, screening reports, posters, and scrapbooks—even Otsu Koshiro's mangled glasses from the riot police attack captured in *Summer in Sanrizuka*. Adding a layer of complication, Kimura Michio also wanted his house returned after two decades of Ogawa Pro occupation. Everything required relocation as soon as possible. The bewildering question was where. And then there was the debt. Disposing of this business naturally provoked passionate feelings about the past, revived sleeping anxieties and angers and desires, and brought a huge number of old companions into sometimes distressingly intimate contact.

Hammer arrived on the scene in the midst of this delicate process, having begun her homework only recently. Immediately, she found herself in an atmosphere of mistrust compounded by cultural miscommunication. Some people were clearly nervous about stories they heard concerning a feminist filmmaker from New York digging into the treatment of women members;

Barbara Hammer and Iizuka Toshio at their interview. *Devotion* (2000) is a precious memento of Ogawa Pro, a gift from both Hammer and the former members who opened their hearts and homes to her. Photograph by Tanaka Junko. Courtesy of Barbara Hammer.

by the 1990s, changes in Japanese society finally had made them highly self-aware of the contradictions in their former politics of liberation and the role of women in the collective. Other former members simply wanted to forget the past or were embarrassed about their fervent political beliefs in an age when redemptive politics have a bad reputation. Still others doubted an outsider, let alone a foreigner who couldn't speak or read Japanese, could adequately represent their own past. Now, however, after the trial of making *Devotion* (2000) it is fair to say she is one of the few foreign experts on Japanese documentary. And the film itself is a precious memento of Ogawa Pro, a gift from both Hammer and the former members that opened their hearts and homes to her. Those that granted interviews to Hammer were amazingly frank and open, trusting her with intimate passages in their life stories. One cannot help being deeply moved at seeing Hatanaka Hiroko and Iizuka Toshio sharing their child's fatherless family portrait or hearing Kawada Yumiko reading passages from her personal diary.

Unfortunately, a number of key people are missing from the film. At least a couple of those who refused Hammer disliked her less-than-subtle approach, clearly a problem of cross-cultural misunderstanding. Her first mistake was initiating her project with a mass mailing to a list of former Ogawa Pro members some one hundred names long, politely asking when she could set up interviews. This is a perfectly reasonable strategy to an American sensibility, but the letter provoked many puzzled calls to the Japanese producers, Yamagata Documentary Film Festival's Ono Seiko, and Pandora's Nakano Rie. Hammer quickly learned that Japanese generally prefer a gently slow approach. Moreover, the director misjudged the importance of "approach" for her subjects (or perhaps we should say "her *taisho*" to emphasize the basic theoretical difference at work here). What sets Ogawa Pro apart from nearly all filmmakers in the history of cinema is the lengths—emotionally and temporally—that the members were willing to go to ease their way into the villages of Heta and Magino. Ogawa Pro was special for its unprecedented, long-term commitment to get inside spaces difficult or supposedly impossible to penetrate. For a filmmaker who based his or her career on such values, it was somewhat distressing to see another filmmaker whip out the camera on the first date. Significantly, many of the people chafed by the swift, direct approach were the ones who did not identify themselves as filmmakers. Practical considerations meant nothing to them; so what if it was inconvenient (and expensive) to preface any formal interview with multiple meetings? Other things are far more vital.

Hammer's efforts at talking to people were hampered by all of these factors. The refusals for interviews came to a spectacular climax in the summer of 1999, when Tamura Masaki visited the University of Chicago for a retrospective of his work. Hammer knew this was her most important interview and was being exceedingly careful and polite in her communication with the cameraman. Despite Tamura's quiet, noncommittal style of speech, Hammer, her assistant, and her producers all thought they had secured an interview in Chicago. I was visiting the retrospective as a spectator, and Hammer asked me to mediate, and perhaps even conduct the interview if that's what the cinematographer preferred. Tamura is a quiet, polite man, and when I confirmed the interview time the day before, he looked grudgingly willing—the very stereotype of Japanese indirection. He certainly hadn't declined.

I have to admit I took Tamura's "I guess" for "yes," and when Tamura left a screening at the appointed time and saw the next-door room with lights ablaze and camera waiting, he was shocked. He assumed he had said, "No!" He stepped into the room, apologized profusely, and told Hammer that he thought she knew he had refused the interview. Hammer pleaded, equally graciously. Tamura told her he just couldn't do it. And Hammer dropped to the floor, forehead to the ground in her best formal Japanese bow. This remarkable scene sums up the intensity of the feelings on both sides of the cultural divide. Tamura's refusal marked the film with his conspicuous absence and points to the many other missing members. (A few years later, he told me the refusal had nothing to do with Hammer; he simply wanted—wants—to wash his hands of Ogawa.) For Hammer's part, it demonstrated the respect she cultivated for "the approach." Perhaps she hadn't internalized it, but she had certainly accorded it the respect it demanded. Tamura's refusal was a terrible blow, and probably pointed her in an increasingly critical direction.

Viewers familiar with Hammer's most celebrated work will probably be surprised by *Devotion's* style. Documentaries, such as *Nitrate Kisses* (1992), *Tender Fictions* (1995) and her earlier experimental films, are highly imaginative and formally innovative. She is one of those filmmakers who has turned the work of optical printing into an art form, and considering the image manipulation tools available to digital editing, it might be surprising to many that she does not take advantage of them here. However, there is another thread of historically based documentaries running through her filmography, and *Devotion* falls into this category.

Hammer has produced what is essentially a talking heads documentary, a style we associate mostly with nonfiction forms on television. Head-and-shoulder interviews with people talking about an absent past are intercut with still and moving images to relieve the monotony of the heads droning on with their stories. Conventionally, this approach relies on first-person testimonials to support a larger argument. Images and various modes of narration supplement people's stories to keep the film visually interesting and bring the past to life. This kind of director strives to use talking heads to portray an adequate, global view of a slice of life—to illustrate "what happened."

While *Devotion* may look pedestrian at first glance, it does tamper with the rules and assumptions about talking-heads documentary in curious and thought-provoking ways. There is the odd camera angle and short reenactment, but these feel like initial attempts at a more experimental structure that might have been abandoned in the production process. What is ultimately fascinating about Barbara Hammer's *Devotion* is the use to which the interviews and images are put. As in the standard approach, a person will be talking about a certain person or incident; an image, if available, will be inserted for the sake of illustration and injecting the image track with some variety. Likewise, the film is predictably framed by amusing and enlightening expert testimony by outside observers, such as Oshima Nagisa, Tsuchimoto Noriaki, Kuroki Kazuo, and Hara Kazuo. (An exception is Robert Kramer who looks lost and only serves to substantiate the fact that Asia is historically off the map of Euro-American filmmakers and film historians.)

At the same time, Hammer is not devoted to the well-trodden stylistic conventions of expert commentary, personal testimony, and audio-visual quotes for illustration. Images serve their usual illustrative function, but only in a curiously ambiguous manner. For example, there are many clips taken from Ogawa's films, but none of them have subtitles explaining which film we are looking at. She uses clips from the actual films in the same indeterminate way she uses outtakes. Hammer shaves off the specificities of all the images to emphasize their function as general place markers for the past. In the most extreme cases, images from Ogawa's first student documentaries shot in his Eiken days serve to illustrate events from Ogawa's own life—for example, an image of a child from *Children Living in the Mountains* is presented as a documentary image of Ogawa himself. Elsewhere, fictional sequences from *Sundial* serve as documentary images of Ogawa Pro's past. Only those familiar with the films will realize the irony. In *Devotion*, a given image represents not "what happened," but "what it was like."

This winnowing out of details that are hardly extraneous, such as what film we are looking at and when it was produced, is indicative of the logic governing *Devotion*. It is a poetic logic, not the approach of a historian who feels a burden of proof or the need to clearly explain the sequence of historical events down to the finest details. Indeed, "details" like the epochal Sanrizuka Struggle are hardly explained here. Unlike the television documentary, which aims at portraying a swath of history in easily understandable terms, Hammer is interested in something more specific and less easy to pin down than public events. There is enormous play in the signifying link between word and image. In the same way, her refusal of voice-over narration means there is no textual cementing of the various interviews into a seamless and easy-to-follow argument or story. In the end, it is apparent she is not all that interested in the history of Ogawa Pro. A viewer coming fresh to the subject of Ogawa Pro, Japanese documentary, and the history of postwar Japanese social movements will come away from *Devotion* learning very little. So if the subject of the film is not this history, then what might it be?

Hammer is ultimately concerned with the web of human relationships constituting this filmmaking group and the paradoxical figure at its center. The filmmakers/activists of Ogawa Pro came together under the ideal of collective filmmaking aligned with progressive causes. By asserting that filmmakers had to take a position, weaving their own subjectivities into the fabric of their final films, they were politicizing the space of production along the lines of the New Left attack on the traditions of documentary of both the government and the Communist Party. Hammer sidesteps the complex task of laying out this kind of contextualization to politicize the space of the collective itself. In doing so, she pits the values underlying their devotion to social justice against the challenges posed by the realities of low-budget, collective filmmaking and communal living amidst the charismatic and vexing figure of Ogawa Shinsuke.

The talking-head approach to documentary style usually assumes a stance of "objectivity," but a smart filmmaker like Hammer would never aspire to any such ideal. Instead, it is likely that she chose this approach to distance herself from the mudslinging, and as a method of critique, literally let people speak for themselves. She recalls, "I saw myself as a witness to the unfolding of each interview not knowing beforehand what I would learn. There were many, many surprises." This alternative does not escape an implicit grab for objectivity to the extent that it deploys the talking-head testimonials like evidence (perhaps of past crimes?). As evidence, the pronouncements of the former members are positioned as (questionable) representations of the past that interact and entwine around one point of contention after another. Through combination, Hammer makes the Ogawa Pro members speak to each other and this interaction, in turn, brings out the full complexity of the social reality.

One might ask, then, where Hammer is in all of this. Where is her voice? Where is her (silent, invisible) head? She may stand apart from the squabbling crowd by virtue of never showing her face, but is she actually hiding through this apparently mundane style we associate with the television documentary? Without the aggressive audio-visual experimentation of her more famous work, she suppresses her directorial presence. We know she is critical, but is she simply an observer?

Watching this film is the ultimate voyeuristic experience. Without the effort to introduce spectators to the back story, what is left is the backstage. There is so little context, the assumed viewer posited by the film's style *must* be someone with great, intimate knowledge of Ogawa Pro. With such little devotion to contextualization, it feels as though it was made specifically for the former members of Ogawa Pro. In the end, Hammer is not an observer; in her trying production process, she became so immersed in the post-Ogawa tangle of interpersonal relationships that she got too far in to pull out clean. Indeed, we could say Barbara Hammer is the last Ogawa Pro member. And *Devotion* is the final Ogawa Pro film.

Piles of Persimmons

The other film that went into production at the end of the decade was Peng Xiao-lian's *Red Persimmons* (*Manzan Benigaki,* which might best be translated *Piles of Persimmons;* the preproduction title was *Benigaki henreki,* or *Red Persimmon Wanderings,* 2001). The project began a few years after Ogawa's passing, and Shiraishi Yoko was the driving force behind this film along with producer Yasui Yoshio. In essence, it completes a film where Ogawa left off, as it finishes one of the segments from *The Sundial Carved with a Thousand Years of Notches,* which Ogawa dropped on the cutting room floor.

In 1984, Ogawa Pro collected stories about dried persimmons, one of the delicacies Yamagata is known for. Each fall around the time the leaves change, the persimmons ripen to a deep red-orange. They remain on the trees long after the leaves drop, making for a spectacle of bare branches decorated with persimmons, fireworks of fruit covering the mountainsides. The filmmakers shot most of the footage they needed, and Ogawa got as far as organizing the material into a rough outline. He worked first on paper and then made a rough cut with their footage. However, by this point they already knew they had a massive film on their hands and something had to go. The first cut of *The Sundial Carved with a Thousand Years of Notches* was extremely rough, and members joke that it would have taken days to screen; apparently, it was some ten hours in length. The second, finer cut was about five and one-half hours long, two hours away from the final running time. Twenty minutes of this was Ogawa's initial version of the persimmons story. Something had to go, and this was one of the sections Ogawa Pro decided to drop, much as it hurt to do so. Ogawa shelved his four hours of rushes but always considered it a pet project on the back burner. He wrote a detailed continuity and intended to return to it before his illness cut all plans short. Shiraishi revived the project in the mid-1990s—perhaps as a way of resurrecting her filmmaking collaboration with her husband—and called Peng Xiao-lian in from Shanghai to direct.

It was an appropriate choice, since this was one of the directors Ogawa staked much hope on in his turn outward to Asia. Peng was one of the women directors that emerged in mainland China's fifth generation, and is well-known for her films *Three Women* (*Nu ren de gu shi*, 1989) and *Shanghai Women* (*Jia zhuang mei gan jue*, 2002). She first met Ogawa at the Hawai'i International Film Festival in 1988, which was the event where I met both directors. Later, she caught up with him once more at the Turin International Film Festival, where she was able to watch *The Sundial Carved with a Thousand Years of Notches*. Impressed, she began to con-

Ogawa Shinsuke's widow, Shiraishi Yoko (left), enlisted the help of Chinese director Peng Xiao-lian to complete an extended sequence on persimmons and modernity that Ogawa left on the cutting room floor. The resulting film posthumously finishes Ogawa's plans to collaborate with other Asian filmmakers. Photograph courtesy of Planet Bibliothèque de Cinéma.

sider attempting some kind of docudrama herself. When Ogawa heard this, he encouraged her to mount a full-fledged documentary in this mode and to shoot it in Japan.

Over the next couple years, they corresponded while Peng developed her idea as a graduate student at the New York University film school. She wanted to make a film on Chinese students who were studying at Japanese universities, and the title was to be *My Dream Japan.* Ogawa liked the idea, especially for the way it tied the contemporary flow of Chinese immigrants into Japan to the previous (forced) movement of Chinese during World War II. Ogawa started contacting critics and other people to create a working committee for the project, and he and producer Fuseya completed the complicated process of securing a long-term visa for a Chinese national. Despite their financial straits, they provided Peng an airplane ticket and allowed her to stay in the Ogikubo apartment while initiating the research for her film. Unfortunately, Ogawa became sick in the middle of this project, and it was never finished.

However, the experience had an enormous impact on Peng. She eventually returned to mainland China, making films for the Shanghai film studio and writing books and essays. In 1996, she published a book about her encounter with Ogawa. Entitled *Burning Attachment,* it uses two intense relationships to discuss her feelings toward Japan. Like many Chinese, Peng harbored a strong dislike for Japan, thanks to both the violence of Japan's wartime invasion and also to the continual retelling of these stories of horror. Peng's family was deeply affected by the wartime experience. Both her mother and father were arrested, and her mother was particularly mistreated while in Japanese hands. The first part of the book explores how this lead to Peng's hatred of the Japanese. The second part discusses the way she met Ogawa, lived in the Ogawa Pro apartment with the crew, and learned to change her attitude about Japan.

Peng's deep admiration for Ogawa made it difficult to accept the assignment to finish the persimmons film. The continuity that Ogawa produced was very much in the spirit of *"Nippon": Furuyashiki Village* and *The Sundial Carved with a Thousand Years of Notches.* On the surface, it is a film describing the details of persimmon farming, punctuated by amusing storytelling from various villagers. For example, one old man ends a discourse on persimmon farming with a story about the first American soldiers to reach the village in the fall of 1945. Tempted by this good-looking fruit, they stole some off the trees and took a bite. Much to the amusement of the farmers, the Americans immediately spit the fruit out, not knowing that persimmons are remarkably astringent before drying. The old man laughs at the memory and finishes off the story with clever symmetry. The

Americans left cans of ketchup with the villagers, who had no idea how to cook with it. They tried eating the ketchup with spoons and then immediately spit it out and fed it all to the livestock. As in previous Ogawa Pro films, this storytelling breathes historical life into the present-day images of nondescript villages. Furthermore, the stories serve to underline larger issues without resorting to pedantic, expository modes of documentary. In these persimmon orchards, they discover the dawning of modernity in village Japan. The parade of elderly farmers narrate the mechanization of persimmon farming, and how a simple fascination with new machines underwrote a massive shift in daily life.

Ogawa begins by introducing the basic process of peeling and drying the persimmons, starting with the traditional way of peeling with a knife. An old woman demonstrates how easy it was to cut one's thumb back in the 1920s, when her new mother-in-law taught her how to do it. Then, she shows a notched knife that pivots around the persimmon's stem for more control, an invention fabricated by her husband for the sake of her thumb. After this, much of the film is devoted to the elaboration of more efficient methods through mechanization. The filmmakers interview an elderly man who invented a peeling machine back in 1931. Basically, he took bicycle parts to a local blacksmith. The end product looked like a small stand with a handle driving bicycle gears that rotate a persimmon impaled on a spindle. As the persimmon spins, a small blade is drawn across the surface of the fruit, enabling the farmer to peel it with a couple turns of the handle. By the end of the film, other farmers have invented electric peelers elaborating on the initial idea.

Just as *The Sundial Carved with a Thousand Years of Notches* was ultimately about finding the universe in a typical rice paddy, *Red Persimmons* strove to discover the dawn of modernity in Yamagata's orchards. The inventor of the first peeler describes how he was "machine mad." And it was thanks to this thrill with modernization that persimmons could be produced in large enough quantities to become a major cash crop. One scene shows a broker in the present day negotiating a price with a distant buyer over the phone, and then coming to an agreement with a local farmer over a space heater and sake. This scene is followed by an interview with an old woman who tells a story about how her mother became the first persimmons broker back in the 1910s. Through this process, which is detailed in the film largely through storytelling, these small Yamagata villages came to engage in the national economy, a market that drives them to spend valuable labor on packaging and waste incredible amounts of food because the shape of the fruit may not be just right.

The film also has the self-reflexivity of Ogawa's *The Sundial Carved with a Thousand Years of Notches*. One of the most memorable scenes is set during the photography of a time-lapse sequence at a huge drying rack. As Nosaka and Ogawa patiently stand around the camera, clicking frames off at regular intervals, an old farmer strolls up, and they introduce themselves: "Oh, you're Ogawa from Magino?" asks the old man, "You're famous!" Their conversation swiftly turns into one of Ogawa's interviews, showing the director's knack for provoking fascinating conversation from villagers. When Ogawa says he heard this village was famous for its dried persimmons, the old man starts sharing his intricate knowledge about the reasons why—why the sun, wind, and soil are just right, why there are dry conditions and little mist, why all the factors that go into good persimmons happily converge on this particular spot. The sequence ends with the footage they were shooting in time-lapse, showing the shadows of a thousand persimmons shifting with the arcing of the sun.

Peng builds Ogawa's approach to reflexivity into her own film. The scenes book-ending the film turn us to both Ogawa and the farmers. In the introduction, Peng and her crew set up a portable screen and watch the rushes they had to work with. At the film's end, a flatbed editor shows freeze-frames of familiar faces from the film we just watched. Subtitles mark the year each person died. The last face is Ogawa's.

Because so many of the people in this film had passed away between the initial filming and the film's realization, the project took on a solemnity that appeared to paralyze Peng. Shiraishi had envisioned a fifty-fifty mix of Ogawa's and Peng's footage, with the latter commenting somehow on the former. However, during the shooting, the Chinese director was torn over her relationship to the earlier footage. It was intimidating to deal with the film of someone she respected so much. In the process of translating Ogawa's continuity into Chinese, Peng converting it into her own rough script, and translating this back again into Japanese, the contours of a frame became distinct. Peng felt compelled to suppress her power as director and retain Ogawa's vision as closely as possible. She and her cinematographer Jong Lin (*Wedding Banquet*, 1992; *Eat, Drink, Man, Woman*, 1994) studied Tamura's work, imagining they were his disciples. Even though 60 to 65 percent of the footage was shot by Tamura, one cannot tell where Tamura's footage stops and Lin's begins. The only trace of Peng is relegated to the reflexive homages book-ending the film. While *Devotion* has the ironic feeling of being Ogawa Pro's last film, *Red Persimmons* actually leaves one with the impression that Ogawa channeled himself through Peng. Indeed, *My Dream Japan* was the closest Ogawa came to his dream of a pan-Asian documentary scene. With *Red Persimmons*, Peng accomplishes more than simply bringing Ogawa's film to completion. She also stands in for the pan-Asian collective Ogawa hoped for—Ogawa's Dream Japan.

The Last Word

The films have been sold, their negatives preserved in ideal archival conditions. The paper materials are in storage and will not be thrown away, even if they are scattered across Japan. Thanks to both the passing of time since Ogawa's death and to the reminiscence forced by these films (and perhaps this book project as well), the former members of Ogawa Pro are coming to terms with their experience. In the end, all that is left are those memories, the films, and the debt.

Notes

Introduction

1. This is my term for the films, a choice I will explain in the chapter that analyzes them.
2. *Ogawa Shinsuke—Shineasuto wa Kataru* 5, ed. Hasumi Shigehiko (Nagoya: Nagoya Cinémateque, 1993), 70.
3. I count most of the people quoted in this book as friends, and their words are largely taken from notes I jotted down over the years. Our conversations rarely took place in formal interview settings. Alcohol and tall tales were often involved. I cannot give dates—as in this particular example from Nosaka—and I hope they trust me in accurately recounting their words. I will be the first to plead guilty to sloppy scholarship, and I hope that the reader will forgive a lack of dates for quotes and information that would usually be scrupulously noted. Friendship and pleasure trumped academics in the writing of this book.
4. Tayama Rikiya, *Gendai Nihon Eiga no Kantokutachi* (Shakai Shisosha, 1991), 168.
5. Kitakoji Takashi. "'Han'tochaku' no Monogatari: Esunogurafii to Shite no Ogawa Puro Eiga," *Jokyo* (May 1999): 123–24.
6. Kawase established her reputation under her maiden name, Kawase Naomi. Shortly after winning a major award at Cannes for her first feature film, she married and actually held a press conference to announce the marriage and her new name. The politics of naming are a complicated and touchy issue in Japan. Although she returned to her maiden name after the divorce, Kawase's insistence at taking her husband's name even though the world knew her by a different one seemed to indicate a certain kind of conservatism whose significance to this book will be apparent by its end. Interestingly, she kept *Kawase* upon remarriage.

Chapter 1. Ogawa as Postwar Documentarist

1. For a thorough history of this film see my *Japanese Documentary Film* (Minneapolis: Minnesota, 2003). In Japanese language, this book's chapter about the atomic bomb film was translated as "Bakushinchi no Shintai—*Hiroshima, Nagasaki ni okeru genshibakudan no koka,*" trans. Shibazaki Akinori, *Hibakusha Shinema* (Tokyo: Gendai Shokan, 1999), 111–44, 244–35.
2. See Hirano Kyoko's *Mr. Smith Goes to Tokyo* (Washington DC: Smithsonian Press, 1992) for an excellent history of this film's censorship and suppression.
3. I found this particular guide in the Tokushima Kenritsu Monjokan, where it was deposited by Shiba Shizuko, a Hiroshima University professor conducting research on the educational reforms of the Occupation. Her "Senryoka no Nihon ni Okeru Kateika Kyoiku no Seiritsu to Tenkai 2: CIE Kyoiku Eiga 'Akarui Katei Seikatsu' no Seisaku," *Annals of Educational Research* (Chugoku Shikoku Kyoikugakkai-hen) 41.2 (1995): 373–78 provides an interesting case study of one film by drawing on primary materials from the U.S. National Archives. Other useful sources are Nakamura Mamori. "Notoko Shikankaku Kyoiku no Bokkaku to Mondaiten," *Shakai Kyoiku* 10.10 (October 1955): 26–30. Robaato B. Tekusutaa, *Nihon ni Okeru Shippai* (Tokyo: Bungei Shunju Shinsha, 1952). "Shikankaku Kyoiku no Ayumi: Natoko no Hatashita Yakuwari," in *Iwate no Kyoiku Gyosei Monogatari* (Tokyo: Rokusansei Kyoiku Kenkyukai, 1960), 25–46.
4. Study guide for *Children's Guardian*, 16.

5. Ibid., 24.
6. Hatano Kanji et al., *Shikankaku Kyoiku Yoran* (Tokyo: Nihon Eiga Kyoiku Kyokai, 1952), 227.
7. Ibid., 148.
8. Abe Akira, *Chiho Kyoiku Seido Seiritsu Katei no Kenkyu* (Tokyo: Fukan Shobo, 1983), 713–16.
9. The following institutional history is deeply informed by conversations with critic-historian Yamada Kazuo and his *Nihon Eiga Hyakuichi-nen* (Tokyo: Shin Nihon Shuppansha 1999).
10. *Kami shibai* is a form of modern storytelling predating the cinema, but loosely aligned with the art of the silent film's *benshi*. A narrator stands before a group of spectators with a set of large drawings, often framed in a stage-like box, telling a story while flipping through the images. Noda Shinkichi and Matsumoto Toshio, "Rensai: 'Taidan' Sengo Dokyumentarii Henkanshi," *Kiroku to Eizo* 1 (May 25, 1964): 3.
11. Noda Shinkichi and Matsumoto Toshio, "Taidan Sengo Dokyumentarii Henkanshi III," *Kiroku to Eizo* 3 (June 16, 1964): 1.
12. *White Mountains* was also the subject of one of the first major debates about *yarase* (faking it). The filmmakers referred to species not known to inhabit their film's setting and even used a stuffed bear for one scene. The outcry provoked a number of thoughtful articles about documentary and truth value from authors like Hani Susumu and Imamura Taihei.
13. The best English-language resource for Kamei is the catalog edited by Yasui Yoshio for a major retrospective at the Yamagata International Documentary Film Festival: *Kamei Fumio 1908–1987* (Yamagata: YIDFF, 2001).
14. Yamada Kazuo, *Nihon Eiga Hyakuichi-nen*, 128.
15. Hani Susumu. "Jisaku o Kataru," *Kiroku to Eizo* 5 (August 16, 1964): 8.
16. Direct cinema and cinema verité are often confused. *Verité* was the approach developed in France by Jean Rouch, one in which the camera is used not only to capture spontaneously unfolding events but also instigate happenings that would not have otherwise taken place had a camera not been present. Filmmakers developing the American version, direct cinema, would follow people around for extended periods, attempting to avoid intervention in the world before them (the fly-on-the-wall approach). Initially, they cloaked themselves in a rhetoric of objectivity, a position from which they quickly retreated upon criticism. Hani's work predates both styles. For an excellent historicization of the direct cinema rhetoric, see Brian Winston. "The Documentary Film as Scientific Inscription," in *Theorizing Documentary*, ed. Michael Renov (New York: Routledge, 1993), 37–57; also Paul Arthur. "Jargons of Authenticity," in *Theorizing Documentary*, ed. Michael Renov (New York: Routledge, 1993), 108–134.
17. Hani's films were international hits on the documentary and educational film circuits so they were purchased by quite a few American libraries. The University of Michigan has a print of the latter film, and a search of research libraries that rented films would probably turn up a print or two.
18. Interview with Tsuchimoto Noriaki, May 27, 2000.
19. Iwanami went out of business in 1999, surviving longer than most documentary film companies that formed to take advantage of the 1950s industrial film boom. Their massive film collection was purchased by Hitachi. The massive electronics company announced plans to convert the films to digital media, but nothing seems to have come of it. Hani Susumu, Takemura Takeji, Yoshihara Junpei, and Ise Chonosuke directed an interesting history of the publishing house: *A Publisher—50 Years* (*Aru shuppansha—50-nen*, 1963). Kubota Yukio was responsible for the film's fascinating soundtrack.
20. Imaizumi Ayako. "Documentarists of Japan, #19: Interview with Tokieda Toshie," *Documentary Box* 21 (May 31, 2003): 5.
21. Kuroki Kazuo. "One Place, One Era," *Yamagata International Documentary Film Festival* main catalog (Yamagata: YIDFF, 2001): 41.
22. Kato Takanobu. "Documentarists of Japan, #17: Otsu Koshiro," *Documentary Box* 19 (April 25, 2002): 3–4.
23. J. Victor Koschmann provides a useful sketch of this larger debate in *Revolution and Subjectivity in Postwar Japan* (Chicago: University of Chicago Press, 1996). Joanne Izbicki writes about the situation within film circles in her dissertation: *Scorched Cityscapes and Silver Screens: Negotiating Defeat and Democracy Through Cinema in Occupied Japan* (Ph.D. diss., Cornell University, 1997).
24. Quoted in Matsumoto Toshio. "*Kiroku Eiga* no Oboegaki," *Eiga Hihyo* 2.3 (March 1971): 95.
25. Ibid., 96.
26. For a discussion of Nakai see Nornes, *Japanese Documentary Film*, 137–47, as well as forthcoming work by Leslie Pincus.
27. Matsumoto Toshio, *Eizo no Hakken* (Tokyo: Sanichi Shobo: 1963), 54.
28. Yamada Kazuo, *Nihon Eiga Hyakuichi-nen*, 144–45; this is a good example of how deep the anger over this film runs forty years after the fact.

29. Noda Shinkichi, *Nihon Dokyumentarii Eiga Zenshi* (Tokyo: Shakai Shisosha, 1984), 10.
30. "Eiga Undo 1961," *Kiroku Eiga* (March 1961): 26.
31. Yamada Kazuo, *Nihon Eiga Hyakuichi-nen,* 146–47.
32. Data from Eikyo, quoted in Tanaka Jun'ichiro, *Nihon Kyoiku Eiga Hattatsu-shi* (Tokyo: Kagyusha, 1979), 227.
33. Ibid., 248.
34. Oshima Nagisa. "Shotto to wa Nanika," *Kiroku Eiga* 3.11 (November 1960): 6–8. Also see Oshima Nagisa. "Sakka no Suijaku: Watakushi no Kiroku Eigaron," *Kiroku Eiga* 3.5 (May 1960): 26–28.
35. Matsumoto Toshio, *Eizo no Hakken,* 86.
36. Umeda Katsumi. "Ogawa Shinsuke no Gakusei Jidai: *Yama ni ikiru kora* o Seisaku Shite," *Eiga Shinbun* 87 (May 1, 1992): 5.
37. Ibid., 1.
38. First published in "Monbusho Shinsa to Watakushi no Taiken," *Sekai Eiga Shiryo* (January 1958); reprinted in *Eiga o Toru* (Tokyo: Chikuma Shobo, 1993), 61–63.
39. *Kenkyukai Kikanshi* 7 (April 1961): 1.
40. *Ogawa Shinsuke—Shineasuto wa Kataru 5,* 25–27.
41. Kubota Yukio, *Kikoetemasu ka, Eiga no Oto* (Tokyo: Waizu Shuppan, 2004), 181.

Chapter 2. Jieiso

1. Kuroki offers a daily account of the conflict from the first discussions about the film in Kuroki Kazuo. "Jijitsu o Kataru," Aru marason rannaa no kiroku *Jiken no Shinjitsu* (Tokyo: "Shinjitsu" Iinkai, August 1964), 4–14. A synoptic explanation of the events behind the incident is Sasaki Mamoru. "Kiroku Eiga Kai no Daisodo o Megutte," *Eiga Geijutsu* 202 (July 1964): 81–84.
2. The preparations for the screening are documented in Eto Ko, "Eigakai: Gogatsu Muika," Aru marason ranna no kiroku *Jiken no Shinjitsu* (Tokyo: "Shinjitsu" Iinkai, August 1964), 26–34.
3. Ibid., 33–34.
4. Matsumoto Toshio, *Eizo no Hakken,* 98.
5. Initially, Kurosawa Akira was to direct; however, he reportedly lost the job when he demanded total control over the staging of the opening and closing ceremonies. He was replaced by the workman-like Ichikawa Kon. For those interested in learning more, look to a roundtable in James Quant's book on Ichikawa [Nornes, A. M., Eric Cazdyn, James Quant, Catherine Russell, and Mitsuhiro Yoshimoto. *"Tokyo Olympiad:* A Symposium," in *Ichikawa Kon,* ed. James Quandt. (Toronto: Cinemateque Ontario, 2001), 315–36]. It is reprinted as an extra in the Criterion Collection's DVD of the film. Aside from a number of interesting perspectives on the film, the discussion includes explanations of the controversies that surrounded the production. Thanks to these controversies, it was by far the highest profile documentary since the prestigious propaganda films of World War II. However, in terms of its relevance to postwar documentary in Japan, it merely stands as a marker for the pinnacle of the PR film and, thus, merits little more than a footnote.
6. This is judging from the narratives of this period offered by both Tsuchimoto and Ogawa. A timeline for the production of *Sea of Youth* is in their first newsletter, *Tsushin* 2 (July 3, 1965): 2–3.
7. "Joei Undo no Shiten to Tenbo," *Jugatsu* 1 (February15, 1968): 1.
8. "Fuji Terebi *Aru Seishun no Mosaku*—Heiwa Undo no Naka De," *Hoei Muki Teiki ni Jogi* (pamphlet, October 25, 1966). [Sanrizuka Archives]
9. "Hihyo no Tame no Angle [sic]," handwritten notes dated September 20, 1966, for a September 20, 1966, meeting. [Jieiso archives]
10. Ogawa never told people about the starting point identified by Kubota, when his script for *Beer Factory* was stolen.
11. *Jishu Joei Undo Shiryo* #3 (unpaginated). [Jieiso Archives]
12. "Kyo no Takasaki Toso o Do Haeru Ka?" *Giansho,* 9. [Jieiso Archives]
13. Ibid., 7.
14. "Takasaki Keizai Daigaku Toso—Jishu Eiga Seisaku Undo ni Mukete," memo dated May 5, 1967: 1–2. [Jieiso Archives]
15. Nosaka Haruo, et al. "Chosabu Rejime #2" budget printed with empty cells filled in and signed by Ogawa (March 29, 1967). [Jieiso Archives]
16. *"Assatsu no mori* Joei Undo Kara no Hokoku," memo circa December 12, 1967, 2. [Jieiso Archives]
17. "Futatsu no Gakusei Kiroku Eiga," *Asahi Journal,* undated magazine clipping, Box 11. [Sanrizuka Archive]
18. Yamada Kazuo. "Torotsukiisuto no Eiga to Eigaron," *Bunka Hyoron* (March 1968): 148–57.

Chapter 3. The Sanrizuka Series

1. *Ogawa Puro Nichiroku 1975,* February 19, 1975, Box 16. [Sanrizuka Archive]
2. "Ogawa Shinsuke Sakuhinshu," leaflet dated April 8–11, 1967. [Jieiso Archive]
3. Ogawa Shinsuke—Shineasuto wa Kataru, 56.
4. The history of the struggle is remarkably complex. For background information and general history, the definitive resource is *Narita Kuko Mondai Shimpojiumu Kirokushu (Sanrizuka, Narita: Narita Kuko Mondai Shinpojiumu Kirokushu Henshu Iinkai,* 1995) and *Narita Kuko Mondai Entaku Kaigi Kirokushu (Sanrizuka, Narita: Narita Kuko Mondai Entaku Kirokushu Henshu Iinkai,* 1995). These are transcriptions of two major conferences led by an organization dedicated to reconciliation between all parties of the struggle. Each volume includes a hard-bound supplement of important historical documents. It may be acquired through the Rekishi Densho Committee, the address for which is in the Filmography of this book. In English, see Suwa Nagayo and David E. Apter's excellent study of the struggle, *Against the State: Politics and Social Protest in Japan* (Cambridge: Harvard University Press, 1984).
5. Kitazawa Yoko. "Vietnam in Japan: Sanrizuka," *AMPO* 9-10 (1970): 3-4.
6. Quoted in Tsuchimoto Noriaki. "Ogawa Shinsuke to wa Donna Otoko Ka," *Eiga Geijutsu* 255 (November 1968): 56.
7. Noël Burch. *To the Distant Observer: Form and Meaning in the Japanese Cinema* (Ann Arbor: University of Michigan Center for Japanese Studies Electronic Reprint Series, 2004), 361.
8. All of these original affidavits are held in the Sanrizuka Archives, along with still photo recreations of the incident, notes, and Otsu's broken glasses.
9. Kitakoji Takashi. "'Han'tochaku' no Monogatari: Esunogurafii to Shite no Ogawa Pro Eiga," 136.
10. "Narita Genchi Ruporutaju," *Jugatsu* 4 (May 15, 1968): 2.
11. The film is perfectly legible and quite powerful for viewers that know little of this context, either through age or nationality. However, even these spectators may gain a sense for the film's incredibly intricate intertext through a thoroughly annotated script in the catalog Ogawa Productions produced at the time. In this sense, it is very much a film of its time.
12. This refers to the curious activity that often accompanies social protest in postwar Japan: participants form a dense line and snake through public spaces in a half-run, almost like a dance. This will be familiar to anyone who has seen films like Oshima Nagisa's *Cruel Story of Youth (Seishun zankoku monogatari,* 1960) or *Hiroshima Mon Amour* (1959).
13. *The Red Army/PFLP: Declaration of World War (Sekigun/PFLP: Sekai senso sengen,* 1971). I will have much more to say about this film in Chapter 4.
14. Kato Takanobu. "Documentarists of Japan, #17: Otsu Koshiro," 7.
15. Noël Burch. *To the Distant Observer,* 360.
16. "Danmaru Eiga Joei ni Tsuite: Rejimeteki na Mono," October 5, 1969, in Tohoku Office Notebook, "Winter, 23 October 1969," Box 16. [Sanrizuka Archive]
17. Ibid.
18. Yokosuka and Sasebo are the locations of two major American military bases. Flier, "Kokaido Happyo ni Mukete," *Nerima Ko Shaken—Shakenbu,* September 8, 1969, Box 10. [Sanrizuka Archive]
19. Nagayo Sawa and David E. Apter. *Against the State: Politics and Social Protest in Japan,* 158.
20. Kitakoji Takashi. "'Han'tochaku' no Monogatari: Esunogurafii to Shite no Ogawa Pro Eiga," 126-7; Ueno Koshi. "Hito to Hito no Tsunagari o Kangaete Yuku Michisuji," *Eiga Shinbun* 91 (September/October 1992): 7.
21. *Narita Kuko Mondai Shimpojiumu Kirokushu,* 290.
22. Noël Burch, *To the Distant Observer,* 361.
23. Indeed, they also had little sense of their own history, since the theorists of the Proletarian film movement (Prokino) laid out the groundwork for a "movement cinema" in the early 1930s but also go entirely unconsidered.
24. Oshima Nagisa. "Ogawa Shinsuke: Toso to Datsuraku," *Eiga Hihyo* 1.3 (December 1970): 17.
25. Abé Mark Nornes. "Documentarists of Japan: An Interview with Suzuki Shiroyasu," *Documentary Box* 2 (April 1993): 14–15.
26. Originally in *Asahi Shinbun* (May 26, 1974); quoted on *Heta Village* flier, Box 030. [Sanrizuka Archives]
27. Fredric Jameson. *The Political Unconscious: Narrative as a Socially Symbolic Act* (Ithaca: Cornell University Press, 1981), 102.
28. Survey taken by Ogawa Productions for *Summer in Sanrizuka* (nd), Box 33. [Sanrizuka Archive]
29. Jane Gaines. "Political Mimesis," *Collecting Visible Evidence,* ed. Jane Gaines and Michael Renov (Minneapolis: University of Minnesota Press, 1999), 84–102.
30. The survey is in the Sanrizuka Archive, Box 12. I have reproduced the formatting of the survey in translation, simply adding figures for the answers. Unfortunately, I did not have enough

time at the archive to tabulate all the surveys. These results are culled from a 200-person sample out of 400 surveys in the folder. The original survey was taken at Ogawa Productions Screenings of *Summer in Sanrizuka* in Tokyo, 1968.

31. *Shiritsu Johoku Koko Shikei Shikko Tomo no Kai*, "Joei Hokokusho," no. 59 (report circa October 1971), in *Joei Hokokusho Rirokubo* (July 4, 1971), Box 50. [Sanrizuka Archive]
32. Jane Gaines. "Political Mimesis," 92.
33. James Tobias. *Music, Image, Gesture: The Graphical Score and the Visual Representation of Music* (Berkeley: University of California Press, forthcoming).
34. Ibid., 100.
35. Ibid., 33.
36. Ibid., 26–27.
37. Ibid., 27.
38. A copy of the suicide note is in the Ogawa Productions archive, suggesting how far into village life they were and how deeply this must have affected the group. It has also been collected in *Narita Kuko Mondai Shinpojiumu Kirokushu: Shiryohen* (Sanrizuka/Narita: Narita Kuko Mondai Shinpojiumu Kirokushu Hanshu Iinkai, 1995), 49–51.
39. *Yumoto Mareo*, production diary, Dai-5 bu Noto #2 (nd), Box 16. [Sanrizuka Archives]
40. Aoyama Shinji, *Ware Eiga o Hakken Seri* (Tokyo Seidosha, 2001), 234.
41. Yumoto Mareo, production diary, Dai-5 bu Noto #3 (September 1, 1972 entry), Box 16. [Sanrizuka Archives]
42. Fukuda Katsuhiko. "Ogawa Shinsuke and Sanrizuka," in *Japanese Documentaries of the 1970s*, ed. Yasui Yoshio, Yano Kazuyuki, Erikawa Ken and Shinkawa Takahiro (Tokyo: Yamagata International Documentary Film Festival and Planet Bibliothèque de Cinéma, 1995), 46–47.
43. Another factor would certainly be their willingness to think of their supply of film stock as endless. *Heta Village* was culled from nearly 21 hours of rushes shot over an 11-month period.
44. Yumoto Mareo, production diary, Dai-5 bu Noto #2 (August 26, 1972 entry), Box 16. [Sanrizuka Archive]
45. *Henshu Sagyo Nishi #1 Heta Buraku* (January 8, 1973 entry), Box 43. [Sanrizuka Archive]
46. Judging from entries in the editing notebooks, *Heta Village* transformed considerably in the course of its construction. An outline written on August 31 puts the Tonojita scene at the end of the film, and includes scenes on the construction of Iwayama Tower and the fights around the tunnels. While this sequencing appears quite different, the outline breaks down into eleven scenes, roughly the same as the finished film. Unsigned (probably Tadorokoro Naoki), *Henshu Kiroku* (nd, Summer–Fall 1972), Box 16. [Sanrizuka Archive]
47. Dipesh Chakrabarty, *Provincializing Europe* (Princeton: Princeton University Press, 2000), 11.
48. Ogawa Shinsuke and Naito Masatoshi. "Karada ni Kizamareta Dokyumento," in *Sennen Kizami no Hidokei* (Tokyo: Ogawa Productions, 1986): 25.
49. Ibid., 66.
50. In *Sanrizuka Ando Soiru* (Tokyo: Heigensha, 2001), Fukuda Katushiko describes their shock at witnessing a village discussion centering on whether or not to ostracize a family that caved in to the Kodan. They had assumed this custom was long dead.
51. Ibid., 93.
52. Yumoto Mareo, production diary, Dai-5 bu Noto #2 (September 7, 1972 entry), Box 16. [Sanrizuka Archive]
53. Renov, Michael. *The Subject of Documentary* (Minneapolis: University of Minnesota Press, 2004).
54. Ei. "'Kyodotai' no Kanosei Kataru," *Asahi Shinbun* (evening edition, May 23, 1973): 8.

Chapter 4. Segue

1. Lithuanian immigrant Jonas Mekas pioneered the diary film in the New York avant-garde with stunning films such as *Memories of a Journey to Lithuania* (1971) and *Lost, Lost, Lost* (1975). He has a wide following in Japan.
2. Suzuki Shiroyasu, *Eiga no Bensho: Sei no Yokubo no Imeji* (Tokyo: Firumu Atosha, 1982) and *Eiga Soshi: Jishu Dokyumentarii Eiga no Shiken* (Tokyo: Gendai Shokan, 1994).
3. Laura Marks. "Naked Truths: Hara Kazuo's Iconoclastic Obsessions," *Independent* 15.10 (1992): 26.
4. Aaron Gerow. "Documentarists of Japan #9: Matsumoto Toshio," *Documentary Box* 9 (December 31, 1996): 13.
5. I am indebted to filmmaker Kato Itaru for convincing me of this.
6. It is unfortunate, however, that virtually no filmmakers of this generation seem willing to work without massive budgets, even though producing amazing films on a shoestring was standard practice at the beginning of their careers. Oshima, in particular, appears to have fallen to the level of self-nude narcissism with his astoundingly self-serving history of Japanese cinema for the BBC centenary project.

7. Pink films were soft-core pornographic films produced on miniscule budgets and were often seen in political terms. Hamano Sachi is one of the most fascinating figures among the women directors, partly because she came to take a feminist position after making several hundred films. She came to know feminist scholars and programmers, and began making interesting films aimed at audiences outside of the pink world, like *In Search of a Lost Writer: Wandering in the Seventh World* (*Dai-nanakankai hoko: Ozaki Midori o sagashite*, 1998) and *Lili Festival* (*Yurisai*, 2001). She claims to have inserted a woman's perspective in her pink films; however, the difference is often, shall we say, subtle. Her very presence—as a talented and strong woman working mostly in the pink film world—challenges the conventional canons of Japanese cinema. For example, she is quick to point out that most people denigrated her work until she made her "respectable" Ozaki Midori documentary. I count her autobiography among the more important in Japanese film history: Hamano Sachi, *Onna ga Eiga o Tsukuru Toki* (Tokyo: Heibonsha, 1995).
8. Yamamoto Masashi. "Interview with Wakamatsu Koji," *In-site Tokyo* (www.insite-tokyo.com/interview/15wakamatsu/content.html).
9. The film is still being distributed on video by the Red Army.
10. While this film is fondly remembered by people with connections to the Red Army and *Eiga Hihyo*, it must be called a curious failure. This could be due to the difficult conditions under which it was shot, and the filmmakers' fear that those interviewed could be subject to retaliation. In any case, a far better film conceived with Adachi and company's *fukei-ron* theory is *AKA Serial Killer* (*Ryakusho: Renzoku shasatsuma*, 1969). This fascinating documentary follows the trail of a convicted serial killer who committed murders across Japan. The filmmakers return to the scenes of his crimes and simply photograph the scenery. They capture the material conditions that produced and barely contained the killer's violence, along with eerie traces of his long-gone presence.
11. Adachi Masao. "Rebanon Kyowakoku Daitoryo e no Kogisho," *Sasho—Visa* 7 (October 25, 1973): 230–32. In the Takezawa Collection, University of Hawai'i.
12. Adachi Masao and Takenaka Tsutomu. "Arabu Gerira to Tomo ni," *Sasho—Visa* 2 (January 18, 1972): 59–60. In the Takazawa Collection, University of Hawai'i.
13. Oshima Nagisa, Adachi Masao, et al. "80-nendai no Nihon Eiga no Tenbo," *Eiga Hihyo*, 4.9 (September 1973): 17. When Sasami Mamoru points to Ogawa and Tsuchimoto as prime examples of a movement cinema, Oshima insists they were actually becoming auteurs at this very moment. In retrospect, Oshima was prescient.
14. Solanas was a key leader and influential theorist of Third Cinema in Latin America. He called for a cinema of imperfection that did not aspire to Hollywood glossiness or get trapped in the logic of capitalism or the bourgeois narcissism of high art. Adachi Masao. "Undo no Shuen—1974—nen Nihon Eiga Jokyo no Bunseki," in *Eiga e no Senryaku* (Tokyo: Shobunsha, 1974), 181. The article was first published in the May 1974 issue of *Scenario*.
15. "'Sakuhin' to 'Ikikata' wa Honto ni Kankei Nai no de Aro Ka?" *Eiga Geijutsu* 49.2 (Autumn 1999): 91.
16. "Tokushu: Eria Kazan no Akademii Tokubetsu Meiyosho o Do Kangaeru Ka," *Eiga Geijutsu* 49.2 (Autumn 1999): 125.
17. Adachi discussed his time in Lebanon in various publications, but the most notable is the book-length interview conducted by Hirasawa Go: *Eiga/Kakumei* (Tokyo: Kawade Shobo Shinsha. 2003).
18. Shiga Nobuo, *Showa Terebi Hososhi, Part 2* (Tokyo: Hayakawa Shobo, 1990), 86.
19. *Ogawa Shinsuke—Shineasuto wa Kataru*,36.
20. *NHK Nenkan* (Tokyo: Rajio Sabisu Sentaa, 1972), 169
21. Ise's father was a well-known documentary film editor, and he began making his own documentaries in his twenties. They include *Run Toward Light: Record of a Blind Baseball Player* (*Hikari ni mukatte hashire: Mojin yakyu no kiroku*, 1983), *And Five Died in a War* (*Soshite gonin wa senshi shita*, 1984), *Trust, Hope, Love: Portrait of Kobori Shiro in his Nineties* (*Shin, nozomi, ai: Kobori Shiro kyujussai no shozo*, 1992), *If You Want to Dance, Dance!* (*Odoraba odore*, 1993) *Skillful* (*Takumi*, 1994) and *Nao-chan* (*Nao-chan*, 1995) and *Loupe* (*Rupe*, 1996) on the famed documentary cinematographer Segawa Jun'ichi.
22. Kanai Katsu graduated from the art department of Nihon University in 1960 and entered the cinematography section of Daiei Studios. He went freelance in 1964 as a cinematographer and turned to documentary in 1968 with made-for-television productions. At the same time, he started making independent films that smudged the line between documentary and avant-garde. They include *Deserted Island* (*Mujin retto*, 1969), *Kingdom* (*Okoku*, 1973) and *Time Blows On* (*Toki ga fukubu*, 1991).
23. Later in *Eiga Shinbun*, Kanai wrote, "Because the perspectives of the four filmmakers diverged so much, we really didn't mesh together . . . but I thought it became lively in the last half when

Fukuda Katsuhiko and Tsuchimoto Noriaki joined the discussion." Kanai Katsu. "Konton Soshite Jiyu no Ba to Shite," *Eiga Shinbun* 144 (December 1, 1997): 4.

24. He didn't tell this story for years, although he mentioned something vague about police visits at the memorial events after Ogawa's death. I heard it in the early 1990s, and this rendering of it cleaves close to his storytelling style. He saved the details for an amusing three-part essay in 2000: Kimura Michio. "Ogawa Shinsuke ga Kita 1," *Yamagata Sanpo* 328 (February 2000): 66–69; Kimura Michio. "Ogawa Shinsuke ga Kita 2," *Yamagata Sanpo* 329 (March 2000): 64–68; Kimura Michio, "Ogawa Shinsuke ga Kita 3," *Yamagata Sanpo* 330 (April 2000): 65–69.
25. *Ogawa Shinsuke—Shineasuto wa Kataru,* 221.
26. Ibid., 223.
27. Kimura Michio, *Gentan Sodoki Mura ni Ikiru* (Tokyo: Jushinsha, 1985).
28. "Sanrizuka no Ogawa Puro Kara Kiroku Eiga no Ogawa Puro E," meeting outline (July 20, 1975), Box 16. [Sanrizuka Archive]
29. These statistics are quoted in "'Kotobuki no Machi' ni Tsuite," *Ogawa Puro Seisaku Nyusu* 1 (June 20, 1974): 1, and are from the city government.
30. "Kiroku Eiga *Kotobuki* Satsuei Kaishi," *Ogawa Puro Seisaku Nyusu* 1 (June 20, 1974): 1.
31. "Furuyashiki," production diary, January 20, 1975. [Furuyashiki Archive]
32. "Ogawa Purodakushon 75-nen Ichinenkan no Ugoki—Sono 1," *Ogawa Pro News* 5 (April 30, 1976): 3.
33. "Furuyashiki," production diary, Furuyashikimura January 10, 1975.
34. "Ogawa Purodakushon 75-nen Ichinenkan no Ugoki—Sono 1," *Ogawa Pro News* 5 (April 30, 1976): 2.
35. *Furuyashiki,* production diary, January 2, 1975. [Furuyashiki Archive]
36. Ibid., January 23, 1975. [Furuyashiki Archive]
37. An alternate title that has been attached to the film is *Song of the Humans,* but Ogawa Pro never used this translation.
38. "Ogawa Purodakushon 75-nen Ichinenkan no Ugoki—Sono 1," *Ogawa Pro News* 5 (April 30, 1976): 6.
39. *Ogawa Puro Nichiroku 1975,* production log, March 18, 1975. [Furuyashiki Archive]

Chapter 5. The Magino Village Story

1. The first line of Makabe Jin's "A Mountain Pass," as translated by Naoshi Koriyama and Edward Lueders in *Like Underground Water—The Poetry of Mid-Twentieth Century Japan,* trans. Naoshi Koriyama and Edward Lueders (Port Townsend, Wash: Copper Canyon Press, 1995): 24.
2. Kitakoji Takashi. "'Han'tochaku' no Monogatari: Esunogurafii to Shite no Ogawa Pro Eiga," 136.
3. The Furuyashiki archive has a box full of these cards.
4. This is evidenced in many places throughout the archive, including ledgers from the Sanrizuka Era detailing the donations collected at each screening.
5. [Furuyashiki archive]
6. Ginza-dori refers to the markets one finds in nearly any city. They borrow the name of the most famous shopping district in Japan, but are usually no more than a nondescript street filled with old mom and pop businesses.
7. Yamazaki Hiroshi, a still photographer known for his beautiful photography of the sun, shot these time-lapse images. In his series entitled Heliography, the sun often appears as a long, brilliant streak plunging into the sea.
8. Laura Marks, *The Skin of the Film: Intercultural Cinema, Embodiment and the Senses* (Durham: Duke University Press, 2000), 24.
9. Ibid., 188.
10. Ibid., 140.
11. Ibid., xvi.
12. Neil Lerner. "Damming Virgil Thomson's Music for *The River,*" in *Collecting Visible Evidence,* ed. Jane Gaines and Michael Renov (Minneapolis: University of Minnesota Press, 1999), 104.
13. Marilyn Ivy, *Discourses of the Vanishing* (Chicago: University of Chicago Press, 1995).
14. Kikuchi actually appeared in three different roles for the film, but two did not make the final cut. A decade later, after Kikuchi's death at the early age of 56, Iizuka Toshio pulled the footage out of the archive and made a short film commemorating Kikuchi's art and life with Hara Tadashi on camera and Kuribayashi Toyohiko capturing sound. It is entitled, *Folk Artist for a Happy Life* (*Kosei no kyodo geinin*) and is available through Iizuka's production company (www004.upp.so-net.ne.jp/iizuka-movie).
15. Ogawa Shinsuke. "Toru ni Atatte," *Itsutsudomoe Jinja Daihokai* (scenario, no date), unpaginated introduction. This printed and bound scenario was probably designed to sell the

sequence to the people of Magino, literally. They actually flipped the bill for the scene by creating a committee to collect donations, supplementing the film's budget with about $40,000 of their own money.

16. Regula König. *Magino Mura Interview: Questions put to Mr. Shinsuke Ogawa* (from the English language press pack): 8. The examples in the next paragraph also come from this interview.
17. Kimura Michio, *Denen no Daigyakushu—Magino-mura Kara* (Yamagata: Studio 1, 1999), 18–19.
18. Name withheld (student, age 21). Survey from *Theater of a Thousand Years* screenings. No date. Erikawa Ken and Kageyama Satoshi, the former editors of *Eiga Shinbun*, kindly granted me access to these files. The other common comment was that four hours sitting on hard dirt was rough, even with cushions.

Chapter 6. After Ogawa

1. Teo's monograph on Kong Kong cinema is mandatory reading for anyone interested in Chinese cinema. Stephen Teo, *Hong Kong Cinema: The Extra Dimensions* (London: BFI Publishing, 1997).
2. Later I found out that Ogawa showed him at least three films in the Ogikubo studio, so perhaps Wu was admitting he slept through them (he would hardly be the first).
3. Deocampo has just finished the first of a projected five-volume history of Philippines cinema, entitled *Cine: Spanish Influences on Early Cinema in the Philippines* (Manila: National Commission for Culture and the Arts, 2003).
4. Our conversations about Ogawa were all in the 1990s. The situation now is completely different thanks to DVD and many impressive film festivals in South Korea.
5. *Xiaochuan Shenjie dishi jie: xun qiu ji lu pian zhong zhi gao wu shang di xing fu* (Taipei: Yuan liu chu ban shi ye gu fen you xian gong si, 1995).
6. "Ogawa Shinsuke Kantoku Saigo no Intabyu," *Eiga Shinbun* 86 (April 1, 1992): 8–13.
7. Ibid., 13.
8. Ogawa Shinsuke and Monica Flaherty. "Furahachi no Eiga o Megutte," *Eiga Shinbun* 61 (November, December 1989): 2.
9. *Ogawa Shinsuke—Shineasuto o Kataru*, 124–125.
10. Tsuchimoto assembled a rough edit of the footage posthumously for Ogawa's public wake at Athénée Français Cultural Center on February 23, 1992. Suzuki Toshiaki finished a similar film about Mori entitled *Butoh, Okura* (*Okura-mura, odoru otoko*, 1999).
11. *Ogawa Shinsuke—Shineasuto wa Kataru*, 215.
12. Jieiso internal memorandum, dated December 31, 1967. [Jieiso Archives]
13. "Ogawa Purodakushon," *Jugatsu* 7 (September 1, 1968): 4.
14. Approximately $1,000,000 at the turn of the century when this extent of the debt was revealed.
15. These are in the Jieiso Archives.
16. Matsuda Masao. "Ogawa Puro—Atarashii Shutsuichi e no Tojo de," in *Best of Kinema Junpo II* (Tokyo: Kinema Junposha, 1994), 768–770; originally published in *Kinema Junpo* 662 (July 15, 1975).
17. Fukuda wrote a wonderfully personal and very thick book on Sanrizuka, and it provides a profound sense for the complexity of the struggle at ground level. His wife published the six-hundred-page tome under the title *Sanrizuka Ando Soiru*. While Fukuda often discusses Ogawa Pro tangentially, the prime focus of the book is on the struggle itself as he experienced and interpreted it.
18. Tamura always kept his distance, and refuses to identify himself completely with Ogawa Pro. He insists he was never a member, even though there was no initiation ceremony or official tattoo or something. He would come in for the Ogawa films late and leave after photography was completed, maintaining his identity as a professional filmmaker and not one of the collective activists. Although the first half of his filmography is heavily weighted with Ogawa Pro films, he gradually established a career as one of Japan's finest cameramen. His most celebrated work is in Kuroki Kazuo's *Assassination of Ryoma* (*Ryoma ansatsu*, 1974), Itami Juzo's *Tanpopo* (1985), Yanagimachi Mitsuo's *Farewell to the Land* (*Saraba itoshiki daichi*, 1982) and *Himatsuri* (1985), Kawase Naomi's *Moe no suzaku* (1997), and Aoyama Shinji's *Eureka* (2000).
19. Sato Makoto, Yamane Sadao, Fukuda Katsuhiko, and Araki Keiko. "From Political to Private: Recent Trends in Japanese Documentary," in *The Pursuit of Japanese Documentary: The 1980s and Beyond* (Tokyo: YIDFF, 1997), 47.
20. Ibid., 46.
21. They include *Artists in Wonderland* (*Mahiru no hoshi*, 1998), *Self and Others* (2000), *Hanako* (2001), a sequel to the first film entitled *Memories of Aga* (*Aga no kioku*, 2004), and *Out of Place* (2004), a biography of Edward Said.

22. It also limits what he can accomplish. After this film, Matsue made the mildly entertaining *Every Woman Knows How to Make Her Own Curry* (*Kare raisu no onnatachi*, 2003), films about his relationships with a series of young women. The structure is something of an homage to a genre of adult video he likes, the twist being each act climaxes with conversation. There are probably fertile connections to be made between Matsue's private film and his love of AV, the ultimate "private film," but Matsue is oblivious to the gender politics he surrounds himself with. That he substitutes sex with women cooking for him—without comment—says a lot. It would seem that in *Annyong Kimchi* made a wonderfully complex and provocative film in spite of himself. Like so many young private filmmakers, he is crippled by his insistent desire to be "non-poli," which too often simply means "proudly unreflective."
23. Hara Kazuo, *Fumikoeru Kyamera—Waga Hoho Akushon Dokyumentarii* (Tokyo: Firumuatosha, 1995), 64–67
24. Clearly, these television documentaries require more comment, however, this is difficult because they have largely been ignored by Japanese film historians, and there are no archives holding them for research purposes. Hara himself started this research in late 1998 through the organization of a kind of "short course" on the subject in Osaka. For the last few years, Hara's production office has been buzzing with the energy of young people as they organize what they call "Cinema Juku," literally Cinema Cram Courses. These are short events where Hara appears with the most famous Japanese actors, directors, and cinematographers to discuss various issues. In total, they constitute an impressive body of research into Japanese film and some of its neglected areas, including television documentary.
25. The festival published a nice catalog that discusses both collectives: *Full Shot & Cinema Juku* (Tokyo: YIDFF, 1999).

Filmography

Works by Ogawa Shinsuke, Jieiso, and Ogawa Productions

Those available with English subtitles are marked with an asterisk (*).

A Small Illusion (Chiisa na gen'ei, 1957)

Produced by Kokugakuin Daigaku Eiga Kenkyukai, black and white, 16mm, 18 minutes

Source: Athénée Français Cultural Center

Production responsibilities: Ogawa Shinsuke, Kawana Tsugio, Sawada Hidenobu

Producer: Takahashi Kichijiro

Direction: Honda Junji, Umeda Katsumi, Jin Kohei, Sato Masatoshi, Yasuda Fumimoto

Photography: Hanaya Akiyoshi, Matsubara Ichiro, Morihara Akiyoshi, Uchida Masakatsu

Scenario: Uchida Masakatsu, Sawada Hidenobu, Yamazaki Kiyoshi, Honda Junji, Umeda Katsumi

Editing: Okumoto Hisashi

Sound: Tojo Akira

Lighting: Doi Mizuho, Hayakawa Shigeaki, Hori Takuo, Yamazaki Kiyoshi

Art direction: Nakano Tadayoshi, Katsuraki Ikuo, Enomoto Toshio

Narration: Tojo Akira

Cast: Kuramoto Masaaki, Shirai Tatsuo

Documentation: Nomura Eiko

Support: Kokugakuin Daigaku Jido Bunka Kenkyukai, Kokugakuin Daigaku Gakuyukai, Kokugakuin Daigaku Jijikai

Children Living in the Mountains (*Yama ni ikiru kora,* 1958)

Produced by Kokugakuin Daigaku Eiken Kenkyukai, black and white, 16mm, 24 minutes

Source: Athénée Français Cultural Center

Production responsibilities: Ogawa Shinsuke, Kawana Tsugio

Production office: Hirose Nobuaki, Matsuo Kenko

Production: Takahashi Kichijiro

Liaison: Sato Masatoshi

Direction: Umeda Katsumi, Jin Kohei, Hayakawa Shigeaki, Ikuma Taiko

Photography: Hanaya Akiyoshi, Sonoda Akito, Matsubara Ichiro, Morihara Akiyoshi

Scenario: Uchida Akikatsu, Takahashi Yoshijiro

Editing: Okumoto Hisashi, Aoki Toshi

Sound: Endo Kazuo

Lighting: Doi Mizuho, Yamazaki Kiyoshi, Kawano Miki

Art direction: Nakano Tadayoshi, Uemoto Norio, Yamazaki Kenji, Noda Hiroko Documentation: Michiko, Nomura Eiko

Location manager: Uchida Masakatsu

Stills: Katsujo Toshio

Song: Hori Takuo

Support: Honda Junji

Instruction: Kiyono Bota

Advisor: Marushige Takeju

Sea of Youth—Four Correspondence Course Students (*Seinen no umi: Yonnin no tsushin kyoikuseitachi*, 1966)*

Produced by *Daigaku tsushin kyoikusei no kiroku eiga* o Tsukuru Kai, black and white, 16mm, 56 minutes

Source: Athénée Français Cultural Center

Direction: Ogawa Shinsuke, Okumura Yuji

Photography: Otsu Koshiro, Kawana Mitsuo, Kubota Yukio, Kuribayashi Toyohiko, Kobayashi Hideko, Jin Kohei, Tamura (Tamra) Masaki, Tateishi Yasuaki, Nakano Ryo, Yamane Makoto, Wada Shu, Iwasa Hisaya

Forest of Oppression—A Record of the Struggle at Takasaki City University of Economics (*Assatsu no mori—Takasaki Keizai Daigaku toso no kiroku*, aka *The Oppressed Students*, *Forest of Pressure*, 1967)

Produced by Kiroku Eiga *Assatsu no mori* Seisaku Jikkoiinkai and Jishu Joei Soshiki no Kai, black and white, 16mm, 105 minutes

Source: Athénée Français Cultural Center

Direction: Ogawa Shinsuke

Assistant director: Jin Kohei

Photography: Otsu Koshiro

Camera assistant: Kawana Mitsuo, Takahashi Hideaki

Sound: Kubota Yukio

Negative cutter: Morizui Fusako

Report from Haneda (*Gennin hokusho—Haneda toso no kiroku*, aka *Eyewitness Report—Chronicle of the Haneda Struggle*, 1967)

Produced by Jishu Joei Soshiki no Kai, Iwanami Film Workers' Union, Eizo Geijutsu no Kai, and Group Vision, black and white, 16mm, 58 minutes

Source: Athénée Français Cultural Center

Production: Kobayashi Hideko

Direction: Ogawa Shinsuke

Assistant director: Matsumoto Takeaki, Katayama Ryuho

Photography: Otsu Koshiro

Camera assistant: Tamura (Tamra) Masaki, Otsuka Noboru

Sound: Kubota Yukio

Negative cutter: Inoue Kazuo

The Battle Front for the Liberation of Japan—Summer in Sanrizuka (*Nihon kaiho sensen—Sanrizuka no natsu*, aka *Japan Liberation Front: Summer in Sanrizuka, Summer at Sanrizuka, Summer in Narita*, 1968)*

Produced by Ogawa Productions, black and white, 16mm, 108 minutes

Source: Athénée Français Cultural Center

Production: Kobayashi Hideko, Fuseya Hiro (Hiroo), Ichiyama Ryuji

Direction: Ogawa Shinsuke

Assistant director: Jin Kohei, Matsumoto Takeaki, Yoshida Tsukasa

Photography: Otsu Koshiro, Tamura (Tamra) Masaki

Camera assistant: Otsuka Noboru

Sound: Kubota Yukio

Transcription: Kuribayashi Toyohiko

Narration: Wada Shu

Negative cutter: Sekizawa Takako

Music: Beethoven's *Ninth Symphony*, Hayashi Hikaru's *The Good Woman of Szechuan*, "Kamigami to Zennintachi no Mubobi Jotai no Uta"

Production manager: Nosaka Haruo

Laboratory: Kinuta Laboratory

Sound recording: Tokyo Studio Center

Prehistory of the Partisans (*Paruchizan zenshi*, aka *Pre-Partisans, Pre-History of the Partisan Party*, 1969)*

Produced by Kansai Ogawa Productions and Ogawa Productions, black and white, 16mm, 120 minutes

Source: Athénée Français Cultural Center

Production: Ichiyama Ryuji (Osaka), Kobayashi Hideko (Tokyo)

Direction: Tsuchimoto Noriaki, Tsusumi Masao

Photography: Otsu Koshiro, Ichinose Masashi

Sound: Kubota Yukio

Editing: Tsuchimoto Noriaki, Matsumoto Takeaki

Negative cutter: Sekizawa Takako

Winter in Sanrizuka (*Nihon kaiho sensen: Sanrizuka*, aka *Front for the Liberation of Japan, Japan Liberation Front, Sanrizuka—Winter*, 1970)

Produced by Ogawa Productions, color, 16mm, 141 minutes

Source: Athénée Français Cultural Center

Production: Kobayashi Hideko, Nosaka Haruo, Fuseya Hiro (Hiroo), Suzuki Tsunezo, Iwasaki Keiichi (Tokyo),

Ichiyama Ryuji, Inoue Akira, Takasaki Keiko, Matsuo Ikuko, Ochiai Miyoko (Kansai Ogawa Productions), Iizuka Toshio, Yumoto Mareo, Tadokoro Naoki, Iwasaki Seiji (Tohoku Ogawa Productions), Shoi Katsuhiro (Sapporo)

Direction: Ogawa Shinsuke

Assistant director: Fukuda Katsuhiko, Honma Shusuke

Photography: Tamura (Tamra) Masaki

Assistant cameramen: Kikuchi Nobuyuki, Shimizu Yoshio

Still photography: Kitai Kazuo

Transcription: Kuribayashi Toyohiko

Production manager: Kawashima Ryoko

Sound: Kubota Yukio

Postproduction sound: Asanuma Yukikazu

Effects: Yoshino Akio

Music: Manabe Riichiro

Editorial assistance: Matsumoto Takeaki

Negative cutter: Sekizawa Takako

Title: Fujinaga Jun

Laboratory: Toyo Genzojo

Sound recording: Kai no Kairokuon Group

Sanrizuka—The Three Day War (*Sanrizuka: daisanji kyosei sokuryo soshi toso*, aka *The Three Day War in Narita, The Third Struggle against Forced Surveying*, 1970)*

Produced by Ogawa Productions, black and white, 16mm, 50 minutes

Source: Athénée Français Cultural Center

Direction: Ogawa Shinsuke

Assistant director: Fukuda Katsuhiko

Photography: Tamura (Tamra) Masaki

Camera assistant: Shimizu Yoshio

Sound editing: Asanuma Yukikazu

Negative cutter: Takahashi Tatsuo

Sound: Mitsuyuki Recording Studio

[As a newsreel, this film did not record credits; these come from the memories of those involved in the production.]

Sanrizuka—Peasants of the Second Fortress (*Sanrizuka—Daini toride no hitobito*, aka *People of the Second Fortress*, 1971)*

Produced by Ogawa Productions, black and white, 16mm, 143 minutes

Source: Athénée Français Cultural Center

Production: Nosaka Haruo, Fuseya Hiro (Hiroo), Honma Shusuke, Mikado Sadatoshi, Nara Noriaki (Tokyo), Iizuka Toshio, Tadokoro Naoki, Iwasaki Seiji, Tanizu Hideko (Tohoku Ogawa Productions), Kikuchi Nobuyuki (Sapporo)

Direction: Ogawa Shinsuke

Assistant director: Fukuda Katsuhiko, Yumoto Mareo

Photography: Tamura (Tamra) Masaki

Assistant cameramen: Shimizu Yoshio, Hara Tadashi

Production manager: Hataya Naoko

Sound editing: Asanuma Yukikazu

Negative cutter: Takahashi Tatsuo

Sound: Mitsuyuki Recording Studio

Laboratory: Toei Kagaku Koyo Kubushikigaisha

Sanrizuka—The Construction of Iwayama Tower (*Sanrizuka—Iwayama ni tetto ga dekita*, aka *The Building of the Iwayama Tower*, 1971)

Produced by Ogawa Productions, black and white, 16mm, 143 minutes

Source: Athénée Français Cultural Center

Direction: Ogawa Shinsuke

Assistant director: Fukuda Katsuhiko (research/liaison)

Location sound: Yumoto Mareo

Photography: Tamura (Tamra) Masaki

Assistant cameramen: Kawakami Koichi, Hara Tadashi

Housework: Shiraishi Yoko, Nakano Chihiro

Production manager: Hataya Naoko

Sound editing: Asanuma Yukikazu

Liaison: Tadokoro Naoki

Location manager: Iwasaki Seiji

Production staff: Iizuka Toshio (photography support, Tohoko screenings), Kikuchi Nobuyuki (Hokkaido screenings), Nosaka Haruo (production office, Kanto screenings), Fuseya Hiro (Hiroo) (distribution office, Chubu screenings), Honma Shusuke (Kyushu screenings), Mikado Sadatoshi (office manager)

Sanrizuka—Heta Village (*Sanrizuka—Heta Buraku*, 1973)*

Produced by Ogawa Productions, black and white, 16mm, 146 minutes

Source: Athénée Français Cultural Center

Production staff: Iizuka Toshio, Tadokoro Naoki, Nosaka Haruo, Fuseya Hiro (Hiroo), Honma Shusuke, Mikado Sadatoshi

Photography staff: Ogawa Shinsuke, Fukuda Katsuhiko, Yumoto Mareo, Iwasaki Seiji, Shiraishi Yoko, Nakano Chihiro

Photograph: Tamura (Tamra) Masaki

Assistant cameramen: Kawakami Koichi, Hara Tadashi

Sound: Kubota Yukio

Sound editing: Asanuma Yukikazu

Negative cutter: Takahashi Tatsuo

Sound studio: Nihon Hoso Rokuon Kyokai

Laboratory: Movie Center

Support: Kagaku Eiga Seisakujo

[To emphasize the collaborative production method, the film lists only the production staff, with no specified roles.]

Filmmaking and the Way to the Village (*Eiga-zukuri to mura e no michi*, 1973)*

Produced by Ogawa Productions, black and white, 16mm, 54 minutes

Source: Athénée Français Cultural Center

Direction, editing, sound: Fukuda Katsuhiko

Production: Iizuka Toshio

Advisor: Asanuma Yukikazu

Photography: Kawakami Koichi

Camera assistant: Hara Tadashi

Assistant editor: Nakano Chihiro

Dokkoi! Songs from the Bottom (*Dokkoi! Ningen bushi—Kotobukicho: Jiyu rodosha no machi*, aka *A Song of Common Humanity, A Song of the Bottom, Song of the Humans*, 1975)*

Produced by Ogawa Productions, black and white, 16mm, 121 minutes

Source: Athénée Français Cultural Center

Photography: Okamura Yuji

Research/liaison: Yumoto Mareo

Transcription: Watanabe Takaaki

Camera assistant: Hara Tadashi

Structure: Ogawa Shinsuke

Editing: Ogawa Shinsuke, Tadokoro Naoki, Yumoto Mareo

Sound: Kubota Yukio

Sound assistant: Kuribayashi Toyohiko

Production: Fuseya Hiro (Hiroo), Shiraishi Yoko, Asahi Setsuko, Iizuka Toshio, Fukuda Katsuhiko, Hayashi Tetsuji

Production assistance: Nosaka Haruo

Calligraphy: Tatsumi Shiro

Poem: Tanaka Yukata

Song: Acid Seven

Still photography: Miyamatsu Hiroshi

Negative cutter: Takahashi Tatsuo

Equipment studio: Kiroku Eizaisha

Laboratory: Sony-PCL

Interview at Clean Center (*Kuriin Sentaa homonki*, 1975)*

Produced by Ogawa Productions, color, 16mm, 57 minutes

Source: Athénée Français Cultural Center

Planning: Kaminoyama City Public Health Section

Producer: Iizuka Toshio

Direction: Ogawa Shinsuke

Photography: Okumura Yuji

Camera assistant: Hara Tadashi

Transcription: Hayashi Tetsuji

Sound: Kubota Yukio

Assistant editor: Mikado Sadatoshi

Editorial assistance: Fukuda Katsuhiko

Recording studio: Kiroku Eizaisha

Support: Mikki Kogyo Kabushikigaisha

Sanrizuka—The Skies of May, the Road to the Village (*Sanrizuka—Satsuki no sora sato no kayoji*, aka *Narita: The Skies of May*, 1977)

Produced by Ogawa Productions, color, 16mm, 81 minutes

Source: Athénée Français Cultural Center

Photography: Tamura (Tamra) Masaki

Photography staff: Ogawa Shinsuke, Fukuda Katsuhiko, Hara Tadashi, Hayashi Tetsuji, Uriu Toshihiko, Kawada Yumiko, Shiraishi Yoko, Watanabe Takaaki

Production staff: Fuseya Hiro (Hiroo), Iizuka Toshio, Mikado Sadatoshi, Asahi Setsuko, Hatanaka Hiroko

Mixer: Kubota Yukio

Tanka: Tsubaki Kiyokatsu

Illustration: Ishige Hiromichi

Negative cutter: Takahashi Tatsuo

Recording studio: Kiroku Eizaisha

The Magino Village Story—Raising Silkworms (*Magino Monogatari—Yosan-hen: Eiga no tame no eiga*, 1977)*

Produced by Ogawa Productions, color, 8mm, 112 minutes

Source: Athénée Français Cultural Center

Producers: Iizuka Toshio, Fuseya Hiro (Hiroo)

Direction: Ogawa Shinsuke

Photography: Hara Tadashi

Sound: Uriu Toshihiko

Editing: Fukuda Katsuhiko

16mm blow-up: Tamura (Tamra) Masaki

Negative cutter: Takahashi Tatsuo

Appearances: Kimura Sato, Kimura Shuichi, Kimura Hatsu, Shiraishi Yoko, Mikado Sadatoshi

The Magino Village Story—Pass (*Magino Monogatari sono 2 Toge—Zao to Makabe Jin—*, 1977)

Produced by Ogawa Productions, color, 16mm, 43 minutes

Source: Athénée Français Cultural Center

Producers: Iizuka Toshio, Fuseya Hiro (Hiroo)

Direction: Ogawa Shinsuke

Photography: Okumura Yuji

Sound: Uriu Toshihiko

Sound editing: Kubota Yukio

Editing: Fukuda Katsuhiko

Assistant directors: Watanabe Takaaki, Mikado Sadatoshi

Camera assistant: Hayashi Tetsuji

Logistics: Shiraishi Yoko, Hatanaka Hiroko

Negative cutter: Takahashi Tatsuo

Appearances: Makabe Jin

"Nippon": Furuyashiki Village (*Nippon koku: Furuyashiki-mura*, aka *A Japanese Village—Furuyashikimura*, 1982)*

Produced by Ogawa Productions, color, 16mm, 210 minutes

Source: Athénée Français Cultural Center

Direction: Ogawa Shinsuke

Production: Fuseya Hiro (Hiroo)

Photography: Tamura (Tamra) Masaki

Location sound: Kikuchi Nobuyuki

Assistant directors: Iizuka Toshio, Mikado Sadatoshi

Camera assistant: Nosaka Haruo, Hayashi Tetsuji

Location logistics: Shiraishi Yoko, Hatanaka Hiroko

Assistant editors: Mikado Sadatoshi, Hirose Satomi

Sound editing: Asanuma Yukikazu

Poem: Kimura Michio

Music: Seki Ichiro

Illustration: Fujimori Reiko

Titles: Shoji Takashi

Charcoal technical advisor: Sato Nikichi

Negative cutter: Takahashi Tatsuo

Sound recording: Ogawa Pro Studio

Laser recording: Minato Rerecording Center

Laboratory: Sony/PCL

Support: Uchiyama Naoaki, Urushiyama Teruhiko, Ogata Masao, Kanai Toshio, Kimura Hatsu, Kiyono Kazuki, Takahashi Masaaki, Tatsumi Shiro, Tomita Tetsunosuke, Naito Masatoshi, Namiki Kikuo, Hoshikawa Seishin, Honda Tsutomu, Mimuro Kiyofumi, Miyada Kiyoshi, Yamane Ichiro, Wada Hidetoku

The Sundial Carved with a Thousand Years of Notches—The Magino Village Story (Sennen kizami no hidokei—Magino-mura monogatari, aka *Magino Village—A Tale,* 1986)*

Produced by Ogawa Productions, color, 16mm, 222 minutes

Source: Athénée Français Cultural Center

Production: Fuseya Hiro (Hiroo)

Direction: Ogawa Shinsuke

Photography: Tamura (Tamra) Masaki

Camera assistant: Hayashi Tetsuji, Nosaka Haruo, Mitsumori Yoko

Assistant director: Iizuka Toshio

Sound: Kubota Yukio, Kikuchi Nobuyuki

Production assistants: Hirose Satomi, Mikado Sadatoshi, Shiraki Yoshihiro

Logistics: Shiraishi Yoko, Hatanaka Hiroko

Lighting: Sato Yuzuru

Music: Togashi Masahiko

Art direction: Tatsumi Shiro, Mikado Sadatoshi

Titles: Ibaragi Shunsuke

Still photography: Naito Masatoshi

Props/sets: Tsuchiya Kozo

Sun photography: Yamazaki Hiroshi, Murakami Shinji

Crane: Ta Masayuki, Mitsui Teruhiko, Yamamoto Naruhito

Music editing: Asahi Sound Studio

Laser recording: Yokohoma Cinema Genzojo

Laboratory: Sony/PCL

Negative cutter: Takahashi Tatsuo

Horikiri Kannon Story

Cast: Hijikata Tatsumi, Miyashita Junko, Kikuchi Masao, Kimura Chiu

Assistant directors: Sato Makoto, Ishiwatari Tetsuya, Zeze Takahisa, Ogawa Izuru Camera assistant: Tanaka Kazamasa

Lighting assistants: Nakayasu Kazunori, Shimizu Yasutoshi, Nakajima Kiyogoro

Makeup: Dewa Yasuo

Wigs: Yamadaya

Replica: Miro Zokei

Costumes/props: Villagers

Accent coach: Kimura Shigeko

Birth of Itsutsudomoe Shrine Story

Cast: Tamura Takahiro, Kawarazaki Choichiro, Ishibashi Renji, Shimada Shogo, Igarashi Ikuo, Inoue Kichizaemon, Kimura Masayoshi, Igarashi Masao, Takahashi Toshiro, Suzuki Toru, Inoue Mitsuru, Kimura Masuo, Sato Akihiro, Kuganuma Norio, Takahashi Toshio, Yoshida Hideaki

Uprising masses: The people of Magino, Haraguchi, and Kaminoyama

Camera assistant: Kasamatsu Norimichi

Lighting assistant: Nakayasu Kazunori, Takahara Ken'ichi, Tsukiyama Makoto

Makeup: Dewa Yasuo

Kimono dressing: Otsuka Chieko

Wigs: Yamadaya

Costumes: Kyoto Isho

Props: Villagers

Handmade ropes: Takebayashi Yoshifusa

Transportation: Kimura Hajime

Production support: Maeda Katsuhiro

Kyoto Demon Market—The Theater of a Thousand Years (*Kyoto oni ichiba—sennen shiataa,* 1987)

Produced by Ogawa Productions, color, 16mm, 18 minutes

Source: Athénée Français Cultural Center

Direction: Ogawa Shinsuke

Production: Fuseya Hiro (Hiroo)

Photography: Maki Itsuo

Camera assistant: Arakawa Toru, Osawa Keiko

Logistics: Yasui Yoshio

Assistant director: Sasaoka Tamotsu

A Movie Capital (*Eiga no miyako,* 1991)*

Produced by Ogawa Productions, color, 16mm, 93 minutes

Source: Athénée Français Cultural Center

Planning: City of Yamagata

Production: Fuseya Hiro (Hiroo)

First shoot

Direction: Iizuka Toshio

Photography: Otsu Koshiro, Kato Takanobu

Sound: Asanuma Yukikazu

Logistics: Masuya Shuichi

Second shoot

Iizuka Toshio, Ogawa Shinsuke, Kuribayashi Masashi

Photography: Kato Takanobu

Technical Advice: Tamura (Tamra) Masaki

Postproduction

Structure: Ogawa Shinsuke

Editing: Ogawa Shinsuke, Tamura (Tamra) Masaki, Iizuka Toshio, Kuribayashi Masashi

Sound editing: Asanuma Yukikazu

Logistics: Shiraishi Yoko, Abe Hiroko

Works about Ogawa Productions

Hijiori Story (*Hijiori monogatari*, 1992)

Produced by Ogawa Productions, color 16mm, 18 minutes

Source: Shiraishi Yoko

Production: Fuseya Hiro (Hiroo)

Line Producers: Shiraishi Yoko, Abe Hiroko

Direction: Ogawa Shinsuke

Photography: Kato Takanobu

Sound editing: Asanuma Yukikazu

Rough cut (1990): Ogawa Shinsuke, Tamura (Tamra) Masaki

Posthumous edit (1992): Tsuchimoto Noriaki

Cast: Mori Shigeya

Red Persimmons (*Manzanbekigaki*, 2001)*

Produced by Kaminoyama Meisan Benigaki no Kiroku Eiga o Tsukuru Kai, color, 16mm, 90 minutes

Source: Planet Bibliothèque de Cinéma, First Run Icarus Films

Production: Shiraishi Yoko, Yasui Yoshio

Initial photography

Direction: Ogawa Shinsuke

Photography: Tamura (Tamra) Masaki

Location sound: Kikuchi Nobuyuki

Assistant director: Iizuka Toshio

Production assistants: Mikado Sadatoshi, Hirose Satomi, Shiraki Yoshihiro

Camera assistants: Nosaka Haruo, Mitsumori Yoko

Production: Fuseya Hiro (Hiroo)

Final photography

Direction: Peng Xiao-lian

Photography: Lin Jong

Location producer: Ogata Mitsuhiro

Sound: Kikuchi Shinpei

Camera assistant: Kato Takanobu

Translation: Ryu Hanfa

Postproduction

Editing: Peng Xiao-lian

Assistant editor: Mikado Sadatoshi

Translation: Ryu Hanfa

Sound editing: Kubota Yukio

Music: Jomontaiko

Calligraphy: Isoda Michiko

Negative editing: Yamada Hiroshi

Support: Kaminoyama MeisanBenigaki no Kiroku Eiga o Tsukuru Kai (Sugano Kenkichi, Sasaki Seichi, Ogata Masao, Urushiyama Teruhiko, Takahashi Yoshiaki)

A Visit to Ogawa Productions (*Ogawa Puro homonki,* 1981/1999)*

Produced by the Japanese Cultural Design Council, color, 16mm, original 48 minutes, 1999 restoration 61 minutes

Source: Planet Bibliothèque de Cinéma, First Run Icarus Films

Direction: Oshige Jun'ichiro

Photography: Hotta Yasuhiro

Interviewer: Oshima Nagisa

Hare to Ke—Das Besondere und der Alltag. Begegnung mit der Ogawa Produktion (Germany/France/Japan, *Hare to Ke—The Ordinary and the Extraordinary,* 1988/1989)*

Produced by Madeleine Remy Filmproduktion, Road Movies, Filmproduktion GmbH, The Japan Foundation, and La Sept, color, 16mm, 88 minutes

Source: Image Forum

Direction, screenplay: Regina Ulwer

Photography: Henrietta Loch

Production: Regina Ulwer, Madeleine Remy, Wim Wenders

Translation: Izumi Isamu, Regula König, Umetsu Yumiko, Kawai Sumi

Subtitles: Annette Eckert, Regina Ulwer

Editing: Henrietta Loch, Susanne Peuscher, Nomura Shinobu

Sound: Kikuchi Noboyuki

Sound editing: Michael Eiler

Narration: Corinna Belz

Music: Frieder Butzmann

*Devotion (USA, 2000)**

Production, direction, photography, editing: Barbara Hammer

Associate producers: Nakano Rie, Ono Seiko

Assistant director: Shimada Yoshiko

Second camera: Iizuka Toshio, Shiraishi Yoko, Masuya Shuichi

Sound: Barbara Hammer and Tanaka Junko

Production assistant: Tanaka Junko, Julie Larson

Assistant editor: Shimada Yoshiko

English subtitles: Linda Hoagland

Japanese subtitles: Shimada Yoshiko, Suzuki Miho

Japanese language consultant: Fukumori Naomi, Sam Morris

Title sequence: Akanuma Akio

Consultant: Abé Mark Nornes

Avid online editors: Paul Hill, Amanda Ault

Distribution Resources

Print Sources

The rights to the films of Jieiso and Ogawa Pro were purchased by the Film School of Tokyo (www.eigabigakkou.com) and Eurospace (www.eurospace.co.jp). They readily lend prints for a modest rental fee through the Athénée Français Cultural Center, one of the epicenters of independent cinema screening in the postwar era. Quite a few English-subtitled films are also distributed by the Japan Foundation, which lends prints for the cost of shipping, as long as permission is secured from the rights holder.

Athénée Français Cultural Center

2-11 Kandasuruga-dai, Chiyoda-ku
Tokyo 101-0062
Japan
Phone: (33) 291-4339
FAX: (33) 291-4340
E-mail: question@athenee.net
Web site: www.athenee.net/culturalcenter

First Run Icarus Films

32 Court Street, 21st floor
Brooklyn, NY 11201
Phone: (718) 488-8900
E-mail: mailroom@frif.com

Image Forum

2-10-2 Shibuya, Shibuya-ku
Tokyo 150-0002
Japan
Phone: 81-3-5766-0114
E-mail: info@imageforum.co.jp
Web site: www.imageforum.co.jp

Japan Foundation

Contact the nearest branch office, which may be found at the Web site, www.jpf.go.jp.

Planet Bibliothèque de Cinéma

206 Shiramo Building
3-41 Banzai-cho, Kita-ku
Osaka 530-0027
Japan
Phone: (6) 6364-2165
Fax (6) 6312-8232
E-mail: planet1@m11.alpha-net.ne.jp
Web site: go.to/planet1

Many of the Japanese documentaries I mention here are available for rental from their producers. For source information, the best place to go is the Tokyo office of the Yamagata International Documentary Film Festival.

Yamagata International Documentary Film Festival, Tokyo Office

ID Kawadacho Building, 3rd floor
7-6 Kawadacho, Shinjuku-ku
Tokyo 990-8540
Japan
Phone: 81-3-5362-0672
Fax: 81-3-5362-0670
E-mail: mail@tokyo.yidff.jp
Web site: www.city.yamagata.yamagata.jp/yidff/home-e.html

Source for Devotion

Barbara Hammer
55 Bethune Street, #523H
New York, NY 10014
E-mail: bjhammer@aol.com
Phone/Fax: (212) 645-9077
Web site: www.barbarahammerfilms.com

Paper Materials

Throughout the notes in this book, I refer to the three "archives" that hold the papers, notebooks, memos, newsletters, photographs, budgets, receipts, broken eyeglasses, and many other items saved by Ogawa Pro. Strictly speaking, only one of these is an archive; I use the term for the sake of convenience. They are probably more akin to "hoards." The materials from the Jieiso days are kept in safekeeping by Nosaka Haruo and Tanaka Nobuko in a closet in the home of Tanaka's parents in Yamagata. The materials from the Magino period are kept in an old, unused house in Furuyashiki. Only the Sanrizuka era collection is properly preserved—in the airport, curiously enough. Just before his untimely death, Fukuda Katsuhiko helped an organization that was trying to mend the hard feelings surrounding the Sanrizuka Struggle (on both sides) acquire the materials. The organization is building an archive for the history of the struggle (the collection from Ogawa Pro is currently its core) and is conducting extensive oral histories with all involved, as well as holding symposia and exhibitions. The materials are preserved in archival conditions and are being catalogued for future public use. So far, a thousand reels of 6-mm audiotape have been converted onto 301 CDs, and more than 10,000 still photographs have been put onto 359 rolls of film. Recently, the organization completed transferring hundreds of reels of rushes onto a digital video format. Long before the boxes were catalogued, and with the blessing of former Ogawa Pro members, the archive was kind enough to grant me access to the collection.

Rekishi Densho Committee

Rinku Kaihatsu Dai-ichi Senta Bldg, Room 411
1-2 Goyo Bokujo, Sanrizuka
Narita City, Chiba Prefecture
Japan 282-0011
Phone: 81-476-32-2586
Fax: 81-476-32-2583
E-mail: info@rekishidensho.jp
Web site: www.rekishidensho.jp

Index

I

N

P

R

S

Y

Z

ABÉ MARK NORNES is associate professor at the University of Michigan, where he teaches in the Department of Asian Languages and Cultures and the Department of Screen Arts and Cultures. He is author of *Japanese Documentary Film: The Meiji Era through Hiroshima* (Minnesota, 2003), also in the Visible Evidence series.